rtial
01

Internet and Surveillance

EUROPEAN
SCIENCE
FOUNDATION

ESF provides the COST Office through an EC contract.

COST is supported by the EU RTD Framework programme.

Routledge Studies in Science, Technology and Society

Internet and Surveillance
The Challenges of Web 2.0 and Social Media

**Edited by Christian Fuchs,
Kees Boersma, Anders Albrechtslund
and Marisol Sandoval**

Routledge
Taylor & Francis Group
NEW YORK   LONDON

First published 2012
by Routledge
711 Third Ave, New York, NY 10017

Simultaneously published in the UK
by Routledge
2 Park Square, Milton Park, Abingdon, Oxon OX14 4RN

*Routledge is an imprint of the Taylor & Francis Group,
an informa business*

© 2012 Taylor & Francis

Typeset in Sabon by IBT Global.

Library of Congress Cataloging-in-Publication Data
    Internet and surveillance : the challenges of Web 2.0 and social media /
edited by Christian Fuchs ... [et al.].
        p. cm. — (Routledge studies in science, technology and society ; 16)
    Includes bibliographical references and index.
    1.   Internet—Social aspects 2.   Electronic surveillance. 3.   Social
media. 4.   Privacy, Right of. 5.   Data protection. I. Fuchs, Christian,
1976-
    HM851.I5696 2011
    005.8—dc22
                                                    2011006083

ISBN: 978-0-415-89160-8 (hbk)
ISBN: 978-0-203-80643-2 (ebk)

About COST

COST—the acronym for European Cooperation in Science and Technology—is the oldest and widest European intergovernmental network for cooperation in research. Established by the Ministerial Conference in November 1971, COST is presently used by the scientific communities of 36 European countries to cooperate in common research projects supported by national funds.

The funds provided by COST—less than 1% of the total value of the projects—support the COST cooperation networks (COST Actions) through which, with EUR 30 million per year, more than 30 000 European scientists are involved in research having a total value which exceeds EUR 2 billion per year. This is the financial worth of the European added value which COST achieves.

A "bottom up approach" (the initiative of launching a COST Action comes from the European scientists themselves), "à la carte participation" (only countries interested in the Action participate), "equality of access" (participation is open also to the scientific communities of countries not belonging to the European Union) and "flexible structure" (easy implementation and light management of the research initiatives) are the main characteristics of COST.

As precursor of advanced multidisciplinary research COST has a very important role for the realisation of the European Research Area (ERA) anticipating and complementing the activities of the Framework Programmes, constituting a "bridge" towards the scientific communities of emerging countries, increasing the mobility of researchers across Europe and fostering the establishment of "Networks of Excellence" in many key scientific domains such as: Biomedicine and Molecular Biosciences; Food and Agriculture; Forests, their Products and Services; Materials, Physical and Nanosciences; Chemistry and Molecular Sciences and Technologies; Earth System Science and Environmental Management; Information and Communication Technologies; Transport and Urban Development; Individuals, Societies, Cultures and Health. It covers basic and more applied research and also addresses issues of pre-normative nature or of societal importance.

Web: http://www.cost.eu

Contents

PART III:
Conclusion

Figures

Tables

Preface

Thomas Mathiesen

I am 77 years old. I remember very well indeed a world without the Internet. I remember the late 1930s in Norway, a humble close-knit society (with some wealthy shipowners on top), where people in fishing villages, rural areas, and towns lived as they always had lived. I remember how the world changed when Norway was occupied by German forces during World War II, I remember vividly our meeting with American soldiers who had come to Northern Europe in 1945 via the disastrous struggles and terrible manslaughter during the Italian campaign, "the soft belly" of German Europe, which turned out not to be soft at all, but which changed my life throughout. I remember how I went to the US with my mother, an American, by steamship in 1946, and came back for school also by steamship in the fall with a new worldview and a large Hershey chocolate bar for each of my classmates. I remember the '50s with more school, partly in the US, and the abolition of restrictions on buying the countless new things that capitalism now had to offer—such as a brand new car, which my father suddenly bought. I remember the '60s, '70s, and '80s, with several marriages in a row whereas the older generation had managed with one, I remember homosexuals coming out of the closet, their sexual secrets being decriminalized, I remember several trips—now by large jet planes—to and back from the US, I remember the oil coming up from the North Sea making us affluent, I remember the struggles I took part in, such as the prisoners' struggles, and the terrifying wars that took place, such as in Vietnam. And all of the instant media came along, such as television. I remember poverty and wealth. There were fast electronic typewriters and equally rapid stencil machines that allowed proofreading and correction with red wax before the duplication process.

I remember all of this and more, tremendous changes in ordinary peoples' lives over say six or seven decades. All of this and more happened without the Internet—although the Internet was in the making.

This makes me wonder: We often hear the saying that with the Internet, the world is entering something brand new, a new societal formation. The world is now leaving the age of the "the industrial society", on the verge of and in fact entering the age of "an information society". Although unskilled and skilled labourers are still around and in demand, production of all the things we need (or think that we need), is increasingly dependent on information.

One of the first to try out the concept of an "information society" was the sociologist Daniel Bell (1973/1976) in his book *The Coming of Post-Industrial Society* from 1973. Bell tried to characterize the shift from what he called the industrial society to "the post-industrial society". According to Bell, the post-industrial society contained two dimensions—a far greater emphasis than before on theoretical knowledge and information, and a tremendous growth in service activities (transport, trade, insurance, banking, public administration, medical, legal, and other types of individual service, travel and so on). The first major change—the far greater emphasis on theoretical knowledge and information—has made us more dependent on science, with the increased role of scientifically based industries. The second change—the increased role of service-oriented trades—has created a strong relative decline of the industrially productive workforce. But Bell also emphasized that the postindustrial society does not *replace* the industrial society. It rather finds its place integrated in that society, erasing some of the features of the industrial society.

Many modern works have gone further. One of them is William H. Davidow and Michael S. Malone's fascinating but problematic book *The Virtual Corporation* from 1992, which contains illustrations from Silicon Valley, Northern Italy, and Japan. According to Davidow and Malone (1992), an industry is "virtual" when it produces material objects very quickly, in principle *in no time*. A perfectly "virtual industry" does not exist, but an industry may *approach* production and operation in no time. They construct a complex theory of information containing four levels, where information is instantaneously converted to complex actions. Neural networks inspired by networks in the brain are referred to.

This is of course just a brief sketch of the main argument. What are we to make of it? Two points:

> *First, I for one do not think we are approaching a situation of virtual production.*

The industrial workforce has declined, and significantly so, in our part of the world. This is partly due to forces such as those pointed to by Davidow and Malone. Information has become an important productive force. But there are also other forces, notably the *outsourcing* to parts of the world where labour is cheap and the *moving* of large-scale industries also to places where labour is cheap (and taxes low). Furthermore, there are limits both of a sociological and a technical nature—strong labour unions in many places, the culture of the workplace, and limits as to how much labour may be mechanized. All of this prevents the transfer of our mode of production from industry to information. It may be too old-fashioned a view, but this is so far where my thinking has gone. If I am right, the significance of this should not be underestimated. It means, essentially, that a basic shift of the mode of production is not occurring, or is occurring only to a limited extent. Unlike the shift from feudal production to industrial capitalism, where whole generations of people originally tied to the land in serfdom were uprooted, fleeing to the cities looking for work in the large new buildings called factories, in which labour was organized in an entirely different way. Industrial capitalism is still with us, albeit with a smaller (un)skilled labour force and to some extent with a shift to service trades and technical expertise. The Internet has made invasions in industrial capitalism, but the Internet basically *promotes* industrial capitalism; it is much more effective as a vehicle of an advanced industrial society. It is not an end point of a mode of production, but an advancement of it.

Second, however, our social relations in our daily lives may be changing more significantly.

Think of it. Students of all grades and classes are now using the Internet, for planning courses, finding out where the courses are given and which courses not to take, receiving exam questions, and a whole string of related things. If they ask a secretary for information, the answer is "look it up on the Net". Approximately 500 million people on a world basis are now daily users of Facebook (information from Wikipedia). In a class (on media and communication) I taught this fall with 70 students, 100% were on Facebook. I was the only person present who was not on Facebook. The prime minister of Norway is an ardent user of Twitter. Research has shown that US politicians increasingly adjust their media appearances on television according to how the messages are received on the Net. Groups on YouTube are able to influence US election campaigns very significantly. Radicals and liberals are ousted or received with warmth. In 1997, 50% of the Norwegian population had access to a computer at home. In 2009 the percentage was 92. In 1997, 13% had access to the Internet. In 2009 the percentage was 91. The same developments can be observed in many countries. The Internet is used for a wide variety of activities. The coffee shop is here for good, and all over the place you see cellphones, which people use as comforters or for calling. Many young people bring their laptops to do their homework. People like to be in places, where they both are alone *and* with other people. Women tend to not go to bars alone, but they can and do go to coffee shops (as a recent doctoral dissertation showed, Dokk Holm 2010). I recently read a research report that showed that Muslim women used the Net for information about dress codes, sexual practice and malpractice, and a variety of other delicate matters (they received *fatwas* in return, which were quite pragmatic and rather women-friendly, see Sardar Ali 2011). Internet use is a worldwide phenomenon. In a streamlined fashion the other modern information media follow suit.

In short, though there are changes in production, I doubt that a new mode of production is coming up. But perhaps there is a new social formation over and above production? Or is there a new way of life? Possibly. The changes are great.

It is not only that. Most of the other changes since 1940 have actually been gradual, relatively speaking. You can trace the development from the combustion engine through various stages to the extremely rapid trains crossing all of Europe in a few hours. You can trace the development from the Spitfire to the jumbo jet. The Internet, and what has followed in its wake, has come more as a break, with whole generations involved within a short span of time. This is, mind you, in open public space, and in spite of the fact that the Internet also has developed and expanded gradually, but more "behind the scenes".

But I have to confess: Though this is a possible interpretation, I am uncertain even here. I wish I could live longer to see how it goes. If you compare 1990 with 2010, the difference in how people behave and act is great. But if you compare 2010 with earlier times, for example with the late 1930s, I am not so sure. This is why I started this little preface with a historical note. The 70 years that have passed since 1940 have been a period of enormous, dramatic social change in the Western world—from modesty to capitalist frenzy, from steamships to large and extremely quick airplanes propelled (or rather, not visibly propelled) by huge jet engines, to social relationships and family principles of a kind completely different from earlier times. Isn't the Internet just a further extension of a whole wave of *social change* over our Western social order, once again with a new technology that elderly people find difficult to learn?

I have doubts. This is where I have arrived—so far.

But is, then, nothing new? Of course there is. The whole period of 70 years, which we have behind us, is characterized by inventions and novelty.

Surveillance is new. Surveillance is the cardinal point of the Internet. Not that we did not have surveillance before. We have had surveillance since the construction of the state, and maybe before that. In the 1970s a man, a Marxist, who lived in the city of Trondheim in Norway found a cord linked to his telephone. He followed the cord—to the police station. This became a standard joke. But much of it was more serious. Many people, especially people of a Marxist or radical leaning, were followed closely by the secret police. I was tailed by the secret police when I participated at prisoners' conferences, and when I received dissident visitors from Eastern Europe under Soviet Rule. Secret police officers reported on my activities to their Norwegian headquarters. The situation was irritating, but at least it was possible to detect that surveillance of a political nature was going on, especially when a special commission was finally set up to control these matters. The commission found much of the surveillance illegal.[1]

> What is new now is *surveillance that is hidden, unseen, and impossible to trace.*

Certainly sensational discoveries occur. One day in 2010 it suddenly turned out that the US Embassy in Norway employed retired Norwegian police officers, making them responsible for the surveillance of Norwegian citizens near as well as somewhat away from the Embassy premises. The Embassy did not trust the standard Norwegian surveillance as far as terrorism was concerned and felt vulnerable. Information was passed on to a US database. On the political level, no one had known: Not the Minister of Justice, not the Prime Minister. Again suddenly, a similar sensation turned up in Denmark. No one had known. Perhaps politicians preferred to be ignorant about the illegal activities of an ally. Perhaps the lower echelons of the Norwegian police, which had cooperated closely with the US Embassy, were aware of this preference and acted accordingly. We will probably never know.

Such sensational scandals do occur. The scandals enter open public space. But they are exceptions that prove the rule. Below the surface there is an enormous hinterland of undiscovered surveillance practices based on the use of the Internet. Surveillance on the Internet is hidden and unseen. So is the vast trail of electronic signs that we leave behind as we go about our daily affairs—in banks, shops, trade centres, and everywhere else, every day of the year. Surveillance becomes a system, or a set of systems, which "silently silences" you—suave, unnoticeable, and undetected surveillance of groups, categories, and large populations, its unnoticeable character in turn silencing opposition (Mathiesen 2004). Processes of corporate and political surveillance on the Internet also act as systems that silence people in a suave and silent way. Some Internet use is official to the extent that formal decisions are made to establish the system in question. An example is the EU Directive 2006/26/EF, passed on March 15, 2006, that concerns the retention of traffic data. That, at least, makes initial protests possible, but not after a while and only when the system is in operation.[2] At any rate, under the Data Retention Directive enormous amounts of data are stored about *all citizens in the country*—who calls who, who e-mails who for how long, start time and end time, place for initiation and place for reception, and so on—and may be used according to vague criteria of crime and terrorism. And most Internet surveillance is beyond any control at all. We simply do not know about it.

This is a very important sign of danger to our society. The surveillance activities and methods that have come up in the wake of the Internet threaten the democratic fibres of our liberal state governed by law. At the same time, the bombing and massacre that cost close to 80 people their lives in Norway in July 2011 make the democratic fibres of Norway potentially more vulnerable. The Norwegian authorities and people therefore use precisely the values of democracy and solidarity as a defence.

The outlined circumstances make the book, which you hold in your hand, most timely. It is a most important volume on a most important feature of our society today.

NOTES

1. Important in this context was the so-called Lund-commission. It was headed by a Supreme Court Judge and set up by Parliament after the Cold War in 1994. The commission's findings were shocking. Illegalities were widespread.
2. Some systems are open rather than hidden also while in operation, such as those that control all passengers at airports.

REFERENCES

Bell, Daniel. 1973/1976. *The coming of post-industrial society: A venture in social forecasting.* New York: Basic Books.

Davidow, William H. and Michael S. Malone. 1992. *The virtual corporation: Structuring and revitalizing the corporation for the 21ˢᵗ century.* New York: Harper Collins.

Dokk Holm, Erling. 2010. *Coffee and the city: Towards a soft urbanity.* Oslo: Arkitekt- og designhøgskolen.

Mathiesen, Thomas. 2004. *Silently silenced: Essays on the creation of acquiescence in modern society.* Winchester, UK: Waterside.

Sardar Ali, Shaheen. 2011. Behind the cyberspace veil: online *fatwas* on women's family rights. In *From transnational relations to transnational laws: Northern European laws at the crossroads,* ed. Anne Hellum, Shaheen Sardar Ali, and Anne Griffiths. Farnham, UK: Ashgate.

1 Introduction

Internet and Surveillance

Christian Fuchs, Kees Boersma, Anders Albrechtslund, and Marisol Sandoval

1.1. COMPUTING AND SURVEILLANCE

Scholars in surveillance studies and information society studies have stressed the importance of computing for conducting surveillance for more than 20 years. This has resulted in a number of categories that describe the interconnection of computing and surveillance: for the new surveillance, dataveillance, the electronic (super)panopticon, electronic surveillance, or digital surveillance.

Gary T. Marx defines the new surveillance as "the use of technical means to extract or create personal data. This may be taken from individuals or contexts" (Marx 2002, 12; see also: Marx 1988, 217–219). He argues that in the old surveillance, it was more difficult to send data, whereas in the new surveillance this is easier. In traditional surveillance, "what the surveillant knows, the subject probably knows as well", whereas in the new surveillance the "surveillant knows things the subject doesn't" (Marx 2002, 29). He says that the new surveillance is not on scene, but remote, and that it is "less coercive" (28) and "more democratized" because some forms are more widely available (28). Computerized surveillance is an important form of new surveillance. "Computers qualitatively alter the nature of surveillance—routinizing, broadening, and deepening it. Organizational memories are extended over time and across space" (Marx 1988, 208).

Dataveillance is the "systematic monitoring of people's actions or communications through the application of information technology" (Clarke 1988, 500). Clarke (1994) distinguishes between personal dataveillance that monitors the actions of one or more persons and mass dataveillance, where a group or large population is monitored in order to detect individuals of interest. Bogard (2006) argues that the computer is a technology that simulates surveillance.

Gordon (1987) speaks of the electronic panopticon. Mark Poster (1990) has coined the notion of the electronic superpanopticon: "Today's 'circuits of communication' and the databases they generate constitute a Superpanopticon, a system of surveillance without walls, windows, towers or guards" (Poster 1990, 93). Mark Andrejevic has coined the notion of the digital enclosure (Andrejevic 2004, 2007), in which interactive technologies generate "feedback about the transactions themselves", and he said that this feedback "becomes the property of private companies" (Andrejevic 2007, 3). Andrejevic (2007, 2) sees the Internet as a virtual digital enclosure. Commercial and state surveillance of consumers would be the result of the digital enclosure. They "foster asymmetrical and undemocratic power relations. Political and economic elites collect information that facilitates social Taylorism rather than fostering more democratic forms of shared control and participation" (Andrejevic 2007, 257). Nicole Cohen argues, based on Mark Andrejevic and Tiziana Terranova, that Facebook profits by the "valorization of surveillance" (Cohen 2008, 8). Parenti (2003, 78) stresses that by digital technology "surveillance becomes more ubiquitous, automatic, anonymous, decentralized, and self-reinforcing".

David Lyon has stressed the role of computers for contemporary surveillance and has used the notion of electronic surveillance: "Contemporary surveillance must be understood in the light of changed circumstances, especially the growing centrality of consumption and the adoption of information technologies" (Lyon 1994, 225). "Although computers are not necessarily used for all kinds of surveillance—some is still face to face and some, like most CCTV systems, still require human operators—most surveillance apparatuses in the wealthier, technological societies depend upon computers" (Lyon 2003, 22). "Electronic surveillance has to do with the ways that computer databases are used to store and process personal information on different kinds of populations" (Lyon 1994, 8). David Lyon (1998; 2001, 101) speaks of the worldwide web of surveillance in order to stress that "all uses of the Internet, the world wide web and email systems are traceable and this capacity is rapidly being exploited as these media are commercialized". He distinguishes three main forms of surveillance in cyberspace that are related to employment, security and policing, and marketing (Lyon 1998, 95). Lyon (1994, 51f) argues that digitalization and networking have changed surveillance: File size has grown, individuals can be more easily traced because databases are dispersed and easily accessed by central institutions, the speed of data flow has increased, and citizens are subjected to increasingly constant and profound monitoring.

Manuel Castells (2001, 172) defines Internet surveillance technologies as technologies that

> intercept messages, place markers that allow tracking of communication flows from a specific computer location, and monitor machine activity around the clock. Surveillance technologies may identify a given server at the origin of a message. Then, by persuasion or coercion, governments, companies, or courts may obtain from the Internet service provider the identity of the potential culprit by using identification technologies, or simply by looking up their listings when the information is available.

Castells considers Internet surveillance as a technology of control (Castells 2001, 171).

Graham and Wood (2003/2007) argue that monitoring across widening geographical distances and the active sorting of subject populations on a continuous, real-time basis are two central characteristics of digital surveillance. They say that under the given economic conditions, "digital surveillance is likely to be geared overwhelmingly towards supporting the processes of indvidualization, commodification, and consumerization" (Graham and Wood 2003/2007, 219).

Many of the discussions about the role of the Internet in surveillance started before the Internet became a popular mass medium in the mid-1990s. Large-scale Internet usage did not take off before 1995, when the Mosaic browser was made available to the public. The World Wide Web (WWW) was created in 1990 by Tim Berners-Lee and was released for the public in 1993. In December 1990, there was one website on the WWW, in September 1993 there were 204 sites, in June 1996, 252,000, in December 2000, 25,675,581, in November 2006, 101,435,253 (data source: Internet time line by Robert Zakon, http://www.zakon.org/robert/internet/timeline/#Growth).

The Internet enables a globally networked form of surveillance. Internet surveillance adds at least two dimensions to computer surveillance: global interaction and networking. The contributors to this book show that it is an important task to discuss how notions such as the new surveillance, dataveillance, the electronic panopticon, and electronic surveillance can be applied to the Internet and what commonalities and differences there are between computer surveillance and Internet surveillance.

1.2. WEB 2.0 AND SURVEILLANCE

Many observers claim that the Internet has been transformed in the past years from a system that is primarily oriented to information provision into a system that is more oriented to communication and community building. The notions of "web 2.0", "social media", "social software", and "social network(ing) sites" have emerged in this context. Web platforms such as Wikipedia, MySpace, Facebook, YouTube, Google, Blogger, Rapidshare, Wordpress, Hi5, Flickr, Photobucket, Orkut, Skyrock, Twitter, YouPorn, PornHub, Youku, Orkut, Redtube, Friendster, Adultfriendfinder, Megavideo, Tagged, Tube8, Mediafire, Megaupload, Mixi, Livejournal, LinkedIn, Netlog, ThePirateBay, Orkut, XVideos, Metacafe, Digg, StudiVZ, etc. are said to be typical for this transformation of the Internet. *Web 2.0/Social media platforms are web-based platforms that predominantly support online social networking, online community-building, and maintenance, collaborative information production and sharing, and user-generated content production, diffusion, and consumption.* No matter if we agree that important transformations of the Internet have taken place or not, it is clear that a principle that underlies such platforms is the massive provision and storage of personal data that are systematically evaluated, marketed, and used for targeting users with advertising. Therefore surveillance is an important topic in the context of web 2.0 studies.

> Web 2.0 is the network as platform, spanning all connected devices; Web 2.0 applications are those that make the most of the intrinsic advantages of that platform: delivering software as a continually-updated service that gets better the more people use it, consuming and remixing data from multiple sources, including individual users, while providing their own data and services in a form that allows remixing by others, creating network effects through an 'architecture of participation', and going beyond the page metaphor of Web 1.0 to deliver rich user experiences. (O'Reilly 2005, online)

Some claim that the Internet has in recent years become more based on sharing, communication, and cooperation. Tapscott and Williams say that web 2.0 brings about "a new economic democracy [. . .] in which we all have a lead role" (Tapscott and Williams 2007). Manuel Castells characterizes social media and web 2.0 as media that enable mass-self communication: "people build their own networks of mass self-communication, thus empowering themselves" (Castells 2009, 421). For Clay Shirky, the central aspect of web 2.0 is "a remarkable increase in our ability to share, to cooperate with one another, and to take collective action" (Shirky 2008, 20f). Axel Bruns sees the rise of produsage—the "hybrid user/producer role which inextricably interweaves both forms of participation" (Bruns 2008, 21)—as the central characteristic of web 2.0. Henry Jenkins (2008) sees a participatory culture at work on web 2.0. Mark Deuze speaks in relation to web 2.0 of the "interactive, globally networked and increasingly participatory nature of new media" (Deuze 2007, 40). Shiffman (2008) sees the emergence of the "age of engage" as result of web 2.0. Yochai Benkler (2006) argues that the Internet advances the emergence of commons-based peer production systems (such as open source software or Wikipedia) that are "radically decentralized, collaborative, and nonproprietary; based on sharing resources and outputs among widely distributed, loosely connected individuals who cooperate with each other without relying on either market signals or managerial commands" (Benkler 2006, 60). Others have stressed for example that online advertising is a mechanism by which corporations exploit web 2.0 users who form an Internet prosumer/produser commodity and are part of a surplus-value generating class that produces the commons of society that are exploited by capital (Fuchs 2011; Fuchs 2010a, b; Fuchs 2009a, b, c; Fuchs 2008a, 195–209, Fuchs 2008b; Andrejevic 2002, 2004, 2007, 2009); that web 2.0 is based on the exploitation of free labour (Terranova 2004); that most web 2.0 users are part of a creative precarious underclass that needs economic models that assist them in making a living from their work (Lovink 2008); that blogging is mainly a self-centred, nihilistic, cynical activity (Lovink 2008); that the web 2.0 economy is still dominated by corporate media chains (Stanyer 2009); that web 2.0 is contradictory and therefore also serves dominative interests (Cammaerts 2008); that web 2.0 optimism is uncritical and an ideology that serves corporate interests (Fuchs 2008b, Scholz 2008, van Dijck and Nieborg 2009); that web 2.0 users are more passive users than active creators (van Dijck 2009); that web 2.0 discourse advances a minimalist notion of participation (Carpentier and de Cleen 2008); or that corporations appropriate blogs and web 2.0 in the form of corporate blogs, advertising blogs, spam blogs, and fake blogs (Deuze 2008).

This short selective overview shows that web 2.0 is a contradictory phenomenon that, just like all techno-social systems, does not have a one-dimensional effect, but complex interconnected effects (Fuchs 2008a). The contributors to this book show the central importance of web 2.0 in the discussion and analysis of Internet surveillance. The working of web 2.0 is based on the collection, storage, usage, and analysis of a huge amount of personal data. Therefore discussing privacy- and surveillance-implications of web 2.0 and the political, economic, and cultural dimensions of privacy and surveillance on web 2.0 becomes an important task. The contributions in this book contribute to the clarification of the surveillance and privacy implications of web 2.0.

The term "web 2.0" can create the false impression that we are experiencing an entirely new Internet. But this is neither the case for the Internet's technological dimension nor for its organizational and institutional contexts. E-mail and information search are still the most popular online activities. In 2010, 61% of all people in the EU27 countries aged 15–74 used e-mail at least once during a three-month period, and 56% used the Internet to search for information about goods and services (data source: Eurostat). The change that has taken place in the past couple of years is that today World Wide Web platforms like Facebook (#2 in the list of most accessed websites, data source: alexa.com, top sites, accessed on January 2, 2011), YouTube (#3), Blogger (#7), Wikipedia (#8), and Twitter (#10) are among the ten most accessed and popular websites in the world. Sharing audiovisual content in public (user-generated content production and diffusion), writing online diaries (blogging), co-creating knowledge with others (wikis), staying in constant contact with friends and acquaintances (social networking sites), sending and sharing short messages online (microblogging, as on Twitter) are relatively new activities that in the 1990s were not supported by the World Wide Web. But there are also many Internet activities, applications, and platforms (like search engines, e-mail, online banking, online shopping, online newspapers, etc.) that have been around longer. The terms "web 2.0" and "social media" do not signify a new or radical transformation of the Internet, but the emergence of specific social qualities (sharing, online cooperation, etc.) supported by the World Wide Web that have become more important (Fuchs 2010b).

The Internet is a technology of cognition, communication, and cooperation (Fuchs 2008a, 2010b). All information is a Durkheimian social fact; it is generated in societal contexts and therefore reflects certain qualities of society and its production contexts. In this sense, we can say that the Internet is and has always been social because it is a vast collection of information and therefore of social facts (Fuchs 2010b). A second mode of sociality is the establishment and reproduction of social relationships (Fuchs 2010b).

Certain Internet applications and platforms support communication and thereby are social in a communicative sense. Cooperation is a third mode of sociality that is reflected in Ferdinand Tönnies' concept of community and Karl Marx's notion of cooperative labour (Fuchs 2010b). The terms web 2.0 and social media are in everyday life frequently employed for meaning that this third mode of sociality (cooperation) has to a certain degree become more supported by the World Wide Web (Fuchs 2010b). One should how-ever bear in mind that this is a specific understanding and mode of sociality and that there are other ones as well (Fuchs 2010b).

One should neither be optimistic nor pessimistic about the transforma-tion of power structures on the Internet. The Internet still is a tool that is used by powerful groups for trying to support their control and domina-tion of other groups just like it is a tool that has potentials for being used in resistances against domination (Fuchs 2011). The difference today is that technologies and platforms like social networking sites, video shar-ing platforms, blogs, microblogs, wikis, user-generated content upload and sharing sites (like WikiLeaks), etc. have come to play a certain role in the exertion of and resistance against domination. The study of online surveillance and web 2.0 surveillance is situated in the context of the con-tinuities and changes of the Internet, conflicts and contradictions, power structures and society.

1.3. THE ROLE OF THEORIES, FOUCAULT, AND THE PANOPTICON FOR ANALYZING INTERNET

Surveillance

Lyon (2006b, 10) argues that modern surveillance theories relate to nation-state, bureaucracy, techno-logic, political economy, whereas postmodern surveillance theories focus on digital technologies and their implications. The contributors to this book show that both modern and postmodern theories are important for discussing Internet surveillance and web 2.0 surveillance.

The notion of the panopticon was conceived by Jeremy Bentham as prison architecture in the nineteenth century and connected to academic discussions about the notions of surveillance and disciplinary power by Michel Foucault (1977, 1994). The concept of the panopticon has strongly influenced discus-sions about computer and Internet surveillance. On the one hand there are authors who find the metaphor suitable. Robins and Webster (1999) argue, for example, that in what they term cybernetic society "the computer has achieved [. . .] the extension and intensification of panoptic control; it has rendered social control more pervasive, more invasive, more total, but also more routine, mundane and inescapable" (Robins and Webster 1999, 180, see also 118–122). Webster (2002, 222) argues that computers result in a panopticon without physical walls. Oscar H. Gandy (1993) has introduced the notion of the panoptic sort: "The panoptic sort is a difference machine that sorts individuals into categories and classes on the basis of routine measurements. It is a discriminatory technology that allocates options and opportunities on the basis of those measures and the administrative models that they inform" (Gandy 1993, 15). It is a system of power and disciplinary surveillance that identifies, classifies, and assesses (Gandy 1993, 15). David Lyon (2003) speaks based on Gandy's notion of the panoptic sort in relation to computers and the Internet of surveillance as social sorting. "The surveillance system obtains personal and group data in order to classify people and populations according to varying criteria, to determine who should be targeted for special treatment, suspicion, eligibility, inclusion, access, and so on" (Lyon 2003, 20). Gandy has analyzed data mining as a form of panoptic sorting (Gandy 2003) and has stressed the role of electronic systems in panoptic sorting: "Electronic systems promise the ultimate in narrowcasting or targeting, so it becomes possible to send an individualized message to each individual on the network" (Gandy 1993, 90). Mathiesen (1997) has introduced the notion of the synopticon as user-oriented correlate to the panopticon and has argued that the Internet is a silencing synopticon (Mathiesen 2004). James Boyle (1997) argues that the works of Foucault allow an alternative to the assumption of Internet libertarians that cyberspace cannot be controlled in order to provide "suggestive insights into the ways in which power can be exercised on the Internet" (Boyle 1997, 184). Gordon (1987) speaks of the electronic panopticon; Zuboff (1988) of the information panopticon; Poster (1990) of the electronic superpanopticon; Elmer (2003, 2004) of diagrammatic panoptic surveillance; and Rämö and Edenius (2008) speak of the mobile panopticon.

On the other hand, there are authors who want to demolish the metaphor of the panopticon (for example Haggerty 2006) and do not find it useful for explaining contemporary surveillance and networked forms of surveillance. They argue that surveillance systems such as the Internet are decentralized forms of surveillance, whereas the notion of the panopticon assumes centralized data collection and control. "Certainly, surveillance today is more decentralized, less subject to spatial and temporal constraints (location, time of day, etc.), and less organized than ever before by the dualisms of observer and observed, subject and object, individual and mass. The system of control is deterritorializing" (Bogard 2006, 102). Haggerty and Ericson (2000/2007) have introduced the notion of the surveillant assemblage and argue that contemporary surveillance is heterogeneous, involves humans and non-humans, state and extra-state institutions, and "allows for the scrutiny of the powerful by both institutions and the general population" (Haggerty and Ericson 2000/2007, 112). Lyon (1994, 26, 67) argues that Foucault's notion of the panopticon does not give attention to two central features of contemporary surveillance: information technologies and consumerism. Connected to this critique of Foucault is the claim that the contemporary Internet makes surveillance more democratic or participatory (for example: Albechtslund 2008; Campbell and Carlson 2002; Cascio 2005; Dennis 2008; Haggerty 2006; Whitaker 1999).

There is no ultimate solution to the question of whether Foucault and the notion of the panopticon are suited for analyzing contemporary surveillance and Internet surveillance; it is an open controversial issue. The contributions in this volume show that the role of Foucault, the panopticon, and George Orwell's Big Brother for surveillance studies continues to be discussed in a controversial manner and that this controversy is also important for Internet studies and web 2.0 studies.

For Gandy, especially, corporations and the state conduct surveillance: "The panoptic sort is a technology that has been designed and is being continually revised to serve the interests of decision makers within the government and the corporate bureaucracies" (Gandy 1993, 95). Toshimaru Ogura (2006, 272) argues that "the common characteristics of surveillance are the management of population based on capitalism and the nation state". Because of the importance of political actors and economic actors in surveillance, we give special attention to aspects of economic and political surveillance on the Internet in this book.

1.4. ECONOMIC IMPLICATIONS OF INTERNET SURVEILLANCE

The production, distribution, and consumption of commodities is one of the defining features of contemporary societies. If the claim that surveillance has become a central quality of contemporary society is true, then this means that surveillance shapes and is shaped by economic production, circulation, and consumption. The economy therefore constitutes an important realm of Internet surveillance that needs to be studied.

Historically, the surveillance of workplaces, the workforce, and production has been the central aspect of economic surveillance. Zuboff (1988) has stressed that computers advance workplace panopticism. As workplaces have become connected to cyberspace, employees tend to produce, receive, transmit, and process more data in less time. They leave digital traces in digital networks that allow the reconstruction and documentation of their activities. The Internet therefore poses new potentials and threats for workplace and workforce surveillance.

Commodities are not only produced, they also circulate in markets and are consumed. Without consumption there is no realization of profit and therefore no growth of the economic operations of firms. The rise of Fordist mass production and mass consumption after 1945 has extended and intensified the interest of corporations to know details about the consumption patterns of citizens. This has not only resulted in the rise of the advertising industry, but also in the intensification of consumer research and consumer surveillance. The rise of flexible accumulation strategies in the 1980s (Harvey 1989) has brought about an individualization and personalization of commodities and advertising. The Internet poses new opportunities for consumer surveillance and new risks for consumers. Technologies such as cookies, data mining, collaborative filtering, ambient intelligence, clickstream analysis, spyware, web crawlers, log file analysis, etc. allow an extension and intensification of consumer surveillance with the help of the Internet. It therefore becomes a central task to analyze how consumer surveillance works on the Internet and which policy implications this phenomenon brings about. Targeted advertising, spam mail, the collection and marketing of e-mail addresses and user data for commercial purposes, detailed consumer profiling, privacy policies, terms of use, the role of opt-in and opt-out solutions, and fair information practices on the Internet are just some of the important and pressing research topics (see for example Andrejevic 2002; Bellman et al. 2004; Campbell and Carlson 2002; Caudill and Murphy 2000; Culnan and Bies 2003; Fernback and Papacharissi 2007; Lauer 2008; Milne, Rohm, and Bahl 2004; Miyaziki and Krishnamurthy 2002; Ryker et al. 2002; Sheehan and Hoy 2000; Solove 2004b; Turow 2006; Wall 2006; Wang, Lee, and Wang 1998).

Only a few randomly selected opinions about the economic dimension of Internet surveillance can be briefly mentioned in this short introduction. "The effectiveness of targeted marketing depends upon data, and the challenge is to obtain as much of it as possible" (Solove 2004b, 19). "Moreover, companies such as Microsoft and Yahoo are beginning to select ads for people based on combining the tracking of individuals' search or web activities with huge amounts of demographic and psychographic data they are collecting about them. Privacy advocates worry that people know little about how data are collected online, or about the factors that lead such firms to reach out to them with certain materials and not others" (Turow 2006, 299). David Wall argues that surveillant technologies of the Internet such as spyware, cookies, spam spider boots, peer-to-peer technologies, and computer-based profiling "make possible the accumulation and exploitation of valuable personal information" (Wall 2006, 341) and "have facilitated the growth in information capital(ism)" (Wall 2006, 340). "The tremendous technical resources of information technology find a vast new field in identifying, tracking, and attempting to channel the consumption activities of householders in the advanced societies. The data gleaned from available records of purchasing patterns and purchasing power are combined both to allure consumers into further specific styles of spending and also to limit the choices of those whose records indicate that at some point they have failed to conform to proper consuming norms, or have transgressed their spending abilities and accrued unacceptable debts" (Lyon 1994, 137). Mathiesen (2004) uses the notion of the synopticon in order to stress that corporations dominate the Internet and manipulate users in order to establish a system of silencing. "Progress in information processing caused the advancement of the segmentation of mass consumers into many categories of consumers" (Ogura 2006, 275).

Economic surveillance includes aspects such as workplace surveillance, consumer surveillance, industrial espionage, or the surveillance of competition. A frequent concern of web 2.0 users is that employers or potential employers could spy on them with the help of Google or social networking sites and could thereby gain access to personal information that could cause job-related disadvantages (Fuchs 2009b). This phenomenon shows that web 2.0 has dramatic implications for economic surveillance that need to be understood and analyzed.

Studying the role of the Internet in economic surveillance is an important task. The contributions in this book contribute to this task.

1.5. POLITICAL IMPLICATIONS OF INTERNET SURVEILLANCE

Internet surveillance has important implications for political regulation, state power, and civil society.

E-government has in recent years emerged as an important phenomenon of online politics. Toshimaru Ogura (2006) argues that e-government is an ideology and advances surveillance by governments.

> E-government creates another route for making consensus with the public by using ICT. ICT allows government to access the constituency online, and monitor their political needs. As public comments online exemplify the case, the government tries to make any interactive discourse with people who want to participate in the policy-making process. This looks more democratic and more effective than the representative decision-making system. However, online democracy only has a narrow basis of permissible scope for discussion because it is based on an 'if/and/or' feedback system of cybernetics. It cannot raise concerns about the fundamental preconditions and essential alternatives or transformation of regime. It ignores the opposition forces outside of partnership strategies that refuse the feedback system itself. (Ogura 2006, 288)

There are different regulatory regimes and options at the policy level that governments and civil society can pursue in dealing with Internet surveillance and its privacy implications at the political level. The US approach in privacy regulation relies on the free market and self-regulation by corporations. It makes some exceptions from the self-regulation rule such as data held by financial institutions and data relating to children (Children's Online Privacy Protection Act 1998). It conceives privacy primarily as a commodity. The EU approach defines privacy as a fundamental right that needs to be protected by the state (Data Protection Directive 95/46/EC of the European Parliament 1995) (Ashworth and Free 2006; Caudill and Murphy 2000).

The terrorist attacks of September 11, 2001, and the subsequent wars in Iraq and Afghanistan have brought about important privacy- and surveillance-policy changes that have implications for Internet surveillance. We can only mention a few examples here. The EU's 2006 Data Retention Directive requires the member states to pass laws that require communication service providers to store identification and connection data for phone calls and Internet communication for at least six months. The USA Patriot Act of 2001 (*Uniting and Strengthening America by Providing Appropriate Tools*

*R*equired to *I*ntercept and *O*bstruct *T*errorism Act of 2001) in section 210 widened the scope of data that the government can obtain from Internet service providers with subpoenas (besides name, address, and identity, data such as session times and durations, used services, device address information, payment method, bank account, and credit card number can also be obtained). The Act extended wiretapping from phones to e-mail and the Web. The use of roving wiretaps was extended from the law enforcement context to the foreign intelligence context, and government no longer has to show that the targeted person is using the communication line in order to obtain surveillance permission from a court. The regulation that surveillance of communications for foreign intelligence requires proof that intelligence gathering is the primary purpose has been changed to the formulation that it must only be a significant purpose. Pen/trap surveillance allows law enforcement to obtain information on all connections that are made from one line. Prior to the Patriot Act, law enforcement agencies had to show to the court that the device had been used for contacting a foreign power in order to gain the permission to monitor the line. The Patriot Act changed the formulation in the law so that law enforcement agencies only have to prove to the court that the information that is likely to be obtained is relevant to an ongoing criminal investigation. This amendment made it much easier for law enforcement agencies to engage in Internet surveillance. Section 505, which allowed the FBI to obtain data on any user from Internet service providers, was declared unconstitutional in 2004. The Combating Terrorism Act that was passed in September 2001 legalized the installation of Carnivore Internet filtering systems by intelligence services at Internet service providers without a judge's permission. The Patriot Act confirmed this rule.

There is a significant debate about the question of whether these regulatory changes bring about conditions that advance a total or maximum surveillance society (see for example Kerr 2003 and Solove 2004a for two opposing views). Such debates show that discussing the continuities and discontinuities of Internet surveillance before and after 9/11 is important. The contributions in this book make a significant contribution to these debates.

Some scholars have argued that the post-9/11 condition is characterized by the ideological normalization of surveillance. "It is also likely that the use of data mining in the so-called 'war against terrorists' will soften the public up for its use in a now quiescent war against global competitors, and the threat to shrinking profits" (Gandy 2003, 41). Bigo argues that surveillance technologies have become so ubiquitous and "are considered so banal [. . .] that nobody (including the judges) asks for their legitimacy and their efficiency after a certain period of time" (Bigo 2006, 49). He speaks in this context of the ban-opticon, which results in the normalization of emergency. "My hypothesis is that surveillance [. . .] is easily accepted because all sorts of watching have become commonplace within a 'viewer society', encouraged by the culture of TV and cinema. [. . .] It is not too much of stretch to suggest that part of the enthusiasm for adopting new surveillance technologies, especially after 9/11, relates to the fact that in the global north (and possibly elsewhere too) the voyeur gaze is a commonplace of contemporary culture" (Lyon 2006a, 36, 49).

Naomi Klein has stressed the connection between corporate and political interests in fostering surveillance in general and Internet surveillance in particular after 9/11.

> In the nineties, tech companies endlessly trumpeted the wonders of the borderless world and the power of information technology to topple authoritarian regimes and bring down walls. Today, inside the disaster capitalism complex, the tools of the information revolution have been flipped to serve the opposite purpose. In the process, cell phones and Web surfing have been turned into powerful tools of mass state surveillance by increasingly authoritarian regimes, with the full cooperation of privatized phone companies and search engines. [. . .] Many technologies in use today as part of the War on Terror—biometric identification, video surveillance, Web tracking, data mining, sold by companies like Verint Systems and Scisint, Accenture and ChoicePoint—had been developed by the private sector before September 11 as a way to build detailed customer profiles, opening up new vistas for micromarketing. [. . .] September 11 loosened this logjam in the market: suddenly the fear of terror was greater than the fear of living in a surveillance society. (Klein 2008, 302f)

The operators of Facebook, the most popular social networking sites, have continuously witnessed user protests against changes of the privacy policy and the terms of use that are perceived to bring about privacy threats and more surveillance. Such protests show the potential of the Internet for the global networked initiation, coordination, and support of protests. Various scholars have in this context coined terms such as cyberprotest and cyberactivism (see for example McCaughey and Ayers 2003; van de Donk et al. 2004). Fuchs (2008a, 277–289) has distinguished between cognitive, communicative, and cooperative cyberprotest as three forms of protest on the Internet. Cyberprotest is an expression of civil society- and social movement-activism. Surveillance as political phenomenon has always been connected to the rise and the activities of citizen groups. The Internet in general and web 2.0 in particular bring about specific conditions for social movement activities that relate to the political topic of surveillance. It is an important task for contemporary Internet studies and surveillance studies to conduct research on the relationship of Internet, surveillance, and social movements.

The Los Angeles Police Department (LAPD) stopped the African-American Rodney King in his car on March 3, 1991, after a freeway chase. King resisted arrest, which resulted in a brutal beating by the police from which he suffered a fracture of a leg and of a facial bone. The four police officers, Briseno, Koon, Powell, and Wind, were tried for police brutality and acquitted by a LA court in April 1992. George Holiday filmed the beating of King with a low technology home video camera. When the news of the acquittal of the officers and the video made their way to the mass media, outrage spread, and many observers came to hold the view that both the LAPD and the justice system engaged in racism against African-Americans. The event triggered riots in Los Angeles in April 2002. John Fiske (1996) discusses the role of video cameras in the Rodney King example and other cases in order to show that the miniaturization, cheapening, and mass availability of video cameras changes surveillance. "Videotechnology extends the panoptic eye of power [. . .], but it also enables those who are normally the object of surveillance to turn the lens and reverse its power" (Fiske 1996, 127). "The videolow allows the weak one of their few opportunities to intervene effectively in the power of surveillance, and to reverse its flow. [. . .] The uses of videolow to extend disciplinary surveillance can be countered [. . .] by those who turn the cameras back upon the surveillers" (Fiske 1996, 224f). Today, we live in an age where the Internet shapes the lives of many of us. The Internet has become a new key medium of information, communication, and co-production. Therefore, paraphrasing Fiske, we can say that the Internet extends the panoptic eye of power, but it also enables those who are normally objects of surveillance to turn the eyes, the ears, and the voice on the powerful and reverse the power of surveillance. We can in such cases speak of Internet counter-surveillance.

Neda Agha-Soltan, a 27-year-old Iranian woman, was shot on June 20, 2009, by Iranian police forces during a demonstration against irregularities at the Iranian presidential election. Her death was filmed with a cellphone video camera and uploaded to YouTube. It reached the mass media and caused worldwide outrage over Iranian police brutality. Discussions about her death were extremely popular on Twitter following the event. The protestors used social media such as Twitter, social networking platforms, or the site Anonymous Iran for coordinating and organizing protests. The Facebook profile image of another Iranian woman, Neda Soltani, was mistakenly taken for being a picture of the killed woman. It made its way to the mass media and caused threats to Ms. Soltani, who as a result had to flee from Iran to Germany. This example on the one hand shows the potential for counter-power that the Internet poses, but also the problems that can be created by information confusion in large information spaces. The newspaper vendor Ian Tomlinson died after being beaten to the ground by British police forces when he watched the G-20 London summit protests as a bystander on April 1, 2009. The police claimed first that he died of natural causes after suffering a heart attack. But a video showing police forces pushing Tomlinson to the ground surfaced on the Internet, made its way to the mass media, and resulted in investigations against police officers.

These examples show that the Internet not only is a surveillance tool that allows the state and corporations to watch citizens and to create political profiles, criminal profiles, and consumer profiles, but that it also poses the potential for citizens to conduct surveillance of the powerful and to try to exert counter-power that tries to create public attention for injustices committed by the powerful against the weak. The Internet is therefore a surveillance power and potentially a counter-surveillance power. There are ways of watching the watchers and surveilling the surveillers. After the Rodney King incident, copwatch initiatives that watch police forces in order to stop police brutality became popular in the US and Canada. Since the turn of the millennium, scepticism against the power of corporations has intensified and has been supported by Internet communication. Corporate watch sites have emerged on the Internet. They document corporate crimes and injustices caused by corporations. Large corporations have huge financial power and have influence so that they are enabled to frequently hide the details, size, nature, and consequences of their operations. Economic and political power tries to remain invisible at those points where it is connected to injustices. Watch sites are attempts to visualize the injustices connected to power; they try to exert a counter-hegemonic power that makes use of the Internet. Alternative online media try to make available critical information that questions power structures that normally remain unquestioned and invisible. The most popular alternative online medium is Indymedia. Indymedia Centres are seen by John Downing (2003, 254; see also 2002) as practices of social anarchism because "their openness, their blend of internationalism and localism, their use of hyperlinks, their self-management, represent a development entirely consonant with the best in the socialist anarchist tradition". For Dorothy Kidd (2003, 64) the Indymedia Centres are "a vibrant commons" among "the monocultural enclosures of the .coms and media giants". Atton (2004, 26f) argues that radical online journalism like Indymedia is "opposed to hierarchical, elite-centred notions of journalism as business" and places "power into the hands of those who are more intimately involved in those stories" so that "activists become journalists". The power of alternative online media derives partly from their open character, which allows citizens to become journalists. WikiLeaks became part of the world news in 2010 because it leaked secret documents about the US wars in Afghanistan and Iraq to the public. Its task is to use the "power of principled leaking to embarrass governments, corporations and institutions"; it is "a buttress against unaccountable and abusive power" (self-description, http://www.wikileaks.org/wiki/WikiLeaks:About, accessed on August 13, 2010). Leaking secret information is understood as a way of watching the powerful and holding them accountable.

But in a stratified society, resources are distributed asymmetrically. Alternative media and watchdog projects are mainly civil society projects that are operated by voluntary labour and are not supported by corporations and governments. They therefore tend to be confronted with a lack of resources such as money, activists, time, infrastructure, or influence. Visibility on the Internet can be purchased and centralized. This situation poses advantages for powerful actors such as states and large corporations and disadvantages for civil society and social movement organizations. It is therefore no surprise that Indymedia is only ranked number 4147 in the list of the most accessed websites, whereas BBC Online is ranked number 44, CNN Online number 52, the *New York Times* Online number 115, Spiegel Online number 152, Bildzeitung Online number 246, or Fox News Online number 250 (data source: alexa.com, top 1,000,000,000 sites, August 2, 2009). Similarly, concerning the example of Neda Soltan, the Iranian government controls technology that allows them to monitor and censor the Internet and mobile phones, which has resulted in the surveillance of political activists. The surveillance technologies are provided or developed by Western corporations such as Nokia Siemens Networks or Secure Computing.

Power and counter-power, hegemony and counter-hegemony, surveillance and counter-surveillance are inherent potentialities of the Internet. But these potentials are asymmetrically distributed. The Internet in a stratified society involves an asymmetric dialectic that privileges the powerful. It has a power to make visible the invisible, which can be the personal lives of citizens, but also the operations of the powerful. But attention is a scare resource on the Internet, although each citizen can easily produce information, not all information can easily gain similar attention by users. There is an Internet attention economy that is dominated by powerful actors: "Surveillance is not democratic and applied equally to all" (Fiske 1996, 246).

The contributors to this volume show that the political dimension of Internet surveillance is an important realm of analysis and that Internet surveillance has practical political consequences that affect civil society, social movements, citizens, governments, and policies.

1.6. DIMENSIONS AND QUALITIES OF INTERNET SURVEILLANCE

Information technology enables surveillance at a distance, whereas non-technological surveillance, for example when a person is tailed by a detective, is unmediated, does not automatically result in data gathering and requires the copresence, closeness, or proximity of surveiller and the surveilled in one space. Internet surveillance operates in real time over networks at high transmission speed. Digital data doubles can with the help of the Internet be copied and manipulated endlessly, easily, and cheaply. Table 1.1 identifies fourteen dimensions of the Internet and summarizes how these dimensions shape the conditions for Internet surveillance and resistance against Internet surveillance or counter-surveillance. It should be noted that Table 1.1 presents an asymmetric dialectic where resistance is only a precarious potential that is less powerful than the surveillance reality. On the Internet we find an unequal resource distribution, unequal technological innovation diffusion, an unequal distribution of power, etc. (see Fuchs 2008a). The contributions in this book all relate to one or more of these 14 dimensions and show that Internet surveillance is embedded into processes of power and counter-power.

Starke-Meyerring and Gurak (2007) distinguish among three kinds of Internet surveillance technologies: 1) surveillance of personal data captured from general Internet use, 2) surveillance of personal data captured by using specialized Internet services, 3) technologies and practices designed to access data from Internet users. Data can be collected, stored, analyzed, transferred,

Table 1.1   Dimensions and Qualities of Internet Surveillance

Dimension	Quality of the Internet	Internet surveillance	Potentials for resisting surveillance
(1) Space	**global communication** global communication at a distance, global information space	**global surveillance** surveillance at a distance is possible from all nodes in the network, not just from a single point; combination and collection of many data items about certain individuals from a global information space	**data storage switching** data can be transferred from one virtual position to another and deleted at the original points, which makes it harder to detect data, but powerful actors possess powerful surveillance tools (e.g., Echelon), and deleted data might still persist in copies at other places
(2) Time	**real-time (synchronous) or asynchronous global communication**	**real-time surveillance** surveillance of real-time communication, surveillance of stored asynchronous communication, surveillance of communication protocols and multiple data traces	**real-time activism** coordination of social movements in real time and asynchronous time (cyberactivism)
(3) Speed	**high-speed data transmission**	**high-speed surveillance** availability of high-speed surveillance systems	**increased surveillance complexity** high-speed transmission enlarges the volume of global data transfer and makes surveillance more complex; but state institutions and corporations due to resource advantages frequently have more efficient and powerful systems than users

(4) Size	**miniaturization** storage capacity per chip increases rapidly (Moore's law)	**surveillance data growth** ever more data on individuals can be stored for surveillance purposes on storage devices that become smaller and cheaper over time	**increased surveillance complexity** users store more data, which makes surveillance more complex; new storage media develop rapidly so that the transfer of surveillance data becomes more complex, which favours surveillance data loss; but powerful institutions benefit from technological advances much earlier than the everyday user (unequal innovation diffusion)
(5) Reproduction	**data multiplicity** digital data can copied easily, cheaply, and endlessly; copying does not destroy the original data	**surveillance data multiplicity** surveillance becomes easy and cheap; if multiple copies of data exist, specific data is easier to find	**data manipulation** data can be consciously manipulated in order to set wrong tracks
(6) Sensory Modality	**multimedia** digital combination of text, sound, image, animation, and video in one integrated medium	**multimodal surveillance** surveillance of multisensory data over one medium	**increased surveillance complexity** messages that are encoded into images, sounds, or videos are difficult to detect (steganography), but there is unequal innovation diffusion
(7) Communication Flow	**many-to-many communication**	**social network surveillance** the multiple personal and professional social networks of individuals become visible and can be traced	**networked cyberprotest** easy and fast coordination of social movements and protests (cyberprotest); protest communication can quickly intensify and spread over the Internet; but political and corporate actors control huge amounts of resources and therefore visibility on the Internet

(*continued*)

Table 1.1 (continued)

Dimension	Quality of the Internet	Internet surveillance	Potentials for resisting surveillance
(8) Information Structure	**hypertext** networked, interlinked, and hyper-textual information structures	**linked surveillance** the links between persons can be more easily observed	**networked individualism in cyber-protest** protest can be easier linked and networked; but protest reduces itself frequently to simple isolated point-and-click activities that do not have the same visual power as mass action protests with physical presence
(9) Reception	**online produsage** recipients become producers of infor-mation (produsers, prosumers)	**economic exploitation of produsage** economic exploitation of produsage, new capital accumulation strategies based on active, creative users that are sold to advertisers as produsage commodity; targeted advertising based on continuous surveillance of user-generated content	**critical produsage** critical information can be easily produced; but visibility is largely controlled by powerful corporations that dominate the Internet
(10) Mode of Interaction and Sociality	**online cooperation** cooperative information production at a distance, information sharing at a distance	**enclosure of digital commons** laws that enable the surveillance of sharing and cooperation, intellectual property rights	**creation of digital commons** copy left; open content; intellectual property rights can easily be under-mined if many users engage in sharing and cooperation; but control of prop-erty rights and attempts to enclose the digital commons are inherent to capitalism and therefore ubiquitous

(11) Context	**decontextualization** decontextualized information and anonymity (authorship, time and place of production, etc. might be unclear)	**intensification of surveillance** decontextualization advances speculative and pre-emptive surveillance	**data anonymity** anonymous data and encrypted messages are harder to trace; but there is an unequal innovation diffusion in this area
(12) Reality	**derealization** the boundaries between actuality and fiction can be blurred	**intensification of surveillance** fictive reality might be taken for actual reality by surveillers, which puts people at risk and intensifies surveillance	**data fakes** fake data might be spread consciously, which makes surveillance more complex, but can also make surveillance more total
(13) Identity and Emotions	**emotive Internet** the Internet is a very expressive medium that allows identity construction and representation online	**personalized surveillance** surveillance of very personal characteristics of individuals and their emotions becomes possible	**fake identities** fake or anonymous online identities make surveillance more difficult; but also allow the intensification of surveillance based on the argument that anonymity is dangerous, might foster antisocial behaviour, and therefore needs to be controlled
(14) Availability	**ubiquitous Internet** the Internet has become ubiquitous in all spheres of everyday life	**ubiquitous surveillance** in a heteronomous society, there is constant and profound surveillance of Internet information and communication for economic, political, judicial, and other aims	**intensified and extended protest capacities** in everyday life, the Internet is likely to attract a large number of users who increase their e-literacy over time; this increases the mobilization potentials for protests; but the violent and ideological policing of protest and the Internet are profound interests of powerful, resource-intensive actors

accessed, monitored, and solicited. Information privacy intrusion is an improper processing of data that reflects one or more of these seven activities and is unwanted by the users (Wang, Lee, and Wang 1998). Table 1.2 presents a classification scheme for Internet surveillance technologies and techniques.

Privacy-enhancing technologies have been defined as "technical and organizational concepts that aim at protecting personal identity" (Burkert 1998, 125). Privacy-enhancing Internet techniques and technologies are, for example: encryption technologies, virus protection, spyware protection tools, firewall, opt-out mechanisms, reading privacy policies, disabling of cookies, spam filters, cookie busters, or anonymizers/anonymous proxy. Dwayne Winseck (2003) cautions that the focus on privacy-enhancing technologies as an answer to surveillance technologies advances "a technocratic approach to managing personal information" and "fails to grasp how power shapes the agenda and overall context in which struggles over technological design occur" (Winseck 2003, 188). Formulated in another way: Privacy-enhancing technologies advance a techno-deterministic ideology that does not question power structures and advances the idea that there is a technological fix to societal problems. Nonetheless it is an important task for Internet studies and surveillance studies to explore ways that privacy-enhancing Internet technologies can be used for minimizing threats. This will not pose solutions to societal problems, but could to a certain extent empower citizens. It is therefore important to take into account that the implementation of privacy-enhancing Internet technologies "forces us to return to social innovation in oreder to successfully implement them" (Burkert 1998, 140).

Classifying privacy-threatening and privacy-enhancing technologies is an important aspect of studying the Internet and surveillance. The contributors to this volume help advance this task.

1.7. CONCLUSION

Howard Rheingold argues that the new network technologies available today that open "new vistas of cooperation also make[s] possible a universal surveillance economy and empower[s] the bloodthirsty as well as the altruistic" (Rheingold 2002, xviii). This book, *The Internet and Surveillance* explores the two sides of the information society that Rheingold mentions. It shows that information technology has a dark and a bright side and that Internet surveillance is deeply enmeshed into the power relations that shape contemporary society.

This book has two parts: Theoretical Foundations of Internet Surveillance Studies (Part I); Case Studies, Applications, and Empirical Perspectives of Internet Surveillance Studies (Part II). The first part predominantly focuses on defining Internet surveillance and web 2.0 surveillance and on identifying its key qualities. The second part presents more applied research, analyses of specific examples of Internet/web 2.0 studies; it is more empirical in character.

Table 1.2   A Classification of Internet Surveillance Techniques (based on Wang, Lee, and Wang 1998)

Technology, practices	Improper data acquisition			Improper data use		Privacy invasion	
	Improper collection	Improper access (to stored data that is only available to single individuals or a small group)	Improper monitoring	Improper analysis	Improper transfer	Unwanted solicitation	Improper storage
spam mail	X					X	X
consumer profiling (including cookies, storage of click-stream data)	X		X	X	X	X	X
online eaves-dropping by state institutions	X	X	X	X	X		X
spyware	X	X	X	X	X		X
selling or transfer of personal data to third parties				X	X	X	X
no opt-out	X		X	X	X	X	X
digital rights man-agement tools	X		X	X	X		X

(continued)

Table 1.2 (continued)

Technology, practices	Improper data acquisition			Improper data use		Privacy invasion	
	Improper collection	Improper access (to stored data that is only available to single individuals or a small group)	Improper monitoring	Improper analysis	Improper transfer	Unwanted solicitation	Improper storage
web bugs	X		X	X	X		X
web crawlers, bots	X		X	X	X	X	X
e-mail and Internet usage surveillance of employees by employers		X	X	X			
targeted online advertising	X		X	X	X	X	X
ISP log file access by government institutions	X	X	X	X	X		X
packet sniffers (e.g., Carnivore)			X	X	X		
phishing, pharming	X	X	X		X	X	X

The theory part of this book has five chapters. *Christian Fuchs* focuses on analyzing and criticizing the political economy of web 2.0 surveillance. Fuchs situates the commercial web 2.0 in the Marxian analysis of capital accumulation and connects this analysis with notions like Dallas Smythe's audience commodity, Oscar Gandy's panoptic sort, Thomas Mathiesen's silent silencing, and Manuel Castells's mass self-communication. *Mark Andrejevic* connects the concept of online surveillance with an analysis of power and control. Andrejevic reminds us that there is a power asymmetry between those engaging in surveillance and those who are the objects of surveillance in the Internet economy. He makes use of Karl Marx's concepts of exploitation and alienation. *Daniel Trottier and David Lyon* provide an empirically grounded identification of five qualities of what they term social media surveillance. These qualities are: (a) collaborative identity construction, (b) lateral ties, (c) the visibility, measurability and searchability of social ties, (d) the dynamic change of social media interfaces and contents, (e) the recontextualization of social media content. *David Hill* connects the notion of Internet surveillance with a detailed interpretation of Jean-François book *The Inhuman*. Hill argues that this inhumanity takes on two predominant forms: the error-prone fetish of algorithmic calculation that can easily advance injustices, and the extension of the capitalist performance principle and consumer culture into all realms of life. *Thomas Allmer* discusses panoptic-oriented and non-panoptic ways of defining Internet surveillance. He points out the importance of economic surveillance in capitalist society and of economic Internet surveillance in contemporary capitalist society. He argues for a critical approach that is grounded in Marxist theory.

The part on case studies, applications, and empirical perspectives of this book consists of eight chapters. *Marisol Sandoval* analyzes the privacy policies and terms of use of more than fifty of the most popular web 2.0 platforms. Her approach is an empirical application of critical political economy to web 2.0 surveillance. The analysis shows that web 2.0 is dominated by corporations that monitor user data in order to accumulate capital by selling user data to advertising companies that provide targeted advertising to the users. The study also shows that commodification tends to be ideologically masked in the privacy policies and the terms of use. *David Arditi* discusses the role of surveillance in the realm of file sharing. He shows that the culture industry tries to use surveillance for on the one hand forestalling music sharing on the Internet and on the other hand for analyzing and exploiting data about music consumption preferences that are commodified. Arditi's chapter is based on a critical understanding of the culture industry that questions corporations' domination of the Internet and culture. *Anders Albrechtslund* analyzes the role of information sharing in web 2.0. He is particularly interested in how such sharing practices shape urban spaces. He interprets online sharing as a form of social, participatory surveillance. He gives particular attention to location-based information sharing, as enabled by applications like Foursquare and Facebook places that are mainly used on mobile phones that support mobile Internet access. *Iván Székély* reports results from an empirical study that analyzed the knowledge, opinion, values, attitudes and self-reported behaviour of IT professionals in the area of handling personal data in Hungary and the Netherlands. Studying the attitudes of IT professionals on privacy and surveillance is crucial because they are the ones who design surveillance systems. The study shows that IT professional tend to have a rather instrumental view of privacy and surveillance in their work practices. *Miyase Christensen and André Jansson* conceptually combine surveillance theory, the concept of transnationalism, and the Bourdieuian notion of the field. They apply this approach for conducting two case studies: The first study deals with transnational migrants of Turkish/Kurdish origin residing in urban Sweden; the second with a Scandinavian expatriate community in Nicaragua, linked to the global development business. *Kent Wayland, Roberto Armengol, and Deborah Johnson* make a conceptual differentiation between surveillance and transparency. They discuss issues of online transparency in relation to the online disclosure of donations in electoral campaigns. They introduce in this context the notion of the house of mirrors. *Monika Taddicken* presents results from a study of attitudes of social web users towards privacy and surveillance, in which focus group interviews were conducted. The study shows a high general concern about online privacy violations and surveillance, a lack of concrete knowledge about online surveillance mechanisms, and the importance of the social and communicative motive of web 2.0 users. *Rolf Weber* discusses legal aspects of online privacy and online surveillance. The chapter shows the importance of discussing which legal understandings of privacy are required in an age where our communication is increasingly taking place online and is mediated by online surveillance systems. The contribution also points out the problems of politically and legally regulating a global space like the Internet with policy frameworks that are primarily national in character.

This book is introduced by a preface written by *Thomas Mathiesen*, who is one of the most frequently cited and influential scholars in surveillance studies, and concluded by a postface written by *Kees Boersma* that identifies the key issues and approaches represented in this book.

ACKNOWLEDGMENTS

This publication is supported by COST—European Cooperation in Science and Technology. It is a result of the COST Action "Living in Surveillance Societies" (IS0807, chair: Dr. William Webster, University of Stirling).

The Living in Surveillance Societies (LiSS) COST Action is a European research programme designed to increase and deepen knowledge about living and working in the surveillance age, in order to better understand the consequences and impacts of enhanced surveillance, and subsequently to make recommendations about its future governance and practice. Further information about LiSS can be found at, URL: http://www.liss-cost.eu/

This publication has emerged from Working Group 2 'Surveillance Technologies in Practice' of the Living in Surveillance Societies COST Action and a number of the contributions were presented and discussed at Working Group meetings and at the Living in Surveillance Societies Annual Conference in London in April 2010. The editors would like to thank the members of LiSS Working Group 2 for their constructive feedback and support.

REFERENCES

Albrechtslund, Anders. 2008. Online social networking as participatory surveillance. *First Monday* 13 (3).

Andrejevic, Mark. 2002. The work of being watched: interactive media and the exploitation of self-disclosure. *Critical Studies in Media Communication* 19 (2): 230–248.

———. 2004. *Reality TV: The work of being watched*. Lanham, MD: Rowman & Littlefield.

———. 2007. *iSpy: Surveillance and power in the interactive era*. Lawrence: University Press of Kansas.

———. 2009. Critical media studies 2.0: an interactive upgrade. *Interactions: Studies in Communication and Culture* 1 (1): 35–51.

Ashworth, Laurence and Clinton Free. 2006. Marketing dataveillance and digital privacy. *Journal of Business Ethics* 67 (2): 107–123.

Atton, Chris. 2004. *An alternative internet*. Edinburgh: Edinburgh University Press.

Bellman, Steven, Eric J. Johnson, Stephen J. Kobrin, and Gerald L. Lohse. 2004. International differences in information privacy concerns: a global survey of consumers. *The Information Society* 20 (5): 313–324.

Benkler, Yochai. 2006. *The wealth of networks*. New Haven: Yale University Press.

Bigo, Didier. 2006. Security, exception, ban and surveillance. In *In Theorizing surveillance*, ed. David Lyon, 46–68. Portland, OR: Willan.

Bogard, William. 2006. Surveillance assemblage and lines of flight. In *Theorizing surveillance*, ed. David Lyon, 97–122. Portland, OR: Willan.

Boyle, James. 1997. Foucault in cyberspace. *University of Cincinnati Law Review* 66 (1): 177–205.

Bruns, Axel. 2008. *Blogs, wikipedia, second life, and beyond: From production to produsage*. New York: Peter Lang.

Burkert, Herbert. 1998. Privacy-enhancing technologies. In *Technology and privacy*, ed. Philip E. Agre and Marc Rotenberg, 125–142. Cambridge: MIT Press.

Cammaerts, Bart. 2008. Critiques on the participatory potentials of web 2.0. *Communication, Culture & Critique* 1 (4): 358–377.

Campbell John E. and Matt Carlson M. 2002. Panopticon.com: online surveillance and the commodification of privacy. *Journal of Broadcasting & Electronic Media* 46 (4): 586–606.

Carpentier, Nico and Benjamin de Cleen. 2008. Introduction: blurring participations and convergences. In *Participation and media production*, ed. Nico Carpentier and Benjamin de Cleen, 1–12. Newcastle: Cambridge Scholars.

Cascio, Jamais. 2005. The rise of the digital panopticon. http://www.worldchanging.com/archives/002651.html (accessed September 5, 2009).

Castells, Manuel. 2001. *The Internet galaxy*. Oxford: Oxford University Press.

———. 2009. *Communication power*. Oxford: Oxford University Press.

Caudill, Eve M. and Patrick E. Murphy. 2000. Consumer online privacy: legal and ethical issues. *Journal of Public Policy & Marketing* 19 (1): 7–19.

Clarke, Roger. 1988. Information technology and dataveillance. *Communications of the ACM* 31 (5): 498–512.

———. 1994. Dataveillance: delivering '1984'. In *Framing technology: Society, choice and change*, ed. Lelia Green and Roger Guinery, 117–130. Sydney: Allen & Unwin.

Cohen, Nicole S. 2008. The valorization of surveillance: towards a political economy of Facebook. *Democratic Communique* 22 (1): 5–22.

Culnan, Mary J. and Robert J. Bies. 2003. Consumer privacy: balancing economic and justice considerations. *Journal of Social Issues* 59 (2): 323–342.

Dennis, Kingsley. 2008. Keeping a close watch—the rise of self-surveillance and the threat of digital exposure. *The Sociological Review* 56 (3): 347–357.

Deuze, Mark. 2007. *Media work*. Cambridge: Polity.

———. 2008. Corporate appropriation of participatory culture. In *Participation and media production*, ed. Nico Carpentier and Benjamin de Cleen, 27–40. Newcastle: Cambridge Scholars.

Downing, John H. 2002. Independent media centres: a multi-local, multi-media challenge to neoliberalism. In *Global media policy in the new millennium*, ed. Marc Raboy, 215–232. Luton: University of Luton Press.

———. 2003. The independent media center movement and the anarchist socialist tradition. In *Contesting media power: Alternative media in a networked world*, ed. Nick Couldry and James Curran, 243–257. Lanham: Rowman & Littlefield.

Elmer, Greg. 2003. A diagram of panoptic surveillance. *New Media & Society* 5 (2): 231–247.

———. 2004. *Profiling machines*. Cambridge: MIT Press.

Fiske, John. 1996. *Media matters*. Minneapolis: University of Minnesota Press.

Foucault, Michel. 1977. *Discipline & punish*. New York: Vintage.

———. 1994. *Power*. New York: New Press.

Fuchs, Christian. 2008a. *Internet and society: Social theory in the information age*. New York: Routledge.

———. 2008b. Book review. Don Tapscott and Anthony D. Williams: *Wikinomics*. *International Journal of Communication* 2 (2008): 1–11.

———. 2009a. Information and communication technologies and society: a contribution to the critique of the political economy of the Internet. *European Journal of Communication* 24 (1): 69–87.

———. 2009b. *Social networking sites and the surveillance society: A critical case study of the usage of studiVZ, Facebook, and MySpace by students in Salzburg in the context of electronic surveillance*. Salzburg/Vienna: Research Group UTI.

———. 2009c. Some reflections on Manuel Castells' book *Communication Power*. *tripleC* 7 (1): 94–108.

———. 2010a. Class and knowledge labour in informational capitalism and on the Internet. *The Information Society* 26 (3): 179–196.

———. 2010b. Social software and web 2.0: their sociological foundations and implications. In *Handbook of research on web 2.0, 3.0, and X.0: Technologies, business and social applications*, ed. San Murugesan, 764–789. Hershey, PA: IGI-Global.

———. 2011. *Foundations of critical media and information studies*. New York: Routledge.

Gandy, Oscar H. 1993. *The panoptic sort: A political economy of personal information*. Boulder: Westview.

———. 2003. Data mining and surveillance in the post-9/11 environment. In *The intensification of surveillance*, ed. Kirstie Ball and Frank Webster, 26–41. London: Pluto.

Gordon, Diana. 1987. The electronic panopticon. *Politics and Society* 15 (4): 483–511.

Graham, Stephen and David Wood. 2003/2007. Digitizing surveillance: categorization, space, inequality. In *The surveillance studies reader*, ed. Sean P. Hier and Josh Greenberg, 218–230. Berkshire: Open University Press.

Haggerty Kevin. 2006. Tear down the walls: on demolishing the panopticon. In *Theorizing surveillance*, ed. David Lyon, 23–45. Portland, OR: Willan.

Haggerty, Kevin and Richard Ericson. 2000/2007. The surveillant assemblage. In *The surveillance studies reader*, ed. Sean P. Hier and Josh Greenberg, 104–116. Berkshire: Open University Press.

Harvey, David. 1989. *The condition of postmodernity.* London: Blackwell.

Jenkins, Henry. 2008. *Convergence culture.* New York: New York University Press.

Kerr, Orin S. 2003. Internet surveillance law after the USA Patriot Act: the big brother that isn't. *Northwestern University Law Review* 97 (2): 607–673.

Kidd, Dorothy. 2003. Indymedia.org: a new communications common. In *Cyberactivism*, ed. Martha McCaughey and Michael D. Ayers, 47–69. New York: Routledge.

Klein, Naomi. 2008. *The shock doctrine: The rise of disaster capitalism.* London: Penguin.

Lauer, Josh. 2008. Alienation in the information economy: toward a Marxist critique of consumer surveillance. In *Participation and media production*, ed. Nico Carpentier and Benjamin De Cleen, 41–53. Newcastle: Cambridge Scholars.

Lovink, Geert. 2008. *Zero comments: Blogging and critical internet culture.* New York: Routledge.

Lyon, David. 1994. *The electronic eye: The rise of surveillance society.* Cambridge: Polity.

———. 1998. The world wide web of surveillance: the Internet and off-world power-flows. *Information, Communication & Society* 1 (1): 91–105.

———. 2001. *Surveillance society: Monitoring everyday life.* Buckingham: Open University Press.

———. 2003. Surveillance as social sorting: computer codes and mobile bodies. In *Surveillance as social sorting*, ed. David Lyon, 13–30. New York: Routledge.

———. 2006a. 9/11, synopticon, and scopophilia: watching and being watched. In *Surveillance and visibility*, ed. Kevin Haggerty and Richard Ericson, 35–54. Toronto: University of Toronto Press.

———. 2006b. The search for surveillance theories. In *Theorizing surveillance*, ed. David Lyon, 3–20. Portland, OR: Willan.

Marx, Gary T. 1988. *Undercover: Police surveillance in America.* Berkeley: University of California Press.

———. 2002. What's new about the "new surveillance"? Classifying for change and continuity. *Surveillance & Society* 1 (1): 9–29.

Mathiesen, Thomas. 1997. The viewer society: Michel Foucault's 'panopticon' revisited. *Theoretical Criminology* 1 (2): 215–234.

———. 2004. Panopticon and synopticon as silencing systems. In *Silently silenced: Essays on the creation of acquiesence in modern society*, 98–102. Winchester: Waterside.

Milne, George R., Andrew J. Rohm, and Shalini Bahl. 2004. Consumers' protection of online privacy and identity. *Journal of Consumer Affairs* 38 (2): 217–232.

McCaughey, Martha and Michael D. Ayers, ed. 2003. *Cyberactivism.* New York: Routledge.

Miyazaki, Anthony and Sandeep Krishnamurthy. 2002. Internet seals of approval: effects on online privacy policies and consumer perceptions. *Journal of Consumer Affairs* 36 (1): 28–49.

Ogura, Toshimaru. 2006. Electronic government and surveillance-oriented society. In *Theorizing surveillance*, ed. David Lyon, 270–295. Portland, OR: Willan.

O'Reilly, Tim. 2005. *What is web 2.0?* http://www.oreillynet.com/pub/a/oreilly/tim/news/2005/09/30/what-is-web-20.html?page=1 (accessed August 10, 2009).

Parenti, Christian. 2003. *The soft cage.* New York: Basic Books.

Poster, Mark. 1990. *The mode of information.* Cambridge: Polity.

Rämö, Hans and Mats Edenius. 2008. Time constraints in new mobile communication. *KronoScope* 8 (2): 147–157.

Rheingold, Howard. 2002. *Smart mobs: The next social revolution.* New York: Basic Books.

Robins, Kevin and Frank Webster. 1999. *Times of the technoculture.* New York: Routledge.

Ryker, Randy, Elizabeth Lafleur, Chris Cox, and Bruce Mcmanis. 2002. Online privacy policies: an assessment of the fortune E-50. *Journal of Computer Information Systems* 42 (4): 15–20.

Scholz, Trebor. 2008. Market ideology and the myths of web 2.0. *First Monday* 13 (3).

Sheehan, Kim Bartel and Mariea Grubbs Hoy. 2000. Dimensions of privacy among online consumers. *Journal of Public Policy & Marketing* 19 (1): 62–73.

Shiffman, Denise. 2008. *The age of engage.* Ladera Ranch, CA: Hunt Street Press.

Shirky, Clay. 2008. *Here comes everybody.* London: Penguin.

Solove, Daniel J. 2004a. Reconstructing electronic surveillance law. *George Washington Law Review* 72 (6): 1264–1305.

———. 2004b. *The digital person: Technology and privacy in the information age.* New York: New York University Press.

Stanyer, James. 2009. Web 2.0 and the transformation of news and journalism. *In Routledge Handbook of Internet Politics*, ed. Andrew Chadwick and Philip N. Howard, 201–213. New York: Routledge.

Starke-Meyerring, Doreen and Laura Gurak. 2007. Internet. In *Encyclopedia of privacy*, ed. William G. Staples, 297–310. Westport, CT: Greenwood.

Terranova, Tiziana. 2004. *Network culture.* London: Pluto.

Tapscott, Don and Anthony D. Williams. 2006. *Wikinomics: How mass collaboration changes everything.* London: Penguin.

Turow, Joseph. 2006. Cracking the consumer code: advertisers, anxiety, and surveillance in the digital age. In *Surveillance and visibility*, ed. Kevin Haggerty and Richard Ericson, 279–307. Toronto: University of Toronto Press.

van de Donk, Wim, Brian Loader, Paul Nixon, and Dieter Rucht, ed. 2004. *Cyberprotest: New media, citizens and social movements.* New York: Routledge.

van Dijck, José. 2009. Users like you? theorizing agency in user-generated content. *Media, Culture & Society* 31 (1): 41–58.

van Dijck, José and David Nieborg. 2009. Wikinomics and its discontents: a critical analysis of web 2.0 business manifestors. *New Media & Society* 11 (5): 855–874.

van Dijk, Jan. 2000. Models of democracy and concepts of communication. In *Digital democracy*, ed. Kenneth L. Hacker and Jan van Dijk, 30–53. London: Sage.

Wall, David S. 2006. Surveillant Internet technologies and the growth in information capitalism: spams and public trust in the information society. In *Surveillance and visibility*, ed. Kevin Haggerty and Richard Ericson, 340–362. Toronto: University of Toronto Press.

Wang Huaiqing, Matthew K.O. Lee, and Chen Wang. 1998. Consumer privacy concerns about Internet marketing. *Communications of the ACM* 41 (3): 63–70.

Webster, Frank. 2002. *Theories of the information society.* New York: Routledge.

Whitaker, Reginald. 1999. *The end of privacy.* New York: New Press.

Winseck, Dwayne. 2003. Netscapes of power: convergence, network design, walled gardens, and other strategies of control in the information age. In *Surveillance as social sorting*, ed. David Lyon, 176–198. New York: Routledge.

Zuboff, Shoshana. 1988. *In the age of the smart machine.* New York: Basic Books.

PART I

Theoretical Foundations of Internet Surveillance Studies

2 Critique of the Political Economy of Web 2.0 Surveillance

Christian Fuchs

2.1. INTRODUCTION

Facebook, YouTube, MySpace, Blogspot/Blogger, Wordpress, Twitter, Flickr—these are just some of the World Wide Web platforms that have become popular in recent years. Blogs, wikis, file-sharing platforms, and social networking platforms are some of the techno-social systems that shape Internet experiences of users in contemporary society. Scholars, the media, and parts of the public claim that the Internet has become more social, more participatory, and more democratic (see Fuchs 2010b). These claims might be overdrawn, techno-optimistic ideologies. E-mail technology was created in the early 1970s, and has for a long time been the most popular and widely used Internet technology, which shows that the Internet was social and communicative right from its beginning. Therefore the claims about "web 2.0" should be more modest. Many web 2.0 sites combine older applications such as forums, guest books, e-mail, multimedia, and hypertext in one user-friendly platform, which increases appeal and ease of use and so supports increased usage. Increased bandwidth and cheaper production technologies (digital cameras, etc.) now allow the easy, fast, and cheap transmission and sharing of audio and video files and has resulted in increased popularity of user-generated content. The discussion of surveillance in web 2.0 is important because such platforms collect huge amounts of personal data in order to work.

I want to start with an example of data commodification and web 2.0 surveillance: Google Buzz. In February 2010, Google introduced a new social networking service called Buzz. Buzz is directly connected to GMail, Google's webmail platform. Google's introduction of Buzz is an attempt to gain importance in the social networking sites market that has been dominated by Facebook and Twitter. In February 2010, Facebook was ranked number 2 and Twitter number 12 in the list of the most accessed web platforms, whereas Google's own social networking platform Orkut, which is only very popular in Brazil, was at number 52 (data source: http://alexa.com, the top 500 sites on the web, February 14, 2010). Popular social networking platforms attract millions of users, who upload and share personal information that provides data about their consumption preferences. Therefore commercial social networking sites are keen on storing, analyzing, and selling individual and aggregated data about user preferences and user behaviour to advertising clients in order to accumulate capital. Google is itself a main player in the business of online advertising. One can therefore assume that Google considers Facebook, Twitter, and other platforms that attract many users as competitors, and that as a result of this competitive situation Google has introduced Buzz. In 2009, GMail had approximately 150 million users (see http://www.tech24hours.com/2009/09/number-of-gmail-users-worldwide-as-of.html, accessed on February 14, 2010), which explains that Google integrated Buzz into GMail in order to start from a solid foundation of potential users.

Buzz supports the following communicative functions: creating postings that are shared with contacts, sharing of images and videos, commenting on and evaluating others' Buzz posts, forwarding of Twitter messages to a Buzz account, linking and integrating images uploaded to Flickr or Picasa, uploading videos to YouTube, generating posts on Blogger, and using Buzz via mobile phones. Buzz messages can either be presented publicly or only to selected groups of followers. Each user's Buzz profile has a list of followers, and users can select which Buzz accounts they want to follow. Buzz mobile phone messages include geo-tags that display the current location of users. Buzz posts of nearby users and information about nearby sites, shops, restaurants, etc. can be displayed on mobile phones. Buzz also recommends postings by other users.

In December 2009, Google's CEO Eric Schmidt commented about online privacy: "If you have something that you do not want anyone to know, maybe you should not be doing it in the first place" (http://www.youtube.com/watch?v=A6e7wfDHzew, accessed on February 14, 2010). This statement is an indication that Google or at least its most important managers and shareholders do not value privacy very highly. Schmidt's statement points towards the assumption that, in the online world, all uploaded information and personal data should be available publicly and should be usable by corporations for economic ends.

When first installing Buzz, the application automatically generated a list of followers for each user based on the most frequent GMail contacts. The standard setting was that this list of followers was automatically visible in public. This design move resulted in heavy criticism of Google in the days following the launch of Buzz. Users and civil rights advocates argued that Buzz threatens the privacy of users and makes contacts that users might want to keep private available in public. Google reacted to public criticism (see: http://gmailblog.blogspot.com/2010/02/new-buzz-start-up-experience-based-on.html, http://www.huffingtonpost.com/2010/02/13/buzz-changes-google-drops_n_461656.html, accessed on February 14, 2010) and changed some of the standard settings of Buzz on February 13, 2010. Some changes were made to the auto-follow option, so that now a dialogue is displayed that shows which users Buzz suggests as followers (see: http://gmailblog.blogspot.com/2010/02/new-buzz-start-up-experience-based-on.html, accessed on February 14, 2010). But still all suggested followers are automatically activated, which does not make this solution an opt-in version of the follow feature. Google also said that Buzz would no longer automatically connect publicly available Picasa and Google Reader items to the application. An options menu that allows users to hide their contact list from their public Google profiles was also announced. The problem here is, again, that this was planned as an opt-out solution, not as an opt-in option (see: http://gmailblog.blogspot.com/2010/02/new-buzz-start-up-experience-based-on.html, accessed on February 14, 2010). From a privacy-enhancing perspective, opt-in solutions are preferable to opt-out solutions because they give users more control over what applications are allowed to do with their data. However, it is clear that opt-in solutions are rather unpopular design options for many Internet corporations because they tend to reduce the number of potential users that are subject to advertising-oriented data surveillance.

Google's economic strategy is to gather data about users that utilize different Google applications in different everyday situations. The more that everyday situations can be supported by Google applications, the more time users will spend online with Google, so that more user data will be available to Google, which allows the company to better analyze usage and consumer behaviour. As a result, more and more precise user data and aggregated data can be sold to advertising clients who then target users with personalized advertising in all of these everyday situations. The introduction of evermore applications does primarily serve economic ends that are realized by large-scale user surveillance. As more and more people access the Internet from their mobile phones, the number of times and the time spans users are online, as well as the number of access points and situations in which users are online, increase. Therefore supplying applications that are attractive for users in all of these circumstances (such as waiting for the bus or the underground, travelling on the train or the airplane, going to a restaurant, concert, or movie, visiting friends, attending a business meeting, etc.), promises that users spend more time online with applications supplied by specific companies such as Google, which allows these companies to present more advertisements that are more individually targeted to users, which in turn promises more profit for the companies. We can therefore say that there is a strong economic incentive for Google and other companies to introduce new Internet and mobile Internet applications.

Google Buzz is part of Google's empire of economic surveillance. It gathers information about user behaviour and user interests in order to store, assess, and sell this data to advertising clients. These surveillance practices are legally guaranteed by the Buzz privacy policy, which says, for example:

> When you use Google Buzz, we may record information about your use of the product, such as the posts that you like or comment on and

the other users who you communicate with. This is to provide you with a better experience on Buzz and other Google services and to improve the quality of Google services. [. . .] If you use Google Buzz on a mobile device and choose to view 'nearby' posts, your location will be collected by Google. (Google Buzz Privacy Policy, February 14, 2010)

A second example of economic surveillance and data commodification on web 2.0 is Facebook. Mark Zuckerberg, Eduardo Saverin, Dustin Mosko-vitz, and Chris Hughes, who were then Harvard students, founded Face-book in 2004. Facebook is the second-most-often accessed website in the world (data source: alexa.com, accessed on 09–10–2010). Facebook's rev-enues were more than $US 800 million in 2009[1] and are likely to increase to more than $US 1 billion in 2010.

Turow (2006b, 83f) argues that privacy policies of commercial Internet websites are often complex, written in turgid legalese, but formulated in a polite way. They would first assure the user that they care about his/her privacy and then spread over a long text advance elements that mean that personal data is given to (mostly unnamed) "affiliates". The purpose would be to cover up the capturing and selling of marketing data. I will now show that Turow's analysis can be applied to Facebook.

Facebook wants to assure users that it deals responsibly with their data and that users are in full control of privacy controls. Therefore as an intro-duction to the privacy issue, it writes: "Facebook is about sharing. Our pri-vacy controls give you the power to decide what and how much you share" (http://www.facebook.com/privacy/explanation.php, accessed on 19–11–2010). The use of advertisement is spread throughout Facebook's privacy policy, which is 35,566 characters long (approximately 11 single-spaced A4 print pages). The complexity and length of the policy makes it unlikely that users read it in detail. Facebook says that it uses the user's data to provide a "safe experience", but also says that it uses targeted advertising to sell user data to advertisers: "We allow advertisers to choose the characteristics of users who will see their advertisements and we may use any of the non-personally identifiable attributes we have collected (including information you may have decided not to show to other users, such as your birth year or other sensitive personal information or preferences) to select the appro-priate audience for those advertisements. For example, we might use your interest in soccer to show you ads for soccer equipment, but we do not tell the soccer equipment company who you are" (Facebook Privacy Policy, revision from October 5, 2010; accessed on November 16, 2010). Face-book avoids speaking of selling user-generated data, demographic data, and user behaviour by always talking of "sharing information" with third parties, which is a euphemism for the commodification of user data and usage behaviour data.

The privacy policy also allows Facebook to collect data about users' behaviour on other websites and to commodify this data for advertising purposes: "Information from other websites. We may institute programs with advertising partners and other websites in which they share information with us" (ibid.). These data can be stored and used by Facebook, according to its privacy policy, for 180 days. Facebook's data collection is not at all transparent; the single user does not know which data exactly it collects from which sources about him/her and to whom these data are sold.

Facebook's privacy policy is a manifestation of a self-regulatory privacy policy regime that puts capital interests first. It is long and written in complex language in order to cover up the economic surveillance and commodification of user data for targeted advertising that helps Facebook accumulate capital. Facebook euphemistically describes this commodification process as "sharing". The privacy policy advances the perception that Facebook always seeks consent from users before selling user data to advertisers, which masks the facts that Facebook does not ask users if they truly wish to have their personal data, user-generated data, and user behaviour data sold for advertising; that users cannot participate in the formulation of privacy policies; and that they are coerced into having to accept Facebook's policy in order to use the platform. Facebook hides an opt-out option from cookie-based advertising deep in its privacy policy and only provides a minimum of advertising privacy options in its settings. It reduces the issue of privacy to controlling the visibility of user information to other users and neglects the issue of control of advertising settings as a fundamental privacy issue. Facebook also collects and commodifies data about user behaviour on other websites. The analysis shows that on Facebook "privacy is property" (Lyon 1994, 189) and that Facebook tries to manipulate the perception of privacy by Facebook users and the public by complexifying the understanding of targeted advertising in its privacy policy, minimizing advertising control settings, implementing a complex usability for the few available advertising opt-out options, and reducing privacy to an individual and interpersonal issue.

Facebook engages in the permanent surveillance of user data and usage behaviour in order to sell these data to advertising clients that provide targeted advertising to Facebook users. Facebook founder and CEO Mark Zuckerberg says that Facebook is about the "concept that the world will be better if you share more" (*Wired Magazine*, August 2010). Zuckerberg has repeatedly said that he does not care about profit, but wants to help people with Facebook's tools and wants to create an open society. Kevin Colleran, Facebook advertising sale executive, says in the *Wired* story that "Mark is not motivated by money". In a *Times* story,[2] Zuckerberg said: "The goal of the company is to help people to share more in order to make the world more open and to help promote understanding between people. The long-term belief is that if we can succeed in this mission then we also be able to build a pretty good business and everyone can be financially rewarded. [. . .] The *Times*: Does money motivate you? Zuckerberg: No". If Zuckerberg really does not care about profit, why is Facebook then not a non-commercial platform and why does it use targeted advertising? The problems of targeted advertising are that it aims at controlling and manipulating human needs, that users are normally not asked if they agree to the use of advertising on the Internet, but have to agree to advertising if they want to use commercial platforms (lack of democracy), that advertising can increase market concentration, that it is not transparent to most users what kind of information about them is used for advertising purposes, and that users are not paid for the value creation they engage in when using commercial web 2.0 platforms and uploading data. Surveillance on Facebook is not only an interpersonal process, where users view data about other individuals that might benefit or harm the latter, it is primarily economic surveillance, i.e., the collection, storage, assessment, and commodification of personal data, user behaviour, and user-generated data for economic purposes. Facebook and other web 2.0 platforms are large advertising-based capital accumulation machines that achieve their economic aims by economic surveillance.

Its privacy policy is the living proof that Facebook is primarily about profit-generation by advertising. "The world will be better if you share more"? But a better world for whom is the real question? "Sharing" on Facebook in economic terms means primarily that Facebook "shares" information with advertising clients. And "sharing" is only the euphemism for selling and commodifying data. Facebook commodifies and trades user data and user behaviour data. Facebook does not make the world a better place; it makes the world a more commercialized place, a big shopping mall without exit. It makes the world only a better place for companies interested in advertising, not for users.

The basic research question of this contribution is: How does the political economy of web 2.0 work and what is the role of surveillance? To answer this question, further questions are asked: What is the role of surveillance in critical political economy studies? What is the role of surveillance in the political economy of capitalism? How does capital accumulation work on web 2.0 platforms? What is the role of surveillance in web 2.0 capital accumulation?

The method employed in this chapter is a combination of social theory and empirical research. To conceptualize the role of surveillance in capitalism and on web 2.0, critical political economy is used as method for theory construction. Data collection about Internet usage and statistical analysis are used for analyzing the political economy of web 2.0. To analyze user perspectives, the results of a quantitative and qualitative online survey are reported.

Political economy focuses on the analysis of the inner constitution and dynamics of the economic system. It is *political* economy because it sees political interests at work in the modern economy. In critical political economy, these interests are conceived as contradictory class interests. Critique of the political economy aims to show the limitations, contradictions, and problems of the capitalist economy; it questions the legitimacy and logic of academic approaches that conceive capitalist phenomena (such as the commodity, exchange value, profit, money, capital, the division of labour, etc.) as universal and not as historically contingent and changeable; and it questions the modes of thinking that postulate the endlessness and reification of existing reality (ideology critique).

To answer the research questions posed in this chapter, first the role of surveillance in the classical critical political economy studies is discussed (section 2). Then, a model that conceptualizes the cycle of capital accumulation and distinguishes between production and circulation of capital is introduced (section 3). Next, the multiple roles of surveillance in capital accumulation are discussed (section 4), and the connection of privacy, surveillance, and capitalism is outlined (section 5). The relationship of capital accumulation, web 2.0, and surveillance is discussed (section 6), the role of the users in this process is empirically studies (section 7), and finally some conclusions that centre on the notion of resistance are drawn (section 8).

2.2. KARL MARX ON SURVEILLANCE

For Karl Marx, surveillance was a fundamental aspect of the capitalist economy and the nation state. "The work of directing, superintending and adjusting becomes one of the functions of capital, from the moment that the labour under capital's control becomes co-operative. As a specific function of capital, the directing function acquires its own specific characteristics" (Marx 1867, 449). Marx argues that the supervision of labour in the production process is "purely despotic" (450) and that this despotism is not directly exerted by the capitalist. "He hands over the work of direct and constant supervision of the individual workers and groups of workers to a special kind of wage-labourer. An industrial army of workers under the command of a capitalist requires, like a real army, officers (managers) and N.C.O.s (foremen, overseers), who command during the labour process in the name of capital. The work of supervision becomes their established and exclusive function" (450).

Marx argues that in the US, population growth in the nineteenth century resulted in the surveillance of states and regions (MEW 7, 434). He says that nation states engage in the surveillance of passenger traffic (MEW 6, 127); the surveillance of the execution of laws (MEW 19, 30); spying (MEW 8, 437); and police surveillance (MEW 2, 78; 7, 313; 9, 511; 17, 401; 18, 387). Like Foucault, Marx talks about disciplinary surveillance power by saying that the state "enmeshes, controls, regulates, superintends and tutors civil society from its most comprehensive manifestations of life down to its most insignificant stirrings" (Marx and Engels 1968, 123).

Although Marx also used the notion of surveillance in the sense of counter-surveillance (watching the watchers) when he said, for example, that "the press not only has the right, it has the duty, to keep the strictest eye on the gentlemen representatives of the people" (Marx 1974, 116), the two main actors of surveillance that he identifies are capital and the nation state. He therefore grounded a critical notion of surveillance that can today still be found in the critical political economy of surveillance. Toshimaru Ogura (2006, 272) argues, for example, that "the common characteristics of surveillance are the management of population based on capitalism and the nation state". Oscar Gandy says that the "panoptic sort is a technology that has been designed and is being continually revised to serve the interests of decision makers within the government and the corporate bureaucracies" (Gandy 1993, 95).

2.3. THE CYCLE OF CAPITAL ACCUMULATION

"Contemporary surveillance must be understood in the light of changed circumstances, especially the growing centrality of consumption and the adoption of information technologies" (Lyon 1994, 225). Capitalism has changed; at the time of Marx consumer surveillance and electronic surveillance were hardly important. Economic surveillance focused on the control of the production process. Nonetheless, the Marxian framework of political economy that describes the cycle of capital accumulation can be used today for systematically locating forms of economic surveillance in the production and circulation process.

In the three volumes of *Capital*, Marx analyzes the accumulation process of capital. This process, as described by Marx, is visualized in Figure 2.1. Introducing some important categories that Marx employs can summarize this account.

Marx's theory is a labour theory of value, which is a theory that draws conclusion from the analysis of the total labour time that is needed for the production of goods. It is also a critique of value, which means that the forms that value takes in capitalism and the practices and ideologies that are based on this form are questioned. The value of a good is the total time that is needed for its production. The more value a good has, the longer its production takes. At the level of prices, this can be observed by the fact that labour-intensive goods are frequently more expensive than goods with low labour intensity. Marx argues that the cell form of capitalism is the commodity, goods that are exchanged in a certain quantitative relationship with money (x amount of commodity A = y units of money). He says that in societies that are based on the economic principle of exchange, goods have a use value and an exchange value. The use value is the qualitative aspect of a good; it is a utility that satisfies certain human needs. In exchange-based societies, humans can only get hold of such goods by exchanging other goods (such as money or their labour power) with the needed goods

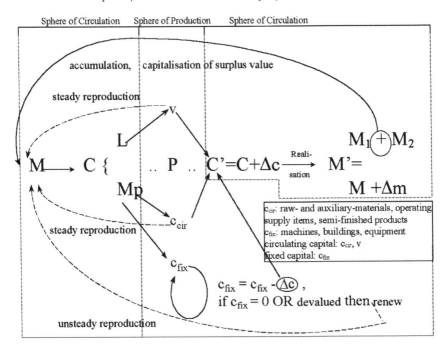

Figure 2.1. The accumulation/expanded reproduction of capital.

in certain quantitative relationships (x commodity A = y commodity B). Concrete labour is a category that is used for describing the creation of the use value of a good by humans. Abstract labour is a category employed for signifying the creation of the value of a good, i.e., the objectified labour time needed for its production. Marx sees money as the general equivalent of exchange; it simplifies the exchange of commodities and is therefore a general commodity.

In the accumulation of capital, capitalists buy labour power and means of production (raw materials, technologies, etc.) in order to produce new commodities that are sold with the expectation to make money profit that is partly reinvested. Marx distinguishes two spheres of capital accumulation: the circulation sphere and the sphere of production. In the circulation sphere, capital transforms its value form: First money M is transformed into commodities (from the standpoint of the capitalist as buyer); the capitalist purchases the commodities labour power L and means of production Mp. M-C is based on the two purchases M-L and M-Mp. In capitalism, labour power is separated from the means of production, "the mass of the people, the workers, [. . .] come face to face with the non-workers, the former as non-owners, the latter as the owners, of these means of production" (Marx 1885, 116). This means that due to private property structures workers do not own the means of production, the products they produce, and the profit they generate. Capitalists own these resources.

In the sphere of production, a new good is produced: the value of labour power and the value of the means of production are added to the product. Value takes on the form of productive capital P. The value form of labour is variable capital v (which can be observed as wages) and the value form of the means of production constant capital c (which can be observed as the total price of the means of production/producer goods).

> That part of capital, therefore, which is turned into means of production, i.e. the raw material, the auxiliary material and the instruments of labour, does not undergo any quantitative alteration of value in the process of production. For this reason, I call it the constant part of capital, or more briefly, constant capital. On the other hand, that part of capital which is turned into labour-power does undergo an alteration of value in the process of production. It both reproduces the equivalent of its own value and produces an excess, a surplus-value, which may itself vary, and be more or less according to circumstances. This part of capital is continually being transformed from a constant into a variable magnitude. I therefore call it the variable part of capital, or more briefly, variable capital. (Marx 1867, 317)

Constant capital consists of two parts: circulating constant capital c_{cir} (the value of the utilized raw materials, auxiliary materials, operating supply items, and semi-finished products) and fixed constant capital c_{fix} (the value of the utilized machines, buildings, and equipment) (Marx 1885, chapter 8). c_{cir} and v together form circulating capital: They transfuse their value totally to the product and must be constantly renewed. c_{fix} remains fixed in the production process for many turnovers of capital. The turnover time of capital is the sum of its circulation time and its production time (Marx 1885, 236). Circulation time is the time that capital takes to be transformed from its commodity form into the money form and later from its money form to its commodity form. Production time is the time that capital takes in the sphere of production.

Fixed constant capital decreases its value in each turnover of capital. Its value is decreased by the amount of Δc, which is a flexible value. Fixed constant capital like machinery does not create value and its value is never entirely transfused to capital at once. It is depreciated by wear and tear, non-usage, and moral depreciation (i.e., the emergence of new machinery with increased productivity).

> A part of the capital value advanced is fixed in this form, which is determined by the function of the means of labour in the process. As a means of labour functions and is used up, one part of its value passes over to the product, while another part remains fixed in the means of

labour and hence in the production process. The value fixed in this way steadily declines, until the means of labour is worn out and has therefore distributed its value, in a longer or shorter period, over the volume of products that has emerged from a series of continually repeated labour processes. (Marx 1885, 237f)

In the sphere of production, capital stops its metamorphosis so that capital circulation comes to a halt. New value V' of the commodity is produced, V' contains the value of the necessary constant and variable capital and surplus value Δs of the surplus product. Surplus value is generated by unpaid labour. Capitalists do not pay for the production of surplus, therefore the production of surplus value can be considered as a process of exploitation. The value V' of the new commodity after production is V' = c + v + s. The commodity then leaves the sphere of production and again enters the circulation sphere, in which capital conducts its next metamorphosis: By being sold on the market it is transformed from the commodity form back into the money form. Surplus value is realized in the form of money value. The initial money capital M now takes on the form M' = M + Δm, it has been increased by an increment Δm. Accumulation of capital means that the produced surplus value is (partly) reinvested/capitalized. The end point of one process M' becomes the starting point of a new accumulation process. One part of M', M_1, is reinvested. Accumulation means the aggregation of capital by investment and exploitation in the capital circuit M-C. .P. .C'-M', in which the end product M' becomes a new starting point M. The total process makes up the dynamic character of capital. Capital is money that is permanently increasing due to the exploitation of surplus value.

Commodities are sold at prices that are higher than the investment costs so that money profit is generated. For Marx, one decisive quality of capital accumulation is that profit is an emergent property of production that is produced by labour, but owned by the capitalists. Without labour no profit could be made. Workers are forced to enter class relations and to produce profit in order to survive, which enables capital to appropriate surplus. The notion of exploited surplus value is the main concept of Marx's theory, by which he intends to show that capitalism is a class society. "The theory of surplus value is in consequence immediately the theory of exploitation" (Negri 1991, 74) and, one can add, the theory of class and as a consequence the political demand for a classless society. The capitalist

wants to produce a commodity greater in value than the sum of the values of the commodities used to produce it, namely the means of production and the labour-power he purchased with his good money on the open market. His aim is to produce not only a use-value, but a commodity; not only use-value, but value; and not just value, but also surplus value [. . .] The cotton originally bought for £100 is for example re-sold at £100 + £10, i.e. £110. The complete form of this process is therefore M-C-M', where M' = M + ΔM, i.e. the original sum advanced plus an increment. This increment or excess over the original value I call 'surplus-value'. (Marx 1867, 293, 251)

Capital is not money, but money that is increased through accumulation, "money which begets money" (Marx 1867, 256). Marx argues that the value of labour power is the average amount of time that is needed for the production of goods that are necessary for survival (necessary labour time), which in capitalism is paid for by workers with their wages. Surplus labour time is all labour time that exceeds necessary labour time, remains unpaid, is appropriated for free by capitalists, and transformed into money profit.

Surplus value "is in substance the materialization of unpaid labour-time. The secret of the self-valorization of capital resolves itself into the fact that it has at its disposal a definite quantity of the unpaid labour of other people" (Marx 1867, 672). Surplus value "costs the worker labour but the capitalist nothing", but "none the less becomes the legitimate property of the capitalist" (Marx 1867, 672).

Capital also developed into a coercive relation, and this compels the working class to do more work than would be required by the narrow circle of its own needs. As an agent in producing the activity of others, as an extractor of surplus labour and an exploiter of labour-power, it surpasses all earlier systems of production, which were based on directly compulsory labour, in its energy and its quality of unbounded and ruthless activity. (Marx 1867, 425)

Surplus value also means that workers are compelled to work more than necessary for satisfying their immediate needs, they produce an excess for free that is appropriated by capitalists: "What appears as surplus value on capital's side appears identically on the worker's side as surplus labour in excess of his requirements as worker, hence in excess of his immediate requirements for keeping himself alive" (Marx 1857/58, 324f).

Marx argues that capitalists are unproductive, they do not produce value, and that profit stems from the production of value by workers that is exploited and appropriated by capitalists. He uses the term productive labour in this context: Productive labour "produces surplus-value for the capitalist, or in other words contributes towards the self-valorization of capital" (Marx 1867, 644). For Marx, capitalism is based on the permanent theft of unpaid labour from workers by capitalists. This is the reason why he characterizes capital as vampire and werewolf. "Capital is dead labour which, vampire-like, lives only by sucking living labour, and lives the more, the more labour it sucks" (Marx 1867, 342). The production of surplus value "forms the specific content and purpose of capitalist production" (Marx 1867, 411); it is "the *differentia specifica* of capitalist production", "the absolute law of this mode of production" (Marx 1867, 769); and the "driving force and the final result of the capitalist process of production" (Marx 1867, 976).

2.4. SURVEILLANCE AND THE CYCLE
OF CAPITAL ACCUMULATION

Following Ogura's (2006) and Gandy's (1993) argument that a common characteristic of surveillance is the management of population based on capitalism and/or the nation state, we can distinguish between economic and political surveillance as two major forms of surveillance. Surveillance by nation states and corporations aims at controlling the behaviour of individuals and groups, i.e., they should be forced to behave or not behave in certain ways because they know that their appearance, movements, location, or ideas are or could be watched by surveillance systems (Fuchs 2008, 267–277). In the case of political electronic surveillance, individuals are threatened by the potential exercise of organized violence (of the law) if they behave in certain ways that are undesired, but watched by political actors (such as secret services or the police). In the case of economic electronic surveillance, individuals are threatened by the violence of the market that wants to force them to buy or produce certain commodities and help reproduce capitalist relations by gathering and using information on their economic behaviour with the help of electronic systems. In such forms of surveillance violence and heteronomy are the ultimo ratio.

The following table discusses the role of surveillance at the various points in the capital accumulation process.

Table 2.1 shows that surveillance is a central method of control and discipline in the capital accumulation process. Corporations conduct a systematic gathering of data about applicants, employees, the labour process, private property, consumers, and competitors in order to minimize economic risks, discipline workers, increase productivity, circumvent theft, sabotage, and protests, control consumers through advertising, and adapt to changing conditions of competition. The overall aim of the employment of multiple surveillance methods and technologies in the capital accumulation process is the maximization of profit and the increased exploitation of surplus value. Surveillance is a method that capital employs for controlling the production and circulation process and for controlling and disciplining the workforce. Economic surveillance is a way of minimizing the risk of incurring losses and maximizing the opportunities for making profits.

Table 2.1 The Role of Surveillance in the Cycle of Capital Accumulation

Sphere of the accumulation process	Surveillance target	Description	Methods (examples)
Circulation	potential variable capital (v)	applicant surveillance: surveillance of potential workforces	access to criminal records, health databases, bank data, employment histories, and other databases; talks with former employers and supervisors; information search on the Internet
Production	variable capital (v)	workplace surveillance: surveillance of labour forces at the workplace	managers, supervisors, workplace surveillance technologies, databases, corporate identities, integrative management strategies, participatory management, identification systems, electronic work flow systems, e-mail surveillance, surveillance of employees' Internet activities, fixation of workers' knowledge, answers to problems, and best practices in databases
Production	variable capital (v)	workforce surveillance: surveillance of productivity	Taylorism: in order to increase productivity, data on the activities of workers are collected, recorded, measured, stored, and analyzed

Production	constant capital (c)	property surveillance: surveillance of private property (commodities, capital, means of production) in order to circumvent theft and sabotage	security guards, alarm systems, CCTV, access control systems, invisible security labelling or electronic tagging of commodities
Circulation	W' => G'	consumer surveillance: consumption interests and processes are systematically observed and analyzed in order to guarantee the selling of as much commodities as possible and the realization of profit	marketing research, consumer research, electronic consumer surveillance (especially on the Internet: cookies, targeted advertising mechanisms, spyware, profiling of Internet usage behaviour, data gathering by intelligent Internet spiders, spam mail databases, data mining, clickstream monitoring, collaborative filtering), loyalty cards, product testing
Circulation	W' => G'	surveillance of competition: corporations have the interest to minimize competition by other firms in order to maximize market shares and profits, therefore they are interested in collecting and analyzing data about the technologies, labour force, organizational structures, commodities, economic performance, etc. of their competitors	marketing research, industrial espionage, information gathering on the Internet

2.5. PRIVACY, SURVEILLANCE, AND CAPITALISM

Privacy is in modern societies an Enlightenment ideal. The rise of capitalism has resulted in the idea that the private sphere should be separated
from the public sphere and not accessible to the public and that therefore
autonomy and anonymity of the individual is needed in the private sphere.
The rise of the idea of privacy in modern society is connected to the rise of
the central ideal of the freedom of private ownership. Private ownership is
the idea that humans have the right to own as much wealth as they want, as
long as it is inherited or acquired through individual achievements. There is
an antagonism between private ownership and social equity modern society. How much and what exactly a person owns is treated as an aspect of
privacy in contemporary society. Keeping ownership structures secret is a
measure of precaution against public questioning or political and individual attack against private ownership. Capitalism requires anonymity and
privacy in order to function. But at the same time, in modernity strangers
enter social relations that require trust or enabling exchange. Whether a
stranger can be trusted is checked with the help of surveillance procedures.
The ideals of modernity (such as the freedom of ownership) also produce
phenomena such as income and wealth inequality, poverty, unemployment,
and precarious living and working conditions. These socio-economic differences pose problems for the maintenance of order and private ownership
(crime, political protests, and violent conflicts) that need to be contained
if modernity wants to survive. As a result, state surveillance is a necessary
component of modern societies. Corporations have the aim of accumulating ever more capital. To do so, they have an interest in knowing as much
as possible about the interests, tastes, and behaviours of their customers.
This results in the surveillance of consumers.

The establishment of trust, socio-economic differences, and corporate
interests are three qualities of modernity that necessitate surveillance.
Therefore modernity on the one hand advances the ideal of a right to privacy, but at the same time it must continuously advance surveillance that
threatens to undermine privacy rights. An antagonism between privacy ideals and surveillance is therefore constitutive for capitalism. This connection
has been observed by a number of authors in surveillance studies (Gumpert
and Drucker 2000, 172; Lyon 2001, 21, 27; Nock 1993, 1; Sewell and
Barker 2007, 356).

Some research has been conducted about public privacy and surveillance
awareness and the awareness of consumers about corporate information
surveillance (for example: Diney, Hart and Mullen 2008; Hoofnagle and
King 2008; McRobb and Stahl 2007; Milne, Rohm and Bahl 2004; O'Neil
2001; Sheehan 2002; Sheehan and Hoy 2000; Turow, Feldman and Meltzer 2005; Wang, Lee and Wang 1998). Some work has also been published
about the relationship of the Internet and economic surveillance (for example: Campbell and Carlson 2002; Fernback and Papacharissi 2007; Odih

2007; Perri 6 2005; Robins and Webster 1999; Solove 2004, 2007; Turow 2006a; Wall 2006).

Mark Andrejevic (2002) and Josh Lauer (2008) argue that the work of being watched in respect to the media is a form of exploitation and productive labour. Andrejecvic speaks of "the interactive capability of new media to exploit the work of being watched" (Andrejevic 2002, 239) and Lauer (2008) of consumer surveillance as alienated labour. Nicole Cohen (2008) has provided remarks on the political economy of Facebook. For her, the economic strategy of Facebook is the "valorization of surveillance" (Cohen 2008, 7). These approaches are critical in character and therefore important contributions to the research landscape. But they lack a systematic theoretical framework that shows how exactly exploitation on the Internet takes place. There is also a lack of discussion and application of the Marxian categories of class and surplus value that are crucial for the concept of exploitation.

This overview shows that web 2.0 is a relatively novel topic in the discussions about Internet surveillance and that systematic critical political economy approaches that give a detailed analysis of capital accumulation on web 2.0 and show the underlying strategies, mechanisms, and interests as well as the role of surveillance are largely missing. The next section aims to contribute to the correction of this deficit.

2.6. WEB 2.0, CAPITAL ACCUMULATION, AND SURVEILLANCE

The rise of popular Internet platforms that are based on user-generated content, co-creation, and information produced by consumers/users (prosumers, produsers), such as Facebook (created in 2004), YouTube (2005), Wikipedia (2001), Myspace (2003), Twitter (2006), Flickr (2003), hi5 (2004), Photobucket (2003), or YouPorn (2005), and usage experiences, have created new narratives about changes of the Internet and society. Many scholars and citizens now claim that a new World Wide Web has emerged—"web 2.0". So for example Axel Bruns sees the rise of produsage—the "hybrid user/producer role which inextricably interweaves both forms of participation" (Bruns 2008, 21) as the central characteristic of web 2.0. He argues that produsage "harnesses the collected, collective intelligence of all participants" (1), that it allows "participation in networked culture" (17), that "open participation" (24, 240) is a key principle of produsage, that a reconfiguration of democracy may result from web 2.0 (34), and that Flickr, YouTube, MySpace, and Facebook are environments of "public participation" (227f). He envisions a "produsage-based, participatory culture" (256) and "a produsage-based democratic model" (372). In relation to social networking sites, Albrechtslund uses the term participatory surveillance for arguing that "the practice of online social networking can be seen as empowering, as it is a way to voluntarily engage with other people and construct identities, and it can thus be described as participatory" (. . .) However, to participate in online social networking is also about the act of sharing yourself—or your constructed identity—with others. [. . .] In this case, participatory surveillance is a way of maintaining friendships by checking up on information other people share" (Albrechtslund 2008). Albrechtslund takes the term participatory surveillance from Mark Poster (1990, 69), who first utilized, but did not define, it. Whitaker (1999), Campbell and Carlson (2002), and Cascio (2005) speak of the emergence of a "participatory panopticon". Koskela (2006, 175) argues the webcams are empowering and "contribute to the 'democratization' of surveillance". Dennis (2008, 350) speaks of the emergence of a "participatory/ social panopticon". For Haggerty (2006, 28), reading weblogs is a form of surveillance that allows "for a leisurely scrutiny of the ruminations and images of otherwise unknown individuals". Haggerty (2006: 30) assumes that the synoptic web brings about democratic surveillance and says that the web "now provides opportunities for a virtual archaeology of the documentary traces of the powerful".

Dataveillance is the "systematic monitoring of people's actions or communications through the application of information technology" (Clarke 1988, 500). Clarke (1994) distinguishes between personal dataveillance that monitors the actions of one or more persons and mass dataveillance, where a group or large population is monitored in order to detect individuals of interest. In web 2.0, the boundaries between these two forms of surveillance become blurred: targeted advertising concerns the large mass of users of commercial web 2.0 platforms because by agreeing to terms of use they agree in most cases to the surveillance of their personal data and their usage behaviour, but this surveillance is fine-tuned in order to detect and store the individual differences and to target each user with a separate mass of advertisings. Web 2.0 surveillance is a form of personal mass dataveillance. Manuel Castells (2009) characterizes web 2.0 communication as mass self-communication.

> because it can potentially reach a global audience, as in the posting of a video on YouTube, a blog with RSS links to a number of web sources, or a message to a massive e-mail list. At the same time, it is self-communication because the production of the message is self-generated, the definition of the potential receiver(s) is self-directed, and the retrieval of specific messages or content from the World Wide Web and electronic networks is self-selected. (Castells 2009, 55)

Web 2.0 surveillance is directed at large user groups who help to hegemonically produce and reproduce surveillance by providing user-generated (self-produced) content. We can therefore characterize web 2.0 surveillance as mass self-surveillance.

So the claim of some is that the web and surveillance on the web become more democratic and participatory. In participatory democracy theory, participation is a broad notion of grassroots control and decision-making that also extends to the economy. A participatory economy requires a "change in the terms of access to capital in the direction of more nearly equal access" (Macpherson 1973, 71) and "a change to more nearly equal access to the means of labour" (73). In a participatory society, extractive power is reduced to zero (74). A participatory society equalizes the access to the means of life, the means of labour, and the protection against invasion by others (access to civil and political liberties): "Genuine democracy, and genuine liberty, both require the absence of extractive powers" (121). Participatory democracy therefore requires for Macpherson that the means and the output of labour are no longer a private property, but become a common property, which is "the guarantee to each individual that he will not be excluded from the use or benefit [. . .]; private property is created by the guarantee that an individual can exclude others from the use or benefit of something" (124). Participatory democracy involves "the right to a share in the control of the massed productive resources" (137). A democratic economy furthermore involves "the democratising of industrial authority structures, abolishing the permanent distinction between 'managers' and 'men'" (Pateman 1970, 43). Pateman terms the grassroots organization of firms and the economy in a participatory democracy "self-management". In order to assess if "web 2.0" is participatory, one therefore has to analyze its ownership structures.

One method for ranking website access is to count the number of unique visitors per website in a country for one month. Table 2.2 shows, based on this method, which web 2.0 platforms are among the top fifty websites accessed in the US in July 2009. If we define web 2.0 platforms as World Wide Web systems that are not predominantly sites for information consumption or search, but offer functions that support social networking, community building, file sharing, cooperative information production, and interactive blogging—platforms that are systems of communication and cooperation rather than systems of cognition (for this definition see 2008), then this allows us to analyze the role web 2.0 platforms play on the WWW: thirteen of fifty websites can be classified as web 2.0 platforms (=26.0%). These thirteen platforms account for 532 million out of a total of 1,916 million monthly usages of the fifty top websites in the US (=27.7%). If 26.0% of the top fifty US websites are web 2.0 platforms and these platforms account for 27.7% of usages, then this means that claims that the web has been transformed into a new web that is predominantly based on sharing, cooperation, and community building are vastly overdrawn. In the US, predominant Internet use is to access sites that allow information search, provide information-, shopping-, and e-mail-services. Web 2.0 platforms have become more important, but they do not dominate the web. Twelve of thirteen of the web 2.0 platforms that are among the top

Table 2.2 Web 2.0 Platforms that are among the Top 50 Websites in the US (data source: quantcast.com, US site ranking, August 13, 2009), Ownership Rights and Advertising Rights of the 13 Most-used Web 2.0 Platforms in the US (data source: terms of use and privacy policies)

Rank	Website	Ownership	Country	Year of Domain Creation	Economic Orientation	Unique Users per Month (million)	Ownership of Uploaded Data	Advertising
4	Facebook	Facebook Inc.	US	2004	Profit, advertising	91	License to use uploaded content	Targeted advertising
6	YouTube	Google Inc.	US	2005	Profit, advertising	72	License to use uploaded content	Targeted advertising
8	Wikipedia	Wikimedia Foundation	US	2001	Non-profit, non-advertising	67	Creative commons	No advertising
9	MySpace	MySpace Inc. (News Corporation)	US	2003	Profit, advertising	63	License to use uploaded content	Targeted advertising
14	Blogspot	Google Inc.	US	2000	Profit, advertising	49	License to use uploaded content	Targeted advertising
19	Answers	Answers Corporation	US	1996	Profit, advertising	39	License to use uploaded content	Targeted advertising

22	Wordpress	Automattic Inc.	US	2000	Profit, advertising	28	License to use uploaded content	Targeted advertising
23	Photobucket	Photobucket.com LLC	US	2003	Profit, advertising	28	License to use uploaded content	Targeted advertising
26	Twitter	Twitter Inc.	US	2006	Profit, no advertising	27	No license to use uploaded content	No advertising
31	Flickr	Yahoo! Inc.	US	2003	Profit, advertising	21	License to use uploaded content	Targeted advertising
32	Blogger	Google Inc.	US	1999	Profit, advertising	20	License to use uploaded content	Targeted advertising
44	eHow	Demand Media Inc.	US	1998	Profit, advertising	14	License to use uploaded content	Targeted advertising
49	eZineArticles	SparkNet Corporation	US	1999	Profit, advertising	13	No license to use uploaded content	Targeted advertising
						532		

fifty US websites are profit-oriented; eleven of them are advertising-based. An exception is Wikipedia, which is non-profit and advertising-free. This shows that although web 2.0 is strongly commodified, it is not totally commodified. There are possibilities for organizing popular non-commercial, non-profit alternatives. Advertising and targeted-advertising are the most important business models among these web 2.0 sites. However, there are some sites that combine this accumulation model with the accumulation model of selling special services to users. So for example Flickr, an advertising-based photo sharing community, allows uploading and viewing images for free, but sells additional services such as photo prints, business cards, photo books. WordPress uses advertising, but also generates revenue by selling VIP blog hosting accounts that have monthly subscription rates and services such as extra storage space, customized styles, a video blogging service, ad-free blogs, and blogs with an unlimited number of community members. Twitter was in August 2009 a profit-oriented corporation without a business model that did not use advertising. This means that Twitter is highly likely to introduce an accumulation model in the next few years because otherwise it will go bankrupt. According to my empirical sample, 92.3% of the most frequently used web 2.0 platforms in the US and 87.4% of monthly unique web 2.0 usages in the US are corporate-based, which shows that the vast majority of popular web 2.0 platforms are mainly interested in generating monetary profits and that the corporate web 2.0 is much more popular than the non-corporate web 2.0.

Google owns three of the eleven web platforms listed in Table 2.2. Eighteen human and corporate legal persons own 98.8% of Google's common stock, Google's 20,000 employees, the 520 million global Google users, the 303 million users of YouTube, and the 142 million users of Blogspot/Blogger are non-owners of Google.[3] All analyzed web 2.0 platforms have to guarantee for themselves a right to display user-generated content, otherwise they are unable to operate and survive. However, Table 2.2 shows that ten of the thirteen web 2.0 sites guarantee themselves in their terms of use a license for usage of user-generated data, which is a de-facto ownership right of the data because such a license includes the right to sell the content. Furthermore eleven of the thirteen web 2.0 platforms guarantee themselves the right to store, analyze, and sell the content and usage data of their users to advertising clients that are enabled to provide targeted, personalized advertisements. This means that the vast majority of the web 2.0 companies in our sample exert ownership rights on user-generated content and user behaviour data. Web 2.0 companies own the data of the users, whereas the users do not own a share of the corporations. This is an asymmetric economic power relation.

Corporations that are profit-oriented and accumulate capital by online advertising and in some cases by selling special services operate the vast majority of web 2.0 platforms. Corporate web 2.0 platforms attract a large majority of users. A few legal persons own the companies that operate web

2.0 platforms, whereas the millions of users have no share in ownership. However, with the help of legal mechanisms (terms of use, privacy policies) most web 2.0 corporations acquire the ownership rights to use and sell user-generated content and to analyze user data and behaviour for implementing third-party operated targeted advertisements in order to accumulate capital. There is a highly asymmetrical ownership structure: web 2.0 corporations accumulate evermore capital that is owned by a few legal persons and not by the users, whereas user data are dispossessed by the firms in order to generate money profit. Web 2.0 does not extend democracy beyond the political sphere into culture and the economy. It does not maximize the developmental powers of humans, it mainly maximizes the developmental powers of an economic class that owns web platforms and holds the extractive power to dispossess users and to exploit workers and users in order to accumulate capital. We can conclude that from the perspective of participatory democracy theory, web 2.0 is not a participatory techno-social system because it is based on capitalist ownership and accumulation structures that benefit the few at the expense of the many, and access is stratified.

This analysis confirms the views of Thomas Mathiesen who argues that the Internet is an undemocratic synopticon, in which the many observe the few, and that this does not bring about a "democratic system where everyone can particpate in interaction" (Mathiesen 2004, 100).

> The Internet becomes to a considerable extent a part of the synoptical system, in as much as it is, to a substantial degree, dominated by powerful economic agents—from newspapers and television agencies to owners having economic capital to invest in sales of lucrative merchandise, including pornography. To the same degree, the structure becomes characterised by a one-way flow, from the relatively few in control of economic capital, symbolic capital and technical know-how, to the many who are entertained or who buy the products" and are thereby silenced. (Mathiesen 2004, 100)

"A basic feature of the Internet is, in other words, that it constitutes an interactive one-way medium, not an interactive two-way or multi-way medium. The agenda is set by those with economic, symbolic or technical capital" (Mathiesen 2004, 100f). The Internet is therefore in its corporate form for Mathiesen a "system of silencing".

Given these empirical results, it seems feasible to theorize the contemporary "web 2.0" not as a participatory system, but by employing more negative, critical terms such as class, exploitation, and surplus value. Such an alternative theory of web 2.0 can here only be hinted at briefly (for a detailed discussion see Fuchs 2010b). It is based on the approach of the critique of the political economy of media and information. Felicity Brown (2006) calls for a combination of the critical political economy of communication and surveillance studies. "The critical political economy of communication has a particularly important role in analysing the mutually productive relationship between surveillance practices and the Internet. In particular, the intense monitoring of cyberspace by private corporations seeking information on consumer behaviour is worthy of critique" (Brown 2006, 10).

Marx highlights exploitation as the fundamental aspect of class in another passage, where he says that "the driving motive and determining purpose of capitalist production" is "the greatest possible exploitation of labour-power by the capitalist" (Marx 1867, 449). He says that the proletariat is "a machine for the production of surplus-value", capitalists are "a machine for the transformation of this surplus-value into surplus capital" (Marx 1867, 742). Whereas Marx had in his time to limit the notion of the proletariat to wage labour, it is today possible to conceive the proletariat in a much broader sense as all those who directly or indirectly produce surplus value and are thereby exploited by capital. This includes, besides wage labour, also house workers, the unemployed, the poor, migrants, retirees, students, precarious workers—and also the users of corporate web 2.0 platforms and other Internet sites and applications. Hardt and Negri (2004) use the term multitude for this multidimensional proletariat of the twenty-first century.

For Marx, the profit rate is the relation of profit to investment costs: p = s / (c + v) = surplus value / (constant capital (=fixed costs) + variable capital (=wages)). If Internet users become productive web 2.0 prosumers, then in terms of Marxian class theory this means that they become productive labourers who produce surplus value and are exploited by capital because for Marx productive labour generates surplus. Therefore the exploitation of surplus value in cases such as Google, YouTube, MySpace, or Facebook is not merely accomplished by those who are employed by these corporations for programming, updating, and maintaining the soft- and hardware, performing marketing activities, and so on, but by them, the users, and the prosumers that engage in the production of user-generated content. New media corporations do not (or hardly) pay the users for the production of content. One accumulation strategy is to give them free access to services and platforms, let them produce content, and so accumulate a large number of prosumers that are sold as a commodity to third-party advertisers. A product is not sold to the users; the users are sold as a commodity to advertisers. The more users a platform has, the higher the advertising rates can be set. The productive labour time that is exploited by capital on the one hand involves the labour time of the paid employees and on the other hand all of the time that is spent online by the users. For the first type of knowledge labour, new media corporations pay salaries. The second type of knowledge is produced completely for free. There are neither variable nor constant investment costs. The formula for the profit rate needs to be transformed for this accumulation strategy:

p = s / (c + v1 + v2), s . . . surplus value, c . . . constant capital, v1 . . . wages paid to fixed employees, v2 . . . wages paid to users

The typical situation is that v2 => 0 and that v2 substitutes v1. If the production of content and the time spent online were carried out by paid employees, the variable costs would rise and profits would therefore decrease. This shows that prosumage in a capitalist society can be interpreted as the outsourcing of productive labour to users who work completely for free and help maximize the rate of exploitation (e = s / v, = surplus value / variable capital) so that profits can be raised and new media capital may be accumulated. Again, this situation is one of infinite over-exploitation. Capitalist prosumage is an extreme form of exploitation, in which the prosumers work completely for free.

That surplus value-generating labour is an emergent property of capitalist production means that production and accumulation will break down if this labour is withdrawn. It is an essential part of the capitalist production process. That prosumers conduct surplus-generating labour can also be seen by imagining what would happen if they stopped using platforms like YouTube, MySpace, and Facebook: The number of users would drop, advertisers would stop investments because no objects for their advertising messages and therefore no potential customers for their products could be found, the profits of the new media corporations would drop, and they would go bankrupt. If such activities were carried out on a large scale, a new economic crisis would arise. This thought experiment shows that users are essential for generating profit in the new media economy. Furthermore they produce and coproduce parts of the products, and therefore parts of the use value, exchange value, and surplus value that are objectified in these products.

Dallas Smythe (1981/2006) suggests that in the case of media advertisement models, the audience is sold as a commodity to advertisers: "Because audience power is produced, sold, purchased and consumed, it commands a price and is a commodity. [. . .] You audience members contribute your unpaid work time and in exchange you receive the program material and the explicit advertisements" (Smythe 1981/2006, 233, 238). With the rise of user-generated content, free access social networking platforms, and other free access platforms that yield profit by online advertisement—a development subsumed under categories such as web 2.0, social software, and social networking sites—the web seems to come close to accumulation strategies employed by the capital on traditional mass media like TV or radio. The users who google data, upload or watch videos on YouTube, upload or browse personal images on Flickr, or accumulate friends with whom they exchange content or communicate online via social networking platforms like MySpace or Facebook constitute an audience commodity that is sold to advertisers. The difference between the audience commodity on traditional mass media and on the Internet is that in the latter case the users are also content producers; there is user-generated content, the users engage in permanent creative activity, communication, community building, and content-production. That the users are more active on the Internet than in the reception of TV or radio content is due to the decentralized structure of the Internet, which allows many-to-many communication. Due to the permanent activity of the recipients and their status as prosumers, we can say that in the case of the Internet the audience commodity is a Internet prosumer commodity. The category of the prosumer commodity does not signify a democratization of the media towards a participatory or democratic system, but the total commodification of human creativity. During much of the time that users spend online, they produce profit for large corporations like Google, News Corp. (which owns MySpace), or Yahoo! (which owns Flickr). Advertisements on the Internet are frequently personalized; this is made possible by surveilling, storing, and assessing user activities with the help of computers and databases. This is another difference from TV and radio, which provide less individualized content and advertisements due to their more centralized structure. But one can also observe a certain shift in the area of traditional mass media, as in the cases of pay per view, tele-votes, talk shows, and call-in TV and radio shows. In the case of the Internet, the commodification of audience participation is easier to achieve than with other mass media.

The importance of the prosumer commodity and extractive power as principles of the contemporary web 2.0 is evidenced by the continuing absolute and relative rise of Internet advertising profits. In 2008, Internet advertising was the third-largest advertising market in the US and the UK. Internet advertising profits were only exceeded in these two countries by advertising in newspapers and on TV (IAB Internet Advertising Revenue Report 2008, 14; Ofcom Communications Market Report 2009, 36).

Surveillance in corporate web 2.0 is surveillance of prosumers who dynamically and permanently create and share user-generated content, browse profiles and data, interact with others, join, create, and build communities, and co-create information. The corporate web platform operators and their third party advertising clients continuously monitor and record personal data and online activities; they store, merge, and analyze collected data. This allows them to create detailed user profiles and know about the personal interests and online behaviours of the users. Web platform operators sell the Internet prosumers as a commodity to advertising clients. Money is exchanged for the access to user data that allows economic surveillance of the users. The exchange value of the Internet prosumer commodity is the money value that the operators obtain from their clients; its use value is the multitude of personal data and usage behaviour that is dominated by the commodity and exchange value form. The surveillance of the prosumers' permanently produced use values, i.e., personal data and interactions, by corporations allows targeted advertising that aims at luring the prosumers into consumption and at manipulating their desires and needs in the interest of corporations and the commodities they offer. Internet prosumers are commodified by corporate platform operators who sell them to advertising clients; this results in an intensified exposure to commodity logic. They are double objects of commodification: they are commodities themselves, and through this commodification their consciousness becomes an object of commodity logic in the form of the permanent exposure to advertisements.

The Marxian cycle of capital accumulation allows distinguishing between workplace surveillance, workforce surveillance, and consumer surveillance. On web 2.0, producers are consumers and consumers are producers of information. Therefore, producer surveillance and consumer surveillance merge into web 2.0 produser surveillance. Web 2.0 surveillance of workplace and workforce (producer surveillance) is at the same time consumer surveillance and vice versa.

Privacy statements are the legal mechanisms that guarantee that personalized advertising can be operated on web platforms. Users have hardly any choice not to agree: if they want to interact with others and make use of the technical advantages web 2.0 poses, they have to agree to these terms. Privacy statements are totalitarian mechanisms that are necessarily not democratically controlled by the users, but under the control of corporations.

"The panoptic sort is a difference machine that sorts individuals into categories and classes on the basis of routine measurements. It is a discriminatory technology that allocates options and opportunities on the basis of those measures and the administrative models that they inform" (Gandy 1993, 15). It is a system of power and disciplinary surveillance that identifies, classifies, and assesses (Gandy 1993, 15). Produsage commodification on web 2.0 is a form of panoptic sorting (Gandy 1993): it identifies the interests of users by closely surveilling their personal data and usage behaviour, it classifies them into consumer groups, and assesses their interests in comparison to other consumers and in comparison to available advertisements that are then targeted at the users.

Facebook is a panoptic sorting machine. It first *identifies* the interests of the users by requiring them to upload personal data for registering and allowing them to communicate in interest groups, with their friends, and to upload personal user-generated content. When registering a Facebook profile, users are required to input the following data: first name, family name, e-mail, gender, date of birth. Other personal data that users can provide are: school, year of school leaving examination, universities attended, year of final degree, programmes studied, employer, former employers, type of job, job description, place of employment, duration of employment, profile picture, place of residence, hometown, district of residence, family members including degree of kinship, relationship status, political attitude, religious belief, activities, interests, favourite music, favourite television programmes, favourite movies, favourite books, favourite quotations, self-description, Internet messenger usernames, mobile phone number, fixed line phone number, address, city, neighbourhood, zip code, website address (information as of September 17,2010). According to the Facebook Privacy Policy (accessed on September 17, 2010), the company also stores the following data about users: type of computer, used browser, cookie data, data about the usage of Facebook applications, data about behaviour on other websites, browsing behaviour on other Facebook profiles, data about users that stems from other profiles. In a second step of the Facebook panoptic sort, all of these data are used for *classifying* users into consumer groups. In the third step, a comparative *assessment* of the interests of users and available advertisements is conducted, and ads that match specific interests are selected and presented to the users. The description of this example process shows that surveillance on Facebook and other commercial web 2.0 platforms is a form of panoptic online sorting that is based on identification, classification, and assessment.

Foucault characterized surveillance: "He is seen, but he does not see; he is the object of information, never a subject in communication" (Foucault 1977, 200). With the rise of "web 2.0", the Internet has become a universal communication system, which is shaped by privileged data control by corporations that own most of the communication-enabling web platforms and by the state that can gain access to personal data by law. On the Internet, the separation between "objects of information" and "subjects in communication" that Foucault (1977, 200) described for historical forms of surveillance no longer exists; by being subjects of communication on the Internet, users make available personal data to others and continuously communicate this data over the Internet. These communications are mainly mediated by corporate-owned platforms; therefore the subjects of communication become objects of information for corporations and the state in surveillance processes. Foucault argues that power relations are different from relationships of communication, although they are frequently connected (Foucault 1994, 337): "Power relations are exercised, to an exceedingly important extent, through the production and exchange of signs", "relationships of communication [. . .] by modifying the field of information between partners, produce effects of power" (Foucault 1994, 338). In web 2.0, corporate and state power is exercised through the gathering, combination, and assessment of personal data that users communicate over the web to others, and the global communication of millions within a heteronomous society produces the interest of certain actors to exert control over these communications. In web 2.0, power relations and relationships of communication are interlinked. In web 2.0, the users are producers of information (produsers, prosumers), but this creative communicative activity enables the controllers of disciplinary power to closely gain insights into the lives, secrets, and consumption preferences of the users.

2.7. HOW AWARE ARE WEB 2.0 USERS OF ONLINE SURVEILLANCE?

Andrés Sanchez (2009) analyzes the resistance of Facebook users against increased surveillance on the platform through the introduction of news feeds and mini feeds. He shows that there are potentials immanent in web 2.0 and social networking sites for protest against web surveillance. The question of whether resistance to online surveillance is possible depends on how conscious users are about potential threats. The author of this chapter conducted an online survey about surveillance on social networking sites (Fuchs 2009). Six-hundred seventy-four students from the city of Salzburg participated in the survey. The two following open-ended questions were part of the questionnaire: What are in your opinion the greatest advantages of social networking platforms as studiVZ, Facebook, MySpace, etc.? What is your greatest concern about social networking platforms as studiVZ, Facebook, MySpace, etc? We identified eighteen categories for the advantages and sixteen categories for the disadvantages and analyzed the answers to the two open-ended questions by content analysis (Krippendorff 2004) so that each text was mapped with one or more categories. The respondents tended to list more than one major advantage and disadvantage. Therefore each answer was mapped with more than one category in most cases.

Figure 2.2 presents the major advantages and disadvantages of social networking sites that our respondents mentioned.

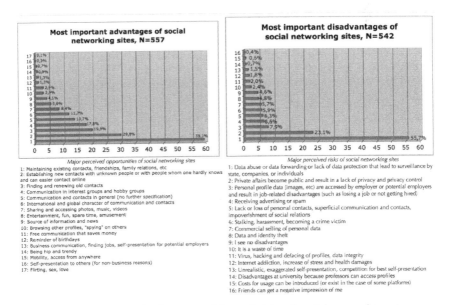

Figure 2.2 Major perceived opportunities and risks of social networking sites.

Here are some typical answers given by students when asked about the main advantages of SNS: "Remaining in contact after a joint period of studying, collaboration, a journey or simply a period of more intensive contact has come to an end, e.g. after relocating etc. You also know years later how/where to find people" (respondent #47). "You have all your friends in one spot, you do not permanently have to ask for mobile phone numbers" (#82). "You can find old acquaintances and stay in touch with them. I have also already contacted students in order to co-operate with them in various seminars and internships" (#93). "Such platforms make it easier to stay in contact also across larger distances—for example with former schoolmates" (#104). "Connects people from all over the world and you find old and new friends" (#123). "It is easy to establish contact with colleagues that you have thus far hardly known" (#199). "To come in touch or stay in touch with people that have the same interests as you; you can build up a small network of friends and acquaintances; finding others and being found" (#267). "Networking of students, exchange between like-minded people" (#377). These typical examples show that students think that social relationship management is an important advantage of SNS. SNS are social spaces for maintaining and extending social networks.

Some typical answers given when asked about the main disadvantages were: "Big Brother is watching you" (respondent #6), "spying by employers" (#65), "My data are sold for advertising. You become too "transparent" for strangers" (#93), "Personal data are sold to different corporations" (#109), "Data surveillance, the transparent human, strangers gain insights into privacy, selling of private data and browsing behaviour" (#224), "To be "spied on" by a third party" (#409), "The surveillance society" (#454). These examples show that surveillance and surveillance for economic ends are big concerns of students who use SNS.

The survey revealed that 55.7% of the respondents say that political, economic, or personal surveillance as a result of data abuse, data forwarding, or a lack of data protection is a main threat of social networking sites. The data of our survey show that 59.1% consider maintaining existing contacts and 29.8% establishing new contacts as major advantage of social networking sites, whereas 55.7% say that surveillance as a result of data abuse, data forwarding, or a lack of data protection is a major threat of such platforms. Communication and the resulting reproduction and emergence of social relations are overwhelmingly considered as major advantage, potential surveillance overwhelmingly as major disadvantage. The impression of the majority of the respondents is that social networking sites enable communicative advantages that are coupled with the risk of surveillance and reduced privacy. How can we explain why they are willing to take the surveillance risk that they are knowledgeable and conscious about? Communication and surveillance are antagonistic counterparts of the usage of commercial social networking platforms: Our data show that students are heavily using social networking sites and are willing to take the risk of increased surveillance although they are very well aware of surveillance and privacy risks.

The potential advantages seem to outstrip the potential disadvantages. It is not an option for them not to use social networking platforms because they consider the communicative and social opportunities associated with these technologies as very important. At the same time they are not stupid, uncritical, or unaware of potential dangers, but rather very conscious of the disadvantages and risks. They seem to fear that they will miss social contacts or otherwise be at a disadvantage if they do not use platforms such as studiVZ, Facebook, or MySpace. Not using these technologies or stopping using them is clearly not an option for most of them because it would result in disadvantages such as reduced social contacts and the feeling of not participating in something that has become important to the young generation. The crucial aspect of the antagonism between communicative opportunities and surveillance risk is that alternative social networking platforms that are non-commercial and non-profit, and therefore do not have an interest in economic surveillance and that see privacy as a fundamental right that needs to be well protected under all circumstances, are hardly available or hardly known. Commercial profit-oriented sites such as studiVZ, Facebook, and MySpace have reached a critical mass of users that is so large that these commercial providers have become cultural necessities for most young people. It is hard for non-commercial platforms to compete with these economic corporations because the latter have huge stocks of financial means (enabled by venture capital or parent companies such as News Corporation or Holtzbrinck), personnel, and technological resources. Capitalist business interests and the unequal distribution of assets that is characteristic of the capitalist economy result in the domination of markets by a handful of powerful corporations that provide services and that make influence by non-commercial, non-profit operators difficult. Given the fact that students are knowledgeable of the surveillance threat, it is obvious that they are willing to use alternative platforms instead of the major corporate ones, if such alternatives are available and it becomes known that they minimize the surveillance threat. Students are not to blame for potential disadvantages that arise from their use of social networking platforms that, in the opinions of our respondents, threaten privacy and advance surveillance. The corporations that engage in surveillance and enable surveillance are to blame. Corporate social networking platforms are for example not willing to abstain from surveillance for advertising because they have profit interests. The antagonism between communicative opportunities and the surveillance threat is not created by students' and young people's usage of social networking platforms, but by the economic and political logic that shapes social networking corporations' platform strategies.

2.8. CONCLUSION: IS RESISTANCE POSSIBLE?

One can observe that there are two predominant ways of defining surveillance: negative and neutral ones (Fuchs 2010a).

Neutral concepts of surveillance make one or more of the following assumptions:

- There are positive aspects of surveillance.
- Surveillance has two faces; it is enabling and constraining.
- Surveillance is a fundamental aspect of all societies.
- Surveillance is necessary for organization.
- Any kind of systematic information gathering is surveillance.

In a negative theory, surveillance is a negative concept that is inherently linked to information gathering for the purposes of domination, violence, and coercion and thereby at the same time accuses such states of society and makes political demands for a participatory, cooperative, free society—a society where cooperative modes of production and ownership replace classes and the exploitation of surplus value and where care and solidarity substitute surveillance.

My personal view is that information is a more general concept than surveillance and that surveillance is a specific kind of information gathering, storage, processing, assessment, and use that involves potential or actual harm, coercion, violence, asymmetric power relations, control, manipulation, domination, or disciplinary power. It is instrumental and a means for trying to derive and accumulate benefits for certain groups or individuals at the expense of other groups or individuals. Surveillance is based on the logic of competition. It tries to bring about or prevent certain behaviours of groups or individuals by gathering, storing, processing, diffusing, assessing, and using data about humans so that potential or actual physical, ideological, or structural violence can be directed against humans in order to influence their behaviour. This influence is brought about by coercive means and brings benefits to certain groups at the expense of others. Surveillance is in my view therefore never cooperative and solidaristic—it never benefits all. Nonetheless, there are certainly information processes that aim at benefiting all humans. I term such information processes monitoring; it involves information processing that aims at care, benefits, solidarity, aid, and cooperation, benefits all, and is opposed to surveillance.

There are a number of problems that neutral surveillance concepts face (for a detailed discussion see Fuchs 2010a).

- A neutral notion of surveillance puts negative and positive aspects of surveillance on one categorical level and therefore may trivialize repressive information gathering and usage.

- Neutral surveillance studies support the ideological celebration and normalization of surveillance.
- A neutral surveillance concept does not allow distinguishing between information gathering and surveillance; therefore no distinctions between a surveillance society and an information society and between surveillance studies and information society studies can be drawn.
- A dialectic should not be assumed at the categorical level of surveillance, but at a meta-level that allows to distinguish between surveillance and solidarity as positive respectively negative side of systematic information gathering.
- Etymologically the term surveillance implies a relationship of asymmetrical power, domination, hierarchy, and violence.

I speak of "neutral" surveillance concepts because identifying potential positive meanings of the term "surveillance" neutralizes the critical potential of the term for engaging in a fundamental critique of power and domination and creates a conceptual confusion and conflationism that is a disservice to a critical theory of society. A fundamental theoretical argument underlying my chapter (and implicitly or explicitly also those of some other authors in this book, for example: Mark Andrejevic, Marisol Sandoval, Thomas Allmer, David Arditi, David Hill, Monika Taddicken, Kent Wayland/Roberto Armengol/Deborah Johnson) is therefore that surveillance in general and therefore also web 2.0 surveillance and Internet surveillance should be used as negative and critical terms, not also as affirmative ones.

Oscar Gandy argues that an alternative to opt-out solutions of targeted advertising are opt-in solutions that are based on the informed consent of consumers. When individuals

> wish information or an information-based service, they will seek it out. It is not unreasonable to assume that individuals would be the best judge of when they are the most interested and therefore most receptive to information of a particular kind. Others with information to provide ought to assume that, unless requested, no information is desired. This would be the positive option. Through a variety of means, individuals would provide a positive indication that yes, I want to learn, hear, and see more about this subject at this time. Individuals should be free to choose when they are ready to enter the market for information. (Gandy 1993, 220)

> The value in the positive option is its preservation of the individual's right to choose. (Gandy 1993, 221)

Culnan and Bies argue that opt-in is a form of procedural justice and a fair information practice: "Fair information practices are procedures that provide individuals with control over the disclosure and subsequent use of their personal information and govern the interpersonal treatment that consumers receive" (Culnan and Bies 2003, 330). Bellman et al. (2004) conducted a survey (N=534 responses from 38 countries) that showed that the highest average agreement (6.30, 7-point Likert scale, 1=strongly disagree, 7=strongly agree) was achieved for the statement "web sites should not use personal information for any purpose unless it has been authorized by the individuals who provide the information". Seventy-nine per cent of US Internet users preferred opt-in solutions in 2000 (Pew Internet & American Life Project Poll, May 2000). Eighty-five per cent said in 2006 that it is very important that they can control who has access to their personal information (Pew Internet & American Life Project Poll, December 2006). These results show that users consider opt-in strongly desirable and opt-out undesirable. Within capitalism, forcing corporations by state laws to implement opt-in mechanisms is certainly desirable, but at the same time it is likely that corporations will not consent to such policies because opt-in is likely to reduce the actual amount of surveilled and commodified user data significantly, which results in a drop of advertising profits. "Historically, members of information intensive industries have tended to be reactive, rather than pro-active, with regard to privacy policy" (Gandy 2003/2007, 296). Therefore capitalist interests are likely to naturally oppose the consumer interest of opt-in. Empirical studies confirm that given self-regulation, only a small portion of companies implements privacy policies that adhere to fair information practices (Federal Trade Commission 2000; Ryker et al. 2002). "Businesses have a great stake in access to individuals' personal information and tend to favor policies that allow self-regulation of privacy practices in engaging with customers" (Starke-Meyerring and Gurak 2007, 301).

In order to circumvent the large-scale surveillance of consumers, producers, and consumer-producers, movements and protests against economic surveillance are necessary. Kojin Karatani (2005) argues that consumption is the only space in capitalism where workers become subjects that can exert pressure by consumption boycotts on capital. I do not think that this is correct because strikes also show the subject position of workers, which enables them to boycott production, to cause financial harm to capital, and to exert pressure in order to voice political demands. However, Karatani in my opinion correctly argues that the role of the consumer has been underestimated in Marxist theory and practice. That in the contemporary media landscape media consumers become media producers who work and create surplus value shows the importance of the role of consumers in contemporary capitalism and of "the transcritical moment where workers and consumers intersect" (Karatani 2005, 21). For political strategies this brings up the actuality of an associationist movement that is "a transnational association of consumers/workers" (Karatani 2005, 295) that engages in "the class struggle against capitalism" of "workers qua consumers or consumers qua workers" (Karatani 2005, 294).

As our study has shown, many young people seem to be aware of the surveillance risks of web 2.0. They possess a critical potential that could be transformed into protest and social movement action if it is adequately triggered and organized.

I recommend that critical citizens, critical citizens' initiatives, consumer groups, social movement groups, critical scholars, unions, data protection specialists/groups, consumer protection specialists/groups, critical politicians, and critical political parties observe closely the relationship of surveillance and corporations and document instances where corporations and politicians take measures that threaten privacy or increase the surveillance of citizens. Such documentation is most effective if it is easily accessible to the public. The Internet provides means for documenting such behaviour. It can help to watch the watchers and to raise public awareness. In recent years, corporate watch organizations that run online watch platforms have emerged.

Examples for corporate watch organizations are:

CorpWatch Reporting (http://www.corpwatch.org),
Transnationale Ethical Rating (http://www.transnationale.org),
The Corporate Watch Project (http://www.corporatewatch.org),
Multinational Monitor (http://www.multinationalmonitor.org),
crocodyl: Collaborative research on corporations
    (http://www.crocodyl.org),
Endgame Database of Corporate Fines (http://www.endgame.org/
    corpfines.html),
Corporate Crime Reporter (http://www.corporatecrimereporter.com),
Corporate Europe Observatory (http://www.corporateeurope.org),
Corporate Critic Database (http://www.corporatecritic.org).

Watchdog organizations and initiatives certainly have limits. They are generally civil society projects because big corporations or governments are unlikely to support initiatives that criticize corporations and governments with big amounts of money. Therefore such projects are frequently based on precarious, self-exploitative labour, and are confronted with a lack of resources such as money, activists, time, infrastructure, influence, etc. If political or economic institutions offer support, then there is a danger that they try to influence the activities of such projects, which can severely damage or limit the autonomy and critical facility of such projects. They seem to be trapped in an antagonism between resource precariousness and loss of autonomy that is caused by the fact that the control of resources is vital for having political influence in contemporary society and that resources in this very society are unequally distributed so that corporations and established political actors have much more power and influence than other actors. Given this situation, it would be a mistake not to try to organize citizens' initiatives, but one should bear in mind that due to the stratified character of capitalism it is more likely that such initiatives will fail and remain unimportant than that they will be successful in achieving their goals.

There are no easy solutions to the problem of civil rights limitations due to electronic surveillance. Opting out of existing advertising options is not a solution to the problem of economic and political surveillance. Even if users opt out, media corporations will continue to collect and assess certain data on them, to sell the users as audience commodity to advertising clients, and to give personal data to the police. To try to advance critical awareness and to surveil corporate and political surveillers are important political moves for guaranteeing civil rights, but they will ultimately fail if they do not recognize that electronic surveillance is not a technological issue that can be solved by technological means or by different individual behaviours, but only by bringing about changes of society. Therefore the topic of electronic surveillance should be situated in the context of larger societal problems in public discourse.

Another recommendation is to create non-commercial, non-profit social networking platforms on the Internet. It is not impossible to create successful non-profit Internet platforms, as the example of Wikipedia, which is advertising-free, has free access, and is financed by donations, shows. But the difficulty is that social networking platforms have to store large amounts of data, especially profile data that contain images, videos, etc., which requires tremendous server capacities. It is certainly easier and probably more efficient to organize such huge data storage endeavours in the form of profit-oriented businesses. But this orientation at the same time brings about the risk of extended and intensified electronic surveillance. I am not saying that non-commercial, non-profit platforms are devoid of this risk, but that there is a reduced likelihood that electronic surveillance for economic reasons will take place on such platforms and an increased likelihood that such platforms will try to protect its users from state surveillance. Within capitalism, it is certainly very difficult to try to organize such non-profit online alternatives because everything that is non-profit and non-commercial tends to be confronted by shortages of resources, which makes sustainable performance difficult. Trying to organize alternatives might be precarious, difficult, and confronted with a high probability of potential failure. But at the same time it might be the only constructive alternative to corporate control and corporate concentration processes in the Internet economy that tend to reinforce processes of economic and political electronic surveillance.

An example for an alternative social networking site is kaioo. It is operated by the Open Networx Initiative, a public trust created in 2007. The users of kaioo can discuss and edit the terms of use and privacy terms in a wiki. Kaioo is advertising-free and non-profit. The most well-known alternative social networking site project is Diaspora, which tries to develop an open source alternative to Facebook. Diaspora defines itself as "privacy-aware, personally controlled, do-it-all, open source social (http://www.joindisaspora.com, accessed on November 11, 2010).

An alternative Internet and alternative Internet platforms could provide the foundation for forms of online communication that are not based on economic surveillance. Slavoj Žižek argues in this context that "the digitalization of our daily lives, in effect, makes possible a Big Brother control in comparison with which the old Communist secret police supervision cannot but look like primitive child's play. Here, therefore, more than ever, one should insist that the proper answer to this threat is not retreat into islands of privacy, but an ever stronger socialization of cyberspace" (Žižek 2001, 256). A commons-based Internet requires a commons-oriented society (Fuchs 2011, chapters 8 and 9).

ACKNOWLEDGMENTS

The research presented in this chapter was conducted in the project "Social Networking Sites in the Surveillance Society", funded by the Austrian Science Fund (FWF): project number P 22445-G17. Project coordination: Dr. Christian Fuchs.

NOTES

1. Reuters: Facebook '09 revenue neared $800 million, http://www.reuters.com/article/idUSTRE65H01W20100618 (accessed on 09–10–2010).
2. *Times*, October 20, 2008, http://business.timesonline.co.uk/tol/business/industry_sectors/technology/article4974197.ece (accessed on ???).
3. Data: Google SEC Filing Proxy Statements 2008. Number of worldwide Internet users: 1,596,270,108 (internetworldstats.com, August 14, 2009).
   3-month average number of worldwide Google users (alexa.com, August 14, 2009): 32.671% of worldwide Internet users (520 million users).
   3-month average number of worldwide YouTube users (alexa.com, August 14, 2009): 18.983% (303 million users).
   3-month average number of worldwide Blogger/Blogspot users: (alexa.com, August 14, 2009): 8.869% (142 million users).

REFERENCES

6, Perri. 2005. The personal information economy: trends in prospects for consumers. In *The glass consumer*, ed. Susanne Lace, 17–43. Bristol: Policy.

Albrechtslund, Anders. 2008. Online social networking as participatory surveillance. *First Monday* 13 (3).

Andrejevic, Mark. 2002. The work of being watched: interactive media and the exploitation of self-disclosure. *Critical Studies in Media Communication* 19 (2): 230–248.

Bellman, Steven, Eric J. Johnson, Stephen J. Kobrin, and Gerald L. Lohse. 2004. International differences in information privacy concerns: a global survey of consumers. *The Information Society* 20 (5): 313–324.

Brown, Felicity. 2006. Rethinking the role of surveillance studies in the critical political economy of communication. IAMCR Prize in Memory of Dallas W. Smythe

2006: http://www.iamcr.org/component/option,com_docman/task,doc_down-load/gid,31/ (accessed on August 28, 2009).

Bruns, Axel. 2008. *Blogs, wikipedia, second life, and beyond: From production to produsage*. New York: Peter Lang.

Campbell John E. and Matt Carlson M. 2002. Panopticon.com: online surveillance and the commodification of privacy. *Journal of Broadcasting & Electronic Media* 46 (4): 586–606.

Cascio, Jamais. 2005. The rise of the digital panopticon. http://www.worldchang-ing.com/archives/002651.html (accessed on September 5, 2009).

Castells, Manuel. 2009. *Communication power*. Oxford: Oxford University Press.

Clarke, Roger. 1988. Information technology and dataveillance. *Communications of the ACM* 31 (5): 498–512.

———. 1994. Dataveillance: delivering '1984'. In *Framing technology: Society, choice and change*, ed. Lelia Green and Roger Guinery, 117–130. Sydney: Allen & Unwin.

Cohen, Nicole S. 2008. The valorization of surveillance: towards a political economy of Facebook. *Democratic Communique* 22 (1): 5–22.

Culnan, Mary J. and Robert J. Bies. 2003. Consumer privacy: balancing economic and justice considerations. *Journal of Social Issues* 59 (2): 323–342.

Dennis, Kingsley. 2008. Keeping a close watch—the rise of self-surveillance and the threat of digital exposure. *The Sociological Review* 56 (3): 347–357.

Dinev, Tamara, Paul Hart, and Michael R. Mullen. 2008. Internet privacy concerns and beliefs about government surveillance—an empirical investigation. *Journal of Strategic Information Systems* 17 (3): 214–233.

Federal Trade Commission. 2000. Privacy online: fair information practices in the electronic marketplace. http://www.ftc.gov/reports/privacy2000/privacy2000.pdf (accessed on September 5, 2009).

Fernback, Jan and Zizi Papacharissi. 2007. Online privacy as legal safeguard: the relationship among consumer, online portal, and privacy policies. *New Media & Society* 9 (5): 715–734.

Foucault, Michel. 1977. *Discipline & punish*. New York: Vintage.

———. 1994. *Power*. New York: New Press.

Fuchs, Christian. 2008. *Internet and society: Social theory in the information age*. New York: Routledge.

———. 2009. *Social networking sites and the surveillance society: A critical case study of the usage of studiVZ, Facebook, and MySpace by students in Salzburg in the context of electronic surveillance*. Salzburg/Vienna: Research Group UTI.

Fuchs, Christian. 2010a. *How can surveillance be defined? Remarks on theoretical foundations of surveillance studies*. Vienna: Unified Theory of Information Research Group. SNS3 Research Paper No.1. ISSN 2219–603X. http://www.sns3.uti.at/wordpress/wp-content/uploads/2010/10/The-Internet-Surveillance-Research-Paper-Series-1-Christian-Fuchs-How-Surveillance-Can-Be-Defined.pdf. (accessed on ???).

———. 2010b. Social software and web 2.0: their sociological foundations and implications. In *Handbook of research on web 2.0, 3.0, and X.0: Technologies, business, and social applications*, ed. San Murugesan, 764–789. Hershey, PA: IGI-Globl.

Fuchs, Christian. 2011. *Foundations of critical media and communication studies*. New York: Routledge.

Gandy, Oscar H. 1993. *The panoptic sort: A political economy of personal information*. Boulder: Westview.

————. 2003. Data mining and surveillance in the post-9/11 environment. In *The intensification of surveillance*, ed. Kirstie Ball and Frank Webster, 26–41. London: Pluto.

————. 2003/2007. Public opinion survey and the formation of privacy policy. In *The surveillance studies reader*, ed., Sean P. Hier and Josh Greenberg, 292–304. Berkshire: Open University Press.

Gumpert, Gary and Susan J. Drucker. 2000. The demise of privacy in a private world. In *Cyberethics*, ed. Robert M. Baird, Reagan Ramsower, and Stuart E. Rosenbaum, 171–187. Amherst, NY: Prometheus.

Haggerty, Kevin. 2006. The new politics of surveillance and visibility. In *Surveillance and visibility*, ed. Kevin Haggerty and Richard Ericson, 3–33. Toronto: University of Toronto Press.

Hardt, Michael and Antonio Negri. 2004. *Multitude*. New York: Penguin.

Harvey, David. 2010. *The enigma of capital*. London: Profile Books.

Hoofnagle, Chris Jay and Jennifer King. 2008. *What Californians understand about privacy online*. Research Report. Berkeley, CA: Samuelson Law, Technology & Public Policy Clinic, UC Berkeley Law.

Karatani, Kojin. 2005. *Transcritique: On Kant and Marx*. Cambridge: MIT Press.

Koskela, Hille. 2006. 'The other side of surveillance': webcams, power and agency. In *Theorizing surveillance*, ed. David Lyon, 163–181. Portland, OR: Willan.

Krippendorff, Klaus. 2004. *Content analysis: An introduction to its methodology*. London: Sage. 2nd edition.

Lauer, Josh. 2008. Alienation in the information economy: toward a marxist critique of consumer surveillance. In *Participation and media production*, ed. Nico Carpentier and Benjamin De Cleen, 41–53. Newcastle: Cambridge Scholars.

Lyon, David. 1994. *The electronic eye: The rise of surveillance society*. Cambridge: Polity.

————. 2001. *Surveillance society: Monitoring everyday life*. Buckingham: Open University Press.

Macpherson, Crawford Brough. 1973. *Democratic theory*. Oxford: Oxford University Press.

Marx, Gary T. 2007. Surveillance. In *Encyclopedia of privacy*, ed. William G. Staples, 535–544. Westport, CT: Greenwood.

Marx, Karl. 1857/58. *Grundrisse*. London: Penguin.

————. 1867. *Capital: Volume I*. London: Penguin.

————. 1885. *Capital: Volume II*. London: Penguin.

————. 1974. *On freedom of the press and censorship*. New York: McGraw-Hill.

Marx, Karl and Friedrich Engels (MEW) *Marx-Engels-Werke*. Berlin: Dietz.

Marx, Karl and Friedrich Engels. 1968. *Selected works in one volume*. London: Lawrence & Wishart.

Mathiesen, Thomas. 2004. Panopticon and synopticon as silencing systems. In *Silently silenced: Essays on the creation of acquiesence in modern society*, 98–102. Winchester: Waterside.

McRobb, Steve and Bernd Carsten Stahl. 2007. Privacy as a shared feature of the e-phenomenon. *International Journal of Technology and Management* 6 (2/3/4): 232–249.

Milne, George R., Andrew J. Rohm, and Shalini Bahl. 2004. Consumers' protection of online privacy and identity. *Journal of Consumer Affairs* 38 (2): 217–232.

Moor, James H. 2000. Toward a theory of privacy in the information age. In *Cyberethics*, ed. Robert M. Baird, Reagan Ramsower, and Stuart E. Rosenbaum, 200–212. Amherst, NY: Prometheus.

Negri, Antonio. 1991. *Marx beyond Marx*. London: Pluto.

Nock, Steven. 1993. *The costs of privacy: Surveillance and reputation in America.* New York: de Gruyter.

O'Neil, Dara. 2001. Analysis of Internet users' level of online privacy concerns. *Social Science Computer Review* 19 (1): 17–31.

Odih, Pamela. 2007. *Advertising in modern & postmodern times.* London: Sage.

Ogura, Toshimaru. 2006. Electronic government and surveillance-oriented society. In *Theorizing surveillance,* ed. David Lyon, 270–295. Portland, OR: Willan.

Pateman, Carole. 1970. *Participation and democratic theory.* Cambridge: Cambridge University Press.

Poster, Mark. 1990. *The mode of information.* Cambridge: Polity.

Robins, Kevin and Frank Webster. 1999. *Times of the technoculture.* New York: Routledge.

Ryker, Randy, Elizabeth Lafleur, Chris Cox, and Bruce Mcmanis. 2002. Online privacy policies: an assessment of the fortune E-50. *Journal of Computer Information Systems* 42 (4): 15–20.

Sanchez, Andrés. 2009. The Facebook feeding frenzy: resistance-through-distance and resistance-through-persistence in the societied network. *Surveillance & Society* 6 (3): 275–293.

Sewell, Graham and James Barker. 2007. Neither good, nor bad, but dangerous: surveillance as an ethical paradox. In *The surveillance studies reader,* ed. Sean P. Hier and Josh Greenberg, 354–367. Maidenhead: Open University Press.

Sheehan, Kim Bartel. 2002. Toward a typology of Internet users and online privacy concerns. *The Information Society* 19 (1): 21–32.

Sheehan, Kim Bartel and Mariea Grubbs Hoy. 2000. Dimensions of privacy among online consumers. *Journal of Public Policy & Marketing* 19 (1): 62–73.

Smythe, Dallas W. 1981/2006. On the audience commodity and its work. In *Media and cultural studies,* ed. Meenakshi G. Durham and Douglas M. Kellner, 230–256. Malden, MA: Blackwell.

Solove, Daniel J. 2004. *The digital person: Technology and privacy in the information age.* New York: New York University Press.

———. 2007. *The future of reputation: Gossip, rumor, and privacy on the Internet.* New Haven: Yale University Press.

Starke-Meyerring, Doreen and Laura Gurak. 2007. Internet. In *Encyclopedia of privacy,* ed. William G. Staples, 297–310. Westport, CT: Greenwood.

Turow, Joseph. 2006a. Cracking the consumer code: advertisers, anxiety, and surveillance in the digital age. In *Surveillance and visibility,* ed. Kevin Haggerty and Richard Ericson, 279–307. Toronto: University of Toronto Press.

———. 2006b. *Niche envy: Marketing discrimination in the digital age.* Cambridge: MIT Press.

Turow, Joseph, Lauren Feldman, and Kimberly Meltzer, 2005. *Open to Exploitation: American Shoppers Online and Offline.* Research Report. Annenberg Public Policy Center, University of Pennsylvania.

Wall, David S. 2006. Surveillant Internet technologies and the growth in information capitalism: spams and public trust in the information society. In *Surveillance and visibility,* ed. Kevin Haggerty and Richard Ericson, 340–362. Toronto: University of Toronto Press.

Wang, Huaiqing, Matthew K.O. Lee, and Chen Wang. 1998. Consumer privacy concerns about Internet marketing. *Communications of the ACM* 41 (3): 63–70.

Whitaker, Reginald. 1999. *The end of privacy.* New York: New Press.

Žižek, Slavoj. 2001. *Did somebody say totalitarianism?* London: Verso.

3 Exploitation in the Data Mine

Mark Andrejevic

3.1. INTRODUCTION:
HOW "ANYTHING" CAN BE PREDICTED

A recent article in the journal *Science* sifted through three months of call records for 50,000 mobile phone users to answer the question: "to what degree are individual human actions predictable?" (Song et al. 2010). More specifically, the authors sifted through location tracking data collected by an unnamed (presumably US) mobile phone operator to track the users' time-space paths. The article concluded, based on its consideration of the large database, "that there is a potential 93% average predictability in user mobility, an exceptionally high value rooted in the inherent regularity of human behavior" (Song et al. 2010, 1018). Even more surprisingly, according to the authors, predictability did not vary greatly across groups sorted by their level of mobility: the highly mobile group was almost as predictable as more stationary groups. The study predicted the level of mobility—not actual location (for which 93% would have been a strikingly high number), but the authors anticipated this might be the next step: "Although making explicit predictions on user whereabouts is beyond our goals here, appropriate data-mining algorithms [. . .] could turn the predictability identified in our study into actual mobility predictions" (1021). The authors conclude that their findings indicate that "the development of accurate predictive models is a scientifically grounded possibility, with potential impact on our well-being and public health" (1021).

The fact that this kind of research has become the province of a premier science journal indicates the important role that the mathematics and theory behind what marketers call "predictive analytics" plays in the digital era. The management, sorting, and mining of huge amounts of information are to the information age what the physics of ballistics was to the space race. The *Encyclopedia of Artificial Intelligence* (Wang, Chen, and Yao 2009) describes predictive analytics as "one of the major future trends for data mining [. . .] They hope to forecast based on the contents of the data [. . .] With predictive analytics you have the program scour the data and try to form, or help form, new hypotheses itself" (421). The best-selling author and Yale Law School professor Ian Ayres provided a more popular gloss on data mining in *Super Crunchers: How Anything Can be Predicted*, when he observed that "Super Crunching will predict what you will want and what you will do" (Ayres 2007, 44).

Prediction is the data-fuelled fantasy of interactive marketing, and is at stake in techniques with names like "cluster analysis", "biological response analysis", "collaborative filtering", and "sentiment analysis". What all of these have in common is their reliance on the capture of large amounts of detailed data about people, products, and their various attributes. Taken to the limit, prediction relies upon increasingly comprehensive forms of commercial monitoring. We have reached the point by now that concerns about commercial surveillance have become a recurring theme in both the academic and the popular literature on the emerging surveillance society. In particular there are developed critiques of the threat to privacy (for example: Rosen 2000; Solove 2006), the pathologies of social sorting (see for example: Gandy 2006; Lyon 2007), and the lack of accountability and transparency in commercial monitoring (Andrejevic 2007).

3.2. EXPLOITATION 2.0

This article focuses on the relationship between surveillance and economic exploitation as a means clarifying the assumptions that undergird both the development of new commercial models and their critique. In particular, I am thinking of Adam Arvidsson's account of the forms of quantitative and qualitative exploitation that characterize what he describes as "the branding of life" (Arvidsson 2005, 251) associated with the "immaterial labour" of consumers. He borrows his analysis of immaterial labour from Lazzarato, who describes it as the "activity that produces the 'cultural content' of the commodity", noting that it "involves a series of activities that are not normally recognized as 'work'—in other words, the kinds of activities involved in defining and fixing cultural and artistic standards, fashions, tastes, consumer norms, and, more strategically, public opinion" (Lazzarato 1996, 137). Such labour corresponds to what Michael Hardt (also following Lazzarato) describes as an "affective" form of immaterial labour: "the production and manipulation of affects", which "requires (virtual or actual) human contact and proximity" (Hardt 1999, 93).

Zwick, Bonsu, and Darmody (2008) also have recourse to the critique of exploitation in their perceptive discussion of the much-hyped marketing paradigm of consumer co-creation (the reliance of producers on consumer participation to help build and communicate brand image) as a form of governance. They argue that the economic success of sites that rely on various forms of user-generated content (including Facebook, MySpace, and Second Life) "expropriate the cultural labour of the masses and convert it into monetary value: each in their own specific way, but all according to the same general logic" (Zwick, Bonsu and Darmody 2008, 180).

The notion of exploitation is a recurring refrain in theoretical approaches that inform recent critical work on the capture of user productivity in a variety of contexts. As Hardt (1999) puts it, "in those networks of culture and communication, collective subjectivities are produced and sociality is produced—even if those subjectivities and that sociality are directly exploitable by capital" (Hardt 1999, 93). In her discussion of the "free labour" provided by chat-room moderators in exchange for access to online services, Terranova (2000) notes that such productive activities can, in some contexts, be described as both voluntary and subject to exploitation: "Free labour is the moment where this knowledgeable consumption of culture is translated into productive activities that are pleasurably embraced and at the same time often shamelessly exploited" (Terranova 2000, 37).

There is in short, much talk of exploitation, but less elaboration of what the term might mean in shifting contexts of labour. The invocation of some notion of exploitation is compelling for a number of reasons including the fact that a critique of privacy invasion does not do justice to the productive character of consumer surveillance. The prospect that advertising might become more effective because it will be able to predict human behaviour with a high degree of reliability and thereby to manage the populace more efficiently in accordance with commercial imperatives is disturbing in a different way from privacy concerns. There is more at stake in such forms of surveillance than profit: specifically the prospect that consumers will be put to work marketing to themselves, and, through this extra work, generate a customized product for which they are required to pay a premium. As Zwick, Bonsu, and Darmody put it: "consumers are asked to pay for the surplus extracted from their own work" (Zwick, Bonsu, and Darmody 2008, 186). Also at stake are issues of power and control, because data in the hands of some promise to provide them with predictive power over others. We need ways of critiquing the promises of control and profit that haunt the imagination of interactive marketers. The concept of exploitation could be a good starting point, but it needs to be clarified and updated for the emerging interactive economy.

One of the dangers of mobilizing the notion of exploitation in online contexts is that it takes a critical concept traditionally associated with industrial labour's sweatshop conditions and transposes it into a realm of relative affluence and prosperity—that is, those with the time and access to participate in online activities. For good reason, it is harder to get worked up about the "exploitative" conditions of user-generated content sites than about the depredations of sweatshop labour and workforce exploitation. In the case of user-generated content, for example, we are talking in many cases about reasonably well-off consumers engaging in what might be described as optional activities: you don't *have* to join Facebook, Twitter, get a Gmail account, or shop online. Even as the distinction between consumer and producer, by many accounts, starts to blur, it is, at times, resuscitated for the purposes of dismissing labour-oriented critiques of consumer activity.

However, to the extent that we are going to take the notion of consumer productivity seriously, it is worth considering the applicability of critiques of exploitation to the online economy. If consumers are generating value, we can interrogate the conditions that structure who is compelled to surrender the economic value generated by their activity and who benefits. Such critiques do more than simply attempt to align consumer (or "prosumer") exploitation with worker exploitation; they also and perhaps more importantly highlight the implications of platform commercialization for the social and political role played by digital media technologies. To speak of consumer exploitation is, in other words, to invoke a strategy for critiquing the emerging online economy against the background of the promise of consumer empowerment and democratization that have accompanied its development. It is also to anticipate potential consequences of the migration of forms of sociability and communication onto a commercially supported platform. By way of comparison, to raise concerns about the commercial model for the development of broadcasting in the US was not just to interrogate the impact of commercials upon viewers, but to evaluate the ways in which a reliance on sponsorship and, eventually, spot advertising, came to structure the medium itself and the kind of stories, news, and entertainment it provided. A similar range of questions needs to be asked about the consequences of the emerging commercial model for the Internet and related interactive platforms: a model that relies upon increasingly comprehensive monitoring of the populace for the purposes of predicting and managing consumption.

It is important to make explicit the wager of the emerging online commercial economy: that comprehensive monitoring will give marketers greater influence over consumers. Reasonable people may disagree over whether such strategies will work, but there is no doubt that they are at the core of the economic model upon which web 2.0 services and platforms are being constructed. That the business literature is hyping the model and businesses are staking billions of dollars in building the databases and developing the hardware and software for storing and sorting data may not mean that the model will work, but that it is worth considering the consequences. In other words, we are increasingly coming to rely on services and communication infrastructure that rely on the effectiveness of targeted marketing, data mining, and predictive analytics. For the purposes of these marketing strategies, more monitoring is better. As one news account put it: "By analyzing or 'mining' large amounts of data, including credit reports, shopping habits, household demographics and real estate records, companies can determine customers who are most likely to buy a product, pay their bills on time, or respond to a marketing campaign. The more data that are gathered and the more powerful the statistical tools that are applied to that information, the more accurate the results" (StarTribune.com 2009). The wager that data-driven marketing will be profitable enough to offset the costs of data collection, storage, and sorting, may, in the end, turn out to be a losing one, but if it is, we should understand that we are staking the future of one of the most important communication media of our era upon it.

3.3. PREDICTIVE ANALYTICS IN THE INTERACTIVE ECONOMY

The way prediction is used in the marketing industry imagines the possibility of managing marketing conditions to induce desired behaviour by determining which conditions lead to certain behaviours and then creating them. Thus, predictive analytics relies not merely on describing existing conditions, but on generating ongoing, large-scale experiments for studying consumer behaviour. As Ayres (2007) puts it: "Academics have been running randomized experiments inside and outside of medicine for years. But the big change is that businesses are relying on them to reshape corporate strategy" (Ayres 2007, 31). Digital interactive environments lend themselves to such experimentation insofar as they make it possible to vary marketing strategies and then to capture the results of this variation in controlled ways. Predictive analytics work to discover which strategies are most likely to result in the desired response and then to vary the commercially supported interactive environment accordingly.

This process might be described as a technique for triggering latent demand—a description that implies consumers are only doing what they would have done anyway, with the added qualification that, after all, the choice they are making is a free one. It is not clear, however, what exactly latency means in contexts in which consumers are systematically exposed to environments designed to influence their behaviour—nor is it clear that the existence of particular dispositions negates marketing strategies for behaviour management and control. If I have certain anxieties and desires that are triggered and enhanced by custom-targeted forms of marketing that result in a response anticipated by marketers, it seems misleading to say that my behaviour has not been subject to deliberate forms of management and control. In this respect, the ability to collect and analyze large amounts of data in order to influence consumer behaviour might be considered a form of power.

This is certainly the way in which marketers and their adjuncts talk about the potential of monitoring-based marketing strategies. Ayres, for example, notes the asymmetry of control over data relied upon by what he calls "super crunching" large amounts of data: "Tera mining sometimes gives businesses a decided advantage over their consumers [. . .] the companies not only know the generalized probability of some behaviour, they can make incredibly accurate predictions about how individual consumers are going to behave" (Ayres 2007, 32f). He goes on to quote the opening lines of the 139th Psalm: "You have searched me and you know me. You know when I sit and when I rise; you perceive my thoughts from afar" (Ayres 2007, 32f). The comparison is telling—it locates the marketers in the position of an omniscient power, a resuscitated "big Other", upon whom our smallest actions register and who knows us better than we know ourselves: "because of Super Crunching, firms sometimes may be able to make more accurate predictions about how you'll behave than you could ever make yourself" (Ayres 2007, 33).

3.4. UPGRADING CRITIQUES OF EXPLOITATION FOR THE DIGITAL ERA

If these characterizations of the power of data mining have some modicum of truth, the marketing strategies it underwrites might be described as manipulation or control, but it takes a few more steps to get to the notion of exploitation. Control and manipulation raise concerns of their own. If indeed data might enable the power of prediction, the concentration of this power in the hands of marketers runs counter to the democratizing promise of the Internet. New media technologies may help level the playing field in some respects by widening access to the means of creating and distributing a range of cultural and informational products, but they also create new asymmetries. Google may know a lot about users' patterns of browsing, emailing, and eventually mobility, but users know very little about what information is collected about them and how it is being put to use.

Thus, the migration of a wide range of social, professional, and personal communication activity onto private, commercially supported platforms raises new questions of accountability: what level of disclosure about the collection and use of personal information is compatible with democratic values? What types of control should be placed on the use of personal information? Are there details of our personal lives, our medical histories, our personal tastes and behaviours that should be off limits to marketers, and where might we draw the line? These are important questions to ask in light of the commercialization of the Internet—questions that societies long focused primarily on public-sector rather than private-sector accountability need to find ways of answering.

The critique of exploitation provides one approach to such questions, at least to the extent that they touch upon economic issues. The notion of exploitation is, in many recent accounts of online exploitation, a relatively under-examined one. In some instances the term exploitation is used simply to describe a situation in which one party benefits from the activity of another. This seems a bit broad, insofar as it would allow us to describe forms of open-source collaboration or co-creation such as Wikipedia and other open source initiatives as inherently exploitative, which would violate any meaningful critical sense of the term. Nor is exploitation reducible to subjective feelings of exploitation (or the lack thereof)—although these certainly may indicate the presence of exploitation.

Because the versions of the critique of exploitation that concern this paper trace their provenance to Marx's critique of capitalism, it is worth exploring the core elements of this critique. Holmstrom offers a concise summary of a Marxist conception of exploitation: "The profits of capitalists, then, according to Marx's theory, are generated by surplus, unpaid and forced labour, the product of which the producers do not control" (Holmstrom 1997, 80). Central to a Marxist account is the notion that coercion is embedded in the relations that structure so-called free choices. As Holmstrom puts it: "Persons who have no access to the means of production other than their own capacity to labour do not need to be forced to work by chains and laws" (Holmstrom 1997, 79)—those are used to ensure that they cannot gain control of resources other than their labour power. The presence of background forms of coercion lurking in what appear to be free choices or exchanges is true not just for industrial wage labour, but also for unwaged domestic labour. Coercion, according to such accounts, is inscribed in the social relations themselves.

The further point to be made is that exploitation is not simply about profit, but also alienation. As Holmstrom puts it: "what workers really sell to the capitalists, according to Marx, is not labour, but the capacity to labour or labour power, which capitalists then use as they wish for the day" (Holmstrom 1997, 79). In selling this capacity, workers relinquish control over their own productive activity—what Marx (1844) also describes as the form of conscious control that distinguishes "species-being" from unreflective life. Alienation takes place not just in the surrender of conscious control over productive activity but also, consequently, in its product. It is a formulation that draws from the description of exploitation in the 1844 manuscripts, where Marx forcefully elaborates the wages of estranged labour: "The worker places his life in the object; but now it no longer belongs to him, but to the object. [. . .] What the product of his labour is, he is not. Therefore, the greater this product, the less is he himself" (Marx 1844, 27).

Exploitation is not simply about a loss of monetary value, but also a diminishment of one's humanity and a loss of control over one's productive and creative activity. As Marx, quoting Hegel, puts it in Volume I of *Capital*: "But by the alienation of all my labour-time and the whole of my work, I should be converting the substance itself, in other words, my general activity and reality, my person, into the property of another" (Marx 1867, 115). The economic aspect of exploitation—the loss of control over the value generated by surplus labour—helps reproduce the forms of scarcity that compel surrender of control over one's labour power. In the end, exploitation is evil, as Holmstrom puts it: "because it involves force and domination in manifold ways and because it deprives workers of control that should be theirs" (Holmstrom 1997, 88). This overtly humanist formulation, it is worth nothing, is perhaps not so distant from posthumanist inflected accounts such as Smith's (2007) conception of an imminent ethics, which is opposed to "anything that separates a mode of existence from its power of acting" (Smith 2007, 68).

It is also worth noting that the empowering promise of the Internet is based, in large part, on an implicit invocation of this notion of exploitation, insofar as it envisions the prospect of overcoming the alienation of control over productive activity. This implied critique of alienation lies at the heart of the celebration of the de-differentiation of consumer and producer, of audience and performer, reader and author, and so on. Such transformations are not to be dismissed out of hand, even if they do refer only to that subset of the population with access to the skills, technology, and resources for using the Internet and related digital technologies. As is frequently pointed out, however, these transformations require a reworking and a revisiting of the critique of exploitation: industrial-age critiques need to be updated for the digital era. The following section explores two attempts to develop a Marxist-inflected critique of exploitation for the digital era and explores their relation to Homstrom's account of alienation. Both accounts could benefit from further clarification that takes into account the productive and, I will argue, alienating role of surveillance in the development of interactive marketing.

3.4.1. Consumer Exploitation

Taking seriously the notion that interactive technologies facilitate enhanced user productivity—that at least in some contexts they reconfigure the (vexed) distinction between production and consumption—means considering how a critique of worker exploitation might apply to the reconfigured realm formerly known as consumption. Zwick, Bonsu, and Darmody's critique of consumer "co-creation" outlines the double dimension of online exploitation: "First, consumers are not generally paid for the know-how, enthusiasm, and social cooperation [. . .] that they contribute to the manufacturing process of marketable commodities. Second, customers typically pay what the marketing profession calls a 'price premium' for the fruits of their own labour" (Zwick, Bonsu, and Darmody 2008, 180). The formulation here is concrete: if someone else realizes a financial profit from one's efforts, and this capture of value is enabled by relations of control and ownership of productive resources, then exploitation is at work. This formula is applied to two distinct forms of interactive participation or user "co-creation"—the model whereby sites like Facebook provide a commercial platform for user-generated activity, and the process of mass customization, whereby users participate in creating a customized product such as a personalized pair of running shoes that they then purchase for a premium. In the former case, profits are captured indirectly, via advertising; in the latter they are captured directly via purchase. In both cases, however, this approach focuses upon what might be described as intentional user-generated content: the conscious creative activity of users, whether in the form of Facebook posts or design modifications and specifications. In both cases the site's owners profit from the activity of users—and although the users may get some benefit, they are not, by definition, compensated according to their contribution (at least not in the case where a profit is realized). This model aligns itself with Fuchs's (2010) account of the exploitation of the labour of so-called "prosumers"—interactive users whose activities help generate value for those who own and control the platforms and applications they use. Fuchs updates the notion of the audience commodity (derived from Smythe 1981)—formerly considered to be something assembled and put to work by media producers—as self-generating: "The difference between the audience commodity in traditional mass media and on the Internet is that in the latter case the user are also content producers" (192). As Fuchs (2010) points out, mere access to interactive platforms does not amount to shared control: "The category of the produsage/prosumer commodity does not signify a democratization of the media toward a participatory or democratic system, but the total commodification of human creativity" (192).

Although all of these approaches to exploitation share a related set of concerns—and all of them align neatly with the critical orientation of this chapter—a number of questions arise regarding this updated conception of exploitation, including: where might we locate coercion, and, in related terms, can a notion of alienation remain operative in these contexts? The presumed benefit of interactivity in both cases is to overcome alienation. The promise of sites like YouTube and Facebook as well as forms of mass customization is precisely that we recognize the results of our productive activity *as our own*. The fact that consumers are willing to pay a premium for a customized commodity both attests to the persistence of alienation (we pay more, at least in part, to overcome the sense of an anonymous, impersonal, alienated product) and gestures towards its overcoming. In both the case of interactive customization and that of Facebook (as well as other user-generated-content sites), users retain control over their productivity, and they do so in the absence of compulsion. Because this labour is free, it does not provide a livelihood—participation is not the result of practical forms of compulsion.

Right away, however, we might want to start making some distinctions. In many examples of customization, the user's contribution is relatively minor; the actual products are manufactured elsewhere, very possibly under sweatshop conditions that lend themselves to the standard critique of exploitation. Mass customization sites that allow users to design their own sneakers or purchase custom-tailored jeans provide industrial forms of exploitation with a veneer of participation. For Zwick et al. (2008), even participatory consumers are subject to exploitation in the sense that they do not realize the full value that they have *added* to the commodity via their participation. That is, they have engaged in value-generating activity, some of which has contributed to the creation of value they do not control.

In the case of user-generated-content, Pasquinelli (2010), following Vercellone (2010), has argued that a more suitable model for exploitation is that of rent. In the digital era, the capture of a productive commons of "cognitive capitalism"—whether in the form of resources for collaboration or the assertion of intellectual property rights, serves as the basis for extracting value from user activity. Thus Pasquinelli argues that Google, for example, "can be described as a global rentier that is exploiting the new lands of the Internet" (2010, 1). The vaunted Google algorithm generates value by building upon the work done by users as they roam the Internet, creating links to web pages. The invocation of the model of land rent, however, raises the question, once again, of coercion. Absent the imperative to, say, earn one's livelihood by using Google, the model whereby rent and profit merge ends up with a somewhat thinner conception of exploitation.

3.4.2. The Role of Coercion

Alternatively, we might develop a more complex notion of exploitation, in which, for example, coercion could be discerned not directly in the consumer relationship (there is no direct compulsion to purchase a customized item or to use a commercial website that collects information about user activity), but in the background labour relations that lead consumers to attempt to overcome alienation in the realm of consumption. Similarly, we might argue that alienation persists in the very misrecognition of the product of sweatshop labour (the customized Nike running shoe for example) as a form of consumer self-expression. The modicum of consumer control serves as an alibi for a process that remains fundamentally about the appropriation of wage labour. These are perhaps plausible, if not particularly galvanizing arguments, and perhaps rightly deflect our concerns back to more traditional forms of exploitation: the sweatshops.

User-generated content sites make a stronger case for overcoming alienation, insofar as user contributions are, in many cases, more compelling examples of creativity than merely picking from among a number of customization options. Even though value is realized from these contributions, the use of such sites does not entail relinquishing control over certain aspects of one's creative activity. The case for alienation, at first glance, seems weak, whereas the case for coercion relies on taking seriously the notion that productive activity, in the digital era, comes to rely increasingly on access to networked resources for communication, distribution, and collaboration. As Arvidsson puts it: "the post-Fordist production process directly exploits the communitarian dimension of social life" (Arvidsson 2005, 241). As a perhaps crude example of this process, consider the example of a Facebook application developed by the "software-as-service" company Appirio that allows employers access to employees' social networks. The application proposes to increase the size of a company's 'virtual account team' by leveraging relationships that employees might already have to approach strategic accounts or build customer relationships [. . .] The employee can see if a friend has become a lead, bought a product, attended an event [. . .] etc. If the employee chooses they can contact their friend through Facebook to make a connection and ultimately help contribute to their company's bottom line (and maybe even their own bonus!). (Market Wire 2009)

The application links data from the social networks of individual employees to a proprietary consumer relationship marketing database in order to "track leads, make follow-up offers, and report on campaign success to see how their viral campaigns stack up to other marketing programs" (Market Wire 2009).

If the increasingly precarious conditions of certain types of labour in a flexible and volatile marketplace require the development of social networking resources by employees, and if forms of so-called immaterial labour similarly rely on networking and communication technologies, companies like Appirio provide ways for employers to capture some of the productivity of these networks. Perhaps, in the not-too-distant future, it may become the case that social networking services become crucial productive resources for certain types of jobs. To the extent that this becomes the case, a stronger case can be made for background forms of coercion that structure access to other privately controlled productive resources. If we need access to such services to earn our living—if employers require the creation and exploitation of such networks—and if access is privately controlled, then the standard critique becomes operative. Whether construed as rent or profit, the value captured relies upon the privatization of productive resources associated with the information economy. In such instances we can make a case for both coercion and unpaid productive activity, but not alienation—again a somewhat thinner conception of exploitation. It is not, however, hard to see how these forms of coercion might, in the end, beget alienation. Consider the example of Appirio's Facebook application: when employers start to view workers' social network as exploitable productive resources, the incentive emerges to develop "high value" networks—as defined by the employers' imperatives. Networks that once reflected a certain degree of autonomy become subject to the control and imperatives of employers.

Arvidsson (2005) supplements this account with a somewhat more abstract analysis of exploitation in his critique of branding in the post-Fordist era. In an argument that fits neatly with that of Zwick et al. (2008), he argues that all brands might be considered "co-creations" insofar as they come increasingly to rely on the immaterial labour of consumers. A brand, he argues, is based, in part, on "values, commitments, and forms of community sustained by consumers" (Arvidsson 2005, 236). Brands can thus be understood as a way of capturing this activity for commercial purposes. In this respect they colonize consumer time and channel the creative potential of the immaterial labour of consumers. He describes this as the "branding of life" (Arvidsson 2005, 251). The result, he argues, is both a quantitative form of exploitation—the "absorption" of "the free time of consumers"—and a qualitative one: "making the productive sociality of consumers evolve on the premises of brands" (Arvidsson 2005, 251). This sounds like a form of alienation—the capture of collective productive activity by commercial imperatives. However, Arvidsson's account does not explore the mechanism whereby this capture and absorption takes place. How might we explain the apparently compelling power of brands to capture, channel, and "filter" consumer activity in accordance with the imperatives of brand managers and owners? Does a brand exert forms of coercions upon consumers? There may be something coercive in this process, but it would require more explication to unearth it.

3.5. PRIVATIZING THE PLATFORM

A discussion of so-called immaterial labour needs to be complemented with a consideration of the material resources that facilitate it. Social networking, always-on communication, and access to the information "commons" depend, increasingly, on commercially supported applications and a privatized, commercial infrastructure. If, on the one hand, it seems fair to say that interactive media technologies facilitate new forms of collaboration and communication as well as the enhanced ability to access and share information rapidly at a distance, they also represent the next stage of the colonization of social life by commerce and marketing. We might think of this as the virtual world equivalent of the replacement of the downtown city centre by the shopping mall, and the consequent privatization and commercialization of social (no longer really "public") space. Our electronic mail, our mobile phone applications, and our social networks will all pepper us with advertising appeals of one kind or another as we go about the course of our wired lives. This is not the result of some autonomous power of "the brand"—it is a consequence of the commercial system that we are creating to support the rapidly growing digital communication infrastructure.

This system is the result of quite concrete, material choices: the decision to privatize the backbone and Internet service delivery and to rely on commercially supported platforms for a range of communication, networking, and information services. The online world thus becomes one where our libraries (in the form of Google books, for example), our directories, and our e-mail services become advertising saturated. As of this writing, even Twitter has developed a system to insert relevant ads in the results when users search the feeds. The next "logical" step, according to one commentator, would be to allow "users to sign up to have, say, every 10th post be an ad placed through Twitter. That ad is related to something the user is talking about (an ad for a nearby restaurant if a user is talking about a neighbourhood), or simply a branded ad placed because the advertiser likes a particular Twitterer's audience" (Singel 2010).

So if we wanted to make a case for Arvidsson's claim that brands come to colonize our social lives, we would want to take a close look at the way in which we are financing new platforms for social life, communication, and information sharing. The commercial infrastructure is by no means a "natural" or inevitable one, as evidenced by the history of the Internet. If it is the case that brands are gaining visibility and marketers are capturing and putting to work the fruit of our online activity, it is the result of our reliance upon the commercial sector to provide the infrastructure for our online communicative, informational, and social lives. There is a striking tendency in contemporary academic and popular accounts of the emerging digital economy to overlook the political economy of the platform. We often talk about "the web" and the networks that support it as unchanging constants—a taken-for-granted and largely neutral infrastructure. In fact, the Internet is a fast-changing and increasingly privatized infrastructure that may look as different in the next twenty years as it did twenty years ago. The affordances of the Internet and the services that run on it change in accordance with the priorities of those who control this infrastructure, and what is taken for granted one day, such as so-called "net-neutrality" may well disappear the next. The same goes for platforms like Facebook, which are constantly tweaked by their private owners to maximize revenues and increase data collection. The flexibility of the virtual environment makes the privatization of cyberspace more malleable than that of physical space: as aspects of users' professional and social lives migrate onto networked, commercial platforms, these platforms continue to adjust to reflect not just technological developments, but also changing economic models. Facebook, for example, continues to tweak its functionality not just to encourage more users to use it more often, but also to continually modify its privacy policy in ways that facilitate the development of its commercial model. Control over the platform and the applications that run on it, in other words, might help explain how the work of "channelling" user activity to profitable ends described by Arvidsson (2005) takes place.

Arvidsson critiques the process of "brand management" for "pushing this production of an ethical surplus [by which he refers to social bonds and shared meanings produced by networked sociability] to the artificial plateau of the brand, and hence depriving it of its real potentiality" (Arvidsson 2005, 252). Once again, an account of how this "pushing" takes place needs to be elaborated—how do brands coerce us? If they seduce us, does that count? The question really is to what extent a compelling account of the way in which force is embedded in relations of seemingly free exchange at the level of consumption can be developed. For Arvidsson, the result of exploitation via branding is an undermining of the very forms of sociability that are captured and put to work: "It comes to work against the productive potential of the social, on which it ultimately builds" (Arvidsson 2005, 252). This is a critique of alienation—a loss of control over the process and product of shared productive activity. Perhaps such a critique is more appropriately directed towards the underlying structure that shapes the imperatives and facilitates the practice of brand management—that is, toward the galloping commercialization of the resources and utilities for networked communication.

3.6. USER-GENERATED VALUE

The decision to privatize the Internet's infrastructure, and, in many cases, to rely upon the commercial sector for the provision of online utilities including e-mail, search engines, document storage, and so on, might be described as a form of enclosure of the digital commons: the separation of crucial productive resources in the digital era from a new generation of productive consumers. In this respect, the notion of exploitation remains relevant to a critique of the online economy and, in particular, to our reliance upon these for-profit utilities that are becoming increasingly indispensable for forms of online work, collaboration, and socializing. However, an account of exploitation needs to be updated to take into account, on the one hand, the possibility of generating economic value from user participation *without apparent alienation* and, on the other, to critique what Arvidsson (2005) describes as a kind of alienation without payment: the channelling of productive activity beyond the confines of the workplace and the wage labour contract. One way to approach such an account is to consider the way in which user activity is redoubled on commercial platforms in the form of productive information *about* user activity.

What makes commercial platforms like Google and Facebook profitable is not just that they can draw an audience, and not just that they can benefit from user activity (including that of constructing links and posting content), but that they can capture detailed information about audience activity. Monitoring becomes an integral component of the online value chain both for sites that rely upon direct payment and for user-generated content sites that rely upon indirect payment (advertising). From a commercial perspective, we can view every action that takes place online, whether a purchase or an online post, as a reflexively redoubled one. Acts of production and consumption both become, in this regard, productive, insofar as they generate information commodities. This redoubling links online productivity with the valorisation process: information about user activity becomes an input into the marketing and production processes.

It is at this level that we might attempt to reintroduce a critique of exploitation and consider whether the activity that produces this information is unpaid, coerced, and alienated. Insofar as the information can generate a surplus, it is by definition not compensated according to its value. An account of coercion would have to enlist a systemic understanding that locates coercion in the social relations that structure access. If we take seriously the notion that online forms of interaction and socializing can double as productive immaterial labour, we might describe the infrastructures that support them as productive resources, access to which is structured by those who own and control the resources. Coercion is then embedded in the process whereby private ownership is asserted and reproduced. In the digital context, we can perhaps see this most palpably in the realm of intellectual property; however a critical account discerns it in the background of private ownership and control of the platforms that are becoming integral to social forms of production.

This is perhaps not a particularly compelling account in an era in which private control over Internet resources has been naturalized. Maybe a more convincing account of coercion can be made indirectly via the notion of alienation. Here, the notion of redoubling usefully highlights the difference between the intentional aspect of user-generated content and its estranged or alienated aspect. In this regard, we might talk about the "dual" character of networked activity: the conscious action and the captured information. In the mobile phone research on mobility described at the start of this chapter, every call made by a user also generated a data point: information about the user's time-space location (not to mention information about who was called and for how long). We might make an analogy here with other forms of user activity: an intentional action such as a purchase, the posting of a photo online, a comment on a Facebook page or a Tweet generates additional *unintentional* information: data about user behaviour captured by the (commercial) platform. Users have little choice over whether this data is generated and little say in how it is used: in this sense we might describe the generation and use of this data as the alienated or estranged dimension of their activity. To the extent that this information can be used to predict and influence user behaviour it is an activity that returns to the users in an unrecognizable form, turned back upon them as a means of fulfilling the imperatives of others. Estrangement, or alienation, in Marx's account, occurs when our own activity appears as something turned back against us as, "an alien power" (Marx 1884/2009).

3.7. CONCLUSION: DIGITAL ALIENATION

The alienated world envisioned by interactive marketers is one in which all of our actions (and the ways in which they are aggregated and sorted) are systematically turned back upon us by those who capture the data. It is, in the end, a decidedly disturbing vision: an informed world in which the very atmosphere through which we move has become privatized, and commercialized. Every message we write, every video we post, every item we buy or view, our time-space paths and patterns of social interaction all become data points in algorithms for sorting, predicting, and managing our behaviour. Some of these data points are spontaneous—the result of the intentional action of consumers; others are induced, the result of ongoing, randomized experiments.

Thanks to market monitoring, the distinctions between alienated and autonomous activity, at least in the context of consumer behaviour, start to blur. Intentional, conscious activity does double duty: it facilitates forms of online sociability and creativity on the one hand and, on the other, the data it generates is captured and returned to consumers in unrecognizable form. The complexity of the algorithm and the opacity of correlation render it all but impossible for those without access to the databases to determine why they may have been denied a loan, targeted for a particular political campaign message, or saturated with ads at a particular time and place when they have been revealed to be most vulnerable to marketing. Much will hinge on whether the power to predict can be translated into the ability to manage behaviour, but this is the bet that marketers are making. Or more accurately, this is the bet that a society makes when it turns to a monitoring-based system of data-mining and predictive analytics as a means for supporting its information and communication infrastructure.

Privacy-based critiques do not quite capture the element of productive power and control at work in the promise of monitoring-based marketing. If privacy violations constitute an invasion—a loss of control over the process of self-disclosure—market monitoring includes an element of control and management: the systematic use of personal information to predict and influence behaviour. The critique of exploitation addresses this element of power and control. Defenders of market monitoring will argue that individual consumer behaviour remains uncoerced. Critical approaches, however, locate coercion not solely at the level of discrete individual decisions, but also in the social relations that structure them. Given an unconstrained choice, individuals may likely choose not to have their information collected, mined, and turned back upon them for screening, sorting, and marketing purposes. However, the decision to privatize the Internet infrastructure and many applications that are becoming important tools for work, creativity, and social life provides those who own these productive resources with control over the terms of access.

Given the difference between post-Fordist forms of productive consumption and industrial modes of production, a critical approach to exploitation needs to be revisited. This chapter argues for the importance of considering how the components of exploitation (the capture of unpaid surplus labour, coercion, and alienation) operate within the context of technologically facilitated forms of commercial surveillance. Although these components are interconnected—alienation, for example, typically implies the existence of background forms of coercion—they appear in different configurations in the realms of consumer productivity or immaterial forms of collective, social labour. Some critics focus on the element of unpaid labour, others on the element of alienation. The challenge is to think these together against the background of the coercion embedded in relations of control over communication resources and the forms of productive surveillance it facilitates.

REFERENCES

Andrejevic, Mark. 2007. *iSpy: Surveillance and power in the interactive era.* Lawrence: University of Kansas Press.

Arvidsson, Adam. 2005. Brands: a critical perspective. *Journal of Consumer Culture* 5 (2): 235–258.

———. 2007. Creative class or administrative class? on advertising and the 'underground.' *Ephemera* 1.

Ayres, Ian. 2007. *Super crunchers: How anything can be predicted.* London: John Murray.

Banks, John and Sal Humphreys. 2008. The labour of user co-creators. *Convergence* 14 (4): 401–418.

De Angelis, Massimo. 2002. Marx and primitive accumulation: the continuous character of capital's "enclosures". *The Commoner.* http://www.commoner.org. uk/02deangelis.pdf (accessed on July 10, 2009).

Fuchs, Christian. 2010. Labor in informational capitalism and on the Internet. *The Information Society* 26 (3): 179–196.

Gandy, Oscar. 2006. Data mining, surveillance, and discrimination in the post 9–11 environment. In *The new politics of surveillance and visibility,* ed. Kevin Haggerty and Richard Ericson, 363–384. Toronto: University of Toronto Press.

Hardt, Michael. 1999. Affective labor. *Boundary* 2 (2): 89–100.

Holmstrom, Nancy. 1997. Exploitation. In *Exploitation: Key concepts in critical theory,* ed. Kai Nielsen and Robert Ware, 81–102. Atlantic Highlands: Humanities Press International.

Lazzarato, Maurizio. 1996. Immaterial labour. In *Radical thought in Italy: A potential politics,* ed. Paulo Virno and Michael Hardt, 133–150. Minneapolis: University of Minnesota Press.

Lyon, David. 2007. *Surveillance studies: An overview.* [city?]: Polity.

Market Wire. 2009. Appirio referral management solution connects social networks with business applications to encourage, manage and measure word-of-mouth referrals. February 2.

Marx, Karl. 1844. *The economic & philosophic manuscripts of 1844.* http://www. marxists.org/archive/marx/works/1844/manuscripts/preface.htm (accessed on July 20, 2009).

Marx, Karl. 1867. *Capital, Volume I: The process of production of capital.* Moscow: Progress Publishers. http://www.marxistsfr.org/archive/marx/works/download/Marx_Capital_Vol_1.pdf. (accessed on December 10, 2010).

Pasquinelli, Matteo. 2010. Google's pagerank algorithm: a diagram of the cognitive capitalism and the rentier of the common intellect. *Pankov,* March 16, 17 (67). http://pankov.wordpress.com/2010/03/16/google%E2%80%99s-pagerank-algorithm-a-diagram-of-the-cognitive-capitalism-and-the-rentier-of-the-common-intellect/ (accessed on December 8, 2010).

Rosen, Jeffrey. 2000. *The unwanted gaze: The destruction of privacy in America.* New York: Vintage.

Singel, Ryan. 2010. Twitter plans search ads like Google's. Wired.com, February 26. http://www.wired.com/epicenter/2010/02/twitter-search-ads/ (accessed on February 26, 2010).

Smith, Daniel W. 2007. Deleuze and the question of desire: toward an immanent theory of ethics. *Parrhesia* 2: 66–78.

Smythe, Dallas. 1981. On the audience commodity and its work. In *Media and cultural studies*, ed. M.G. Durham and Douglas Kellner, 230–256. Malden, MA: Blackwell.

Solove, Daniel. 2006. *The digital person: Technology and privacy in the information age*. New York: New York University Press.

Song, Chaoming, Zehui Qu, Nicholas Blumm, and Albert-László Barabási. 2010. Limits of predictability in human mobility. *Science* 327 (February 19): 1018–1021.

StarTribune.com. 2009. Predictive analytics: What is it? October 11. http://www.startribune.com/business/63907602.html?elr=KArks:DCiU1OiP:DiiUiacyKUUr (accessed on February 20, 2010).

Terranova, Tiziana. 2000. Free labor: producing culture for the digital economy. *Social Text* 63 (18): 33–57.

Vercellone, Carlo. 2010. The new articulation of wages, rent and profit in cognitive capitalism. http://www.generation-online.org/c/fc_rent2.htm. (accessed on December 10, 2010).

Wang, John, Qiyang Chen, and James Yao. 2009. Data mining fundamental concepts and critical issues. In *Encyclopedia of Artificial Intelligence,* ed. Juan Rabunal, Julian Dorado, and Alejandro Sierra, 418–423. Hershey, PA: IGI Global.

Weed, Julie. 2009. Finding new employees, via social networks. *The New York Times*, May 30. http://www.nytimes.com/2009/05/31/jobs/31recruit.html?_r=1&scp=2&sq=appirio&st=cse. (accessed on June 1, 2009).

Zwick, Detlev, Samuel Bonsu, and Aron Darmody. 2008. Putting consumers to work: 'co-creation' and new marketing govern-mentality. *Journal of Consumer Culture* 8 (2): 163–196.

4 Key Features of Social Media Surveillance

Daniel Trottier and David Lyon

4.1. INTRODUCTION

A German law governing privacy at the workplace recently made it illegal for bosses to look up prospective employees on Facebook (Jolly 2010). In doing so this law attempts to restrict Facebook's presence in the job hiring process and illustrates one of the many ways in which social media have surveillance dimensions. The rapid uptake of social media as well as their spread into virtually every social realm prompts such action in a number of spheres.

Social media refers to a set of web-based services that enable users to share content with each other. Many of these sites are used to exchange specific kinds of media: YouTube for videos, Flickr for photographs, Digg and del.ici.ous for news. Their reliance on user-generated content provides them with a cultural and contextual versatility. As Internet-based services compatible with mobile technology they also benefit from spatial versatility, all of which means that the opportunities for surveillance multiply. Personal data proliferates and flows promiscuously.

Social media facilitates information exchange between individuals and institutions. When used to convey personal details they augment their users' visibility, not only to their chosen "friends" but also to other agencies and institutions. This chapter uncovers key features of surveillance practices using data emanating from social media platforms. Although a wealth of surveillance literature has explored the role of the Internet and electronic databases, social media sites like Facebook, MySpace, and Twitter generate an unprecedented amount of user-generated information. This research explores the surveillance features of these platforms by considering how the "social" in social media contributes to a more social surveillance.

Using Facebook as a case study, five features are considered. First, users participate in a collaborative identity construction with other users. Second, friendships provide unique surveillance opportunities as users often engage with a particular audience in mind. Third, the construction of a personal social network means social ties become visible, measurable, and searchable. Fourth, an ever-changing interface and privacy controls alter users' visibility through the site. Fifth, social media content is easily recontextualized. Information leaks are now a common outcome.

The first three features illustrate interpersonal aspects of social media with an emphasis on social ties. The final two highlight its growth into social life, institutions, and culture. These features are supported by findings from three sets of semi-structured in-depth interviews. The first set is with thirty university students at a mid-sized Canadian university who use Facebook to exchange personal information. The second set is with fourteen university administrators who use social media to communicate with students. This includes professors, campus security, residence life, human rights advisors, and marketing and communications. The third set of interviews is with twelve professionals who use the aggregated data available on Facebook as a business tool, including marketers, consultants, and software developers.

In order to understand social media surveillance, scholars should turn to recent developments in this field. The following section provides a theoretical background rooted in sociological and surveillance studies material. This will contextualize the five features of social media surveillance that are explored in the following section. Upon providing both a theoretically and an empirically rich description of these five features, this chapter concludes by situating this research alongside a growing scholarship on social media surveillance, and recommends directions for subsequent research.

4.2. SURVEILLANCE, SOCIAL MEDIA, AND SOCIAL RELATIONS

The background to studies of social media surveillance includes at least three items, discussed briefly below: social science research on Internet surveillance in general, a rapidly growing body of knowledge on the dynamics of social media, and some broader discussions of digitally mediated social relations. However, it is worth noting that the specific "key features" of social media surveillance are also located within large-scale social and cultural shifts that both inform and are informed by them. Above all are the ways that contemporary conditions are characterized by what Zygmunt Bauman calls "liquid modernity" (Bauman 2000).

As Bauman says, the shift from a solid to a liquid phase of modernity means that social forms do not keep their shape for long and thus cannot serve as frames for human action and life strategies (Bauman 2007, 1). Yet while this is so, it does not mean that liquid modernity is entirely shapeless, still less that the structural and institutional facilitators and constraints on human activities and life strategies have somehow melted away. To the contrary—and this is especially visible in the context of new media—surveillance itself is liquefying, with new implications for everyday life chances and opportunities that affect new media users in particular ways.

Liquid surveillance (see Lyon 2010) bespeaks a world in which older institutions of marketing or crime control have become malleable and adaptive. Indeed they "modulate" to use the word favoured by Gilles Deleuze in his work on the "society of control". In social media such as Facebook, friends are fluid and surveillance is multifaceted. Although the forms of social order produced in part by surveillance are no longer relatively static, their pulsating, morphing shapes are no less significant for the reproduction of social class positions, for example, than the productive relations that they are replacing.

Yet for many social media users, surveillance, and especially surveillance-as-control, does not seem to flicker on the horizon. Indeed, it seems that for them, control is in their hands as they choose whom to accept or deny as friends and build their networks of like-minded acquaints. The notion that the Internet could have this connective capacity in a world pulled apart by ever-increasing mobility has been prominent since its inception. Manuel Castells, for instance, spoke in the nineties of the "vast array of virtual communities" enabled by computer-mediated communication (Castells 1996, 22), in which identity construction is an organizing principle. Sociologists such as Barry Wellman extensively researched the emergence of such communities, linked by new media, arguing, notably, that they tend to be characterized by "networked individualism" (Wellman et al. 2003).

The advent of social networking sites in the early twenty-first century offered new opportunities for contact, networked individualism and perhaps even for community. Scholars have examined such sites, sometimes in celebratory, sometimes in more sober, fashion, including in its surveillance dimensions. One recent study, of Anders Albrechtslund, argues that for social media users, surveillance is empowering and does not involve forms of violation. As he rightly observes, users share activities, beliefs, tastes, and preferences online, precisely so that they can socialize. This Albrechtslund dubs "participatory surveillance" (Albrechtslund 2008), in part to distinguish it from Andrejevic's (see below) "lateral surveillance", which for Albrechtslund is compromised by its association with panoptic metaphors.

For Albrechtslund—and no doubt many users—social media are empowering and are a mutual "sharing practice". Voluntary engagement with others and with identity-construction is seen as key to the practice of participatory surveillance. Such findings as Albrechtslund's offer a cautionary tale for surveillance studies, which are all-too-often preoccupied with the Orwellian and the panoptic. Genuine insights into surveillance processes are available through the exploration of users' actual involvement in social media, in analogous ways in which diverse public responses to camera surveillance or employee interaction with workplace surveillance may be viewed. Albrechtslund does not deny the role of socially negative uses of social media; his claim is that those should not dominate forms of analysis.

So how exactly did the Internet become a key surveillance site? This may be grasped by considering the development of Internet surveillance over a period of almost two decades. The key moment, as Manuel Castells notes, was when the Internet was opened to commercialization. This spelled the "transformation of liberty and privacy on the Internet" (Castells 2001, 170). Why? Because from a marketer's viewpoint "surfing" data could be added to the already highly profitable geo-demographic data to create new nuance and depth in understanding consumer profiles (Lyon 2002). And what was useful to marketers was equally important for employers, police, and others.

What Mark Andrejevic (among others) called a "digital enclosure", that is, "an interactive realm wherein every action and transaction generates information about itself" (Andrejevic 2007, 2), creates a condition of surveillance. For all the benefits of interactivity to those thus enabled to "stay in touch" with their social media contacts, each click permits more data to be accumulated, to circulate. And, as in other cases, as more information is gathered, so there is less accountability of data-gatherers to the general public. Yet the consequences are considerable. As Andrejevic also observes, social sorting is at the core of what organizations do with Internet-generated personal data (Andrejevic 2007, 125–128).

The advent of geo-tagging or of locating users in space as well as in time simply takes surveillance potential one stage further (Lyon 2007, 43). It builds on ways that geo-demographic marketing has increasingly sorted consumer populations since the 1990s, by adding online data to other more conventional kinds. The use of software and statistics to socially sort all manner of populations has now become a basic mode of organization in almost any enterprise, public or private. And the consequences for life chances and opportunities are considerable, such that, as Burrows and Gane (2006) argue, such surveillance is salient not only for those individuals affected but also for the production and reproduction of social class differences. That this is also visible on the Internet, and in the development of the so-called web 2.0, is explored further in Beer and Burrows (2010).

Much then hangs on the frame within which social media surveillance is understood and how its key features are construed. On the one hand are the analyses of those like Albrechtslund, who rightly highlight the interactive, participatory, mutual, voluntary, and empowering aspects of social media, while acknowledging that negative surveillance also occurs. On the other hand are those like Andrejevic, who see social media in a "digital enclosure" or, more strongly, Christian Fuchs, who insists that social media users are an "audience commodity" sold to advertisers. The fact that they are also content producers means not that the media are thus being democratized, but rather that this is the advent of the "total commodification of human creativity" (Fuchs 2010, 148–149).

Part of the point of this paper is to show that the key features of social media surveillance are best understood by acknowledging both the aspects discussed above. The liquidity of today's surveillance may be seen in the ways that social media sites are constantly mutating as users cooperate with providers to develop new modes of contact and identity-construction, but simultaneously in the ways that, however fluid and flexible, all online surveillance contributes to social sorting and to the reproduction of difference.

Another key point, made in the following section, is that because surveillance is not the first thing that springs to mind in discussions of new media, it is helpful to explore the issues from the perspective of those who consider themselves as users. Collaborative identity construction, lateral ties, social ties, changing interfaces, and recontextualization, discussed below, each connect the generation of personal data by users with the ways that such data are available for surveillance "uses". Such uses, we suggest, are also liquid, but there are discernible and often powerful currents within those flows.

These perspectives build a theoretically informed understanding of the five features discussed in the following section. Liquid surveillance facilitates participatory surveillance and online sociality. Yet it also enables data commodification and other types of large-scale scrutiny. Identity becomes more liquid as a result of ubiquitous opportunities for speaking about one's self as well as about one's peers. This is typically fuelled by participatory motives, but also enhances other kinds of online surveillance. Second, lateral ties become a dispersed and versatile conduit for intentional as well as accidental leaks. These connections allow sharing between trusted colleagues. Yet this information is also held by Facebook, who may sell it to advertisers or hand it over to policing and intelligence agencies. The connection between participatory and more problematic social media practices is further exemplified by the visibility of social ties. Social media is used for empowering purposes, but this rests on the creation of social ties that contribute to visible social networks.

The final two features speak more broadly to the volatility of social media. Social media interfaces constantly add and modify features. Facebook does this to such an extent that we can consider change to be a permanent feature of social media. This has the effect of enabling unanticipated forms of visibility. These changes enhance the scope of peer-to-peer sociality and scrutiny, all while facilitating the commodification of these exchanges. Additionally, information on social media platforms is easily recontextualized, such that participatory surveillance may generate content that will be used for marketing or other purposes. Both interpersonal activity and institutional information management share Facebook. It stands to reason that a theory of social media surveillance should acknowledge both empowering and exploitative practices.

4.3. KEY FEATURES

Five key features of social media highlight a shift in the collection of personal information on the Internet and illustrate the growing liquidity of surveillance. New forms of visibility and transparency afforded by social media are coupled with user practices to manage these possibilities.

4.3.1. Collaborative Identity Construction

Users increasingly participate in a collaborative identity construction with their peers. Facebook allows users to share information about their friends with those friends. Profiles are composed of fields where both users and their friends can add personal information about that user. By default this information is shared with both users' networks of friends. Thus, speaking to a colleague also means speaking about that colleague to an extended audience of users. This occurs on four principal locations: walls, photos, tags, and comments.

Walls are a prominent feature on user profiles, where friends can post messages and other content as a series of chronologically ordered entries. This serves a dual purpose: content is used to communicate with friends, but also offer a kind of public testimony about that person to their network of friends. Students acknowledge that the kind of postings a user will receive from friends is treated as a reflection on the their personality and character:

> I guess the type of wall posts they get also kind of reflects who they are as well and, again someone who has a lot of really nasty wall posts from the people added on Facebook as friends might not exactly seem the most appealing person in the world. (interview #24)

With this reflection in mind, users are tactical about the content that they post on their friends' walls. They are careful how they portray their friends, relegating sensitive or compromising content to the private message feature:

> I love the walls and I post on people's walls all the time—but at the same time I'm very careful about what I post on other people's walls and I also send a lot of messages because it's like 'This is wall appropriate, this is message appropriate'. And [. . .] it's just a fact of life that people are going to read my conversations. [. . .] We all know what we're saying to each other. (#19)

The above respondent suggests that scrutinizing other user's conversations is a taken-for-granted feature of social media. Likewise, users report having to scrutinize their own wall for problematic postings from their friends:

> Especially people have a tendency to throw things on your wall and you're like 'Uh, you forget that I've got a dozen friends who are still friends with this person and they could see this and could see this on their News Feed' and that kind of thing. (#22)

Users will not only monitor what other users will say about each other, but also actively monitor what is being said about themselves. In employing these tactics, users increasingly frame the wall as featuring content that is entirely public and visible to others:

> Like, when you write like you know, hilarious comment on one of your friends' walls, it's not necessarily to communicate with that person, but to show everyone who comes and visits their page that you are communicating with that person. So, it's intended to be viewed by others, in its very nature. (#28)

Users can also upload photographs of their friends. With over three billion photos uploaded to Facebook every month (FB Statistics 2010), it stands to reason that they are a central feature for interpersonal assessments. Indeed, most users report that when adding a new contact to their network, they will immediately scrutinize the photos on their profile: "You can get to know someone by looking at their information [. . .] you can see all the comments people have made on their photos and all the photos of them and all the photos that they've posted" (#19).

Friends can further augment a user's visibility by tagging them in a photo. By creating a link between the photo and the user's profile, tags facilitate browsing often hundreds or thousands of photos featuring any single user from dozens of sources. As an added feature, the act of tagging someone is itself content to be distributed. Following default privacy controls, if friend A tags friend B in a photo—which may belong to friend C—this will be featured on both walls as well as both users' friends' news feeds. The politics of tagging has become a sticking point for some users, especially those who have struggled with incriminating material about them being publicized:

> There's a picture of me someone took randomly in an awkward position. It looks like I'm doing something bad to the teacher, but I was actually not. That was like a hundred comments on it. That took a week to get it off. (#7)

Through this experience, the above respondent developed a series of tactics to cope with incriminating photos:

> First of all, especially people who are taking photos of you doing something destructive at parties, if I know they've taken it, I will go tell them like the next day after the party: 'Do not upload these. Please delete them'. And if they do upload, I would tell them again. And, first of all un-tag myself. And then, I would report to Facebook. (#7)

As this is a growing concern, campus security is increasingly involved in cases where students have been defamed through social media:

Within Facebook itself, if someone comes to us and says 'subject A is slandering my name and has several entries on their Facebook sites about me that are grossly injurious to me', then we will check that out. (#37)

Through tagging users are publicly identified by their friends. This feature has been extended to text-based content like notes as well as status updates. When a user is tagged in someone else's note or status update, this content will then appear on both users' profiles as well as both friendship networks' news feeds. This feature has also raised concern for the tagged person's reputation. Many students are concerned with how their friends' opinions will reflect on them:

You can make a note on Facebook [. . .] and you can mention people in the note. I find that a little bit difficult just because a lot of the time the views they'll sometimes post aren't something that you agree with. (#22)

Comments are another way users can be made visible by their friends. This involves adding a text-based response to content like photographs, status updates, notes as well as actions like adding a friend or joining a group. Comments add a conversational feature to activity on Facebook, such that users can comment indefinitely about any content or activity on the site. This feature ensures that users do not have exclusive claims over how they present themselves on social media. Upon receiving an accusatory comment on a note she posted, one student used the comment feature herself to manage her online presence:

But like an acquaintance of mine [. . .] flamed my post and in the comments he accused me of being like tacitly supporting the murder of all these civilians and posted a picture, a link to a picture of someone who I had participated in the murder of. I was just like what the hell is this? I didn't delete it, I instead wrote my response underneath it hoping that anyone who came across it was like, so he is a whacko. (#28)

Users rely on what others say about their friends to make inferences about them. Given the difficulty involved in managing what potentially hundreds of friends are saying about a user, this is seen as a more authentic representation of who that person is. This is not to suggest that users are void of any tactics. They can choose to remove wall posts, photo tags, or comments, and can report inappropriate content. They can also disable their wall and hide all tagged photos as a means to minimize their friend's influence. But the absence of a wall or photos on a profile is often read as an admission of guilt in that the user is attempting to conceal something.

4.3.2. Lateral Ties Provide Unique Surveillance Opportunities

Marketers, employers, and other institutional watchers access a rich knowledge of users when those individuals are bound to a network of colleagues to whom they wish to remain transparent and trustworthy. Users have a particular audience in mind when uploading and sharing personal details. Yet that audience makes up only a small portion of the people who have access to their information.

Institutional surveillance typically occurs in fixed and readily identifiable settings, including the border crossing, the interrogation room, and the census form. These allow for a degree of deceit and subterfuge on the part of the person under scrutiny. In contrast, Facebook is a site of social convergence, with other users belonging to several social spheres. Personal information is not authored with all potential audiences in mind. Thus, other watchers can intervene in ties between a Facebook user and that user's intended audience. The majority of respondents claimed that they upload information for their closest friends and occasionally their relatives. There is some variance in terms of ideal audiences, as some use Facebook for geographically proximate ties whereas others use it mostly for long distance ones. With these kinds of friendship ties shaping the way users understand Facebook, they will provide information meant for a personal audience. As one student notes:

> That's the best way to get a measure of someone [. . .] when they think they're in their own space. The things people post on Facebook can be very telling. Right or wrong, if you want to know about someone, look on Facebook because that's sort of where they bare their souls to the world. (#19)

These social ties are manifest as a kind of soft coercion, with pressure from a network of friends pushing users to engage with the site. The majority of respondents report joining Facebook at the behest of their friends, and then being expected to submit biographical content. These friendship ties regulate the kind of information provided through a passive yet ongoing scrutiny. When uploading information, users only identify a portion of their audience. This suggests a self-presentation geared towards friends, ensuring a degree of comfort with sharing otherwise sensitive personal information. For example, users are routinely asked by friends to post their phone number on Facebook. Given the site's quasi-public status, this troubles some student users:

> I've seen a lot of people being like 'I've lost my cell phone, please give me your phone number' and you'll just have walls full of people's phone numbers with their name attached and I think that's really stupid. (#21)

The user's social ties with their friend network compel them to share personal information. What's more, the information they share is expected to be consistent with how they would otherwise present themselves to those peers. This is not to suggest that deception and identity play are absent from Facebook. Rather, this becomes the kind of deception that would normally exist between friends and colleagues. Instead of actively resisting online surveillance, these tactics are akin to a Goffmanian form of self-presentation (1959) based on the use of explicit and implicit cues to maintain a favourable public image.

4.3.3. Social Ties are a Visible, Measurable, and Searchable Kind of Content

Sites like Facebook turn social connections into visible, measurable, and searchable content. This adds a dimension of visibility to the study of social ties and social capital, which indicates that "who you are" has always been a reflection of "who you know". With social media this has become a standard feature for profiling individuals. Not only are a user's social ties visible, but others can also make inferences about private information on the basis of friends' publically accessible information.

The notion that social ties are a form of personal information often escapes users' scrutiny simply because they do not submit it in the same way they submit photographs and other content. As a result, "friends" and "friends in common" are accessible features on user profiles, even when most other content is kept private. Following the default settings, everybody would be aware of the company that everyone else keeps. This information is used internally by Facebook to recommend new friends based on existing ones. Respondents look at other users' friends not only to confirm their identity, but also to make inferences about users. Too few friends and too many friends are both seen as cause for concern. Several assumptions are made: too few friends suggests either the user is too socially withdrawn, or employing a false identity. Too many friends suggest social promiscuity, a lack of privacy concerns, or lack of knowledge about privacy controls. As one student reports:

> You can't have that many friends. [. . .] There were people on the site being like 'Add me!', like 'I'll add anybody'. And it's just like you're going to have way too many friends and way too many people who you actually don't know. (#21)

Another respondent suggests that the kind of scrutiny cast on friends also applies to the self: "There are people who have over 1000 [friends]. And, okay, you can know a lot of people, but I have too many right now" (#19).

Beyond this immediate discomfort, there's a growing realization among users that friends, when taken in aggregate, can be used as a window into a users' innermost thoughts and intentions. Social ties are descriptive in and of themselves, but they also allow one user's personal details reflect on their peers. Users may choose not to disclose their sexual orientation or political affiliations, either by omitting these details or hiding them with privacy controls. Yet a portion of their friends will openly share these details about themselves. By monitoring this information in aggregate, researchers claim that it can be used to make assessments about users (Wills and Reeves 2009; Jernigan and Mistree 2009). If the average user has 130 friends, and one fifth of those friends have partially transparent profiles, those users provide a substantial sample of information that may reflect on the individual. Current privacy settings are not able to prevent these exploits, as the user in question is essentially bypassed. The inferences made through users' friends may not be accurate, although that's hardly the point. Through social sorting this information shapes social outcomes.

The fact that a user's friends reflect them presents some unique challenges to self-presentation on social media. Many are clearly ambivalent about this kind of exposure, as evidenced by the number of users who hide this information. Yet by default, users are sharing this information with the public. Users are beginning to realize the extent to which their friends reflect their identity, and many have expressed discomfort with this. Yet this discomfort is mixed with fascination about the insight these features provide. One student states: "I don't think everyone should be able to view who my friends are. Interestingly enough I do go look at other people's friends" (#26).

4.3.4. The Interface and Its Contents are Always Changing

Social media platforms are dynamic. Not only do they perpetually solicit new input from users, but they also forge new avenues for that information. Likewise, user engagement is shifting in response to changes to the interface. This illuminates a broader vision of how Facebook operates, the culture in which it is situated, and the way its users position themselves in it.

Users report that Facebook itself is continuously changing. Revisions to the interface push some information to the foreground, while hiding other details. New features and third party applications require further personal details from users. Facebook's front page prominently invites users to make new friendship connections and send new content to existing ties. Each revision to Facebook's interface is accompanied by new privacy settings, which by default are left open to a broad public. These changes indicate a tension, where Facebook's developers purport to offer users greater control over their information while promoting open and unrestricted access to their personal information. The 2007 decision to make this content searchable through Google indicates that Facebook is increasingly linked to additional settings.

These changes to the interface and privacy settings are met with a degree of distrust among users, who link them to attempts to monetize personal information:

> I really don't trust Facebook at all because, they're there to make money, obviously, and it's like 'Oh, we don't sell your personal information' and then it's like 'Oh, headline story: Facebook selling your personal information'. (#19)

In addition to these features research on the topic should consider the complexity of the users themselves, who may transpose this information to separate contexts. They may save a photograph to their hard drive and e-mail it or upload it to a separate site, repost it in their own photo album, or simply tag or comment on it. In all these cases that photo leaks from its original setting to another, and is thus made more public. Yet the latter methods require less user intervention, suggesting that these kinds of leaks are increasingly a built-in feature of the social media.

As users continually catch up with a changing interface, it stands to reason that information they post about themselves or others will be more widely distributed than anticipated. This suggests an ongoing learning curve for using Facebook that leads users to perceive each other as potential liabilities. Photos of a mature student's children were leaked when a day-care employee posted them online:

> Now I think she had intended to put them up privately and that was just the mistake. However still, she made those pictures available to everybody that goes to the day-care, all the other parents that were there and it was done without my consent and I was actually very upset by that. That's a violation of my privacy and my child's privacy. (#26)

Recognizing these shifts, users themselves treat their engagement with Facebook as an ongoing project. Many users report that they have revised their personal content; either modifying or removing content as well as pruning ties with their peers. These measures are framed as a way to cope with the emerging risks associated with Facebook's changes. As one student states: "I go through my privacy settings every couple months and just make sure that everyone is still how I want it to be" (#19).

Although very few respondents are willing to predict how Facebook would change in the immediate future, they anticipate that its content will become more and more public with time. As for how they would use Facebook in the future, student respondents treat the job market as a catalyst for major revisions to their engagement: "I will probably start locking down profiles and stuff, un-tagging myself from scandalous photos" (#4). Another student claims: "When I'm applying for jobs and stuff I think I'm going to turn off my Facebook" (#20).

Despite uncertainties about new features and issues, respondents who approach Facebook from an institutional perspective regard it as a growing aspect of their responsibilities. A university web coordinator comments on the sudden emergence of a new set of responsibilities:

> When I first started, social media and Facebook weren't necessarily part of my daily routines, but there's been an explosion in the last few months especially in the area of higher education and we developed this social media task force. (#36)

Likewise, a marketing coordinator indicates that the only certainty is their continued engagement with the social media: "I really can't predict, I really don't know, but I do know we're going to continue to be part of it, whatever it is (#35).

4.3.5. Social Media Content is Easily Recontextualized

The conditions described in the above section suggest that information on Facebook circulates to an ever-increasing amount of social spheres. Information is increasingly free from its initial context when uploaded to Facebook, augmenting the scope of any single act of surveillance. This speaks to some of the key features of most contemporary surveillance: where information is gathered in a particular setting and context, is scrutinized elsewhere, and the consequences of this scrutiny may occur in yet another context. This in turn is why simplistic notions of privacy, including those relating to privacy settings found on social media sites, are inadequate to contemporary conditions. Context is crucial (Nissenbaum 2010).

This is an acceleration of the leaks previously considered in information databases (Lyon 2001). It's no novelty that information tied to a particular context may migrate elsewhere. This can be caused by technological error or the deliberate and often malicious intention of a particular operator. Yet social media platforms privilege the open distribution of personal information through "sharing" and "publishing". As a result, the leak becomes a standard feature for information exchange in social networks.

Facebook is especially susceptible to recontextualization. Personal information is appraised in a distinct context, typically one that differs from the context in which it was authored. A profile may be treated as a personal—if collaborative—diary. Yet its contents are generally handled as a public broadcast. As Facebook gains prominence as a de facto location for self-representation, information found on user profiles will be assessed in several contexts. These features illustrate an interpretation of the social in social media: these services endeavour to bridge as many social contexts as possible.

Social networks first emerged as a service used exclusively by trusted colleagues. When it was limited to a number of American universities users were under the impression that they were sharing information with their fellow students. As a result Facebook emerged in a climate where university students were relatively comfortable sharing personal information with known peers. Starting in September 2006, their siblings, parents, and non-university colleagues began to join the site. Although this provoked some discomfort, they were more likely to use their privacy settings rather than remove personal information. As employers, politicians, and other institutional representatives joined the site, users had grown accustomed to the degree of authenticity they offered. Facebook is now a hub of social convergence. A student's friend list still contains university colleagues, but they are situated alongside family, friends, co-workers, and strangers.

Students author a wealth of information about themselves in a particular context. Many participants report either joining or augmenting their Facebook presence during the first few weeks of school. This activity is tied to a specific agenda: to create a publicized identity, make new friends, and socialize in a context linked to recreational drinking and casual romantic encounters. The "party photo" is a kind of interpersonal currency in this context, yet it is treated as a liability during job applications. In light of these possibilities, researchers should explore the principal trajectories by which information leaks. Conversations and photographs from this context are perceived as potentially leaking into a postgraduate context, whether that involves graduate school, law school, or job applications. In a more general sense, respondents describe consistent leaks between personal and professional contexts:

> Obviously at work you have your professional self and at home you have your private self and your private life, but that's the part of you that gets reflected on Facebook. So, whereas before Facebook, there was this definite distinction between walking through the doors of the office and once you're out of there [. . .] with Facebook and with the Internet, your private life can follow you around 24/7. (19)

One student offers a scenario where a childcare employee's photos are leaked into the public and the dilemma this presents for parents who are evaluating their professional image:

> And I'm thinking, you put that information on your page, that you happily work at a child care facility A and here you are in a drunken state—and that's not to suggest that I believe that people who work at child care facilities should live cloistered lives and not party and have a great time, but am I left with that one snapshot of this person and is that the person that I want to hand my child over to? (#27)

The above respondent acknowledges that Facebook users have the right to their private lives, but also concedes that if information about lifestyle is made public, this person would act on it. The kinds of leaks that are possible are difficult to anticipate, but it stands to reason that they will threaten interpersonal boundaries that users would prefer to maintain. A human rights advisor offers such a scenario:

> Let's say you're a person of a particular religious background that isn't particularly supportive of intimate relationships before marriage. Right? And somebody sends that out. Imagine how your family in Egypt is going to feel seeing those kinds of things. I mean, there are huge ways to devastate people in very fast terms by using that technology. (#40)

Unlike more tangible kinds of surveillance regimes it is the indeterminate nature of later scrutiny that evokes some anxiety. Users do anticipate this, but admit to not knowing the outcome, or being fully capable of preventing this. Even if the user adopts some tactics to avoid the worst consequences, it is difficult to anticipate all the outcomes of publishing information. Different populations of people are engaging with the user's profile, different kinds of institutions are taking an interest in personal information, Facebook introduces new features, and users adopt new practices. Past activity is coupled with future conditions in a way that poses unique challenges.

4.4. DISCUSSION AND DIRECTIONS FOR SUBSEQUENT RESEARCH

Social media's growth makes it a pressing concern for surveillance studies. A key tension underlies research on this topic: managing personal information on social media is largely a user-initiated task, but a lot of activity on these sites is beyond the control of users themselves, and may further the increased liquidity of surveillance. Recent scholarship has considered the surveillance consequences of social media. Although some (for example: Albrechtslund 2008) highlight the voluntary and empowering potential of managing online visibility, others (for example: Andrejevic 2007; Fuchs 2010) warn that these services augment institutional surveillance while enabling new ways of exploiting everyday sociality. By exploring the key features of information exchange on Facebook, this chapter offers an understanding of the "social" in social media based on the increased visibility of its user base. Although the consequences that Andrejevic and Fuchs describe are a reality for users, many are aware of these consequences and are adopting tactics to prevent or at least manage the risks associated with living through social media.

Changes to the interface, coupled with emerging practices, complicate users' attempts to manage their online presence, although they are developing new tactics in response to these challenges. Despite this apparent growth, a director of campus security comments on how social media is still at an early formative stage of its development: "It's like a toddler. It's not a newborn anymore, it's a toddler, it still needs some direction, some guidance" (#34). How such direction, such guidance, will emerge, and where from, remains to be seen. It is unlikely that those charged with responsibilities for campus security will be able to offer such tutelage for "toddlers" without extensive collaboration with a number of other stakeholders. But this is an area beyond the scope of this chapter.

To conclude: This chapter draws on empirical research that is limited to one particular social media platform and illustrates from a user perspective some of the novel dimensions and directions of today's liquid surveillance. Although Facebook's sharply growing population and emerging features justify the decision to focus on Facebook, subsequent research will expand this scope by contributing empirical findings from other platforms (see Andrejevic's chapter in this book). The growth of surveillance studies requires increased specialization, especially in the field of emerging "social" technologies. Although scholars scarcely understand the full consequences and potential of these technologies, they are rapidly accumulating a significant user population. As sites like Facebook and Twitter become a mainstay in everyday life, indefinite retention becomes the de facto outcome for personal information, which has clear and consequential implications for surveillance. How many of these implications are also a cause for concern will be shown by subsequent research.

REFERENCES

Albrechtslund, Anders. 2008. Online social networking as participatory surveillance. *First Monday* 13 (3). http://firstmonday.org/htbin/cgiwrap/bin/ojs/index.php/fm/article/view/2142/1949 (accessed on ???).

Andrejevic, Mark. 2007. *iSpy: Surveillance and power in the interactive era*. Lawrence: University Press of Kansas.

Bauman, Zygmunt. 2000. *Liquid modernity*. Cambridge UK/Malden MA: Polity.

Beer, David and Roger Burrows. 2010. Consumption, prosumption and participatory web cultures: an introduction. *Journal of Consumer Culture* 10 (3): 3–12.

Burrows, Roger and Nick Gane. 2006. Geo-demographics, software and class. *Sociology* 40 (5): 793–812.

Castells, Manuel. 1996. *The rise of the network society*. Oxford UK/Malden MA: Blackwell.

———. 2001. *The Internet galaxy*. Oxford/New York: Oxford University Press.

FB Statistics. 2010. Statistics. http://www.facebook.com/press/info.php?statistics (accessed on ???).

Fuchs, Christian. 2010. Labor in informational capitalism and on the Internet. *The Information Society* 26 (3): 179–196.

Goffman, Erving. 1959. *The presentation of self in everyday life*. New York: Anchor Books.

Jolly, David. 2010. Germany plans limits on Facebook use in hiring. *The New York Times*, August 25. http://www.nytimes.com/2010/08/26/business/global/26fbook.html (accessed on ???).

Lyon, David. 2001. *Surveillance society: Monitoring everyday life*. Buckingham: Open University Press.

————. 2002 Surveillance in cyberspace: the Internet, personal data and social control. *Queen's Quarterly* 109 (3): 135–149.

————. 2010. Liquid surveillance: the contribution of Zygmunt Bauman to surveillance studies. *International Political Sociology* 4 (4).

Nissenbaum, Helen. 2010. *Privacy in context: Technology, policy, and the integrity of social life*. Palo Alto, CA: Stanford University Press.

Wellman, Barry, Anabel Quan-Haase, Jeffrey Boase, and Wenhong Chen. 2003. The social affordances of the Internet for networked individualism. *Journal of Computer-Mediated Communication* 8 (3). http://jcmc.indiana.edu/vol8/issue3/wellman.html/ (accessed on ???).

5 Jean-François Lyotard and the Inhumanity of Internet Surveillance

David W. Hill

5.1. INTRODUCTION

As we have moved towards an information society so too has surveillance become increasingly informational in its object and operation. In our day-to-day exchanges we are uploading and sharing valuable quantities of information, making possible unprecedented levels of surveillance. David Lyon (1994) notes that surveillance in this context is about storing and processing personal information. This definition places a desirable emphasis on information storage, highlighting that surveillance is not just about how information is used but also the amassing of it in the first place. With this in mind, Gary T. Marx's (2002) characterization of the "new surveillance" as the use of technologies to extract personal data adds a pertinent dimension; surveillance is not merely "snooping" but any technological means of extracting exploitable information from users—this, I suggest, is just as applicable to social networking as it is to more cloak-and-dagger methods. With the rise of new media, or web 2.0, surveillance hides in the open; we are seduced into giving up the information in the name of social commerce, creating what Mark Andrejevic (2007) calls a digital enclosure from which information can be extracted for corporate gain. On top of this, many of the surveillance technologies used in this context, such as "social ad" generating programs, operate algorithmically, processing information according to set parameters with minimal human input. A significant change in surveillance today can be detected, as visual modes are replaced with algorithmic software.

What we need are new theoretical tools for framing this shift in emphasis. In what follows I will argue that the work of Jean-François Lyotard in *The Inhuman* (2004) will assist us in keeping up with the advances in surveillance technologies. What Lyotard offers that, say, Michel Foucault does not is an emphasis on the informational. As Mark Poster (1990, 91) notes, Foucault had failed to take notice of new forms of surveillance and, I would add, the panoptic emphasis on the visual should be seen as today limited in scope. By drawing out the key arguments and concepts in Lyotard's *The Inhuman*, I will demonstrate that this remains an important text for understanding the conditions of our information society in general, and new forms of surveillance in particular. Lyotard highlights the complicity of new technologies with capitalist extension whilst raising urgent ethico-political problems surrounding the impact of this dynamic and the inhuman functioning of new technologies (their difference and indifference to the human). This will provide a framework for a critique of surveillance through social media focused on its impact upon what it means to be human. I will argue that such surveillance is inhuman, serving to extend the capitalist system according to a dangerous logic—performative, heterophobic—whilst making the user complicit in the whole shoddy process. The approach here is theoretical, with examples of surveillance in web 2.0 (as well as other relevant examples) used illustratively.

5.2. LYOTARD AND THE INHUMAN

First published in 1979, Lyotard's *The Postmodern Condition* has been his most famous and most commented-upon text, a work that has been taken up by sociologists, philosophers, and literary theorists, amongst others. However, this popular focus has as its consequence the neglect of another key text, *The Inhuman*, published nine years later. This text is largely philosophical in nature and has yet to have the same impact in the social sciences as its more heralded predecessor. In this section I will introduce Lyotard's work in *The Inhuman* in order to show its usefulness for understanding surveillance in our information society (see also Gane 2003 for a reading of this text that demonstrates its relevance to contemporary media theory).

Of course, *The Postmodern Condition* remains an important text and, before proceeding, I will highlight two elements of it that both illuminate a reading of *The Inhuman* and augment an approach to surveillance. First, Lyotard introduces "performativity" as the operating principle of what he calls "techno-scientific capitalism" (the combined force of technological and scientific R&D and advanced capitalism). Performativity is the optimization of the relationship between input and output (Lyotard 2005, 11). That is, the system works to constantly optimize its performance, and the only legitimation for the power that it possesses is its very efficiency (Lyotard 2005, xxiv). The decision-makers—states but, increasingly, corporate leaders—apply "input/output matrices" to all elements of their purview and, also, to "us" allocating "our lives for the growth of power" and introducing a level of terror to the performance: "be operational [. . .] or disappear" (Lyotard 2005, xxiv). This operation is nothing to do with justice or truth—or any of the key tenets of humanist progress—but is purely technological:

> [Technologies] follow a principle, and it is the principle of optimal performance: maximising output (the information or modifications obtained) and minimizing input (the energy expended in the process). Technology is therefore a game pertaining not to the true, the just, the beautiful, etc., but to efficiency: a technical "move" is "good" when it does better and/ or expends less energy than another. (Lyotard 2005, 44)

Everything must be translated into quantities of information, which are easily communicable, in order to gain optimal performance through efficiency. Anything that cannot be translated is abandoned (Lyotard 2005, 4). This leads to "the hegemony of computers" (Lyotard 2005, 4), the rule of performative logic, and the dominance of a computerized form of capitalism. Here Lyotard identifies complicity between new technologies and the capitalist system, both sharing the same logic and the former allowing for the optimized performance of the latter. Deeply wary of this, his second useful move is to pose the question: "who will know?" (Lyotard 2005, 6). That is, who can acquire the information? Who decides what of this proliferating information is true? Who gets to make the decisions based on this information? Who even knows the decision to be made? "Increasingly, the central question is becoming who will have access to the information these machines must have in storage to guarantee that the right decisions are made" (Lyotard 2005, 14).

The turn to *The Inhuman* is motivated by the more nuanced work on these two elements and by the more critical reading Lyotard gives, utilizing the notion of inhumanity to pose ethico-political problems that will allow us to frame and critique contemporary forms of surveillance. The book is a collection of commissioned lectures given by Lyotard that all seek, in different ways, to approach two questions: "what if human beings, in humanism's sense, were in the process of, constrained into, becoming inhuman (that's the first part)? And (the second part), what if what is 'proper' to humankind were to be inhabited by the inhuman?" (Lyotard 2004, 2). This notion of the inhuman is taken in two separate senses:

1. the inhumanity of the system (the techno-scientific development that results in the ascendancy of computerized capitalism);
2. the inhumanity that "haunts the human from the inside" (Gane 2003, 439), taking the soul hostage, as Lyotard puts it (2004, 2).

The second kind of inhumanity—hostage-taking—is somewhat opaque, but I find Stuart Sim's reading here to be instructive, he says, in part: "the inhumanity of our social conditioning: the pressure to conform to prescribed modes of behaviour" (Sim 1996, 130). However, as we will see, this does not quite cover the range of inhumanity of the second kind found in Lyotard's text, and so I would add to this social conditioning the usurpation of properly human roles as a defining example.

5.2.1. Development through Translation

In *The Inhuman,* Lyotard redeploys his concept of performativity, now framed in terms of "saving time," in order to examine the nature of "development": the utilization of technological and scientific advances for the extension of computerized capitalism. He observes: "'Development' is the ideology of the present time", and the saving of time is its modus operandi (Lyotard 2004, 3). Because it operates solely by this performative principle, development has no goal other than its own furtherance. The principle way of achieving this, according to Lyotard, is through an incessant and all-encompassing digitalization. What we see today is the rewriting of everything as bits or units of information. This is the main effect of our technological environment (rather than the proliferation of simulacra, pace Baudrillard). These bits of information conform to the chief principle of development: performativity. Lyotard writes: "Any piece of data becomes useful (exploitable, operational) once it can be translated into information" (Lyotard 2004, 50); it is easily read, quickly transmitted. Further: "The availability of information is becoming the only criterion of social importance" (Lyotard 2004, 105). That is, the hegemony of computers places demands on the individual to make available personal information in digital form such that it is operational (computer-readable).

The increasing computerization of all aspects of society is directly linked to new potentials for all-encompassing surveillance. With the demand for everything to become translated into information comes the storage of vast amounts of personal data and an indelible electronic trail. These can be of immense value to corporations, for example, the detailed amount of personal information that is utilized in a credit check. Lyotard draws attention to the connections between a demand for development through increased efficiency, digitalization and the extension of the capitalist system through the exploitation of this "digital enclosure" (Andrejevic 2007). Development (as ideology) is inextricable from capitalist extension; information is big business—and surveillance essential to it.

5.2.2. Dominance

Our information society, observes Lyotard, heralds the dominance of computerized capitalism. Four points in this regard can be identified. First, the computerization of society, with its demand that everything be translated into information, creates the conditions for this dominance. Information can be frictionlessly exchanged, which means that once anything is translated it becomes easily commodified. The possibility of resistance is foreclosed, as any sort of counterculture or subversion can be translated and so becomes "commercializable" (Lyotard 2004, 76)—and, thereby, consumed by the system. Lyotard remarks: "The question of a hegemonic teleculture on a world scale is already posed" (Lyotard 2004, 50). Second, there is the question of legitimacy. Who is responsible for this translation into information and who takes responsibility for it? Usually the state would be held responsible, but now the challenge to state power by corporations that Lyotard remarked upon in *The Postmodern Condition* has been completed, such that telegraphic breaching now goes well beyond state control. This means that multinational corporations are manipulating what is stored and what is considered "good" information. By extension, they are then also deciding what is irrelevant, what is not operative, and so what should not be inscribed in memory. That which cannot be translated or that is not efficient (i.e., dissenting or inoperative narratives, cultures, data resources, etc.), is forgotten, as "those parts of the human race which appear superfluous" for the goal of continued development are "abandoned" (Lyotard 2004, 77). So we see that the question of legitimacy (or the lack thereof) is intimately related to the question of transparency (who bears witness to the process when the perpetrators are not accountable in the way politicians would have been) and ultimately betrays Lyotard's concern that the system is intolerant of difference. Finally, this whole process of development is inhuman; humans are more its vehicle than its beneficiary. There is no "progress" here, only a process of complexification (the growth of the complexity of the system, or negentropy). As Lyotard puts it elsewhere: "It is no longer possible to call development progress. It seems to proceed of its own accord, with a force, an autonomous motoricity that is independent of ourselves. It does not answer to demands issuing from man's needs" (Lyotard 1992, 91–92). Development is an end in itself, striving only to achieve higher performance/efficiency and greater profits. "It is reproduced by accelerating and extending itself according to its internal dynamic alone" (Lyotard 2004, 7).

Lyotard's reflections on the dominance of computerized capitalism draw attention to the increasing role of corporations in surveillance, and the complicity of surveillance technologies with the capitalist order. Through the surveillance of electronic trails (websites visited, purchases made, etc.) it becomes possible to directly market goods and services, and the collection of geo-demographic data makes it possible to prioritize premium customers (see, for example, Burrows & Gane 2006; Lyon 2003; Solove 2004). By removing friction (the inefficiency of acting without such information), both approaches result in faster capitalism. The opacity of this practice is alarming: who can be held to account? And how is the algorithmic software that processes personal information, making possible such marketing and prioritizing, written? (That is, *who will know?*) What makes this inhuman is that, unlike surveillance by the state—where the justification is some form of human good (civil order, the reduction of crime, etc.)—the only goal of this corporate surveillance is increased performativity and therefore the extension of the system of computerized capitalism.

5.2.3. Hostage-Taking

The translating impact and dominance of computerized capitalism demonstrates inhumanity in the first sense: the internally inhuman functioning of the system, the translation of everything into information, and the dominance of computerized capitalism, along with its intolerance for difference and its development with disregard for human needs. Our final reading of Lyotard will indicate an example of inhumanity in the second sense, (both) social conditioning (our actions taken hostage) and the usurpation of roles (that which is proper to the human taken hostage), illustrating the way that we become forced to think like computers or be replaced by computers—human (reflexive) thought replaced with computer (determinant) thought.

With information "there's no longer any question of free forms given here and now to sensibility and the imagination"—just bits (Lyotard 2004, 34). That is, there is nothing to think through—just data to process. Lyotard is here concerned with what is lost when we move from a human to a computer mode of thinking. Human thought does not operate in binary code. It does not work solely with bits, with processed units of information. Rather, human thought takes in the full picture; it is focused, like the computer processor, but lateral too, taking in side effects and marginal data. Human thought can sift through data quickly, discovering what is useful and what is not without the need to run a series of trial and error tests. Most importantly, it is "a mode of thought not guided by rules for determining data, but showing itself as possibly capable of developing such rules afterwards on the basis of results obtained 'reflexively'" (Lyotard 2004, 15). This is what Immanuel Kant called reflective judgement, which stands in contrast to determinant judgement wherein rules are pre-given. Kantian reflexive judgement is described by Lyotard elsewhere as "the synthesis we are able to make of random data without the help of pre-established rules of linkage" (Lyotard 1988, 8) whereas the way of thinking that techno-science would impose—"programming, forecasting, efficiency, security, computing, and the like"—is "the triumph of determinant judgement" (Lyotard 1988, 21). Computers cannot defy rules or create their own: they simply follow them, lacking creativity.

Lyotard's reflections on the disparity between human and computer thinking contain two warnings. First, that as the demand in our information society to work with information increases, we become more like the machines with which we work. We begin to think as computers—in terms of efficiency, processing, etc.—losing what is valuable about the human mode of thought. As Nicholas Gane notes, human thought is reduced "to the immediate *processing* of information, and to the selection of preprogrammed, and thus standardized, options from the framework of the system" (Gane 2003, 441). This is inhuman in Sim's sense, as the demand to operate in a computerized society puts pressure on us to conform to computerized (and capitalist) ways of thinking. Second, that in an information society the human is in danger of being replaced by the computer (in the workplace, say) and so creative human thought is replaced by limited computer thought. This is inhuman in the sense of the usurpation of human roles. Lyotard demands that we consider the way that technologies are today replacing us in many activities and the way that their inhuman mode of thinking is inadequate and dangerous.

This account of the paucity of computer thought becomes increasingly urgent as more and more operations are given over to algorithmic software. The sort of "smart" surveillance technologies prevalent today can combine not only data collection, but also decision-making—not only about what information is relevant, but increasingly what actions human or non-human actors should take in response to it.

5.3. INTERNET SURVEILLANCE TECHNOLOGIES

Many commentators highlight the present or near-future nature of "thinking things" (see, for example, Beer 2007; Hayles 2005; Mitchell 2005). These thoughtful objects take over many of the tasks that were previously the preserve of humans. I suggest, amongst others (Beer 2009; Lyon 2007), that it is important to situate surveillance in this context. A large part of surveillance today has become computerized. It is no longer so much about the visual tracking of persons—although this remains a large element of contemporary surveillance (see, for example, the debate in the UK about ubiquitous surveillance in cities such as Birmingham; for an example of press coverage see Lewis 2010)—but about the processing of information. To this end, many surveillance technologies now work algorithmically, sorting data through a series of set instructions. In what follows I will use examples that have already entered academic thinking in order to initiate a critique of, first, the operating logic of "inhuman" surveillance technologies and, second, their complicity with the extension of capitalist development.

5.3.1. The Inhumanity of Usurpation

In our contemporary "surveillance society", we are under the impression that our every move is being watched, with ubiquitous CCTV cameras supposed markers of this. Yet it is more common that we are watched only retrospectively, if something happens that requires it. Being recorded by CCTV is not the same thing as being watched. Often nothing happens to the data recorded other than it being stored for possible later access—if, for example, we are the victims of crime or commit a crime. However, new "intelligent" CCTV cameras change this situation. Although we are still not being watched, something is happening to the data that is collected: it is processed algorithmically by software. These technologies are leading us towards the "automation of street surveillance" (Graham 2005, 572), wherein human input to the process, after the writing of the software, is marginalized.

Event-driven CCTV is an example of the inhumanity of usurpation. Such technologies are programmed to recognize "apparently abnormal behaviours, presences, and people", for example "the signature walking styles that are deemed to be most often used by those committing criminal acts"

(Graham 2005, 572). They work by having first been programmed to recognize deviation from normal (i.e., expected) behaviours. This human input—which of course raises the Lyotardian problem of who knows/decides what is expected/normal—then retreats, with software left to do the "thinking". As Stephen Graham reports, a foot moving backwards and forwards is interpreted as a kick, a rapid arm movement as a violent act (Graham 2005, 573). What we see is the migration of thinking from the human to technology. But will the software be able to tell the difference between a peaceful protest and a riot? Or a *parkour* runner and a burglar? Or street theatre and a street brawl? The problem here is the rigidity of the algorithmic mode of processing data compared with the human's ability to ascertain the contextual difference between what can be exactly similar movements.

The importance of this technology should not be underestimated when considering Internet surveillance. With all the video content uploaded to web 2.0 sites—Facebook, YouTube, etc.—the application of such behaviour-recognition software cannot be ruled out. At the time of writing, student protests against tuition fees in the UK are gaining a considerable amount of media coverage. With some of these protests escalating into acts of vandalism or violence there is a perceived need to identify agitators. How might a seemingly innocuous video of one of the protests posted online by a student be processed? Might one student be loitering at the edge of the frame with a suspicious gait? It is presently unclear whether such techniques have been used in this context, but the potential is very real. Consider the "Recognizr" facial recognition technology discussed in Marisol Sandoval's contribution to the present volume. She observes that "Recognizr", developed by The Astonishing Tribe and designed to cross-reference social networking sites with photographs taken on camera phones in order to recognize faces of photographed individuals, could be used for precision-targeted marketing by finding out an individual's buying practices through using images of faces to locate their social networking profile. This, as Lyotard would observe, would make for a more efficient capitalist system, but, in relation to usurpation, it is possible to imagine further applications. An individual's associations could be easily traced through such software, facial recognition applied to group photos posted online, and offering an ambiguous account of with whom s/he has met. "Ambiguous" because being in a photograph with someone says nothing more than that they have met; and yet dangerous because of the guilt by association—with, say, known terrorists or exuberant protestors. If nothing else, the use of facial recognition technology in mobile photography suggests that behaviour-recognition through online videos on social networking sites is not too far-fetched.

We see with this computerized surveillance the inhuman with which Lyotard was so concerned. When surveillance is achieved through algorithmic processing it can be identified as inhuman in the sense of usurpation in four ways. First, a role that would ordinarily belong to the human comes to be technological. The decision-making power of these software algorithms challenges human agency (Beer 2009, 987). Humans are taken out of the decision-making process when analyzing surveillance data, taking human thought with them; more performative computer software takes our place, and decision-making becomes a question of processing information according to set instructions. Second, this mode of technological "thinking" is impoverished in comparison with human thinking. Sim (2001, 35) gives a good example of this when discussing *The Inhuman:* if I get part of an address wrong when sending a letter, the deliverer will in many cases be able to work out where it needs to go, and so it will reach its destination; get an e-mail address wrong, and it will be bounced back to the sender. Lyotard argues that human thought can work with imprecise or ambiguous data, data that is not selected by pre-established codes; that it "doesn't neglect side effects or marginal aspects of a situation"; and that humans can intuit, think laterally, and operate without rules (Lyotard 2004, 15). Compared to the strict algorithmic functioning of computers, where thinking is reduced to passing information through a determined sequence of operations, our thought is far more flexible. These "intelligent" surveillance devices are making decisions ordinarily entrusted to humans, with serious consequences (far more so than unsent correspondence), and yet with a vastly inferior mode of reaching that decision. Third, Lyotard's concern for saving time in *The Inhuman* plays out here, as such technologies operate in computerized time—or what Manuel Castells called "timeless time" (Castells 2006). The speed at which these technologies operate does not reflect the more thoughtful periods at which the human operates. As Nicholas Gane and David Beer note, "timeless time refers to a regime of instant communication and information exchange in which there is little time for reflection" (Gane and Beer 2008, 21). Without time for reflection, the sorts of decisions these technologies make are compromised, as instantaneous processing responds to spontaneous situations without pause for thought. Finally, this way of thinking instantiates computerized capitalism's disregard for difference. With event-driven CCTV, ludicrously, certain ways of walking or moving or behaving in general are identified as abnormal and, if not criminalized, deemed worthy of further surveillance. As Graham notes, such systems risk further demonization of minority groups, something already entrenched in "neoliberal [. . .] landscapes of power" (Graham 2005, 574). For Lyotard, this would illustrate the inhuman effect of a system that operates in "gross stereotypes, apparently leaving no place for reflection and education" (Lyotard 2004, 64).

5.3.2. The Inhumanity of the System I

The (so-called) thinking surveillance technologies in our human environment can also be understood in terms of the inhuman in Lyotard's first sense: the inhumanity of the system. Take, for example, the RFID (radio frequency identification) tag. RFIDs have entered the academic imaginary in recent years (see for example: Beer 2007, 2009; Gane and Beer 2008, 62–64; Gane et al. 2007; Mitchell 2005) as part of the "thinking" environment. These tags are implanted in consumer goods to allow objects and consumers to be tracked through time/space; they can be "pinged" much like a barcode, but from a distance. With RFIDs there are "unprecedented capacities for surveillance and control, for RFID technologies now allow physical objects and bodies to be positioned and tracked through the Internet" (Gane and Beer 2008, 63). In an interview with N. Katherine Hayles, Gane remarks: "RFIDs are the dream of the capitalist marketplace, being able to identify and track consumers" (Gane et al. 2007, 331); track, that is, the *right* consumers. These tags allow goods and services to be targeted at specific groups of consumers in a faster, more efficient way—creating a smoother, frictionless system. With RFIDs those who are being tracked are often unaware, but we see also examples where something similar is a consumer "choice". Many applications on Apple's iPhone give users the choice to have their position located by GPS. This allows the application to present to the user nearby retail/leisure facilities, for example (as is the case with Wetherspoon's Pub Finder application). Similarly, the voluntary "checking-in" via a mobile Internet device of a user's location through Facebook's Place application allows for the location of the user and the offer of discounts at nearby shops, restaurants, etc. Is this tracking a nightmarish surveillance or the offer of a convenience culture?

Lyotard shows us that this dichotomy is a false one. That is, convenience in a system of computerized capitalism comes with surveillance as its price: for mechanisms of consumption to be sped up the means of exchange needs to be sped up—and this means digitalized. More than this, though, the surveillance/convenience binary can be restated as an opposition between control and freedom; yet freedom here is only freedom to consume more efficiently, to move through frictionless channels. The choice of freedom/convenience is a *choiceless choice* as we would merely be choosing to operate according to the performative logic of the system. *Choiceless* because this performativity is the very demand of the system: be operative or be obsolete (Lyotard 2005, xxiv). The danger is that those groups of people that do nothing to enhance and extend the development of the system (by making *themselves* convenient—trackable) are abandoned (Lyotard 2004, 77). The façade of "convenience" merely indicates what Lyotard calls "Mr Nice Guy totalitarianism" (Lyotard 1993, 159).

5.3.3. Pause for Thought

The technologies surveyed in this section highlight the state of surveillance and/through the Internet and further afield. We have seen how Lyotard allows us to understand the way these technologies work in terms of their inhuman "thinking" (processing) and their complicity with the extension of computerized capitalism. We can understand this latter process as "software sorting" (Graham 2005) or "social sorting" through surveillance (Lyon 2003) or as "knowing capitalism" (Thrift 2005); however Lyotard's notion of the inhuman captures not only this element—the way new technologies are complicit with the system, shaping the social for its furtherance—but the way that the very mode of technological operation works according to its logic: performative (or time-saving) and intolerant of difference. Gross stereotypes are written into surveillance software, and those who do not submit to surveillance become obsolete.

5.4. SURVEILLANCE THROUGH SOCIAL NETWORKING

The technologies above go some way towards supporting Scott Lash's (2007) claim that power operates through the algorithm. As social life becomes "mediatized" (Lash 2007, 70) so does power extend into the every-day, through software: "A society of ubiquitous media means a society in which power is increasingly in the algorithm" (Lash 2007, 71). Beer (2009) has shown how this (Lyotardian) notion of power ought to be applied to "participatory web cultures" (or, web 2.0), and so my focus below is on surveillance through social networking sites. Lyotard has highlighted the complicity of technological development with capitalist extension. The potential of web cultures to be incorporated into capitalist culture was slow to be seen, with the early Internet (web 1.0) being a site of what Felicia Wu Song (2009, 136) calls "visionary communal" groups where strangers met with strangers to form online communities. Needless to say, this curious disconnection of technological development and capitalist extension was bridged, and, in what follows, I will frame this history and the present practice of surveillance of social networking profiles for commercial ends as part of what Lyotard calls the inhumanity of the system. This includes three key observations: the opacity of the algorithmic functioning of this surveillance; the transformation of web cultures into capitalist cultures; and the system's disregard for difference. I will conclude this section with some reflections on the volunteering of information by individuals through social networking sites, or the inhumanity of social conditioning.

5.4.1. The Inhumanity of the System II

The Internet was not always a site of economic interests, early groups such as the WELL being formed with countercultural, communal ideals in mind (Wu Song 2009, 82). But with the mid-90s boom came online advertising: first, hypertext links that allowed users to navigate to advertising pages; these were largely ineffective because relatively few users "clicked-through", so, second, banner adverts became the norm, with the advert situated on the page the user was already accessing; third, more imposing forms then came to be used, such as pop-up adverts and flash banners; these were largely seen to be too aggressive, and so, finally, what we now most commonly encounter are text adverts, small and situated to the side/s of web pages—such as those we see when we perform a Google search (Wu Song 2009, 84–85). However, advertising is only half the story. When the bubble burst in the early '00s, ushering in the end of web 1.0, media companies began a period of acquisitions, such that previously non-commercial sites— sites that were fundamentally communal, despite their reliance on selling "space" for advertising—became part of media stables (such as when the WELL was acquired by the online media company Salon.com in 1999) (Wu Song 2009, 82–83). It was only so long before corporations realized the value of the very form these communities took.

Take, for example, the Facebook profile: here are collected together various key items of information: name, age/date of birth, location, hobbies and interests, musical tastes, and so on. Users input this to present an identity to others. At the same time this is highly valuable information. Wu Song notes that "personal data become a form of currency in online participation" (Wu Song 2009, 88)—a form, I would add, of cultural currency that becomes a valuable commodity to corporations. The information contained in these profiles can be collected and analyzed to look for preferences and patterns of behaviours amongst the social network, allowing for precision targeting—an efficient mode of advertising, in tune with the Lyotardian principle of performativity. Anecdotally, I remember clearly being surprised when adverts for B.B. King tickets and Stevie Ray Vaughan t-shirts regularly appeared on my Facebook page: *how did they know?* As Wu Song notes: "Although the rhetoric and discourse of most online communities never even hint at the ubiquitous data collection and surveillance that normally occur, such activities are buried in the fine print of the Terms of Service and Privacy Policy that most members never bother to read" (Wu Song 2009, 89). Facebook's privacy statement reads:

> We allow advertisers to choose the characteristics of users who will see their advertisements and we may use any of the non-personally identifiable attributes we have collected (including information you may have decided not to show to other users, such as your birth year or other sensitive personal information or preferences) to select the appropriate audience for those advertisements. (Facebook Privacy Policy 2010)

Along with this personalized advertising, Facebook also collects site activity information and information on the kind of device used to access Facebook (including browser type, IP address, location, and the sites the user visits) (Facebook Privacy Policy 2010). When shared with third parties, such information can be used for precision targeting of markets and consumers.

What is unclear, however, is how the information is processed. The controversy over Facebook Beacon, the advertising system that ran from its inception in 2007 to its deactivation in 2009, is illustrative (see http://

en.wikipedia.org/wiki/Facebook_Beacon). This system used data from other websites—for example, online transactions—in order to target advertising on Facebook. Users complained that the process was opaque, and confusion about what data was being collected—which online actions tracked—was widespread. Although Beacon was shut down, this obfuscation continues: nowhere in Facebook's literature is it clearly stated quite how their data mining and surveillance works. The question Lyotard asks in *The Postmodern Condition* is posed once more: who will know? The power is in the algorithmic functioning of data-processing software, and yet its functioning is unknown to the users of social networking sites. Who writes the software? What commands does it follow? How does it target data? And what does it collect?

Whereas Lyotard's *The Postmodern Condition* prompts us to explore the hidden power of such technologies, and already warns of the commodification of (personal) information, it is his *The Inhuman* that can take us further in examining the impact of the logic that motivates it. Lyotard observes here that as cultures and subcultures begin to operate through telecommunications technology they run the risk of being consumed by capitalist culture. Their key elements—memory (taking in and storing knowledge) and recall (regulating access to knowledge)—are digitalized, causing cultures to become spatially-temporally "unanchored", therefore easily transmissible and "exploitable" (Lyotard 2004, 49–50). Cultures and subcultures begin to have a market value; once translated into information they can be packaged and sold. For Lyotard, nothing can escape this process as even the most subversive of countercultures can be marketed and so become profitable. What is so surprising in hindsight about the early stages of the Internet is that, despite being comprised of digital "webcultures" and communities, commercialization was slow to come. What we see with participatory webcultures such as Facebook is the way that they are increasingly being exploited for profit. The various diffuse subcultures and communities that exist within the Facebook framework have been colonized by the "hegemonic teleculture" (Lyotard 2004, 50) of computerized capitalism—the only real game in town.

This observation also highlights an ethico-political problem raised by Lyotard. When virtual communities become commercialized, different communities become different markets. This has two effects. First, as Wu Song (2009, 95) notes, when minority groups come to be seen as niche markets, the inequalities between groups are masked: all that is relevant is what data can be gathered about what they consume so that goods and services can be marketed accordingly. Instead of seeing unequally advantaged citizens, this process sees dissimilarly consuming customers. Lyotard feared that such groups would be abandoned by the system unless they became performative (Lyotard 2004, 76–77). What we see today is that such groups are tolerated because, through data mining, their inequality can be exploited for profit—which is to say, they have become performative. The effect is a systemic quietism towards social inequality, because it represents another space into which the system can extend. Second, as different cultural groups are exploited for profit "their members are homogeneously approached as consumers" (Wu Song 2009, 95). Instead of respecting the differences of cultural groups, this process sees only the cult of consumption. For example, one's identity as a lesbian or black man is redefined as one's identity as a consumer who buys the kinds of things bought by lesbians or black men. Here we see the disregard of the system for difference: it is only tolerated to the extent that it can be used to market diverse goods and services—in effect subsuming it under the overriding sameness of consumption. In effect, as Christian Fuchs notes in his contribution to this volume, users are sold as a commodity to advertisers, fine-grained identity distinctions lost in the conformity of commodity.

5.4.2. The Inhumanity of Social Conditioning

The final exploration through Lyotard of this mode of surveillance involves returning to the second kind of the inhuman, the inhumanity "of which the soul is hostage" (Lyotard 2004, 2), understood in Sim's sense as "the inhumanity of our social conditioning: the pressure to conform to prescribed modes of behaviour" (Sim 1996, 130).

Social networking profiles, design flourishes aside, tend to be more or less the same. As noted above, standard items of information are displayed, such as name, age/date of birth, relationship status, location, hobbies and interests, and so on, and alongside the user's photograph this makes up the core of the profile. This information was important for building online communities and initiating friendships with previously unknown individuals in web 1.0, as some marker of shared characteristics and interests was necessary for such formations to be practicable. These standard profiles, as we saw above, were also eventually seen to be beneficial to corporations, as useful demographic data and consumption patterns could be read straight off them. As Wu Song notes, social networking in web 2.0 has moved away from the old "visionary communal" ideals of many web 1.0 communities: we seem no longer to be interested in "meeting anyone from anywhere" (Wu Song 2009, 136). Instead, sites such as Facebook are about maintaining communications with offline friends (loosely defined) with some geographically defined commonality: school friends, university friends, work colleagues, and so on. Why, then, this vestigial profile?

It seems, as Zygmunt Bauman (2008) notes, that we have become accustomed to putting the private into the public domain, as if we no longer see any distinction between the two. The trouble is that this incessant posting of personal information is exactly what speeds up and smoothes out the extension of computerized capitalism by facilitating targeted adverts and marketing strategies (Hill 2009). We translate our identities into valuable information and post it online, taken hostage by the very logic by which the system operates. One example, recent at the time of writing, will be illustrative. Coca-Cola ran a promotion for its Dr Pepper soft-drink brand on Facebook that involved users allowing their profile status to be hijacked by the corporation (see Dodd 2010). According to Facebook's Privacy Policy (2010), this interaction with a third party means that they can subsequently access information about the user. These kinds of promotions show how users proactively allow personal information to be collected by third-party corporations. Perhaps more worrying, the Dr Pepper example demonstrates the willingness of users to relinquish control over the profile status update, usually a personal expression of current ideas or activities, to a product promotion. On the one hand, the expression of thoughts and feelings; on the other hand, the shameless hawking of fizzy pop: the willingness of the user to allow the latter to be represented as the former demonstrates the success of a system that conditions the human to act towards the system's ends, with little regard for that which is proper to the human. Another example, discussed in Mark Andrejevic's contribution to this volume, suggests the further extension of this process. A Facebook application designed by Appirio gives employers access to their employees' social networks, allowing for direct marketing through "word of mouth referral" within that network; the company increases profits, and the employee may earn a bonus dependent on the suitability of their social network. The idea that one's social network might be not only profitable to companies but to the social networker him/herself suggests a yet further conditioning for individuals to treat something as vital as social relations according to an exploitative logic. And if the canny employee, with an eye for the bonus, begins to build social networks with the potential for profiteering in mind, then the degeneration is yet more marked. If the human is a social animal, then we are witnessing the submission of that which is special to "being human" to the demands and scrutiny of computerized capitalism.

It is not so much that we are thinking like computers (as Lyotard also worried): we are thinking, communicating, and expressing ourselves online like humans. The problem is, we are thinking, communicating, and expressing ourselves in accordance with the operating logic of computerized capitalism, extending its operation. We translate everything about us into information in order to exchange it as cultural currency; at the same time, we make information exploitable by corporations according to the very operating principles—translation, exchange—of the system itself. A reading of Lyotard here allows us to reflect upon how surveillance through social networking impacts upon our very core of humanity, an approach that I suggest is complementary to Mark Andrejevic's account of exploitation in web 2.0 in the present volume; whereas Andrejevic's focus is on the economic—alienation from the product of labour—a Lyotardian approach would suggest that we consider also our alienation from species-being. The inhumanity of this surveillance is that we internalise, not the gaze (pace Foucault), but the performative logic of computerized capitalism. We are haunted from within, the soul taken hostage (Lyotard 2004, 2) by this dehumanizing spectre.

5.5. CONCLUDING REMARKS

I have attempted here to demonstrate the usefulness of a Lyotardian theoretical understanding of the computerized surveillance that operates though the Internet. Such an account crucially includes the commodification of information; the highlighting of the opacity of surveillance software; and an understanding of the complicity of new technologies of surveillance with the capitalist system, both functioning according to the principle of performativity. Further, the notion of the inhuman was shown to be a tool for opening up several ethico-political questions concerning the paucity of computerized thinking in "smart" surveillance technologies; the disregard for difference in computerized capitalism played out through surveillance software; and the social conditioning of citizens into active information sources.

Lyotard asks: "What else remains as 'politics' except resistance to this inhuman?" (Lyotard 2004, 7). Resistance can take many forms. Sociological research into the functioning of surveillance software is necessary to address the problem of *who will know*. That way we can bear witness to the programs that "social-sort" or that threaten difference, whilst keeping tabs on what and how much information is collected. The problem of our own complicity is great in the context of resistance. Lyotard offered few solutions, and no programs of resistance. However, remarks in his *Postmodern Fables* (Lyotard 2003) may prove helpful. In resistance to flows of communication (such as social networking sites) becoming streams of capitalism, Lyotard suggests we become "subterranean streams", underground yet springing up in undetermined locations on the surface (Lyotard 2003, 5). Although I partly agree with Gane that Lyotard is advocating a "radical 'underground' existence" (Gane 2003, 448) that would resist the capitalist order, it is important to emphasize the relevance of the spring. Resistance cannot merely be about opting out, but about participating in unpredictable ways—such that the surveillance technologies of the capitalist order cannot keep up. Resistance might follow from more research into the algorithms that contain the power. The information we glean could allow us to shape our profiles (in the loose sense) in ways that cannot so easily be read and that work to *our* benefit; in such a way we might remain underground whilst springing up when necessary or desired. This kind of *streaming* may not resist the capitalist order, but it would go some way to putting the ball in the court of the individual—and not the inhuman.

ACKNOWLEDGMENTS

I would like to thank Nick Gane and Jenny Hambling for their helpful comments on an earlier draft.

REFERENCES

Andrejevic, Mark. 2007. *iSpy: Surveillance and power in the interactive era.* Lawrence: University Press of Kansas.

Bauman, Zygmunt. 2008. *Liquid modernity.* Cambridge: Polity.

Beer, David. 2007. Thoughtful territories: imagining the thinking power of things and spaces. *City,* 11 (2): 229–238.

———. 2009. Power through the algorithm? participatory web cultures and the technological unconscious. *New Media & Society* 11 (6): 985–1002.

Burrows, Roger and Nick Gane. 2006. Geodemographics, software and class. *Sociology* 40 (5): 793–812.

Castells, Manuel. 2006. *The rise of the network society.* 2nd ed. Oxford: Blackwell.

Dodd, Vikram. 2010. Coca-Cola forced to pull Facebook promotion after porn references. *Guardian,* July 18. http://www.guardian.co.uk/business/2010/jul/18/coca-cola-facebook-promotion-porn (accessed on ???).

Facebook Privacy Policy. 2010. http://www.facebook.com/policy.php (accessed on ???).

Gane, Nicholas. 2003. Computerised capitalism: the media theory of Jean-François Lyotard. *Information, Communication & Society* 6 (3) 430–450.

Gane, Nicholas and David Beer. 2008. *New media: The key concepts.* Oxford: Berg.

Gane, Nicholas, Couze Venn, and Martin Hand. 2007. Ubiquitous surveillance: an interview with Katherine Hayles. *Theory, Culture & Society* 24 (7/8): 349–358.

Graham, Stephen. 2005. Software-sorted geographies. *Progress in Human Geography,* 29 (5): 562–580.

Hayles, N. Katherine. 2005. Computing the human. *Theory, Culture & Society* 22 (1): 131–151.

Hill, David W. 2009. Reflections on leaving Facebook. *Fast Capitalism* 5 (2). http://www.uta.edu/huma/agger/fastcapitalism/5_2/Hill5_2.html (accessed on ???).

Lash, Scott. 2007. Power after hegemony: cultural studies in mutation. *Theory, Culture & Society* 24 (3): 55–78.

Lewis, Paul. 2010. Surveillance cameras in Birmingham track Muslims' every move. *Guardian,* June 4. http://www.guardian.co.uk/uk/2010/jun/04/surveillance-cameras-birmingham-muslims (accessed on ???).

Lyon, David. 1994. *The electronic eye: The rise of surveillance society.* Cambridge: Polity.

———. 2003. *Surveillance as social sorting: Privacy, risk and digital discrimination.* London: Routledge.

———. 2007. *Surveillance studies: An overview.* Cambridge: Polity.

Lyotard, Jean-François. 1988. *Peregrinations: Law, form, event.* Guildford: Columbia University Press.

———. 1992. *The postmodern explained to children: Correspondence 1982–1985,* trans. Don Barry et al., ed. Julian Pefanis and Morgan Thomas. London: Turnaround.

———. 1993. *Toward the postmodern,* trans. Kenneth Berri et al., ed. Robert Harvey and Mark S. Roberts. Atlantic Highlands, NJ: Humanity Books.

———. 2003. *Postmodern fables,* trans. George Van Den Abbeele. London: University of Minnesota Press.

———. 2004. *The inhuman: Reflections on time,* trans. Geoffrey Bennington and Rachel Bowlby. Cambridge: Polity.

———. 2005. *The postmodern condition: A report on knowledge,* trans. Geoffrey Bennington and Brian Massumi. Manchester: Manchester University Press.

Marx, Gary T. 2002. What's new about the "new surveillance"? classifying for change and continuity. *Surveillance & Society* 1(1): 9–29.

Mitchell, William J. 2005. *Placing words: Symbols, space, and the city.* Cambridge: MIT Press.

Poster, Mark. 1990. *The mode of information: Poststructuralism and social context.* Cambridge: Polity.

Sim, Stuart. 1996. *Jean-François Lyotard.* Hemel Hempstead: Prentice Hall/Harvester Wheatsheaf.

———. 2001. *Lyotard and the inhuman.* Duxford: Icon Books.

Solove, Daniel J. 2004. *The digital person: Technology and privacy in the information age.* New York: New York University Press.

Thrift, Nigel. 2005. *Knowing capitalism.* London: Sage.

Wu Song, Felicia. 2009. *Virtual communities: Bowling alone, online together.* Oxford: Peter Lang.

6 Critical Internet Surveillance Studies and Economic Surveillance

Thomas Allmer

6.1. INTRODUCTION

Surveillance has notably increased in the last decades of modern society. Surveillance studies scholars like David Lyon (1994) or Clive Norris and Gary Armstrong (1999) stress that we live in a surveillance society. Although there are a lot of other features in contemporary society, such as information, neoliberalism, globalization, or capitalism, surveillance in general and Internet surveillance in particular are crucial phenomena. For instance, web 2.0 activities, such as creating profiles and sharing ideas on Facebook, announcing personal messages on Twitter, uploading or watching videos on YouTube, and writing personal entries on Blogger, all enable the collection, analyses, and sale of personal data by commercial web platforms.

The overall aim of this chapter is to clarify how we can theorize and systemize such phenomena. Lyon (1998, 95; 2003b, 163) emphasizes that economic surveillance on the Internet, such as monitoring consumers or the workplace, is a central aspect of modern surveillance societies. The approach that is advanced in this chapter recognizes the importance of the role of the economy in contemporary surveillance societies. To do so, the following thematically grouped research questions are subjects of this contribution:

Foundations of Internet surveillance studies
- How is Internet surveillance defined in the existing literature?
- What are commonalties and differences of various notions of Internet surveillance?
- What are advantages and disadvantages of such definitions?

Critical Internet surveillance studies
- Which theory provides a typology in order to systemize Internet surveillance in the modern economy?
- What are examples of Internet surveillance in the spheres of production, circulation, and consumption?

This chapter can be fruitful for scholars who want to undertake a systematic analysis of surveillance in general and Internet surveillance in particular in the modern economy and who want to study the field of surveillance critically. It deals with surveillance in the modern economy and is a critical contribution to surveillance studies insofar as it is based on the foundations of a critical political-economy approach (MECW 28; MEW 23). The term modern economy refers to the capitalistic economy of modern societies. Modern society is the historical period that began with the Enlightenment and continues today.

This contribution constructs theoretically founded typologies in order to systemize the existing literature of Internet surveillance studies and to analyze examples of surveillance. Therefore, it mainly is a theoretical approach combined with illustrative examples, advancing from the abstract to the concrete level. Based on the research questions and the described methodology, the following structure can be outlined:

Section 2 analyzes how Internet surveillance is defined in the existing literature, what commonalties and differences of various notions of online surveillance exist, and what advantages and disadvantages such definitions have. Furthermore, section 2 describes how different notions deal with economic surveillance on the Internet and makes clear if there is a gap in the existing literature in order to study Internet surveillance in the modern economy. The specific economic mode of Internet surveillance is studied in section 3. Based on the foundations of a critical political-economy approach and the distinction of surveillance in the economy into the spheres of production, circulation, and consumption, a typology of online surveillance in the economy can be constructed. Constructing a theoretically founded typology of economic surveillance is important in order to undertake a systematic analysis of surveillance in the modern economy. Economic surveillance on the Internet in the spheres of production, circulation, and consumption will be outlined. Section 4 concludes with a summary and makes some political recommendations for overcoming Internet surveillance in the modern economy.

6.2. FOUNDATIONS OF INTERNET SURVEILLANCE STUDIES

In this contribution, Internet surveillance is understood as a special form of surveillance. Since Michel Foucault published his book *Surveiller et punir,* in French in 1975 and in English in 1977, the amount of literature on surveillance has increased enormously and represents a diffuse and complex field of research. Lyon (1994, 6–7) stresses: "Michel Foucault's celebrated, and contentious, historical studies of surveillance and discipline had appeared that mainstream social theorists began to take surveillance seriously in its own right". David Murakami Wood (2003, 235) emphasizes that "for Surveillance Studies, Foucault is a foundational thinker and his work on the development of the modern subject, in particular Surveillir et Punir (translated as Discipline and Punish), remains a touchstone for this nascent transdisciplinary field". According to Google Scholar (2010), Foucault's book *Discipline and Punish* (1977) is cited more than 17,000 times. According to the *Encyclopedia of Philosophy* (Pryor 2006, 898) and to the *Routledge Encyclopedia of Philosophy* (Gutting 1998, 708–713), Foucault is one of the most important historians and philosophers of the twentieth century and has had wide influence in different disciplines.

The overall aim of this section is to elucidate how Internet surveillance is defined in the existing literature, what commonalties and differences of various notions of online surveillance exist, and what advantages and disadvantages such definitions have. To do so, Foucault's understanding of surveillance and the idea of the panopticon are introduced (subsection 1). Based on these findings, and by establishing a typology of the existing literature and discussing their commonalities and differences, subsections 2 and 3 contain a systematic discussion of the state of the art of Internet surveillance. To analyze the existing literature on a more abstract level and identify advantages and disadvantages, it is essential to discuss commonalties and differences and to find certain typologies. Finally, subsection 4 gives a summary, discusses how different notions deal with Internet surveillance in the modern economy, and makes clear if there is a gap in the existing literature.

6.2.1. Foucault's Notion of Surveillance and the Panopticon

Foucault (1995; 2002; 2003; 2007) analyzes surveillance in the context of the emergence of disciplinary societies. He stresses an evolution from feudal societies of torture, to reformed societies of punishment, and on to modern disciplinary societies. In the age of torture, arbitrary penalties and public spectacles of the scaffold took place in order to exterminate bodies. Afterwards, in the age of punishment, defendants were punished and exterminated. In the age of disciplines, direct violence has been replaced with softer forms of power in order to discipline, control, and normalize people in respect of drilling docile bodies and "political puppets" (Foucault 1995, 136).

For Foucault (1995, 195–210), Jeremy Bentham's panopticon is a symbol for modern disciplinary society: "On the whole, therefore, one can speak of the formation of a disciplinary society in this movement that stretches from the enclosed disciplines, a sort of social 'quarantine', to an indefinitely generalizable mechanism of 'panopticism'" (Foucault 1995, 216). The panopticon is an ideal architectural figure of modern disciplinary power. It exists of an annular building divided in different cells and a huge tower with windows in the middle. Prisoners, workers, pupils, as well as patients stay in the cells and a supervisor occupies the middle tower. The architecture allows the supervisor to observe all individuals in the cells without being seen. Not every inmate is observed at every moment, but no one knows if she or he is monitored. Observation is possible anytime. As a result, everyone acts as if kept under surveillance all the time—individuals discipline themselves out of fear of surveillance. The panopticon creates a consciousness of permanent visibility as a form of power, where no bars, chains, and heavy locks are necessary for domination any more. Foucault (1995, 228) finally asks: "Is it surprising that prisons resemble factories, schools, barracks, hospitals, which all resemble prisons?"

In summary, Foucault analyses surveillance in the context of the emergence of modern disciplinary societies. He understands disciplines as forms of operational power relations and technologies of domination in order to discipline, control, and normalize people. For Foucault, the panopticon is an ideal symbol of modern surveillance societies. Foucault's understanding of surveillance and the panopticon allows to distinguish panoptic (affirmation of Foucault's notion) and non-panoptic (rejection of Foucault's notion) approaches of defining Internet surveillance that can be used for constructing a typology of existing surveillance literature and for discussing commonalities and differences of definitions of Internet surveillance: The task of the following two subsections is to give a representative, but still eclectic, overview about different definitions of online surveillance.

6.2.2. Non-Panoptic Notions of Internet Surveillance

Lyon understands the "world wide web of surveillance" (Lyon 1998) as a neutral concept that identifies positive consequences such as protection and security as well as negative consequences such as control. Computerization of surveillance makes bureaucratic administration easier (Lyon 2003b, 164), and surveillance in cyberspace permits "greater efficiency and speed, and may well result in increased benefits for citizens and consumers, who experience them as enhancing their comfort, convenience, and safety" (Lyon 2003a, 69). Nevertheless, Lyon says that the nation state and the capitalist workplace are the main sites of surveillance on the Internet (1998, 95; 2003a, 69; 2003b, 163) and argues that surveillance technologies such as the Internet reinforce asymmetrical power relations on an extensive and intensive level (Lyon 1998, 92): "So surveillance spreads, becoming constantly more routine, more intensive (profiles) and extensive (populations), driven by economic, bureaucratic and now technological forces" (Lyon 1998, 99). The Internet has become a multibillion dollar industry, because it is primarily corporations that are interested in collecting, analyzing, and assessing a huge amount of personal consumer data in order to target personalized advertisement (Lyon 2003b, 162).

Similarly to Lyon's notion of Internet surveillance that assumes there are enabling and constraining effects, Seumas Miller and John Weckert (2000) articulate advantages and disadvantages of being monitored. Their paper examines monitoring at the workplace in general and observing of e-mail and the Internet usage in particular. Although the authors claim that privacy is a moral right (Miller and Weckert 2000, 256) and criticize existing approaches that stress benefits of workplace monitoring for both employers and employees (Miller and Weckert 2000, 258–259), they argue that "surveillance and monitoring can be justified in some circumstances" (Miller and Weckert 2000, 255) and reason: "The proposition must be rejected that the extent and nature of the enjoyment of rights to individual privacy is something to be determined by the most powerful forces of the day, be they market or bureaucratic forces" (Miller and Weckert 2000, 256).

For Anders Albrechtslund (2008; see also Albrechtslund's contribution in this volume), positive aspects of being under surveillance are worth mentioning, and he argues that online surveillance also empowers the users, constructs subjectivity, and is playful. Internet surveillance as social and participatory act involves mutuality and sharing.

> Online social networking can also be empowering for the user, as the monitoring and registration facilitates new ways of constructing identity, meeting friends and colleagues as well as socializing with strangers. This changes the role of the user from passive to active, since surveillance in this context offers opportunities to take action, seek information and communicate. Online social networking therefore illustrates that surveillance—as a mutual, empowering and subjectivity building practice—is fundamentally social. (Albrechtslund 2008)

Hille Koskela (2004; 2006) emphasizes the individual's active role in the context of surveillance in general and online surveillance in particular. For instance, reality shows are based on viewer participation, mobile phones with cameras create an active subject, and home webcams generate new subjectivities. Koskela wants to analyze "the other side of surveillance", which has resistant and liberating elements: "Webcams can also be argued to contribute to the 'democratization' of surveillance" (Koskela 2006, 175). In addition, Koskela (2004, 204) argues that webcams have an empowering role and that the active role of individuals with surveillance equipment shows that the lines of control are blurred.

In conclusion, non-panoptic notions of Internet surveillance either use a neutral concept that assumes there are enabling effects, such as protection and security, as well as constraining effects, such as control or a positive concept that identifies comical, playful, and amusing characteristics of surveillance, and where everyone has the opportunity to surveil. In addition, these approaches tend to reject the proposition that surveillance mechanisms are dominated by political and economic actors and see monitoring not necessarily as annoying and disturbing. In non-panoptic notions, Internet surveillance is understood as a useful and effective management tool and as a fair method and procedure of monitoring individuals online. Now, we move on to panoptic notions of Internet surveillance.

6.2.3. Panoptic Notions of Internet Surveillance

Based on a diagrammatic understanding of panoptic surveillance, Greg Elmer (1997) predominantly understands the Internet as a powerful space of economic surveillance. "The Internet is first mapped, through indexical search engines, and then diagnosed, via 'spiders' and 'cookies', to actively monitor, survey, solicit and subsequently profile users' online behavior" (Elmer 1997, 182). Corporations map consumer profiles including demographic and psychographic data in order to target advertising and to accumulate profit (Elmer 1997, 186, 189–190).

Likewise, in *The Internet Galaxy,* Manuel Castells (2001, 168–187) describes the Internet not only as a space full of opportunities, but also as a technology of control, which has primarily emerged from the interests of economic and political actors such as corporations and state institutions. He argues that these institutions make use of such technologies in order to locate individual users. State institutions such as governments and corporations like Microsoft and Google use special surveillance technologies that allow the monitoring of online behaviour in one central database.

> Surveillance technologies . . . often rely on identification technologies to be able to locate the individual user . . . These technologies operate their controls under two basic conditions. First, the controllers know the codes of the network, the controlled do not. Software is confidential, and proprietary, and cannot be modified except by its owner. Once on the network, the average user is the prisoner of an architecture he or she does not know. Secondly, controls are exercised on the basis of a space defined on the network, for instance, the network around an Internet service provider, or the intra-network in a company, a university, or a government agency. (Castells 2001, 171–173)

Castells understands the rise of the Internet as an emergence of a powerful electronic surveillance system and concludes: "If this system of surveillance and control of the Internet develops fully, we will not be able to do as we please. We may have no liberty, and no place to hide" (Castells 2001, 181). Castells (2001, 171–173) considers, just like Foucault, surveillance to be negative and centralized and being connected to control and power. Hence, although Castells does not refer to the concept of the panopticon directly, his contribution to online surveillance can be considered as being a panoptic notion of Internet surveillance.

Michael Levi and David Wall (2004, 201–203) emphasize the new politics of surveillance in a post-9/11 European information society and the increase of the panoptic power of the EU member states as mediated through surveillance techniques such as identity/entitlement cards, asylum seekers' smartcards, data-sharing schemes, and smart passports in order to create a suspect population. Wall (2003; 2006) analyzes the growth of surveillant Internet technologies in the information society. He draws on Foucault's understanding of panoptic power relations (Wall 2006, 344) and distinguishes between personal and mass surveillance (Wall 2006, 342). For Wall, the Internet as a multidirectional information flow has brought new opportunities for individuals in the context of surveillance. Techniques such as spyware, spam spider bots, and cookies allow a synoptic effect where the surveilled can surveil the surveillers (Wall 2006, 342–343).

> The Internet is not simply a 'super' (Poster, 1995), 'virtual' (Engberg, 1996) or 'electronic' (Lyon, 1994, ch. 4) Panopticon: an extension of Foucault's conceptualization of Bentham's prison design—'seeing without being seen' (Foucault, 1983, p. 223), as has become the conventional wisdom. It is important to emphasize that Internet information flows are simultaneously panoptic and synoptic—not only can the few watch the many, but the many can watch the few. (Mathiesen, 1997, p. 215) (Wall 2003, 112)

Wall argues that the balance between personal surveillance on the one hand and mass surveillance on the other hand is "rarely even" (Wall 2006, 346) and lists powerful corporations such as DoubleClick and Engage that are able to undertake large-scale surveillance (Wall 2006, 343). In addition, he emphasizes the growth of surveillance and privacy threats as tradable commodities in information capitalism (Wall 2003, 135) and presents an empirical case study of the spam industry such as e-mail list compilation and unsolicited bulk e-mails (Wall 2006, 350–352).

Joseph Turow (2005; 2006) speaks about marketing and consumer surveillance in the digital age of media. He stresses that online media are interested in collecting data about their audience in order to sell these data to advertisers. In a next step, the advertisers use these data in order to increase the efficiency of marketing (Turow 2005, 103–104; 2006, 280). Furthermore, customer relationship management constructs audiences and produces a surveillance-driven culture, where consumers understand surveillance as a cost-benefit calculation and are willing to contribute to data collection by media and advertisers (Turow 2005, 105, 119–120). Turow's understanding of surveillance can be seen in the context of Foucault's notion of panoptic surveillance. He considers, just like Foucault, surveillance to be negative and centralized and connected to discipline, control, and power (Turow 2005, 115). Similarly to Foucault, Turow (2005, 116–117) stresses that surveillance is predominately undertaken by powerful institutions such as corporations. Also interesting in this context is the national survey of Internet privacy and institutional trust by Joseph Turow and Michael Hennessy (2007). In 2003, they undertook 1,200 quantitative telephone interviews in the US with adults (18 years and older), who go online at home (Turow and Hennessy 2007, 304). The authors analyzed what US citizens think about institutional surveillance and concluded "that a substantial percentage of Internet users believes that major corporate or government institutions will both help them to protect information privacy and take that privacy away by disclosing information to other parties without permission" (Turow and Hennessy 2007, 301).

Mark Andrejevic (2002; 2007b; also 2007a 135–160; see also Andrejevic's contribution in this volume) wants to offer an alternative approach of online privacy in the era of new media. Andrejevic studies the economic surveillance of interactive media such as interactive TV (2002) and Google's business model of free wireless Internet access (2007b) and analyzes interactive surveillance in the digital enclosure: "the model of enclosure traces the relationship between a material, spatial process—the construction of networked, interactive environments—and the private expropriation of information" (Andrejevic 2007b, 297). He argues that Foucault's panopticon is a suitable approach to study surveillance and hierarchical power asymmetries in the online economy and speaks about a "digital form of disciplinary panopticism" (Andrejevic 2007b, 237). Andrejevic argues that just as workplace surveillance rationalized production in the era of scientific management, online surveillance rationalizes and stimulates consumption (Andrejevic 2007b, 232; 244) and produces customized commodities and the crucial capital of the economy (Andrejevic 2007b, 234). "Viewers are monitored so advertisers can be ensured that this work is being done as efficiently as possible. Ratings, in this context, are informational commodities that generate value because they help to rationalize the viewing process" (Andrejevic 2007b, 236).

Also in the context of economic surveillance, John Edward Campbell and Matt Carlson (2002) revisit Foucault's idea of the panopticon as well as Gandy's notion of the panoptic sort. They apply these notions to online surveillance and the commodification of privacy on the Internet:

> The Panopticon was seen as a way of organizing social institutions to ensure a more orderly society by producing disciplined and 'rational' (read predictable) citizens. With Internet ad servers, the goal is to provide marketers with the personal information necessary to determine if an individual constitutes an economically viable consumer. The enhanced consumer profiling offered by these third-party ad servers increases the effectiveness and efficiency of advertisers' efforts, reducing the uncertainty faced by producers introducing their goods and services into the marketplace. (Campbell and Carlson 2002, 587)

Summing up, panoptic notions of Internet surveillance argue that power, control, and surveillance have increased in the era of the Internet.

Furthermore, the rise of the Internet has brought a space of electronic surveillance, where the powerful will appropriate the Internet as a technology of control for their own instrumental advantage. These approaches consider online surveillance to be negative and being connected to coercion, repression, discipline, power, and domination. For these authors, power is primarily centralized and society tends to be repressive and controlled.

6.2.4. Discussion

The overall aim of this section was to clarify how Internet surveillance has been defined in the existing literature, what the different notions of online surveillance have in common, and what distinguishes them from one another. Based on the distinction of panoptic and non-panoptic notions of surveillance, a systematic discussion of the state of the art of Internet surveillance was conducted by establishing a typology of the existing literature and introducing a discussion of commonalties and differences. Table 6.1 summarizes the results:

Table 6.1   Foundations of Internet Surveillance Studies

		Non-panoptic notions of Internet surveillance	Panoptic notions of Internet surveillance
Non-panoptic notions of Internet surveillance	Non-panoptic notions of Internet surveillance either use a neutral concept that assumes there are enabling as well as constraining effects or a positive concept that identifies comical, playful, and amusing characteristics of online surveillance.	*David Lyon (1998; 2003a; 2003b), Seumas Miller and John Weckert (2000), Anders Albrechtslund (2008), Hille Koskela (2004; 2006)*	
Panoptic notions of Internet surveillance	Panoptic notions of Internet surveillance consider online surveillance to be negative. These approaches argue that power, domination, coercion, control, discipline, and surveillance have increased in the era of the Internet.		*Greg Elmer (1997), Manuel Castells (2001), David Wall (2003; 2006), Joseph Turow (2005; 2006), Mark Andrejevic (2002; 2007a; 2007b), John Edward Campbell and Matt Carlson (2002)*

In conclusion, non-panoptic notions of Internet surveillance use either a neutral concept, which assumes that enabling as well as constraining effects exist or a positive concept, which identifies comical, playful, and amusing characteristics; they are represented by scholars such as David Lyon and Hille Koskela. In contrast, panoptic notions of Internet surveillance consider online surveillance to be negative. These approaches argue that power, domination, coercion, control, discipline, and surveillance have increased in the era of the Internet; they are represented by scholars such as Greg Elmer, Manuel Castells, and Joseph Turow.

Although private actors monitor and watch over other individuals in everyday life experiences (for example parents taking care of their children, providing personal information on weblogs, and using social networking sites on the Internet), these acts are processes to which people agree and which involve no violence, coercion, or repression. In comparison, economic and political actors use surveillance and exercise violence in order to control certain behaviours of people, who in most cases do not know that they are surveilled. To accumulate profit and guarantee the production of surplus value, corporations control the economic behaviour of people and coerce them to produce or buy specific commodities. Corporations and state institutions are the most powerful actors in society and are able to undertake mass surveillance extensively and intensively (such as for example the collection and gathering of information on Internet user profiles in order to implement targeted advertising), because the amount of available resources shapes the intensity and extension of surveillance. In the modern production process, primarily electronic surveillance documents and controls workers' behaviour and communication to guarantee the production of surplus value. The commodification of privacy is important to target advertising for accumulating profit. State institutions have intensified and extended state surveillance of citizens in order to combat the threat of terrorism (Gandy 2003, 26–41; Lyon 2003c). Therefore, one can assume that corporations and state institutions are the main actors in modern surveillance societies, and surveillance is a crucial element for modern societies.

Those who hold non-panoptic notions of Internet surveillance understand surveillance in cyberspace in a non-hierarchical and decentralized way, where everyone has the opportunity to surveil. This argument overlooks the fact that corporations and state institutions are the most powerful actors in society and are able to undertake mass surveillance online—what private actors are not able to do. Neutral concepts of surveillance on the Internet tend to overlook power asymmetries of contemporary society and therefore tend to convey the image that private actors are as powerful as corporations and state institutions. Hence, a general and neutral understanding of surveillance in cyberspace is not fruitful for studying online surveillance as it does not take asymmetrical power relations and repressive aspects of society into consideration. Approaches that stress that everyone today has the opportunity to surveil, that online surveillance is a useful and effective management tool, and that Internet surveillance has playful and amusing characteristics are typical for postmodern scholars and disguise the fact of power and domination in contemporary surveillance societies.

Surveillance studies scholars like Lyon (1998, 95; 2003b, 163) argue that economic surveillance on the Internet such as monitoring consumers or the workplace are central aspects of modern surveillance societies. The following explanations indicate that most of the panoptic notions of Internet surveillance recognize the importance of economic aspects of surveillance in cyberspace: So for example Elmer (1997, 186; 189–190) investigates economic Internet surveillance predominantly in the sphere of consumption and analyzes how corporations map consumer profiles in order to target advertising and to accumulate profit. In contrast, Castells (2001, 173–174) mentions economic Internet surveillance in the sphere of production and in the sphere of consumption. When Wall (2006, 350–352) presents an empirical case study of the spam industry, such as e-mail list compilation and unsolicited bulk e-mails, he solely emphasizes surveillance in the sphere of consumption. Turow (2006, 114–118) analyzes consumer surveillance in the digital age and marks a development from customized media of one-to-one marketing to walled gardens as an online environment to interactive television such as video-on-demand. Andrejevic (2007b, 242–243) is primarily interested in analyzing consumer surveillance. In addition, Campbell and Carlson (2002, 587) understand online surveillance in the context of the commodification of privacy, consumer profiling, and advertising. In conclusion, panoptic notions of Internet surveillance primarily analyze economic aspects of surveillance on the Internet in the context of consumption. The following table summarizes these example approaches:

Although panoptic notions of Internet surveillance recognize the importance of the economy, they tend to focus on the sphere of consumption and to overlook online surveillance in the spheres of production and circulation as important aspects of contemporary surveillance societies. Furthermore, panoptic notions of Internet surveillance claim that there are particular forms of economic surveillance without a theoretical criterion for a certain typology.

Table 6.2 Economic Aspects in Panoptic Notions of Internet Surveillance

Internet surveillance in the sphere of production	*Internet surveillance in the sphere of circulation*	*Internet surveillance in the sphere of consumption*
Manuel Castells (2001)		*Greg Elmer (1997)* *Manuel Castells (2001)* *David Wall (2003; 2006)* *Joseph Turow (2005; 2006)* *Mark Andrejevic (2002; 2007a; 2007b)* *John Edward Campbell and Matt Carlson (2002)*

In summary, non-panoptic notions of Internet surveillance are in my view not fruitful for studying online surveillance as they do not take asymmetrical power relations and repressive aspects of society into consideration. In addition, panoptic notions of Internet surveillance tend to overlook online surveillance in the spheres of production and circulation as important aspects of contemporary surveillance societies. Therefore, a critical contribution to Internet surveillance studies is needed.

6.3. CRITICAL INTERNET SURVEILLANCE STUDIES

A critical contribution to Internet surveillance studies strives for the development of theoretical and empirical research methods in order to analyze surveillance in the context of domination, asymmetrical power relations, resource control, social struggles, and exploitation. It critically analyzes Internet surveillance as an important aspect of guaranteeing the production of surplus value and accumulating profit (Fuchs 2008, 268–270; 2010, 19–21; see also the contributions by Fuchs, Sandoval, and Andrejevic in this volume). Furthermore, a typology of Internet surveillance in the modern economy, which is based on Marx's theory and critique of the political economy, allows to systemize economic surveillance on the Internet and to distinguish between online surveillance in the spheres of production, circulation, and consumption (see also Fuchs' analysis of surveillance in the cycle of capital accumulation in this volume). A theoretically founded typology of economic Internet surveillance is important in order to undertake a theoretical analysis of online surveillance in the modern economy. Based on the foundations of a critical political-economy approach, the distinction of production, circulation, and consumption within the economy is introduced (6.3.1) in order to establish a typology of online surveillance in the economy and to study Internet surveillance in the spheres of production, circulation, and consumption (section 6.3.2).

6.3.1. The Spheres of the Economy

In the Introduction to a Contribution to the Critique of Political Economy, Karl Marx (MECW 28, 26–37) distinguishes between (a) production, (b) circulation (distribution and exchange), and (c) consumption as dialectically mediated spheres of the capitalistic economy (a). The sphere of production appears as the point of departure. In the capitalist mode of production, entrepreneurs consume purchased commodities (means of production and labour power) in order to produce new commodities and surplus value. (b) Circulation is the "mediation between production and consumption" (MECW 28, 27). In the process of circulation, consumers purchase commodities for daily life and proprietors sell the produced commodities to realize profit. (c) In the sphere of consumption as the final point of the process, "the product drops out of this social movement, becomes the direct object and servant of an individual need, which its use satisfies" (MECW 28, 26). Whereas in production the person receives an objective aspect, in consumption the object receives a subjective aspect. The "consumption, as the concluding act . . . reacts on the point of departure thus once again initiating the whole process" (MECW 28, 27). Although production, circulation, and consumption are separated spheres, they correlate in an interconnected relationship (see Figure 6.1):

In the sphere of production, means of production are consumed, and in the sphere of consumption, labour power is (re)produced. "Production is consumption; consumption is production. Consumptive production. Productive consumption" (MECW 28, 30). Production is not possible without demand, and consumption does not take place without material: "No consumption without production; no production without consumption" (MECW 28, 30). Moreover, the process of production is determined by circulation of labour power as well as by means of production, whereas circulation itself is a product of production. Production, circulation, and consumption are not "identical, but . . . they are all elements of a totality, differences within a unity [. . .] There is an interaction between the different moments" (MECW 28, 36–37). Nevertheless, production, circulation, and consumption are not equal spheres in the economy; production is rather "the dominant moment, both with regard to itself in the contradictory determination of production and with regard to the other moments. The process always starts afresh with production [. . .] A definite [mode of; TA] production thus determines a definite [mode of; TA] consumption, distribution, exchange and *definite relations of these different moments to*

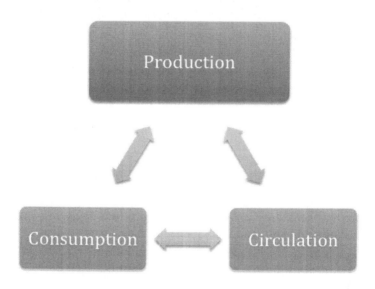

Figure 6.1 Production, circulation, and consumption as dialectically mediated spheres of the modern economy.

one another. Production *in its one-sided form*, however, is in its turn also determined by the other moments" (MECW 28, 36).

Based on the distinction of production, circulation, and consumption, a typology of surveillance in the economy can be constructed. Such a typology will be outlined in the next subsection.

6.3.2. Internet Surveillance in the Spheres of the Economy

Illustrative examples of economic online surveillance in the spheres of production, circulation, and consumption will be presented. The next three subsections are therefore structured according to this distinction.

6.3.2.1. Internet Surveillance in the Sphere of Production

The *Electronic Monitoring and Surveillance Survey* (American Management Association and the ePolicy Institute 2008) offers interesting examples of Internet surveillance in the sphere of production: according to the American Management Association and the ePolicy Institute (2008), who undertake an annual quantitative survey about electronic monitoring and surveillance with approximately three hundred US companies, "more than one fourth of employers have fired workers for misusing e-mail and nearly one third have fired employees for misusing the Internet". More than 40% of the studied companies monitor e-mail traffic of their workers, and 66% of the corporations monitor Internet connections. In addition, most companies use software to block non-work-related websites such as sexual or pornographic sites, game sites, social networking sites, entertainment sites, shopping sites, and sport sites. The American Management Association and the ePolicy Institute (2008) also stress that companies track "content, keystrokes, and time spent at the keyboard [. . .] store and review computer files [. . .] monitor the blogosphere to see what is being written about the company, and [. . .] monitor social networking sites". Furthermore, about 30% of the companies were also firing employees for non-work related e-mail and Internet usage such as "inappropriate or offensive language" and "viewing, downloading, or uploading inappropriate/offensive content" (American Management Association and the ePolicy Institute 2008). This example shows that companies use surveillance and exercise violence in order to control certain behaviour of workers. Corporations control the economic behaviour of people and coerce individuals in order to produce specific commodities for accumulating profit and for guaranteeing the production of surplus value. In the modern production process, primarily electronic surveillance is used to document and control workers' behaviour and communication to guarantee the production of surplus value.

6.3.2.2. Internet Surveillance in the Sphere of Circulation

An interesting phenomenon of surveillance in the sphere of circulation is applicant surveillance: Rosalind Searle (2006, 343) states in this context that "checking procedures are increasingly utilised to authenticate candidates' data. In several countries financial services authorities have sanctioned formal vetting, often outsourcing it to external contractors [. . .] such as Kroll and Carratu International". The corporate investigation company Carratu International is headquartered in London. The company operates around the world, serving national and multinational corporations, insurance companies, law firms, and financial institutions, which are primarily found in the Fortune 500 and the Financial Times Top 100 rankings (Carratu International). Carratu International offers background screening services for companies and government agencies who want to check personal information about new job applicants. If Carratu International realizes a company's application procedure, job candidates have to complete a detailed questionnaire on the Internet as part of their application, which is sent invisibly to Carratu International (Searle 2006, 343). Carratu International argues that pre-employment screening is crucial, because up to 80% of new job candidates give incorrect information about themselves.

According to Carratu International, the only opportunity to "know that the information provided is complete and honest" is to undertake a systematic off- and online check of information such as personal data and information on civil litigation, credit history, bankruptcy, employment history, educational achievements, professional qualifications, and professional or occupational licensing. In addition, Carratu International provides three levels of off- and online pre-employment screening at different prices: the basic service includes data analyses of items such as address, educational qualification, and employment history. The intermediate service includes the basic service plus searches of the media, ownership records, company directorship, and judicial data. Finally, the professional level includes an investigation of "all details contained on the application document, carry[ing; TA] out all checks as detailed in Level Two validations, together with additional relevant research and investigations to confirm the probity and standing of the applicant" (Carratu International). Carratu International is a threat to the job candidates' privacy, because the applicants assume their personal information is only shared with the company where they are applying, but the candidates do not know that their information is sent to Carratu International. Carratu International and their entrepreneurial clients use surveillance and exercise violence in order to control certain behaviour of people. Carratu International also offers surveillance services of existing employees such as monitoring e-mail traffic and Internet usage (Internet surveillance in the sphere of production). This indicates that economic surveillance also occurs in combinations of different spheres and that forms of surveillance in the sphere of production, circulation, and consumption are interconnected.

6.3.2.3. Internet Surveillance in the Sphere of Consumption

To examine Internet surveillance in the sphere of consumption, the example of Google and DoubleClick can be outlined: According to Alexa Internet, of the top websites, Google has the most visits on the Internet. Google uses a wide range of methods to collect data about its users, namely click tracking (to log clicks of users), log files (to store server requests), JavaScript and web bugs (to check users' visits), as well as cookies (to record individual actions) (Stalder and Mayer 2009, 102). DoubleClick is one of the main projects of Google (Google 2008). It is a global leader in ad serving and has developed sophisticated methods in order to collect, analyze, and assess huge amounts of users' data on the Internet (Campbell and Carlson 2002, 596–597). Google (2007; 2008) acquired DoubleClick in 2008 for $US 3.1 billion. DoubleClick is headquartered in New York City. It was founded in 1996 and works for leading digital publishers, marketers, and agencies around the world, such as About, Durex, Ford, Friendster, Optimedia, Scripps, and MTV (Double-Click). Ad-serving companies such as DoubleClick use methods by placing advertisements on websites and analyzing their efficiency. DoubleClick develops and provides Internet ad serving services that are sold primarily to advertisers and publishers. DoubleClick's main product is known as DART (Dynamic Advertising, Reporting, and Targeting). DART is an ad-serving programme that uses a complex algorithm; it is primarily developed for publishers and advertisers to "ensure" that they "get the right message, to the right person, at the right time, on the right device" (DoubleClick). Double-Click collects personal data such as users' individual behaviour, preferences, and interests from many websites with the help of automated computer processes and sells these data to advertising agencies in order to guarantee the production of surplus value and to accumulate profit.

In this section, Internet surveillance in the context of the economy was analyzed. Based on the foundations of a critical political-economy approach, the distinction of production, circulation, and consumption in the economy was introduced in order to establish a typology of Internet surveillance in the economy. Illustrative examples of economic online surveillance in the spheres of production, circulation, and consumption were presented.

6.4. CONCLUSION

The overall aim of this chapter was to clarify how we can theorize and systemize Internet surveillance in the modern economy. The chapter constructed theoretically founded typologies in order to systemize the existing literature of Internet surveillance studies and to analyze examples of surveillance. Therefore, it mainly was a theoretical approach combined with illustrative examples, advanced from the abstract to the concrete level.

Foundations of Internet surveillance studies were discussed in the second section. In the third section, a critical contribution to Internet surveillance studies was drawn in order to distinguish Internet surveillance into the spheres of production, circulation, and consumption. Based on these findings, we were able to systemize illustrative examples of Internet surveillance in the modern economy such as the Electronic Monitoring and Surveillance Survey, Carratu International, and DoubleClick into the spheres of production, circulation, and consumption.

As shown in this chapter, economic actors such as corporations undertake surveillance and exercise violence in order to control certain behaviours, and in most cases people do not know that they are being surveilled. To guarantee production of surplus value and accumulate profit, corporations control economic behaviour of people and coerce them to produce or buy specific commodities. Therefore, one can assume that economic online surveillance is a negative phenomenon of modern societies, which should be questioned and struggled against. Based on Gandy (1993, 230–231), Castells (2001, 182–184), Parenti (2003, 207–212), Ogura (2006, 291–293), Lyon (1994, 159–225; 2001, 126–140; 2007a, 159–178; 2007b, 368–377), Fuchs (2009, 115–117) and Sandoval (in this volume), some political recommendations can be drawn in order to overcome economic online surveillance:

- The first recommendation is that support is needed for critical privacy movements on the Internet in order to develop counter-hegemonic power and advance critical awareness of surveillance.
- As Lyon suggests: "Such public awareness of surveillance issues could further be raised through professional groups and organizations, especially those directly concerned with computing, information management, and so on" (Lyon 1994, 223).
- Lyon also (2001, 127) identifies the importance of political activism by critical citizens: "Films, consumer groups, Internet campaigns and international watchdogs are just some of the ways that ongoing surveillance practices are brought to the surface of our consciousness, and thus overtly into the realm of ethical evaluation and political response."
- According to Fuchs (2009, 116), "critical citizens, critical citizens' initiatives, consumer groups, social movement groups, critical scholars, unions, data protection specialists/groups, consumer protection specialists/groups, critical politicians, critical political parties observe closely the relationship of surveillance and corporations and document instances where corporations and politicians take measures that threaten privacy or increase the surveillance of citizens".
- In addition, Lyon recommends supporting cyber-activism and "counter-surveillance" (Lyon 1994, 159) in order to surveil corporate surveillants or rather to watch the watchers.
- Parenti (2003, 212) suggests civil disobedience, rebellion, and protest: "It will compel regulators to tell corporations, police, schools, hospitals, and other institutions that there are limits. As a society, we want to say: Here you may not go. Here you may not record. Here you may not track and identify people. Here you may not trade and analyze information and build dossiers".
- A further recommendation is to create non-profit, non-commercial social networking platforms on the Internet such as Kaioo (Fuchs 2009, 116; Sandoval in this volume argues for an alternative web 2.0). Kaioo

is owned by the non-profit organization OpenNetworX, has been available since 2007, and has currently about 30,000 users. Kaioo's privacy terms are created in common and can be edited online by every user. In addition, the data belong to their users (Kaioo). OpenNetworX can do so, because they are not interested in targeting advertising and they do not need to produce surplus value and accumulate profit.

- "To try to advance critical awareness and to surveil corporate and political surveillers are important political moves for guaranteeing civil rights, but they will ultimately fail if they do not recognize that electronic surveillance is not a technological issue that can be solved by technological means or by different individual behaviours, but only by bringing about changes of society" (Fuchs 2009, 116). Therefore, Internet surveillance has to be put into the larger context of societal problems in public discourse. "We should look at the whole macro picture." (Ogura 2006, 292)
- Finally, Internet surveillance is caused by economic and political issues and is inherent in modern society. It is neither just a technical issue, nor an individual problem, but a societal problem. Internet surveillance is a crucial phenomenon, but there are a lot of other features influencing contemporary society, such as information, neoliberalism, globalization, and capital.

ACKNOWLEDGMENTS

The research presented in this paper was conducted in the project "Social Networking Sites in the Surveillance Society", funded by the Austrian Science Fund (FWF): project number P 22445-G17. Project coordination: Dr. Christian Fuchs.

REFERENCES

Albrechtslund, Anders. 2008. Online social networking as participatory surveillance [cited 07.09.2010]. http://firstmonday.org/htbin/cgiwrap/bin/ojs/index.php/fm/article/view/2142/1949 (accessed on ???).

Alexa, Internet. [cited 07.09.2010]. http://www.alexa.com (accessed on ???).

American Management Association and The ePolicy Institute. 2008. *Electronic monitoring and surveillance 2007 survey* [cited 07.09.2010 http://www.amanet.org/training/seminars/2007-Electronic-Monitoring-and-Surveillance-Survey-41.aspx (accessed on ???).

Andrejevic, Mark. 2002. The work of being watched: interactive media and the exploitation of self-disclosure. *Critical Studies in Media Communication* 19 (2): 230–248.

———. 2004. *Reality TV: The work of being watched.* Lanham: Rowman & Littlefield.

———. 2007a. *iSpy: Surveillance and power in the interactive era.* Lawrence: University Press of Kansas.

———. 2007b. Surveillance in the digital enclosure. *The Communication Review* 10 (4): 295–317.

Campbell, John Edward and Matt Carlson. 2002. Panopticon.com: online surveillance and the commodification of privacy. *Journal of Broadcasting & Electronic Media* 46 (4): 586–606.

Carratu, International. [cited 07.09.2010]. http://www.carratu.com/ (accessed on ???).

Castells, Manuel. 2001. *The Internet galaxy: Reflections on the Internet, business, and society.* Oxford: Oxford University Press.

DoubleClick. [cited 07.09.2010]. Retrieved on ??? at: http://www.doubleclick.com (accessed on ???).

Elmer, Greg. 1997. Spaces of surveillance: indexicality and solicitation on the Internet. *Critical Studies in Mass Communication* 14 (2): 182–191.

Foucault, Michel. 1995. *Discipline and punish: The birth of the prison.* New York: Vintage.

———. 2002. The eye of power: a conversation with Jean-Pierre Barou and Michelle Perrot. In *CTRL [Space] Rhetorics of surveillance from Bentham to Big Brother*, ed. Thomas Y. Levin, Ursula Frohne, and Peter Weibel, 94–101. Karlsruhe: ZKM Center for Arts and Media.

———. 2003. *"Society must be defended": Lectures at the Collège De France, 1975–1976.* New York: Picador.

———. 2007. *Security, territory, population: Lectures at the Collège De France, 1977–1978.* New York: Palgrave Macmillan.

Fuchs, Christian. 2008. *Internet and society: Social theory in the information age.* New York: Routledge.

———. 2009. *Social networking sites and the surveillance society: A critical case study of the usage of studiVZ, Facebook, and MySpace by students in Salzburg in the context of electronic surveillance.* Salzburg: Research Group Unified Theory of Information.

———. 2010. Social networking sites and complex technology assessment. *International Journal of E-Politics* 1 (3): 19–38.

Gandy, Oscar. 1993. *The panoptic sort: A political economy of personal information.* Boulder: Westview.

———. 2003. Data mining and surveillance in the post-9/11 environment. In *The intensification of surveillance: Crime, terrorism and warfare in the information era*, ed. Kirstie Ball and Frank Webster, 26–41. London: Pluto.

Google. 2007. *Press center: Google to acquire Doubleclick: Combination will significantly expand opportunities for advertisers, agencies and publishers and improve users' online experience* [cited 07.09.2010]. http://www.google.com/intl/en/press/pressrel/doubleclick.html (accessed on ???).

———. 2008. *Press center: Google closes acquisition of Doubleclick* [cited 07.09.2010]. http://www.google.com/intl/en/press/pressrel/20080311_doubleclick.html (accessed on ???).

———. 2010. *Google Scholar* [cited 10.09.2010]. http://scholar.google.com/ (accessed on ???). .

Gutting, Gary. 1998. Foucault, Michel (1926–84). In *Routledge encyclopedia of philosophy. Volume 4*, ed. Edward Craig and Luciano Floridi, 708–713. London: Routledge.

Kaioo. *About Kaioo* [cited 07.09.2010]. http://kaioo.com/toro/resource/html?locale=en#wiki.9 (accessed on ???).

Koskela, Hille. 2004. Webcams, TV shows and mobile phones: empowering exhibitionism. *Surveillance & Society* 2 (2/3): 199–215.

———. 2006. 'The other side of surveillance': webcams, power and agency. In *Theorizing surveillance: The panopticon and beyond*, ed. David Lyon, 163–181. Cullompton: Willian.

Levi, Michael and David Wall. 2004. Technologies, security, and privacy in the post-9/11 European information society. *Journal of Law and Society* 31 (2): 194–220.

Lyon, David. 1994. *The electronic eye: The rise of surveillance society.* Minneapolis: University of Minnesota Press.

———. 1998. The World Wide Web of surveillance: the Internet and off-world power-flows. *Information, Communication & Society* 1 (1): 91–105.

———. 2001. *Surveillance society: Monitoring everyday life.* Issues in society. Maidenhead: Open University Press.

———. 2003a. Cyberspace, surveillance, and social control: the hidden face of the Internet in Asia. In *Asia.Com: Asia encounters the Internet,* ed. K.C. Ho, Randy Kluver, and Kenneth C. Yang, 67–82. London: Routledge.

———. 2003b. Surveillance technology and surveillance society. In *Modernity and technology,* ed. Thomas J. Misa, Phlip Brey, and Andrew Feenberg, 161–184. Cambridge: MIT Press.

———. 2003c. *Surveillance after September 11.* Cambridge: Polity.

———. 2007a. *Surveillance studies: An overview.* Cambridge: Polity.

———. 2007b. Resisting surveillance. In *The surveillance studies reader,* ed. Sean Hier and Joshua Greenberg, 368–377. Maidenhead: Open University Press.

Marx, Karl (MEW 23). 2005. *Das Kapital: Kritik der politischen Ökonomie: Erster Band: Der Produktionsprozeß des Kapitals.* Berlin: Dietz.

Marx, Karl and Friedrich Engels (MECW 28). 1986. *Collected works, Volume 28.* New York: International.

Miller, Seumas and John Weckert. 2000. Privacy, the workplace and the Internet. *Journal of Business Ethics* 28 (3): 255–265.

Murakami Wood, David. 2009. Situating surveillance studies. *Surveillance & Society* 6 (1): 52–61.

Norris, Clive and Gary Armstrong. 1999. *The maximum surveillance society: The rise of CCTV.* Oxford: Berg.

Ogura, Toshimaru. 2006. Electronic government and surveillance-oriented society. In *Theorizing surveillance: The panopticon and behind,* ed. David Lyon, 270–295. Portland, OR: Willan Publishing.

Parenti, Christian. 2003. *The soft cage: Surveillance in America from slavery to the war on terror.* New York: Basic Books.

Pryor, Benjamin. 2006. Foucault, Michel (1926–1984). In *Encyclopedia of philosophy, Volume 3,* ed. Donald M. Borchert, 698–702. Detroit: Thomson Gale.

Searle, Rosalind. 2006. New technology: the potential impact of surveillance techniques in recruitment practices. *Personal Review* 35 (3): 336–351.

Soanes, Catherine and Angus Stevenson. 2005. Surveillance. *The Oxford dictionary of English* [cited 07.09.2010]. http://www.oxfordreference.com/pub/views/home.html (accessed on ???).

Stalder, Felix and Christine Mayer. 2009. The second index: search engines, personalization and surveillance. In *Deep search: The politics of search beyond Google,* ed. Konrad Becker and Felix Stalder, 98–116. Vienna: Studienverlag.

Turow, Joseph. 2005. Audience construction and culture production: marketing surveillance in the digital age. *The ANNALS of the American Academy of Political and Social Science* 597 (1): 103–121.

———. 2006. Cracking the consumer code: advertising, anxiety and surveillance in the digital age. In *The new politics of surveillance and visibility,* ed. Kevin Hagerty and Richard V. Ericson, 279–307. Toronto: University of Toronto Press.

Turow, Joseph and Michael Hennessy. 2007. Internet privacy and institutional trust: insights from a national survey. *New Media Society* 9 (2): 300–318.

Wall, David. 2003. Mapping out cybercrimes in a cyberspatial surveillant assemblage. In *The intensification of surveillance: Crime terrorism and warfare in the information age,* ed. Kirstie Ball and Frank Webster, 112–136. London: Pluto.

———. 2006. Surveillant Internet technologies and the growth in information capitalism: spams and public trust in the information society. In *The new politics of surveillance and visibility,* ed. Kevin Haggerty and Richard V. Ericson, 340–362. Toronto: University of Toronto Press.

PART II

Case Studies, Applications, And Empirical Perspectives Of Internet Surveillance Studies

7 A Critical Empirical Case Study of Consumer Surveillance on Web 2.0

Marisol Sandoval

7.1. INTRODUCTION

Who are the owners of web 2.0 sites, and what are their motivations for providing their services? Often the owners of web 2.0 platforms are media corporations. Google for example owns YouTube and Blogger, Yahoo owns Flickr, and News Corporation owns Myspace. According to the Forbes 2000 ranking[1] News Corp's assets are $US 56.13 billion, the assets of Google amount to $US 40.5 billion, and the assets of YouTube are $US 14.49 billion. Obviously the aims of these companies are generating profits and increasing their capital stock. At the same time access to the mentioned 2.0 platforms is free of charge. Thus, why do these companies provide web 2.0 services for free? In this context critical scholars (Fuchs 2009b; Scholz 2008) have stressed that web 2.0 is about new business models, based on which user-generated content and user data are exploited for the profit purposes. In this case users receive access to web 2.0 platforms for free, and profit is generated by selling user data and space for advertisements. Selling user data for profit generation requires the surveillance of web 2.0 users for collecting these data. In order to understand how far capital accumulation in web 2.0 is connected to surveillance, in this chapter I address the following question:

> *How does surveillance contribute to capital accumulation on web 2.0, and how do the owners of commercial web 2.0 sites collect and disseminate user information?*

In order to answer this question, first some hypotheses about and theoretical foundations of consumer surveillance on web 2.0 are outlined (section 2). Section 3 describes the method used for the empirical case study. In section 4 the results are described and interpreted. Conclusions are drawn in section 5.

7.2. CONSUMER SURVEILLANCE ON WEB 2.0: THEORETICAL FOUNDATIONS AND HYPOTHESES

In the following I will give a brief outline of the central notions and concepts that are used in this chapter: surveillance, consumer surveillance, and web 2.0.

Neutral definitions of surveillance argue that surveillance does not necessarily imply coercion, domination, or oppression. They focus on the collection, storage, processing, and transmission of information about individuals, groups, masses, or institutions, irrespective of the context, motivations and consequences of surveillance. They either do not refer to the purposes of surveillance and the interests behind surveillance (see for example Ball/Webster 2003, 1; Solove 2004, 42; Bogard 2006, 101; Bogolikos 2007, 590) or they do not judge whether these purposes are normatively desirable or not (see for example or Ball 2006, 297; Clarke 1988, 499; Rule 1973/2007, 21). Sometimes neutral definitions explicitly point at the ambiguity of surveillance (see for example Hier and Greenberg 2007, 381; Lyon 2007, 137; Clarke 1988, 499; Haggerty 2006, 41; Lyon 2003, 13). In contrast to neutral definitions, negative notions of surveillance consider the latter always as a form of domination. Such understandings stress the coercive, hierarchical, and dominative character of surveillance and can for example be found in the work of Michel Foucault (1977/2007), Oscar Gandy (1993), Toshimaru Ogura (2006), and Christian Fuchs (2008; 2009a). So there are on the one hand neutral concepts of surveillance and on the other hand negative ones.

Consumer surveillance can be understood as a form of surveillance that aims at predicting and, in combination with (personalized) advertising, controlling the behaviour of consumers (Turow 2006, 282). Unlike workers, consumers for a long time were not under the control of capital. They were an anonymous mass, buying standardized mass products (Ogura 2006, 273). But as Campbell and Carlson state the "last decades of the twentieth century also saw a massive expansion of efforts to use surveillance technologies to manage consumers" (Campbell and Carlson 2002, 587).

According to Mark Andrejevic, the increased tendency towards consumer surveillance is a reaction to the growing amount and variety of consumer products, which make necessary "techniques to stimulate consumption" (Andrejevic 2002, 235). To stimulate consumption means controlling the behaviour of consumers, that is, to make them buy certain commodities or services. Advertising is used as a means for influencing consumer behaviour. As Turow puts it: "the goal of advertising is straightforward: to persuade people to purchase or otherwise support the product, service or need" (Turow 2006, 282). The more knowledge an advertiser has on consumers and their behaviour, the more specifically they can be addressed by advertising campaigns. Ogura stresses that the main motive for consumer surveillance is to know as many details as possible about the behaviour of unknown customers (Ogura 2006, 271). This allows the creation of personalized marketing campaigns, which are tailored to the habits, lifestyles, attitudes, hobbies, interests, etc. of specific consumers or consumer groups. The idea behind personalized advertising is that the more appealing an ad is to a specific individual the more likely it is that s/he will buy a certain product.

For personalized sales strategies to be successful, marketing campaigns need to create the illusion that individuality and authenticity can be achieved by buying certain consumer products. Contemporary sales strategies thus rest on the surveillance and categorization of consumers as well as on an ideology that ties individuality to specific consumption patterns. Mass media play an important role in disseminating this ideology. In this context Mathiesen has coined the notion of the synopticon. In his view "synopticism, through the modern mass media in general and television in particular, first of all directs and controls or disciplines our consciousness" (Mathiesen 1997, 230). Controlling the behaviour of consumer, that is to make them buy certain commodities and services, also requires controlling their mind. Surveillance and manipulation are two complementary strategies for influencing consumer behaviour. Capital can only be accumulated when commodities and services are sold and surplus is realized. The more commodities people buy, the more capital can be accumulated. Capital is therefore interested in influencing consumer behaviour in order to sell evermore commodities and services. Thus, if consumer surveillance stimulates consumption, it serves the interest of capital.

The term web 2.0 is used for describing technological changes and/or changes in social relations and/or changes in technology usage and/or new business models. It has also been argued that the term web 2.0 describes nothing really new because web 2.0 is not based on fundamental technological advancements (see for example boyd 2007, 17 Scholz 2008, online). Some critical scholars have argued that these terms function as a market ideology for stimulating profit generation. Christian Fuchs for example argues that "the main purpose behind using these terms seems to be a marketing strategy for boosting investment" (Fuchs 2009b, 80; see also Scholz 2008, online).

However, irrespective of whether these terms describe technologically new phenomena or whether they have been used as ideologies for advancing new spheres for capital accumulation, the fact is that the term web 2.0 today is widely used for describing an increasing amount of commercial and non-commercial web applications that have in common the involvement of users in the production of content. Technological refinements have made it much easer for users to produce their own media (Harrison/Barthel 2009, 157, 159).

Most understandings of web 2.0 have in common that they point at this active involvement of users in the production of content, that is user-generated content, as the central characteristic of web 2.0 (boyd 2007, 16; Fuchs 2008, 135; 2009, 81; Cormode/Krishnamurthy 2008, online; O'Reilly 2005, online; Bruns 2007, online; van Dijck 2009, 41; Allen 2008, online; Harrison/Barthel 2009, 157; Kortzfleisch et al. 2008, 74; Jarrett 2008, online; Beer/Burrows 2007, online).

The main hypothesis that underlies this empirical study is:

H: The terms of use and privacy statements of commercial web 2.0 platforms are designed to allow the owners of these platforms to exploit user data for the purpose of capital accumulation.

Zizi Papacharissi and Jan Fernback (2005) conducted a content analysis of privacy statements of 97 online portal sites. They tested the credibility as well as the effectiveness of these statements and found that "privacy statements frequently do not guarantee the protection of personal information but rather serve as legal safeguards for the company by detailing how personal information collected will be used" (Papacharissi and Fernback 2005, 276). Their study focused on the language used in these statements but did not evaluate which information online portal sites do collect and use. In a subsequent discourse analysis of privacy statements they analyzed the rhetoric of four corporate web 2.0 (MSM, Google, Real.com, and Kazaa) applications and found out that privacy statements support profit generation (Fernback and Papacharissi 2007).

The business model of most commercial web 2.0 platforms is to generate profit through selling space for advertisements (Fuchs 2009b, 81; Allen 2008, online). Thus web 2.0 platforms provide their services for free in order to attract as many users as possible (Fuchs 2008, 2009b). Selling space for advertisements in order to generate profit is nothing new. Traditional media companies also employ this strategy. Dallas Smythe (1981) has in this context pointed out that media companies generate profit by selling media consumers as a commodity to advertisers.

Fuchs (2009b) has applied Smythe's notion of the audience commodity to web 2.0. He argues that in contrast to traditional media environments on web 2.0, users are not only recipients but, at the same time, also producers of media content. They can therefore be characterized as prosumers or produsers (Fuchs 2009b; Bruns 2007, online; van Dijck 2009, 4; see also Toffler 1980). Advertisers favour personalized advertisements over mass advertisements because personalized advertisements increase the effectiveness of marketing campaigns (Charters 2002; Fuchs 2009). As personalized advertisements for advertisers are more valuable than mass advertisements, the owners of web 2.0 platforms can charge higher rates for personalized ads. Because personalized advertising is based on information about consumers, I assume that the owners of commercial web 2.0 platforms, in order to increase their profits, surveil users, and sell information about them to advertisers.

This main hypothesis will be tested along with the following three topics and six sub-hypotheses:

1. Advertising (H1a and H1b)
2. Data Collection (H2a and H2b)
3. Data Dissemination (H3a and H3b)

1. Advertising

H1a: The majority of commercial web 2.0 platforms are allowed to target users with personalized advertisements directly on the platform.

H1b: The majority of commercial web 2.0 platforms is allowed to target users with personalized advertisements via e-mail.

The average user of user-generated content sites is highly educated and well paid (van Dijck 2009, 47). Thus, "all UGC [user generated content] users—whether active creators or passive spectators—form an attractive demographic to advertisers" (van Dijck 2009, 47). Furthermore the technical features of Internet technologies such as web 2.0 provide various means for personalized advertising (see for example: Campbell and Carlson 2002; Starke-Meyerring and Gurak 2007; Wall 2006).

Because the aim of every company is to increase its profits, it is likely that the owners of web 2.0 platforms will make use of the technical possibilities and the available information about users for purposes of profit accumulation. Because selling space for personalized advertisements is a potential source for profit accumulation (Allen 2008, online; Fuchs 2009; van Dijck 2009), I hypothesize that commercial web 2.0 companies will place such ads directly on the platform (see H1a) as well as distribute them via e-mail (see H1b).

2. Data Collection

H2a: The majority of commercial Web 2.0 platforms are allowed to track the surfing behaviour of users for advertising purposes.

User information available on web 2.0 platforms not only includes information that users provide by themselves, but also information about their surfing behaviour, IP address, and their technical equipment, which is collected automatically while they are using the platform.

José van Dijck (2009) argues that especially automatically tracked data about the surfing behaviour of users is of interest for advertisers. Petersen (2008, online) also stresses that what is valuable on web 2.0 sites is not content, but context data. Advertisers are not only interested in user data but also in their actual behaviour. Tracking data about consumer behaviour and providing this information to advertisers constitutes another potential source of profit for web 2.0 companies.

H2b: In order to use commercial web 2.0 platforms, users in a majority of cases have to provide the following personal information: e-mail address, full name, country of residence, gender, and birthday.

Although data about the surfing behaviour and IP addresses of users can be tracked automatically, other personal information has to be actively provided by users. Van Dijck states that in order to use a web 2.0 site, users have to register and provide information about themselves such as name, gender, e-mail address, nationality, etc. (van Dijck 2009, 47). Web 2.0 users are both "content providers" and "data providers" (van Dijck 2009, 47). The more data web 2.0 users provide, the more data can be sold and the more profit can be generated. Thus the owners of web 2.0 platforms are interested in gathering as much information about users as possible. One possibility for forcing users to provide data about themselves is an obligatory registration on the platform.

3. Data Dissemination
    H3a: The majority of commercial web 2.0 platforms are allowed to sell aggregated information.
    H3b: The majority of commercial web 2.0 platforms are allowed to sell personally identifiable information.

Web 2.0 companies can increase their profits by selling not only space for advertisements, but also information about users to advertising companies. These companies use this information in order to create targeted advertisements. In terms of the panoptic sort (Gandy, 1993) this means that web 2.0 platforms identify information about consumers and pass it on to marketing companies that categorize and assess this information in order to create personalized advertisements.

A common distinction in regard to personal data is the differentiation between personal information and personally identifiable information (PII). PII is generally conceived as information that reveals the identity of a unique person (Krishnamurthy and Wills 2009, 7; Reis 2007, 383). It is "a unique piece of data or indicator that can be used to identify, locate, or contact a specific individual" (Reis 2007, 383). PII includes full name, contact information (mail address, e-mail address, phone number), bank and credit information, and social security number (Reis 2007, 383). Information that is collected anonymously (for example, age, gender, race, purchasing habits), as well as aggregate information about a group of individuals, is generally not considered as PII (Reis 2007, 383).

Both kinds of personal information can potentially be sold to advertisers. Thus selling this information is another possibility for satisfying a web 2.0 company's desire for capital accumulation.

7.3. RESEARCH METHOD

The hypotheses described in section 2 were addressed by conducting a content analysis of the terms of use and privacy statements of commercial web 2.0 platforms. It mainly focused on quantitative measures. Nevertheless the quantification of results needs to be based on a qualitative analysis of the sample. As Krippendorff states, "the quantitative/qualitative distinction is a mistaken dichotomy" (Krippendorff 2004, 86) because "all reading of texts is qualitative, even when certain characteristics of a text are later converted into numbers" (Krippendorff 2004, 16). Krippendorff mentions four important components of a content analysis (compare: Krippendorff 2004, 83). These components are:

- Unitizing (selecting those texts that are of interest in order to answer the research questions)
- Sampling (selecting a manageable subset of units)
- Recording/coding (transforming texts into analyzable representation)
- Narrating (answering the research questions)

The methodological procedure employed in this empirical study was oriented on these principles. First relevant texts (units), were identified. Second, a sample of all units was selected, which was subsequently coded. In a fourth step, the hypotheses were answered by evaluating the results of the coding (see section 4).

The units, on which this content analysis is based, are the terms of use and privacy statements of web 2.0 platforms. These documents constitute a legal contract between owners and users of web 2.0 platforms, and define rights and responsibilities of both platform owner and users. Because they describe what platform owners are allowed to do with user data (Papacharissi and Fernback 2005; Fernback and Papacharissi 2007; van Dijck 2009, 47; Campbell and Carlson 2002, 59), these documents are a viable source for figuring out how far platform owners are allowed to collect and disseminate user data.

The sample selection was based on the Alexa Top Internet Sites Ranking. Alexa provides a daily updated ranking of the 1,000,000 most popular sites on the Internet. The ranking is compiled based on a combination of the number of daily visitors and page views (see Alexa.com). The sample was selected based on the 1,000,000 most popular sites ranking from April 27, 2009. All web 2.0 platforms that were among the top 200 sites were selected.

For the purpose of this study web 2.0 sites were defined as sites that feature content that is entirely or almost entirely produced by users (see section 2). According to this understanding, web 2.0 involves wikis, weblogs, social networking sites, and file-sharing sites (sharehoster).

The selection process resulted in a sample of 71 sites that mainly feature user-generated content. Two of these had to be excluded because they provided neither terms of use nor privacy statements.[2] Another four sites were excluded because they are subsites of sites that were listed earlier in the ranking.[3] Thirteen sites had to be excluded because of language barriers. On these sites, the privacy policies and terms of use were not available in English, German, or Spanish[4] and therefore could not be coded. The final sample consisted of 52 web 2.0 platforms. The terms of use and privacy statements of these platforms were downloaded on April 27, 2009, and analyzed according to a predefined coding scheme.

The construction of the coding scheme followed the six subhypotheses, underlying this study. As a pretest, the privacy policies and terms of use of ten randomly selected platforms were analyzed according to the initial coding scheme. After the pretest, the coding scheme was redefined and extended.

The final coding scheme was structured along the following four main categories:

- General characteristics
- Advertising
- Data collection
- Data dissemination

Within the category "general characteristics", two subcategories were used in order to evaluate under which conditions users can access the platform and how the user has to accept the terms of use. The category "advertising" aimed at grasping the advertising practices of web 2.0 companies and consisted of five subcategories that addressed advertising, personalized advertising, third-party advertising, e-mail advertising for the platforms own products and services and e-mail advertising for third-party products and services. The category "data collection" consisted of four subcategories. These were used in order to find out how and what information about users is collected on web 2.0 platforms. The subcategories included: employment of behavioural tracking techniques for advertising purposes, association of automatically tracked data with a user's profile information, required information for platform usage, and data combination. The category "data dissemination" comprised three subcategories concerning whether platform owners are allowed to sell statistically aggregated, non-personally identifying information and personally identifying information about users to third parties. If the analyzed terms of use and privacy policies did not contain information on a specific category, this category was coded 99, i.e., "not specified".

7.4. RESULTS

The content analysis was based on a sample of 52 web 2.0 platforms: 51 of them are commercial. The only non-commercial platform among the sample is Wikipedia. Since the hypotheses refer to commercial web 2.0 platforms, Wikipedia was excluded from the data evaluation. Thus the following results are derived from a content analysis of 51 commercial web 2.0 platforms. Section 7.4.1 describes the quantified results of the content analysis and answers the hypotheses. In section 7.4.1 the results are interpreted and supplemented with some qualitative findings.

7.4.1. Description of Results

The following description of results is structured along three main topics of the content analysis

1. Advertising
2. Data Collection
3. Data Dissemination

1. Advertising
   H1a: The majority of commercial web 2.0 platforms is allowed to target users with personalized advertisements on the platform.

Of all analyzed commercial web 2.0 platforms, 94.2% display advertisements. Only on 5.8% of all analyzed platforms advertisements will never be shown to users. Figure 7.1 illustrates that on 74.5% of all analyzed platforms personalized advertisements can be found. In these cases the user does not have any way to deactivate this feature (opt-out). On another 15.7%, personalized advertising is activated as a standard setting, but the user is allowed to opt out. This means that in total, on 90.2% of all analyzed web 2.0 platforms personalized advertisements are potentially shown to users. Only 9.8% of all analyzed platforms never feature personalized advertisements.

Of all commercial web 2.0 platforms, 58.9% explicitly state in their privacy statements that they allow third-party advertising companies to place cookies on users' computers for personalized advertising purposes,

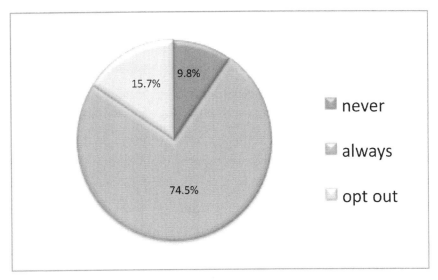

Figure 7.1. Personalized advertising on commercial web 2.0 platforms, N=51.

without giving the user a way to opt out. Another 7.8% allow users to opt out of third-party cookies. This means that on 66.7% of all analyzed platforms third-party cookies are activated as a standard setting. Only 3.9% of all commercial web 2.0 platforms explicitly state that they do not allow third parties to use cookies in order to collect information about users. The remaining 29.4% of all analyzed privacy statements do not refer to whether or not they support third-party cookies.

These results confirm H1a: On the vast majority of commercial web 2.0 platforms, users receive personalized advertisements; on 74.5% of all analyzed platforms personalized advertisements are always shown to users; 15.7% provide the possibility to deactivate personalized ads. Furthermore 56.9% of all analyzed platforms allow third parties to place cookies on a user's computer. On 7.8% third-party cookies are allowed unless a user explicitly deactivates this feature.

> H1b: The majority of commercial web 2.0 platforms are allowed to target users with personalized advertisements via e-mail

On 58.9% of all analyzed commercial web 2.0 platforms, the default setting is set so the user's e-mail addresses are used for advertising the platforms' own products and services. On 19.7% of all analyzed platforms this standard setting is unchangeable, but 39.2% do permit users to modify this default setting and to opt out of receiving such advertising e-mails. Another 17.6% allow users to opt in for receiving advertising e-mails regarding the platforms products and services, and 23.5% never use the user's e-mail address for their own advertising purposes (see Table 7.1).

Of all analyzed commercial web 2.0 platforms, 62.7% do not use users' e-mail addresses for advertising third-party products and services; 25.5% by default send advertising e-mails for third-party products and services; 15.7% give users a way to deactivate this feature (opt-out). On 9.8% of all analyzed sites users are not allowed to opt out of receiving advertising e-mails for third-party products and services. On 11.8% of all commercial web 2.0 platforms users can opt in for receiving third-party advertising e-mails (see Table 7.1).

Using the contact information provided by users for advertising products and services is a common practice on web 2.0. Nevertheless, on the majority of sites (56.8%), the user is put in the position to choose whether or not s/he wants to receive advertising e-mails (opt-in or opt-out). Less frequently the user's e-mail address is used for advertising third-party products and services. On the majority of sites (62.7%) users will not receive third-party advertising e-mails.

2. Data Collection
> H2a: The majority of commercial web 2.0 platforms are allowed to track the surfing behaviour of users for advertising purposes.

Table 7.1 Advertising E-mails on Commercial Web 2.0 Sites, N=51

	Advertising e-mails for the platforms products and services	Advertising e-mails for third-party products and services
Never	23.5%	62.7%
Always	19.7%	9.8%
Opt-out	39.2%	15.7%
Opt-in	17.6%	11.8%

The data evaluation confirms this hypothesis and shows that the vast majority of commercial web 2.0 platforms are allowed to track the surfing behaviour for advertising purposes: 94.1% of all commercial web 2.0 platforms use behavioural tracking techniques for surveilling the behaviour of users on the site; 80.4% use the gathered information for advertising purposes.

H2b: In order to use commercial web 2.0 platforms, users in a majority of cases have to provide the following personal information: e-mail address, full name, country of residence, gender, and birthday.

On all analyzed commercial web 2.0 platforms, users have to complete a registration form for receiving full access to all services. During the registration process, users are required to provide certain information. On all platforms, users have to provide their e-mail address. Name as well as birthday is required on 54.9%, gender on 43.10%, and country on 37.3 % of all analyzed web 2.0 platforms.

3. Data Dissemination
     H3a: The majority of commercial web 2.0 platforms is allowed to sell aggregate information.

Of all analyzed privacy statements of commercial web 2.0 platforms, 86.3% state that platform owners are allowed to pass on aggregate information about users to third parties for any purpose. In these cases the user does not have a way to opt out. Only 2% allow users to opt out of passing on aggregate information about themselves; 5.9% do not explicitly state whether or not circulating aggregate information is allowed. Only 5.9% declare that aggregate information is never handed on to advertisers (see Figure 7.2). Aggregated information involves all kind of information that does not personally identify a specific user. Thus it can include demographic information and other information provided by users (except of name contact information and social security number), as well as information regarding the surfing patterns of users.

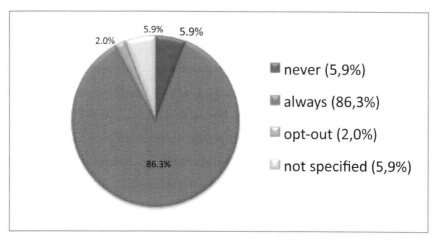

Figure 7.2. Dissemination of aggregate information on commercial web 2.0 platforms, N=51.

Furthermore the privacy statements also indicate that 58.9% of all commercial platforms allow third parties to track the surfing patterns of users directly on the platform (see H1a). In this case instead of gathering and selling aggregated information about users, platform owners sell access to user data to third parties that gather information about users on their own.

These results confirm H3a and show that almost 90% of all commercial platforms are allowed to aggregate information about users and sell this information to advertisers.

> H3b: The majority of commercial web 2.0 platforms are allowed to sell personally identifiable information.

On the one hand 29.4% of all analyzed commercial web 2.0 platforms in their privacy statements state that they under no circumstances pass on any information that identifies a user personally. On the other hand 27.5% are by all means allowed to circulate personally identifiable information. On 13.7% of all platforms, personally identifiable information is only handed onto third parties until a user opts out: 21.60% have to ask for a user's permission to pass on personally identifiable information—that is, users have to explicitly opt in. And 7.8 % of all platforms in their privacy statements do not state how they deal with data that personally identifies an individual (see Table 7.2).

As these data show, personally identifiable information is less frequently passed on to third parties than aggregated information. In approximately one-third of all cases (35.3%) users are allowed to choose (opt-in, opt-out) whether or not they want to allow the dissemination of information that personally identifies them. In approximately a second third (29.4%) of all

Table 7.2   Dissemination of Personally Identifiable Information on Commercial
Web 2.0 Platforms, N=51

	Never	Always	Opt-out	Opt-in	Not specified
Dissemination of personally identifiable information on commercial web 2.0 platforms	29.4%	27.5%	13.7%	21.6%	7.8%

cases personally identifiable information will under no circumstances be passed on to third parties. Approximately a third (27.5%) of all platforms do sell PII under all circumstances.

7.4.2. Interpretation of Results

The first important result of this study is that there is only one non-commercial platform among the 52 most popular web 2.0 sites (1.9%). The fact that contemporary web 2.0 is mainly a commercial web 2.0 has far-reaching consequences for users, because the main aim of these platforms is profit maximization. As will be shown, this motive of profit maximization at the same time creates financial benefits for platform owners and a broad range of disadvantages for individuals and society.

This study has confirmed the assumption that the business model of commercial web 2.0 platforms is based on advertising. Thus, users receive access to web 2.0 platforms for free, and profit is generated by selling space for advertisements. The content analysis has shown that in more than 90% of all cases these advertisements are even personalized. Personalized advertising aims at targeting specific individuals or groups of individuals in a way that fits their lifestyle, interests, habits, or attitudes. It is based on the assumption that the more specifically an ad is directed towards an individual, the more likely it will influence his/her actual shopping behaviour. Thus this form of advertising is considered more effective than mass advertising. Therefore the owners of web 2.0 platforms can charge higher advertising rates for personalized advertisements, which allow them to increase their profits.

Because web 2.0 is based on user-generated content it potentially constitutes a useful data source for advertisers. Apart from selling space for advertisements, selling these data is another convenient strategy for web 2.0 platform owners to generate profits. But before this information can be sold, it needs to be collected and stored. The more user information is available to platform owners, the more information can be sold and the more profit can be generated. This study shows that there are two main ways to collect data in web 2.0: First, users provide information about themselves either in the course of using the site or during the registration process. The fact that on 100% of all analyzed sites, registration is required for receiving full access to the platform's services ensures that every user provides at least a minimum of information about him/herself. As the following quotation from the terms of service of Tagged.com illustrates, commercial web 2.0 platforms try to learn as much as possible from each user:

> During registration, users also complete survey questions that provide information that is helpful for us to understand the demographics and consumer behavior of our users, such as identifying the users' eye color, style, personality type, favorite color, sport, food, activity or TV show, post-graduation plans or graduation year. (Tagged Privacy Policy, accessed on April 27, 2009)

Second, on most commercial platforms (94.1%) behavioural tracking methods are used to automatically store data on a user's hardware, software, or site usage patterns. This double strategy for collecting information about users that can be used for personalized advertising is for example expressed in the YouTube privacy policy:

> We may use a range of information, including cookies, web beacons, IP addresses, usage data and other non-personal information about your computer or device (such as browser type and operating system) to provide you with relevant advertising. (YouTube Privacy Policy, accessed on April 27, 2009)

As such the fact that this information about users is available is not necessarily problematic; risks for users rather arise through the usage of this data, particularly when this information is disseminated to third parties. This content analysis illustrates that, in fact, around 90% of all commercial web 2.0 platforms are allowed to pass on aggregated information about users to third parties. Aggregated information includes all kinds of statistical data about users, which do not identify an individual personally. This kind of information is thus ranging from site usage patterns to sociodemographic information to information about social relationships with other users, etc. Furthermore, according to this study up to 63% of all commercial web 2.0 platforms even sell information that identifies an individual personally.

The majority of all commercial platforms allow third-party advertising companies to place cookies on the computer of users in order to collect information about them for advertising purposes. The ways in which these third parties deal with user information is not described in the platforms' own terms of use, but subject to the third party's terms of service. This is for example pointed out in the Fotolog privacy policy:

> In some cases, our business partners may use cookies on our site. For example, an advertiser like Google may place a cookie on your computer to keep track of what country you are from so they show ads in

the correct language. Fotolog has no access to or control over these cookies. (Fotolog Privacy Policy, accessed on April 27, 2009)

Whereas in terms of profit, personalized advertising is beneficial for advertisers (because it increases the effectiveness of advertising) as well as for the owners of web 2.0 platforms (because it allows them to charge higher advertising rates and to sell user information), it brings along a number of disadvantages and risks for web 2.0 users. These risks for users arise due to the fact that the creation of personalized ads requires detailed information about a consumer's habits, attitudes, lifestyles, etc., that is, the surveillance of users. In the following three main undesirable consequences of consumer surveillance and personalized advertising for users are identified:

1. Negative consequences for the personal life of web 2.0 users:

The fact that web 2.0 users are surveilled and information about them is sold to third parties can have undesirable consequences for individual users. The available information about them, which is stored in databases, can be combined with information from other sources and can produce a detailed picture about the life of an individual. As the following quotation from the Netlog privacy policy illustrates, advertising networks can access many different web 2.0 sites and are thus able and allowed to combine information from various sources. This quotation furthermore shows the limited reach of terms of services and privacy policies: Third parties are indeed allowed to access user information on a specific web 2.0 site; however, the ways that they deal with this information is not covered by the specific website's privacy policy, but rather is subject to the third party's policies.

> Your online profile will also be used by other websites in the BlueLitihium Network to provide you with targeted advertising. These websites may combine the personal data collected on the Netlog website with personal data collected from other sources. Consult the privacy policies of our advertisement providers to learn more about how your personal data are used by them. (Netlog Privacy Policy, accessed on April 27, 2009)

It therefore becomes almost impossible to determine which information is collected and to whom it is disseminated. The more commercial web 2.0 applications an individual is using, the more likely it is that widespread information about him/her is available and disseminated to various companies. This is problematic because it is not determinable for what purposes this information will be used and if the individual agrees to all these uses of his/her data. The possible undesirable consequences for an individual are manifold and range from political surveillance to professional and economic disadvantages due to employer surveillance to disadvantages regarding health or life insurance. In the light of newly developed mobile applications such as the face recognizer "Recognizr" from the software company The Astonishing Tribe (TAT), the fact that a broad range of information about individuals is stored in databases becomes increasingly threatening. "Recognizr" is a facial recognition application for mobile phones, which retrieves information about strangers from web 2.0 sites if they are photographed with a cameraphone. Thus this application potentially allows the identification of every web 2.0 user everywhere and any time. It also allows instant retrieval of a broad range of information about users from their 2.0 profiles simply by taking a user's picture. In economic contexts, such an application could be used as another tool for enhancing capital accumulation by personalizing shop offers according to a person's shopping habits, which can be instantly retrieved from a person's web 2.0 profiles. In political contexts, it can have negative effects on individuals (e.g., the identification of protesters during a demonstration) and as a consequence limit the right to political opposition and protest. At the moment "Recognizr" only allows identifying individuals who are using this application as well (The Astonishing Tribe, 2010, online). Nevertheless it could potentially also be used for identifying persons that have not given their permission.

2. Exploitation of web 2.0 users:

In addition to potentially causing personal disadvantages for individuals, a second problem is that realizing profit out of personalized advertising also constitutes a form of exploitation of web 2.0 users (Fuchs 2010). Christian Fuchs (2010) has pointed out that on web 2.0 sites, users are productive workers because they create media content and usage data that result in profit. Without this content, web 2.0 sites would not be attractive to users, and the owners of these sites would therefore be unable to sell user data for advertising purposes and no profit could be generated. Tiziana Terranova has in this context spoken of "unwaged, enjoyed and exploited, free labor" (Terranova 2000, 33).

Advertising on web 2.0 platform is only rewarding for advertisers if the site's users form an attractive demographic audience of potential consumers. Thus only if a platform has enough users, will advertisers be willing to buy space for ads. User data can only be sold when enough users leave their information on the site. This shows that without the work done by users who produce and upload content, it would be impossible to generate profit. Thus the owners of web 2.0 platforms exploit the labour power of users in order to satisfy their profit interests.

3. Manipulation and the reinforcement of a consumer culture:

Another undesirable consequence of this web 2.0 business model is that users are permanently confronted and annoyed with ads that try to foster the illusion that individuality and authenticity can be achieved by buying certain consumer products. Because most web 2.0 sites are commercial and employ an advertising-based business model, for users it becomes nearly impossible to escape from this atmosphere of consumption.

As the terms of use and privacy statements of most commercial web 2.0 platforms ensure that platforms owners are allowed to sell space for advertisements and user data to third parties, commercial web 2.0 users do not have any way to protect themselves from these undesirable consequences unless they refrain from using these commercial platforms. If users do not agree to the terms set by platform owners they are excluded from using their services. The results of this content analysis confirm that the terms of use allow the platform owners to force users to provide data about themselves by threat of exclusion. This unequal power relation between platform users and owners, which puts platform owners in the position to set the terms of the contract, is expressed in the following passage of Google's privacy policy:

> You can decline to submit personal information to any of our services, in which case Google may not be able to provide those services to you. (Google Privacy Policy, accessed on April 27, 2009)

The business practices of commercial web 2.0 providers do not only have undesirable consequences for the individual user, but also negatively affect society as a whole. Personalized advertising brings about a commodification of information because data are increasingly turned into a tradable commodity. The web 2.0 business model thus contributes to the commercialization of the Internet on the one hand because the omnipresence of advertising creates an atmosphere of consumption and, on the other hand, because this business model is based on the transformation of user information into commodities.

Personalized advertising has undesirable consequences for web 2.0 users and society as a whole, but it is beneficial for business interests of the owners of commercial web 2.0 platforms and advertisers. It allows owners to charge higher advertising rates, and it increases the effectiveness of advertisers' marketing campaigns.

This unequal relation of advantages for owners and advertisers and disadvantages for users and society is not reflected in the terms of use and privacy statements of commercial web 2.0 platforms. These documents rather aim at creating the illusion that personalized advertising is beneficial for web 2.0 users. The language used obviously intends to approach users in a personal way to create an atmosphere of friendship; but these documents ideologically mask the unequal power relation between owners, who design the terms of use in a way that allows them to generate profit out of users' work and information, and users, who have to accept them. In this spirit Hyves.com for example writes

> Hyves consists of a network of friends. We deal with your information as you would expect from friends. So Hyves takes your privacy very seriously and will deal with your information with due care. (Hyves Privacy Policy, accessed on April 27, 2009)

Furthermore the language of the terms of use and privacy statements describes personalized advertising as beneficial for web 2.0 users, because it will ensure that users only receive "relevant and useful" information, "improve user experience", and "prevent" them from seeing uninteresting ads. YouTube for example writes:

> YouTube strives to provide you with relevant and useful advertising and we may use the DoubleClick cookie, as well as other third-party ad-serving systems, to do so. (YouTube Privacy Policy, accessed on April 27, 2009)

Similarly Facebook emphasizes that personalized advertising benefits the user:

> Facebook may use information in your profile without identifying you as an individual to third parties. We do this for purposes such as aggregating how many people in a network like a band or movie and personalizing advertisements and promotions so that we can provide you Facebook. We believe this benefits you. You can know more about the world around you and, where there are advertisements, they're more likely to be interesting to you. (Facebook Privacy Policy, accessed on April 27, 2009)

The fact that in most privacy policies the word "selling" does not appear constitutes another aspect of the ideological character of the analyzed terms of use and privacy policies. Instead of "selling" the word "sharing" is used, which again reinforces the illusion of friendship and mutual benefits:

> From time to time, Tagged may share the email address and/or other personally identifiable information of any registered user with third parties for marketing purposes. In addition, Tagged may share a registered user's email address with third parties to target advertising and to improve user experience on Tagged's pages in general. (Tagged Terms of Service, accessed on April 27, 2009)

The results of the content analysis confirm that the terms of use and privacy policies of commercial web 2.0 sites are designed to allow the owners widespread use of user information. At the same time, a qualitative reading of these documents shows that their language, style, and structure is confusing, misleading, ideological, or even manipulative. The main ideology, on which these statements rest, is one of friendship, of equality, of sharing, and of user benefits. They try to create the impression that the only aim of these platforms is to provide to its users an attractive high-quality service and experience that allows them to produce their own media content and to connect with friends. The fact that these platforms are owned by commercial companies that aim at increasing their profits by selling user information and space for advertisements remains hidden.

Apart from this ideological character, another problem concerning the privacy policies and terms of use of commercial web 2.0 platforms is their limited reach. Most platforms give third-party advertising companies access to user information. Nevertheless the privacy policies and terms of use of these platforms do not cover how third parties deal with user information. In fact these documents explicitly state that once data are handed over to a third party, the platform owners no longer have any control over further usage of this data. This fact can be illustrated with the following quotation from the privacy policy of Megaupload:

> We use third-party advertising companies to serve ads when you visit our website. These companies may use information (not including your name, address, e-mail address or telephone number) about your visits to this and other websites in order not only to provide advertisements on this site and other sites about goods and services that may be of interest to you, but also to analyze, modify, and personalize advertising content on Megaupload.com. We do not have access to or control over any feature they may use, and the information practices of these advertisers are not covered by this Privacy Policy. (Megaupload Privacy Policy, accessed on April 27, 2009)

This qualitative analysis shows that the privacy statements and terms of use of commercial web 2.0 platforms ideologically mask the unequal power relationship between platform owners and users, conceal the profit motivations of platform owners, and downplay the risks for users that arise due to personalized advertising. Some privacy statements and terms of use even create the impression that platform owners intentionally want to delude users.

7.5. CONCLUSION

In summary, the analysis and interpretation of the results of the conducted content analysis shows that the main hypothesis underlying this study can be confirmed:

> H: The terms of use and privacy statements of commercial web 2.0 platforms are designed to allow the owners of these platforms to exploit user data for the purpose of capital accumulation.

This case study of consumer surveillance on web 2.0 has shown that contemporary web 2.0 mainly is a commercial web 2.0 and that the business model of web 2.0 corporations rests on economic surveillance. The terms of use and privacy statements of commercial web 2.0 platforms allow the widespread use of user data in a way that supports the profit interests of platform owners. The business model of most commercial web 2.0 platforms is based on personalized advertising. Capital is accumulated by selling space for advertisements as well as by selling user data to third-party advertising companies. Furthermore these documents try to advance an ideology of friendship and mutual benefits and thus mask and downplay the unequal power relationship between platform owners and users. Whereas personalized advertising satisfies the profit interests of platform owners it has undesirable consequences for individual users as well as for society. Thus, in terms of reducing economic surveillance and its negative effects on individuals and society the search for and support of an alternative web 2.0 is of specific importance. The launch of the newly developed non-commercial social networking site Diaspora might be an important step into this direction: "Diaspora doesn't expose your information to advertisers, or to games you play, or to other websites you visit".[5]

NOTES

1. See *Forbes Magazine* (2010): The Global 2000. http://www.forbes.com/2010/04/21/global-2000-leading-world-business-global-2000–10_land.html (accessed December 13, 2010).
2. xvideos.com [rank 107] and xnxx.com [163].
3. orkut.co.in [rank 54] and orkut.com [106] belong to orkut.com.br [11]; files.wordpress.com [127] belongs to wordpress.com [7]; and wikimedia.org [192] belongs to wikipedia.org [3].
4. The following 13 sites had to be excluded because of language issues: 2 Russian sites (vkontakte.ru [rank 28]; odnoklassniki.ru [48]); 6 Chinese sites (youku.com [53]; ku6.com [94]; kaixin001.com [110]; 56.com [116]; xiaonei.com [132]; people.com.cn [188]); 2 Japanese sites (mixi.jp [84]; nicovideo.jp [119]); 1 Taiwanese site (wretch.cc [97]); 1 Polish site (nasza-klasa.pl [100]); 1 Persian site (blogfa.com [179]).
5. See Diaspora: what is diaspora. http://blog.joindiaspora.com/what-is-diaspora.html (accessed on December 14, 2010).

REFERENCES

Allen, Matthew. 2008. Web 2.0: an argument against convergence. *FirstMonday* 13 (3) http://firstmonday.org/htbin/cgiwrap/bin/ojs/index.php/fm/article/view/2139/1946 (accessed June 20, 2010).
Andrejevic, Mark. 2002. The work of being watched: interactive Media and the explotation of self-disclosure. *Critical Studies in Media Communication* 19 (2): 230–248.

Ball, Kirstie. 2006. Organization, surveillance and the body: towards a politics of resistance. In *Theorizing Surveillance: The panopticon and beyond*, ed. David Lyon, 296–317. Portland, OR: Willan.

Ball, Kirstie and Frank Webster. 2003. The intensification of surveillance. In *The intensification of surveillance*, ed. Kirstie Ball and Frank Webster, 1–16. London: Pluto.

Beer, David and Roger Burrows. 2007. Sociology and, of and in web 2.0: some initial considerations. *Sociological Research Online* 12 (5). http://www.socresonline.org.uk/12/5/17.html (accessed June 20, 2010).

Bogard, William. 2006. Welcome to the society of control. In *Surveillance and visibility*, ed. Kevin Haggerty and Richard Ericson, 4–25. Toronto: University of Toronto Press.

Bogolicos, Nico. 2007. The perception of economic risks arising from the potential vulnerability of electronic commercial media to interception. In *Handbook of technology management in public administration*, ed. David Greisler and Stupak, 583–600. Boca Raton: CRC.

boyd, dannah. 2007. The significance of social software. In *BlogTalks reloaded: Social software research & cases*, ed. Thomas Burg and Jan Schmidt, 15–13. Norderstedt: Books on Demand.

Bruns, Axel. 2007. Produsage, generation C, and their effects on the democratic process. *Media in Transition* 5. http://eprints.qut.edu.au/7521/ (accessed September 14, 2009).

Campbell, Edward John and Matt Carlson. 2002. Panopticon.com: online surveillance and the commodification of privacy. *Journal of Broadcasting & Electronic Media* 46 (4): 586–606.

Charters, Darren. 2002. Electronic monitoring and privacy issues in business-marketing: the ethics of the DoubleClick experience. *Journal of Business Ethics* 35: 243–254.

Clarke, Roger. 1988. Information technology and dataveillance. *Communications of the ACM* 31 (5): 498–512.

Coates, Tom. 2005. An addendum to a definition of social software. http://www.plasticbag.org/archives/2005/01/an_addendum_to_a_definition_of_social_software/ (accessed September 14, 2009).

Cormode, Graham and Balachander Krishnamurthy. 2008. Key differences between web 1.0 and web 2.0. *First Monday* 13 (3). http://firstmonday.org/htbin/cgiwrap/bin/ojs/index.php/fm/article/view/2125/1972 (accessed September 14, 2009).

Fernback, Jan and Zizi Papacharissi. 2007. Online privacy as legal safeguard: the relationship among consumer, online portal, and privacy policies. *New Media and Society* 9 (5): 715–734.

Foucault, Michelle. 1977/2007. Panopticism. In *The surveillance studies reader*, ed. Sean P. Hier and Josh Greenberg, 67–76. Berkshire: Open University Press.

Fuchs, Christian. 2008. *Internet and society: Social theory in the information age.* New York: Routledge.

———. 2009a. *Social networking sites and the surveillance society.* Salzburg/Vienna: Unified Theory of Information Research Group.

———. 2009b. A contribution to the critique of the political economy of the Internet. *European Journal of Communication* 24 (1): 69–87.

———. 2010. Labor in informational capitalism and on the Internet. *The Information Society* 26 (3): 179–196.

Gandy, Oscar. 1993. *The panoptic sort: A political economy of personal information.* Boulder: Westview.

Haggerty, Kevin and David Lyon. 2006. Tear down the walls. In *Theorizing surveillance: The panopticon and beyond*, 23–45. Portland, OR: Willan.

Harrison, Teresa M. and Brea Barthel. 2009. Wielding new media in web 2.0: exploring the history of engagement with the collaborative construction of media products. *New Media & Society* 11 (1): 155–178.

Hier, Sean P. and Josh Greenberg. 2007. Glossary of terms. In *The surveillance studies reader*, ed. Sean Hier and Josh Greenberg, 378–381. Berkshire: Open University Press.

Jarrett, Kylie. 2008. Interactivity is evil: A critical investigation of Web 2.0. *First Monday* 13 (3). http://firstmonday.org/htbin/cgiwrap/bin/ojs/index.php/fm/article/view/2140/1947 (accessed September 14, 2009).

Kortzfleisch, Harald, Ines Mergel, Shakib Manouchehri, and Mario Schaarschmidt. 2008. Corporate web 2.0 applications. In *Web 2.0*, ed. Berthold Hass, Gianfranco Walsh, and Thomas Kilian, 73–87. Berlin/Heidelberg: Springer.

Krippendorff, Klaus. 2004. *Content analysis: An introduction to its methodology.* Thousand Oaks: Sage.

Lyon, David. 2003. Surveillance as social sorting: computer codes and mobile bodies. In *Surveillance as social sorting*, ed. David Lyon, 13–30. London: Routledge.

———. 2007. Everyday surveillance: personal data and social classifications. In *The surveillance studies reader*, ed. Sean P. Hier and Josh Greenberg, 136–146. Berkshire: Open University Press.

Mathiesen, Thomas. 1997. The viewer society: Michel Foucault's panopticon revisited. *Theoretical Criminology* 1: 215–237.

Ogura, Toshimaru. 2006. Electronic government and surveillance-oriented society. In *Theorizing surveillance: The panopticon and beyond*, ed. David Lyon, 270–295. Portland, OR: Willan.

O'Reilly, Tim. 2005. What is web 2.0?: design patterns and business models for the next generation of software. http://oreilly.com/web2/archive/what-is-web-20.html (accessed September 14, 2009).

Papacharissi, Zizi and Jan Fernback. 2005. Online privacy and consumer protection: an analysis of portal privacy statements 49 (3): 259–281.

Petersen, Soren Mark. 2008. Loser generated content: from participation to exploitation. *First Monday* 13 (3). http://firstmonday.org/htbin/cgiwrap/bin/ojs/index.php/fm/article/view/2141/1948 (accessed September 14, 2009).

Reis, Leslie Ann. 2007. Personally identifiable information. In *Encyclopedia of privacy*, ed. William G. Staples, 383–385. Westport/London: Greenwood.

Rule, James B. 1973/2007. Social control and modern social structure. In *The surveillance studies reader*, ed. Sean P. Hier and Josh Greenberg, 19–27. Berkshire: Open University Press.

Scholz, Trebor. 2008. Market ideology and the myths of Web 2.0. *First Monday* 13 (3). http://firstmonday.org/htbin/cgiwrap/bin/ojs/index.php/fm/article/view/2138/1945 (accessed September 14, 2009).

Smythe, Dallas. 1981/2006. On the audience commodity and its work. In *Media and cultural studies*, ed. Meenakshi Gigi Durham and Douglas Kellner. Malden: Blackwell.

Solove, Daniel. 2004. *The digital person: Technology and privacy in the information age.* New York: New York University Press.

Starke-Meyerring, Doreen and Laura Gurak. 2007. Internet. In *Encyclopedia of privacy*, ed. William G. Staples, 297–310. Westport/London: Greenwood.

The Astonishing Tribe. 2010. *Recognizr covered by FOX News and SC Magazine.* Press Release. May 3, 2010. http://www.tat.se/site/media/news_1.php?newsItem=42 (accessed June 20, 2010).

Toffler, Alvin. 1980. *The third wave.* New York: Bantam.

Turow, Joseph. 2006. Cracking the consumer code: advertisers, anxiety, and surveillance in the digital age. In *The new politics of surveillance and visibility*, ed. Kevin Haggerty and Richard Ericson. Toronto: University of Toronto Press.

Van Dicjk, José. 2009. Users like you? theorizing agency in user-generated content. *Media, Culture & Society* 31 (1): 41–58.

Wall, David. 2006. Surveillant internet technologies and the growth in information in information capitalism: spams and public trust in the information society. In *The new politics of surveillance and visibility*, ed. Kevin Haggerty and Richard Ericson, 240–261. Toronto: University of Toronto Press.

8 Disciplining the Consumer
File-Sharers under the Watchful Eye of the Music Industry

David Arditi

8.1. INTRODUCTION

There has been a considerable amount of discussion over the past decade about the legality of downloading music.[1] Copyright and intellectual property have been at the centre of this debate, but few scholars have set aside the legal questions to consider the timing of file-sharing lawsuits and the mechanisms deployed to find and prosecute downloaders. Understanding the mechanisms and timing of file-sharing lawsuits can point to structural political-economic changes in the way people are encouraged to consume. By using surveillance on the Internet, the major players in the music industry have successfully re-established the dominance that they had at brick-and-mortar retailers on the Internet.

In 2000, the Recording Industry Association of America (RIAA)[2] began its crackdown on Napster. Napster started as a peer-to-peer (p2p) file-sharing program[3] where users could share content directly with other users online. By alleging that Napster (and later other p2p programs such as Kazaa) knowingly created a service to foster copyright infringement, the RIAA successfully compelled the US Federal court system to shut down Napster on the grounds that they violated the Digital Millennium Copyright Act (DMCA). Along with the court case shutting down Napster, there was quite a bit of publicity surrounding file-sharing that portrayed p2p users explicitly as copyright violators. File-sharing became synonymous with "piracy", and the practical reasons for using p2p programs were drowned in the rhetoric of copyright infringement; it was entirely lost that these programs could also be used by independent artists and labels to circumvent the Big Four's dominance in distribution. The RIAA and the four major record labels (also known as the Big Four[4]) won the linguistic battle over file-sharers by equating the downloading of music to "piracy"; this is significant because it implied that everyone that used p2p file-sharing programs were in fact criminals.

In 2003, the first major Internet music store, iTunes, was launched. At this point the RIAA began using surveillance tools, including hacking into p2p networks to monitor music downloads and uploads, to directly target "pirates". Prior to 2003, all RIAA affiliated lawsuits were aimed at p2p programs and ignored the people downloading and consuming music on the Internet. Spectacular displays of lawsuits against individuals participating in file-sharing began in September of 2003, five months after the launch of the iTunes store. As Steve Knopper points out in *Appetite for Self-Destruction* (2009), the major record labels worked with Steve Jobs (CEO of Apple) to create a profit-making alternative to p2p file-sharing. Knopper argues that Major record labels realized that without a structured alternative to p2p networks, suing users would have been self-defeating because it would push music consumers away from their labels. Creating a digital music store before lawsuits against individuals began allowed record labels to discipline digital music consumers, with surveillance technologies and lawsuits, into digitally mediated consumer capitalism.

File-sharers immediately began to fear that their anonymous online transactions could in fact be monitored by the RIAA at anytime because the trade association was demonstrating its capacity to hack into p2p programs to discover personal information about users. How do major record labels and the RIAA use p2p surveillance to (re)produce ideas about the economy and consumption practices that previously existed in brick-and-mortar retail stores on the Internet? This paper will argue that ever since the Big Four major record labels gained the ability to monitor the usage of file-sharing networks through the RIAA, they began to use their surveillance capabilities to not only deter users from downloading music using p2p services, but also to monitor the market of what users were downloading/consuming.

The methodological framework that I use to analyze this p2p networks is critical theory, which allows the research object's description to reveal its own internal contradictions as described by Theodor Adorno in *Negative Dialectics* (1983). This methodological framework is applied to understand the role of p2p networks in the production and consumption of music on the Internet and how that process is a reappropriation of the mode of production. Adorno and the Frankfurt School delve deeper into the effects of science and technology than to simply accept the narrative of "progress" (Adorno 2003). By illuminating the negative side of new technologies we can see the contradictions that exist in a digital media environment.

BigChampagne began as a company, in 2000, engaged in consolidating online media data to inform the Big Four and other corporations about demographic information regarding media consumers. The surveillance mechanisms that corporations use on p2p networks create new techniques to monitor the consumption of music and are in effect creating new subjects[5] that unknowingly work for the record industry. Downloaders are labouring for the record industry so that record labels can better market their product, even as some of the same users are being prosecuted for downloading that product without paying for it. Through p2p technology the Big Four can use illegal, in addition to legal, downloads as raw data to get a heads up on new markets and essentially structure the norms and laws that govern consumption patterns of music downloaders.

Downloaders in effect become "indirect knowledge workers" (Fuchs 2010, 186) because although they create surplus value for the major record labels, they are not directly producing knowledge, but rather produce that data that is used as knowledge. The act of consuming digital music creates an audience commodity (Smythe 1981) that can be measured and used to generate profit. This data makes record labels more efficient in getting artists' music to their fans, and the data can be sold to other companies for cross-promotional/advertising purposes.

Although the Internet presents new ways for information to be shared, it also permits the increasing surveillance of those communications. Throughout this chapter I am using the term surveillance for the monitoring of human behaviour with the goal of altering behaviour. Michel Foucault's concept of "governmentality" (Foucault 1978) is important to this concept because it deals with altering a subject's behaviour to coincide with the norms, practices, and laws of a society. Through the use of surveillance, domination can be extended to every aspect of a subject's life. As capitalism has shifted from one phase to another,[6] the superstructure that serves the mode of production has undergone transformations to re-establish the rate of profit. These adaptations are rarely sought by corporations, but rather these changes are happening with the transformation of capitalism and corporations scramble to create an advantage using the superstructure. In this case record labels have had to use surveillance on the Internet to re-create their dominant position in the production and distribution of music.

8.2. INDUSTRY HESITATION
FOR A DIGITAL MUSIC ECONOMY

The story of surveillance of the Internet by the music industry comes out of a history of slow adaptation to new media formats. The Big Four major record labels were not only slow to adapt to digital music, but were more importantly hostile to the active development of mp3 technology (Knopper 2009, 113). However, it has never been the music industry that has taken the lead on developing new mediations of music; it has always been the technology producing companies that take the lead on creating new technologies because technology companies develop new media products (in this case music players) that then need content to drive the consumption of the technology (Kittler 1999). Record labels own the content that producers of music players need to drive the consumption of their commodities and have an interest in maintaining the mediated status quo to keep current profit levels.

Because record labels produce music as their commodity, it only makes sense for them to oppose the development of new technologies. It is a highly risky maneuver for corporate CEOs to change their means of production because it can result in the loss of profit and the monopolistic/oligopolistic power that they hold in their industry. As Karl Marx describes in Volume III of *Capital*, "No capitalist ever voluntarily introduces a new method of production, no matter how much more productive it may be, and how much it may increase the rate of surplus value, so long as it reduces the rate of profit" (2000, 528). In other words, the consumption that compels the changes in mediation of music is not driven by the desires of the music industry itself, but rather, technological change is stimulated by the pursuit of profits by those companies that produce technology. Companies that manufacture record players/eight-track machines/compact disc players/mp3 players force record labels to adapt to new mediations by producing new products and generating demand for content to play on those products. Companies that produce music players sell the players to make a profit and record labels cannot even sell records in a given format until a player is widely available. However, record labels are never sure what will happen with the rate of profit until the new mediations are instituted on a large scale.

Part of the music industry resistance to adapting to the digital mode of production is because record labels have historically benefitted from people that purchase the music that they already own in a new media format, also known as "repeat sales." For instance, the change from vinyl records to compact discs (CDs) forced music listeners to purchase their already owned albums in the new format if they wanted to hear the music on their new players. When people began listening to music in digital formats, all that they had to do is rip their already purchased music onto a hard drive, but one of the sources of profit that the major record labels have always relied on is the repurchasing of music in recently developed formats (Park 2007). Arguably, cassette tapes had the same effect, but digital rips of CDs are of the same quality as the original whereas every copy on analog tape is degraded from the original. Therefore, when people began purchasing mp3 players (or listening to music on their computers), there was not a jump in record sales from music fans re-purchasing music that they had in another format.

The Big Four's resistance to changes in music formats, although understandable in political-economic terms, has made it so that the major record labels have had a lot of space to cover in order to catch up to independent labels and artists in their use of digital music distribution. Similar to large corporations in other cultural industries,[7] the major record labels have maintained their dominance in the music industry because of their control of the distribution networks, i.e., brick-and-mortar stores. As music consumers turned to online sources for their music, the Big Four lacked a way to make a profit from selling music to consumers, and the consumers turned to legally questionable sources for digital music. In an attempt to regain control in the market, the Big Four turned to surveillance to re-establish their dominant power within the music industry by both disciplining users to use online stores to avoid lawsuits and by tracking users' consumption habits. The surveillance techniques that the Big Four developed have been at various times draconian, extralegal, arbitrary, and deceitful. In the next section, I describe the ways that brick-and-mortar record stores differ from online music distribution in order to demonstrate the way that Internet surveillance re-creates the dominance of the Big Four on the Internet later in this chapter.

8.3. BRICK-AND-MORTAR RECORD STORES
VS. ONLINE MUSIC DISTRIBUTION

When a person walks into a brick-and-mortar record store, she is faced with any number of options from purchasing music to stealing music, from leaving empty handed to asking the clerk to make a special order. Any of these options are viable, and very little qualitative information remains of the person's visit beyond any transaction that may have been made while in the store. Surveillance, although present, is primarily geared towards preventing shoplifting. A clerk is present to keep a, generally distracted, eye on the store, convex mirrors may help the clerk see around blind spots, cameras may provide a permanent record that monitors shoplifting, and magnetic fields may lead a shoplifter to believe that an alarm will sound if she takes the merchandise through the doors.

However, these mechanisms have no way of monitoring what a person does after she leaves the store with her legally purchased album. She can go home, make a thousand copies (compact discs or cassettes), and give them away to all of her friends and/or sell them to people on the street. There is also no way to tell how much she listens to the music that she purchased (if at all). She may have purchased an album as a gift for someone else, rendering most demographic information about the purchaser useless, or she may have determined that she did not like the album and left it on her shelf to collect dust. With the invention of Nielsen SoundScan in 1991, a new layer of surveillance was introduced to the record store by allowing the music industry to track the sale of specific albums using bar codes and point-of-sale technology (Watkins 2005). This tracking system allows record labels to get near-instantaneous feedback on the albums that are selling at any given record store. Although SoundScan gives an accurate picture of what is purchased, it fails to monitor how and by whom the music is consumed. There is little information available about the use of any music purchased by this customer.

Furthermore, there is qualitative information missing altogether on this imaginary customer's trip to the record store. There is no data stored on what she specifically came to the store looking to purchase. If she is visiting the record store simply to browse, then she is limited by what is available at the store; although she may ask a clerk (or search a catalogue) for something specific that she has in mind, there is no way to track what she did not know she was looking for through her browsing.

With the transmediation (Kittler 1999) of music from a material media to a digital media, the surveillance of a person searching for music dramatically changes. With any change in mediation, the uses of any new media can only be known after the media has become widely used because technology is limited by the way that people use it. It is equally the case that industries that benefit from previous mediations will develop ways to use new mediations to reinforce their dominance in a given market. Changes in communication technology related to music have tended to favour the Big Four record labels and the same holds true for digital mediations.

With the digital availability of music, the actions of our imaginary record store customer can be observed in profoundly new ways as digital technologies radically increase the information collected about consumption habits. If she logs onto a p2p network, her shared files are immediately available for viewing by other people on the network. First, the most visible bits of information about her are her genre preferences as articulated by the specific music that she possesses in her shared music folder. Second, there is a record of her search history. Third, there is data stored on the music she samples and the music she downloads. Finally, a computer savvy person can identify personal characteristics about her from her zip code and other websites that she visits. The information obtained from the users' p2p network usage can then be paired with her preferences on other websites. It is possible to combine information from her p2p network with songs that she purchases from the iTunes Store or radio stations that she creates at Pandora.com. This information can be processed and used to produce music that is directly marketed towards her specific market segment, which can in turn be continually refocused towards that segment's changing "tastes". Whereas it was very difficult to tell exactly which music interested our customer in the record store, it becomes very easy to monitor her music interests on the Internet.

8.4. DIALECTIC SURVEILLANCE

As this hypothetical scenario demonstrates, the Internet has dramatically changed the surveillance of music consumers. It is important to understand the dialectic nature of p2p surveillance in order to analyze the role that large corporations (both within and outside of the music industry) play in reproducing the means and the mode of production (i.e., the relationship between labour and capital) during the creation of new technologies; this relationship is dialectic because the two types of surveillance described here are opposites and rely on the internal logic of the other to be effective.

First, the surveillance of p2p networks structure consumption habits by separating legality from illegality and encouraging users to self-regulate themselves out of concern for being monitored and punished by industry associations such as the RIAA. Downloading music using p2p file-sharing networks has become ubiquitous with music "piracy". In the discourse about downloading music, very little room has been left to discuss the *legal* downloading of music. It is not my intention here to explore the nuances of copyright law as this has been done ad nauseam (Lessig 2004; Kohli 2001; Seadle 2006; Jeweler 2002; Langenderfer and Cook 2001), but rather to call attention to the way people have been forced to change their habits because of the RIAA intimidation that has occurred through surveillance. The RIAA has created spectacular events by suing thousands of people of all ages, from teenagers to grandmothers, for millions of US dollars in some cases, for downloading (or rather sharing) music online. Although "due process" has been absent from all of these cases, the RIAA has successfully deprived thousands of people of their life savings by suing each individual for $2,500 per shared song and muscling defendants out of a fight by threatening to tie them up in court for more money than they can afford to pay (Park 2007; Knopper 2009).

Although the RIAA could not possibly sue every user on any given p2p network, the spectacle produced by the RIAA in the news media and courts acted as a deterrent for most people by convincing them that lawsuits exceeded their opportunity cost of downloading free music. The panoptic (Foucault 1977) effect of Internet surveillance creates a situation where p2p file-sharers are always unaware of whether the RIAA is watching them, which consequently structures their Internet habits. To further produce a sense of omnipresence the RIAA was even messaging users on p2p networks and warning them to not break the law because file-sharing is equivalent to "stealing music" (Park 2007, 85). Some music downloaders began to think that their every move on the Internet was being watched and began to conceive of p2p networks as telescreens reporting their habits back to Big Brother RIAA. Convincing p2p users that they were being watched by the RIAA and that downloading music could result in an astronomical fine was the strategy that the RIAA chose to convince people to use an online retailer as opposed to sharing music online. Not only did surveying p2p networks create a questionable legal environment for those downloading music, but it also brought an increased consciousness to Internet users that they were in fact not anonymous.[8] Because people never know if and when the RIAA is monitoring their p2p usage, the RIAA's surveillance acts as a panopticon and disciplines users' Internet habits. Whether or not the RIAA is in fact watching p2p users' habits and whether or not their use is legal becomes secondary to their fear of being caught downloading music. The risk of being watched and subsequently sued drove a number of users away from p2p networks and onto online-retail stores. The simultaneity between the timing of lawsuits and the launching of the iTunes store (the iTunes store started in April 2003 and the lawsuits began in September of 2003) points to a desire by the RIAA and the major record labels to force people that had become used to downloading music into using an Internet store, which would enable the major record labels, whose interests the RIAA protects, to profit from the new technology (Knopper 2009).[9] iTunes has acted as a reasonable alternative to the legal gray area of the panoptic p2p programs for those consumers downloading mass-marketed music, but the acquiescence of popular music listeners does not effectively deal with the legality and usefulness of p2p programs.

Getting p2p users to think that the RIAA was always watching is one important way that record labels have used the surveillance of the Internet to re-create their production and distribution advantages on the Internet. The disintermediation of the Internet presented risks to the record labels because it destroys the advantage that the major record labels have had over independent labels and artists in the production, storage, and distribution of music. Without an online music retailer designed to assert the dominance of the Big Four, the major record labels would be forced to compete[10] with a greater number of independent artists.

However, the recording industry's surveillance of the Internet is not restricted to the repressive tactics of identifying music pirates; there has been an increasing nuance to record industry spying. The second method of surveillance is a more savvy technique used by individual record labels to measure where there is demand for its music.

Whereas it used to be difficult for record labels to determine the demographic information of consumers, the Internet has created an atmosphere where any information about consumers can be constructed by monitoring a music consumer's Internet consumption patterns. Sound-Scan, discussed in my description of brick-and-mortar distribution, made it slightly easier for record labels to monitor the sales of albums at retail stores, but the data collection was limited to purchases. With the Internet, the music industry can see not only what is being sold in online and offline stores, but also what is being downloaded on p2p networks, what music is being streamed on Internet radio stations, what sites users are visiting, what people are searching for on music sites, how long they are viewing these sites, and where site visitors are coming from and going to before and after they visit a site. The composite data collected on Internet music listeners as immaterial labor can be used in a number of ways to generate profit for large corporations.

The market surveillance of music habits on the Internet allows for the music industry to fundamentally shift its strategies for selling music. Over the past several years, major record labels have become increasingly interested in services such as those provided by BigChampagne, a company dedicated to tracking demographic information from p2p software and online retailers to provide data about who is downloading particular songs online. A 2003 *Wired Magazine* article explains that "[b]y matching partial IP addresses to zip codes, the firm's software creates a real-time map of music downloading" (Howe). There is a need to stress that although the RIAA is not directly suing users anymore (Reardon and Sandoval 2009), BigChampagne was providing this information for the Big Four during the zenith of music piracy lawsuits. Ava Lawrence explains that at the same time that the Big Four labels "are doggedly fighting to prevent online piracy, these companies are monitoring file-sharing and selling that information to the record companies for a hefty price. WebSpins and BigChampagne monitor what Internet users are sharing on peer-to-peer fileswapping services" (Lawrence 2004, 30). Lawsuits and the media measurement of p2p networks have existed concurrently since the first lawsuits were filed. It is equally important to mention that BigChampagne is not intended for use by everyone; the cost of using BigChampagne is anywhere from $2,000 per month for an individual to track an album to $40,000 per month for a record label to monitor its market. BigChampagne's scope of services changes depending on the money customers have to spend; this is important because it means that only corporations heavily endowed with capital can access and leverage data from BigChampagne whereas independent artists and labels cannot afford this information.

Data collected by BigChampagne is important for the major record labels because it can give them insight into where exactly a certain artist is popular. Where brick-and-mortar retail stores could provide data on the consumption of specific genres and artists, it was quite limited by what was available and the assumptions that record labels and distributors had about specific geographic demographics (Leslie 1995). Eliot Van Buskirk of *Wired Magazine* goes as far as to argue that "BigChampagne's music panopticon does a fine job of summing [complete data] up in a neat package to give insiders an easy way to see what's going on in their world" (Buskirk 2009). With BigChampagne's data, record labels can pressure radio stations in a particular region to play an artist's hit song by arguing that the music has been downloaded X number of times during the past week in that region. The record label can also insist that radio stations in a specific region conduct on-air interviews or promos because of the artist's celebrity power in that region. Furthermore, the record labels can make sure that the artist's concert tour passes through the regions in which the artist is most popular. This data can in turn have an impact on how other products are marketed using musicians as sponsors by directly targeting fans while at the same time understanding specific demographics' consumption preferences.

> Say a marketer has discovered that fans of the band Kings of Leon have a particular affinity for the beer brand she represents. According to the [data from August 2009], she should consider seeking out users of Last. fm, Napster, iTunes and Rhapsody, but not file sharing networks (represented by the TopSwaps category) or Yahoo Music, where the song didn't make the top ten. (Buskirk 2009)

This type of market monitoring allows advertising synergy to function in increasingly parasitic ways by not only creating advertisements within advertisements (LaFeber 2002), but also by directly targeting people based on their perceived personal consumption tastes.[11]

Whereas BigChampagne mentions that major record labels use its services, the labels try to keep their usage under the radar because the RIAA's lawsuits assert that every use of p2p programs is an act of piracy. Record labels are in a position of contradiction when they in turn use p2p programs to obtain information about their consumers' consumption habits by using surveillance because of the dialectic tension between RIAA lawsuits and BigChampagne. "If the labels acknowledge a legitimate use for P2P programs, it would undercut their case as well as their zero-tolerance stance" (Howe 2003). The litigation that creates the RIAA's panopticon is a thin veil that has protected the absolute interests of the Big Four record labels: i.e., to profit from the sale of music. But consumers always-already know that they are participating in the commodification of music because as Guy Debord explains "The spectacle is the stage at which the commodity has succeeded in totally colonizing social life. Commodification is not only visible, we no longer see anything else" (Debord 1994, 21). It is not that consumers fail to see that the major record labels are becoming more directly in touch with demographic desires, but rather that consumers have begun to see this process as ubiquitous.

Although the two methods of Internet surveillance used by the major record labels may appear at first glance to be contradictory, they actually constitute a dialectic that has become necessary for the functioning of the music industry on the Internet. Market surveillance by BigChampagne is only possible because of the RIAA's opposition to the illegal downloading of music. RIAA lawsuits create a layer of panoptic protection for the RIAA hackers who are maliciously accessing p2p networks to litigate downloaders of corporate music. Legal respect for intellectual property rights, created through various laws developed by the World Intellectual Property Organization (WIPO), secures legal protection for these RIAA hackers; the pretext of fighting pirates in the US makes it difficult for p2p network advocates to appeal to privacy rights because that would protect the pirates in a country that "governs through crime" (Simon 2007). As the RIAA's panoptic surveillance has increasingly scared music listeners away from p2p networks, the infrastructure for that surveillance has cleared the way for BigChampagne to monitor Internet music consumption.

On a certain level, the music industry must ideologically sell itself as the only legitimate source of music in order to allow its rhetoric to function. Music listeners are sold the idea that downloading music could destroy the music industry, but the gap between the music *industry* and music as *culture* is rarely identified. In turn, people are led to believe that the death of the music industry is the same thing as the death of music itself. The RIAA has been arguing that what will end music is the "illegal" use of Internet technologies, but what the RIAA is actually wary of is the end of the Big Four's oligopoly.

The industry has alienated consumers by using surveillance to discipline its consumers and if the surveillance created by BigChampagne were broadly publicized, the industry's shell game would be exposed. Because the major players of the music industry act separately in their respective forms of surveillance of the Internet and because only the RIAA's panopticon garners attention in the media, the dialectic of Internet surveillance functions to reinforce the Big Four's power in digital capitalism. If consumers were aware of this dialectic, then they may not be as docile in accepting record industry conceptions of ideal Internet usage. However, the record industry surveillance strategies have allowed current Internet use models to become so ubiquitous that the downloading of music through online retailers has become the standard model for music consumption.

8.5. RIPPLES OF MUSIC SURVEILLANCE

The Big Four's use of both the RIAA to sue p2p users and BigChampagne to monitor the market are direct, and intrinsically linked, forms of surveillance. The music industry has not stopped at the monitoring of digital music downloads on the Internet. Digital music can be surveilled long after its initial download by computer code called Digital Rights Management (DRM). DRM acts as an additional level of surveillance for corporations and causes music listeners to further conform to a digitized post-industrial mode of production. Record labels and online retail stores code music with DRM to limit the number of devices and computers that a song can be played on, and DRM can track the movement of a song when the computer or device is connected to the Internet. This not only allows record labels to limit the flow of "free" music, but also forces music listeners to change their music listening habits in very specific ways.

After numerous copyright lawsuits over the legality of copying purchased music through previous transmediations of music and other media, the RIAA (along with the Motion Picture Association of America) preempted copyright ambiguity and helped create the US Digital Millennium Copyright Act (DMCA) in 1996, which implemented DRM. This coding, which consumers purchase with their music, in turn has an effect on how people use music in everyday life by precluding people from listening to their music in particular ways.

Digital downloads from online retailers complicate the social practices that have developed around the exchanging of music and in many ways end the ability of people to actually share (in the non-p2p sense) music with friends. Music fans create mix-tapes of their favourite songs to demonstrate feelings and alert their friends to new music. The CD greatly increased the ease through which people could share music by allowing traders to burn multiple copies of the same mix without losing quality, an attribute for which cassette tapes were infamous. Among some subculture circles, mix-tapes act as a way for people to share new music with other members of their circle; this is especially true with hip-hop (Harrison 2006). In the case of hip-hop, most of the recordings shared in this way are underground (independent of label influence), but there is a risk that as the number of artists that rely on getting their music out using iTunes (and other DRM encoded services) grows, the more difficult it will be for them to share music. Although there are ways to get around DRM,[12] encoding music qualitatively shifts the way people listen to new music as they can only make a definite number of copies from their original copy.

The DRM code attached to music files prohibits people from purchasing digital music and giving it to another person as a gift. Gifting was one of the reasons why it was difficult to tell the actual use of music purchased by the hypothetical shopper discussed earlier. The result of DRM prohibiting people from giving music as a gift (in digital form only) is that instead of buying someone a specific album as a gift, the only way to gift digital music is by purchasing gift cards through online music retailers. This has a number of effects both formally and informally in the way people give and receive gifts. Generally, people try to remove the price tag from a gift before giving it, but this has never been a possibility with a gift card: i.e., people always know the exact value of a gift card whereas other forms of gifts are more hidden. A gift card also lacks a personal touch because it is equivalent to giving money to a person to purchase his or her own gift at a specific store. But there are broader political economic problems with giving gift cards that generates even more profit for the music industry. If a person were to purchase an iTunes gift card, for example, then that gift giver is giving a specific amount of music to the gift receiver without putting much thought into the receiver's aesthetic music inclinations. A $10 gift card for iTunes allows the receiver to purchase ten songs at $0.99/song charging the gift card $9.90; this means that there is an additional $0.10 on every $10 gift card that cannot be used by the gift receiver. The extra money remains as profit for iTunes where the direct purchase of a compact disc, for instance, as a gift would earn no more profit for the retailer than the profit extracted from labour in the original price of the CD.

When people purchase gift cards, it has the potential to change relationships that surround gifting in general. As Marcel Mauss describes it, a "gift economy" is based on three obligations "to give, to receive, to reciprocate" (Mauss 1990, 39), but a gift qualitatively changes when the receiver knows exactly how much money went into the purchasing/making of the gift. Arguably, in a gift economy, the value of a gift is not directly known in monetary terms, but with gift certificates the gift is given an exact monetary value. Every item exchanged becomes valued by an exact monetary value in a digitally mediated economy. In this way, the surveillance associated with the Internet has effectively transformed earlier ("primitive") economic forms into the digitized post-industrial mode of production.

8.6. PERPETUAL SURVEILLANCE CONSUMPTION MODEL

Although the Big Four record labels were slow to acknowledge the effects that digital music would have on the music industry (Knopper 2009), they more than made up for lost time with the aggressiveness with which they cornered the digital music market. Major record labels use lawsuits for Intellectual Property violations and media measurement companies to create a media environment that benefits the Big Four business models over independent record labels and independent artists; the tactic is to scare people from using p2p networks while at the same time monitoring music downloaders' actions to know where to market music. After the realization of competition from independent artists on Napster (Arditi 2007), the major record labels responded with a strategy to re-establish their power in a new sales medium. David Park explains that the Big Four re-created their hegemonic power on the Internet with a four-pronged approach:

> First, it wanted to give the public the option to purchase individual tracks and albums online, but at higher profit margins. Second, it wanted to offer some digital tracks for sale online before they were available in other formats . . . Third, the industry wanted to create subscription services where consumers have to pay to access and purchase music and last, it wanted to divide music through various labels and exclusive content throughout a number of online distribution services. (Park 2007, 94)

These strategies have been the cornerstone for enticing consumers to buy more music online; indeed, fans of particular artists will inevitably seek out bonus tracks by subscribing to any service if it means being able to hear more music by a particular artist. However, if the music is available somewhere online for free, that fan is likely to seek it there first.

Forcing customers to buy music from multiple online outlets seemed like a great idea in theory, but the major record labels' plan that Park outlines failed because too many online services developed between 1998 and 2003. Without a gatekeeper to restrict access to the music market, consumers tend to get lost in different sites of consumption on the Internet. Accessibility to a wide range of online sites of consumption could have created more niche outlets for genres and multiplied those genres because there would have been less centralized control of distribution. This could have in turn created more room for competition from independent artists. Although BigChampagne monitors most conceivable ways of accessing music online, it alone does not create the dominance of the four major record labels that brick-and-mortar stores have allowed through expensive distribution. Monitoring the market does little to re-create the advantages that the Big Four hold on distribution, and transmediation still threatens the long-term dominance of the major labels unless they can successfully discipline consumers to listen to their music. In this case, there is no substitute for the disciplinary apparatus that the RIAA has for monitoring and prosecuting p2p file-sharers for "piracy". Internet surveillance, particularly the surveillance of p2p networks, helps the Big Four to reassert their market dominance in the newly digitized music distribution networks. It is the dialectic relationship between the RIAA's surveillance and BigChampagne's surveillance that has re-created the oligopoly of the Big Four through the transmediation of music on the Internet.

NOTES

1. See Lessig (2004); Kohli (2001); Seadle (2006); Jeweler (2002); Langenderfer and Cook (2001).
2. The RIAA is the trade association that represents the music industry's interests in the US by lobbying Congress and conducting public relations campaigns. Its board consists primarily of representatives from the major record labels, but also includes minority representation from smaller labels (many of which are owned by the major record labels).
3. Peer-to-peer (p2p) file-sharing programs and networks are tools that Internet users use to exchange various types of files on their computers with one another. Users can directly view, access, and download shared files on other users' computers.
4. The Big Four consists of the major record labels Sony Music Entertainment, EMI, Universal Music Group, and Warner Music Group. The Big Four constitute the main interests of the RIAA and is what people generally mean when they claim that the RIAA represents the music industry. Combined, the Big Four accounted for 87.64 percent of album sales in 2006 in the US (Cashmere 2007).
5. Here Michael Hardt and Antonio Negri's concept of "immaterial labour" is useful. By immaterial labour Hardt and Negri mean "labour that produces an immaterial good, such as a service, a cultural product, knowledge, or communication" (2000, 290). Immaterial labour is not only produced while at work, but also while the labourer is at home supposedly at "leisure". The act of consuming becomes an act of production in an information economy, and this becomes accelerated with digital consumption (Dyer-Witheford 1999).
6. There are numerous descriptions of shifts from the industrial to the post-industrial, from Fordism to post-Fordism or from a material to an information economy (Benkler 2006; Fuchs 2007; Dyer-Witheford 1999; Bell 1976; Castells 1996). All of these iterations describe a historical materialist development of capitalism. Also, see Harvey (2005).
7. As Nicholas Garnham (1990) explains in relation to the movie industry, the media content available is severely limited by distribution networks. Whereas the cost of reproduction of media content is generally low, the access to extensive distribution networks is quite limited. The size and cost of these distribution networks creates monopolies and oligopolies for media corporations and allows them to dominate the content distributed on these networks. Small

record labels and independent artists cannot get their albums to record stores and outlet centers across a wide geographic area, whereas major record labels can distribute music in a near universal manner.

8. For more discussion on the way that Internet users perceive privacy on the Internet see Monika Taddicken's chapter in this book.

9. Steve Knopper's *Appetite for Self Destruction* (Knopper 2009) provides a detailed journalistic account of the discussions that took place between the major record labels and Apple (specifically Steve Jobs) during the development of iTunes.

10. As David Harvey explains in *A Brief History of Neoliberalism* (2005), the language of competition that neoliberals use is never truly about a "free market." Instead, corporations constantly seek ways to have governments create laws that exclude new actors from a given market. The DMCA is no different in this respect because it creates an advantage for copyright owners in a digital environment by limiting the use of copyrighted material. By creating Digital Rights Management and redefining piracy, the DMCA outlaws software technologies that violate the new copyright standards. These new technologies are precisely what would allow for broader competition.

11. At the same time, working away from a music industry based on album sales to one that thrives on performances could be a hidden benefit to this model. This could mark a shift toward Jacques Attali's concept of "composing" (1985) where the music ceases to function as a commodity. If the musicians become increasingly concerned with getting fans to their shows, then the recorded music becomes more of a promotional tool for the live product. Although the Big Four's dominance in the surveillance of industry trends on the Internet still favors the interests of artists on the major record labels, it could help change the way that people conceive of the commodification of music. This could be a move away from the industry fetishization of the recorded product and signify a move back to the importance of live performance. However, the continued disciplining of consumers to purchase music online contradicts any move towards a music industry that is unconcerned with the monetization of the recorded product.

12. A song that is in the iTunes format can be converted to WAV format and burned onto a disc, but the digital song owner must be careful to not copy the file in the original format because this will count as one of the copies allowed by DRM. There are other ways to get around DRM, but they are time intensive and often require an advanced level of computer skill.

REFERENCES

Adorno, Theodor W. 1983. *Negative dialectics*. New York: Continuum.
———. 2003. Progress. In *Can one live after Auschwitz?: A philosophical reader*, ed. Rolf Tiedemann. Stanford, CA: Stanford University Press.
Arditi, David. 2007. *Criminalizing independent music: The Recording Industry Association of America's advancement of dominant ideology*. Saarbrücken: VDM Verlag. Original edition, October 25, 2007.
Attali, Jacques. 1985. *Noise: The political economy of music*. Minneapolis: University of Minnesota Press.
Bell, Daniel. 1976. *The coming of post-industrial society: A venture in social forecasting*. New York: Basic Books.
Benkler, Yochai. 2006. *The wealth of networks: How social production transforms markets and freedom*. New Haven: Yale University Press.

Buskirk, Eliot Van. 2009. Inside BigChampagne's music panopticon. *Wired*, 8/5/09.
Cashmere, Paul. 2007. Review. Universal the biggest label of 2006. November 14, 2010. *Undercover.fm*, January 4, 2007.
Castells, Manuel. 1996. *The rise of the network society.* Cambridge, MA.: Blackwell.
Debord, Guy. 1994. *The society of the spectacle.* New York: Zone Books.
Dyer-Witheford, Nick. 1999. *Cyber-Marx: Cycles and circuits of struggle in high-technology capitalism.* Urbana: University of Illinois Press.
Foucault, Michel. 1977. *Discipline and punish: The birth of the prison.* 1st American edition. New York: Pantheon Books.
———. 1978. *The history of sexuality.* 1st American edition. New York: Pantheon Books.
Fuchs, Christian. 2007. Transnational space and the 'network society'. *21st Century Society* 2 (1): 49–78.
———. 2010. Labor in informational capitalism and on the Internet. *The Information Society* 26 (3): 179–196.
Garnham, Nicholas and Fred Inglis. 1990. *Capitalism and communication: Global culture and the economics of information.* London/Newbury Park: Sage.
Hardt, Michael and Antonio Negri. 2000. *Empire.* Cambridge, MA: Harvard University Press.
Harrison, Anthony Kwame. 2006. 'Cheaper than a CD, plus we really mean it': Bay Area underground hip hop tapes as subcultural artifacts. *Popular Music* 25 (2): 283–301.
Harvey, David. 2005. *A brief history of neoliberalism.* Oxford/New York: Oxford University Press.
Howe, Jeff. 2003. BigChampagne is watching you. *Wired* (10), http://www.wired.com/wired/archive/11.10/fileshare.html (accessed on ???).
Jeweler, Robin. 2002. Copyright issues in online music delivery. Washington, DC: Congressional Research Service.
Kittler, Friedrich A. 1999. *Gramophone, film, typewriter.* Stanford, CA: Stanford University Press.
Knopper, Steve. 2009. *Appetite for self-destruction: The spectacular crash of the record industry in the digital age.* New York: Free Press.
Kohli, Vanita. 2001. Mutilating music: a critical look at the copyright a business issues in online music distribution. *Entertainment Law Review* 12 (1): 15–24.
LaFeber, Walter. 2002. *Michael Jordan and the new global capitalism.* New York: W.W. Norton.
Langenderfer, Jeff and Don Lloyd Cook. 2001. Copyright policies and issues raised by *A&M Records v. Napster*: "The shot heard 'Round the World'" or "Not with a Bang but a Whimper?" *Journal of Public Policy & Marketing* 20 (2): 280–288.
Lawrence, Ava. 2004. Market research in the Internet age: how record companies will profit from illegal file-sharing. *Journal of the Music & Entertainment Industry Educators Association* 4 (1).
Leslie, D.A. 1995. Global scan: the globalization of advertising agencies, concepts, and campaigns. *Economic Geography* 71 (4): 402–426.
Lessig, Lawrence. 2004. *Free culture: The nature and future of creativity.* New York: Penguin Press.
Marx, Karl. 2000. *Capital: Volume 3.* In *Selected writings*, ed. David McLellan. Oxford/New York: Oxford University Press.
Mauss, Marcel. 1990. *The gift: The form and reason for exchange in archaic societies.* Trans. W.D. Halls. London: Norton.
Park, David J. 2007. *Conglomerate rock: The music industry's quest to divide music and conquer wallets.* Lanham, MD: Lexington Books.

Reardon, Marguerite and Greg Sandoval. 2009. Verizon tests sending copyright notices. *CNET*, 11/12/2009.

Seadle, Michael. 2006. Copyright in the networked world: copyright police. *Library Hi Tech* 24 (1):153–159.

Simon, Jonathan. 2007. *Governing through crime: How the war on crime transformed American democracy and created a culture of fear.* Studies in crime and public policy. Oxford/New York: Oxford University Press.

Smythe, Dallas Walker. 1981. On the audience commodity and its work. In *Dependency road: Communications, capitalism, consciousness, and Canada*, ed. Dallas W. Smythe. Norwood, NJ: Ablex.

Watkins, S. Craig. 2005. *Hip hop matters: Politics, pop culture, and the struggle for the soul of a movement.* Boston: Beacon.

9 Socializing the City
Location Sharing and Online Social Networking

Anders Albrechtslund

9.1. INTRODUCTION

In the mid-1990s Microsoft founder Bill Gates claimed that computers and the Internet were making geography less important (1995). This statement illustrates a common theme of the early Internet days: that the "information highway" and "cyberspace" would connect people with similar interests and thus bridge gaps of distance, culture, and language. To some extent this has become reality, but mostly it has remained a beautiful vision of a potential global society. However, in later years the focus moved from this anti-geographical understanding of the Internet to a location- or place-based understanding. A number of Internet-connected surveillance-capable technologies have been introduced to everyday life and especially adapted in urban spaces. These include a variety of mobile devices that allow for location tracking, which along with more familiar technologies, such as closed-circuit television (CCTV), make up a network of surveillance-enabling technologies in urban spaces. The technologies facilitate both new surveillance practices and practitioners, as not only city authorities and private businesses have access to surveillance equipment. Ordinary citizens, tourists, restaurant guests, drivers, pedestrians, and many other inhabitants of the city carry mobile devices, which distribute the surveillance capabilities to a wide variety of actors.

The increase in surveillance technologies and practices has already been thoroughly explored and analyzed (for example: Andrejevic 2006, Fuchs 2008, Lyon 2006); however, this chapter offers an alternative perspective on surveillance technologies and the Internet that focuses on the "locative turn" (de Lange 2009, 56) in new media practices and approaches this topic phenomenologically. The questions that guide this focus are (a) what is online sharing? (b) what does location mean to online sharing?, and (c) how can we understand the popularity of this practice?

9.2. WHAT IS ONLINE SHARING?

A central characteristic of Internet usage is the sharing of information. Today, in its broadest interpretation, this includes activities at commercial and corporate websites, private websites dedicated to personal interests, multiplayer games, web applications, blogging, media websites, forums and message boards, social networking sites, and many other platforms for computer-mediated communication. More specifically, when we think about online sharing, we often refer to social practices that have come to prominence during the last decade. Websites such as Twitter, Foursquare, MySpace, and, in particular, Facebook have changed how we connect to each other on the web, which in turn has changed web culture, professional relations, as well as consumer behaviour. Even though social life is not new to the web (boyd and Ellison 2007), i.e., only a "web 2.0" phenomenon, the majority of Internet traffic today is related to social network sites (Lenhart and Madden 2007). Therefore, in order to explore online sharing, I will focus on this main social activity on the web.

In this section I will further discuss online sharing in three ways: First step is to elaborate the definition of the social web to get a better grasp on this dominating practice. Second, the focus is on whom we are sharing with, especially those people, agencies, and organizations that are not necessarily our friends. The final step is to broaden this surveillance perspective from potential privacy breaches with regard to the recipients of the shared information to the online social networking as social surveillance practice in itself. I suggest that online sharing can be viewed as a practice of exchanging more or less personal information, and thus, social networking has the characteristics of other surveillance practices. However, there are notable differences with regard to power relations, reasons for engagement, and the structure of transparency, and I will explore these alterations brought on by this practice of social surveillance.

9.2.1. The Social Web

Social interaction in its many varieties is the dominant Internet activity today, and especially online social networking has grown considerably with Facebook (500 million users as of 2010[1] driving the development. To distinguish these activities from other types of computer-mediated communication, danah boyd and Nicole Ellison offer this three-fold definition of social network sites (SNS):

> We define social network sites as web-based services that allow individuals to (1) construct a public or semi-public profile within a bounded system, (2) articulate a list of other users with whom they share a connection, and (3) view and traverse their list of connections and those made by others within the system. The nature and nomenclature of these connections may vary from site to site. (boyd and Ellison 2007)

According to this definition, a SNS includes making visible a network of friends to this very network and possibly to people outside the network.

The level of transparency of the network depends on the particular user's privacy settings, which can be more or less determined by the design of the SNS. Sharing your life with others on the web can also be about meeting strangers; however, studies show that most people rather develop and maintain the same social relations online as well as offline (Ellison, Steinfield, and Lampe 2007; Lenhart and Madden 2007). Observing SNSs today and considering the rise of Twitter, Foursquare, and the News Feed-feature in Facebook, it seems that the importance of the first point of the definition (the profile) has diminished compared to the flow of a "news stream", "tweets", or "check-ins".

An important consequence of this behaviour is that the alleged gap between offline and online worlds has been bridged. Previous discourses about the Internet have described it as a transcendent space (for example "cyberspace", "information highway", or "global village") with its own conventions, structure, types of activities, and even as a separate moral universe. Opposed to cyberspace was the "real world", that is, our physical, mundane reality. These two supposedly separate worlds have been woven together; this is especially obvious in connection with our social interactions, which take place in the mixed spaces, i.e., online and offline. In other words, the activities and general social life we experience with our circle of friends take many forms offline and online—sometimes these are performed at the same time with different audiences. These co-online/offline social activities can be observed especially in relation to smartphones, where we can physically be together with (some) friends and simultaneously interact via, e.g., Twitter "tweets", picture uploads to Flickr, and Foursquare check-ins to our network of online friends, including those physically present with us.

A second significant observation about SNSs compared to other forms of computer-mediated communication has to do with the online persona. The general idea is that profiles should reflect the "real" person, group, project, or organization, i.e., the offline identity of the profile holder. Thus, when we share our social life on the web, our profiles are not supposed to be an alter ego, but rather a more or less accurate representation of ourselves. Facebook even insists that profiles must be personal and use real names,[2] whereas Foursquare and Twitter allow for alias names—and the latter for multi-person accounts (e.g., groups, organizations, and projects). Similarly, it is common to use a personalized photo and provide profile information that is grounded in something outside the Internet.

9.2.2. Sharing With Whom?

We share information with a number of connections, our online social network, but we also more or less involuntarily share beyond our circle of friends. This is in part a result of the SNS design including privacy options and in part how the user configures these options. The sharing of information beyond the network occurs in numerous ways, including with the service itself, application developers, search engines, and other third-party stakeholders. A wide range of stakeholders will presumably have an interest in detailed information about individuals. Here I will mention two: commercial and government interests.

From a commercial point of view such data are valuable, because they provide insights into customer interests, preferences, and activities. To know what people do, what they want, and what they think makes it much easier to market products. Thus, the insights gained from SNSs can be used to better profile and target consumers. Fuchs (2008), Andrejevic (2007), and others argue that this knowledge is the foundation for corporate exploitation of users.

Further, some government organizations and agencies can have an interest in gaining information about their own citizens and even about foreign organizations and citizens. It is not difficult to understand why governments have an interest in SNSs. To effectively profile and investigate individuals, an organization needs to combine a wide variety of information, including circle of friends, activities, preferences, beliefs, opinions, views—all types of personal information that only a few years ago were very difficult to collect. Here, people themselves publish this kind of information and this makes online social networking appear as a "snoop's dream" (Marks 2007). The purposes for government interest in this kind of information can range from suspicion of tax fraud to possible involvement in terrorism. This might contribute to what Mark Andrejevic has termed "lateral surveillance" (2007), the process of mixing social, policing, and government technologies and practices, and thus spreading panopticism further.

When we take part in online social networking and when we more or less involuntarily share information beyond our circle of friends, it can have serious consequences. Commercial exploitation, including targeted marketing, can be extremely annoying and privacy invading, and on a societal level it can contribute to social sorting by including or excluding people (Gandy 1993; Lyon 2002). Moreover, to be (wrongly) suspected of terrorism is even more unpleasant, if not dangerous. Accordingly, when our everyday social musings are shared with commercial and government stakeholders, it represents the boundary of free social interaction.

9.2.3. Online Sharing as Social Surveillance

As a result of certain surveillance practices, there can be undesirable or even malicious side effects when we take part in social interactions online (Zimmer 2008). However, my interest here is directed towards another perspective on the possibilities of surveillance. This perspective emphasizes the social, playful, and potentially empowering aspects of surveillance practices, and it is therefore radically different from the dominant ways of understanding the practices, as described above. I have introduced the concept "participatory surveillance" elsewhere as a theoretical framework that allows for this understanding (Albrechtslund 2008).

Many types of surveillance practices can have social, playful, and potentially empowering aspects, but these are especially recognizable in connection with online social networking. When we use social media such as Facebook, Twitter, and Foursquare, the basic practice that facilitates social interactions (distributing and collecting information) is—perhaps surprisingly—surveillance. This is certainly a departure from well-known concepts, including Orwell's iconic Big Brother figure and Bentham's prison design, Panopticon. However, rather than replacing these ways of thinking about surveillance, I introduce participatory surveillance as an alternative concept, as it is clearly not applicable to all kinds of surveillance practices. Similarly, the Panopticon and Orwellian ways of thinking about surveillance do not adequately help us to better understand all types of surveillance practices—at least they do not exhaust every possible perspective. My aim with this alternative conception is to better explain the reasons and intentions that people might have for taking part in their own surveillance—a practice which is very difficult to meaningfully explain from an Orwellian or Panoptic conception of surveillance. In this way I hope to contribute to a pluralistic approach to surveillance studies that emphasizes the many possible motives, means, ends and conceptions at play.

Participatory surveillance is the kind of practice we take part in voluntarily. The prisoners in the Panopticon also take part in their own surveillance when they internalize the gaze, and the characters in *1984* participate in their "love" for Big Brother; however, there are a number of important differences. The panoptic and Orwellian concepts of participation are both the result of processes of mind control and, thus, cannot be described as voluntary engagements, but rather as a form of forced pseudo-participation. The kind of practices of self-surveillance that are consistent with what is here described as participatory surveillance must be pursued actively and truly voluntarily. Of course, absolute freedom of will—complete, unconditional free choices—are probably not a practical possibility for anyone, as even voluntary choices always have to be made in specific situations. Thus, a number of conditions, expectations, specific circumstances, etc. are always also considered when making a choice. Similarly, free choices might be motivated by other circumstances, expectations, conditions, etc. Still, the practice of online sharing remains highly voluntary by comparison.

As a consequence, the gaze plays a different role in the context of participatory surveillance. To be exposed to the gaze is not necessarily equal to being vulnerable. In the Panopticon, the gaze of the guards is a powerful way to discipline the prisoners, and in *1984*, the gaze of Big Brother is an almost destructive force that transforms people into victims. In connection with practices of participatory surveillance, visibility is not associated with vulnerability or victimization. Rather, being visible is an important part of these practices, which transforms the gaze into something desirable. This also leads to significant changes in how we can understand the power relations of surveillance practices. Instead of being intimidating and potentially damaging, certain surveillance practices demonstrate that it can be empowering to be on the receiving end of the gaze. Accordingly, the power relation between watcher and watched is not always a one-way connection that puts the former in control; some surveillance practices empower the watched and, thus, sometimes reverse the panoptic and Orwellian understanding of gaze and power.

9.3. WHAT DOES LOCATION MEAN TO ONLINE SHARING?

To share a location with other people is more than simply conveying geographical information. Embedded in our locations is partial information about activities, interests, opinions, patterns of movement, and much more. In the context of online social networking these types of information are already available, but location sharing on the one hand works as a "handle" that holds together manifold types of information, and on the other hand expands and enriches this information. In the following I begin with an example—"a day in the life"—to illustrate how location sharing combines with online social networking. In the second subsection I discuss the idea of "mixed places", i.e., the necessary connection between physical locations and shared locations in the context of online social networking. The final subsection explores how the process of social interaction and location sharing can be better understood as a mapping process that involves two aspects of mastering.

9.3.1. A Day in the Life: An Example

An example can illustrate how location sharing combined with online social networking adds more information to the picture than the sum of its parts. Someone named Anders uses Foursquare to check in to a venue called "IMV Helsingforsgade 14 Wiener Building" most weekdays sometime between 9:11 and 9:18 in the morning. This particular venue is located in Aarhus, Denmark. About one and half hours earlier he checked into a venue called "Skorping station", which is at a railroad station ca. 80 km north of Aarhus. Sometime during the morning, he responds to a few tweets as well as posting one himself saying "working on book chapter". This tweet is automatically imported into Facebook and broadcast on his wall and, thus, included in his network's news feed (depending on individual settings). This status update—which it is called here—spurs a few comments that lead to a brief discussion about location sharing. At about 11:30 most weekdays, he uses Foursquare to check in to the venue "INCUBA Science Park Katrinebjerg". He is back at IMV Helsingforsgade 14 Wiener

Building about 30 minutes later. In the afternoon, at about 16:30, he is back at Skorping station, and for the rest of the day there are no other Foursquare check-ins, but a few Twitter tweets as well as occasional comments on Facebook posts by people in his network.

Anders is the "mayor" of several venues, including Skorping station and IMV Helsingforsgade 14 Wiener Building. He holds a number of Foursquare badges, including "Bender", "Overshare", and "Babysitter". Because he is the mayor of more than ten venues (currently 17 venues), he also holds the "Supermayor" badge. Some of his mayorships include "Rebild Bakker", "Rold Skov", "Troldehaven", and "Legepladsen, Stentoften". All of these venues have few or even no check-ins by other people and, looking at a map, most of them are located in a specific rural area. Also, the dominant categories of these venues are park, playground, and train station. However, Anders is also mayor of the urban-located venue IMV Helsingforsgade 14 Wiener Building, and, here, a number of other people also check-in frequently, most of whom are in Anders' network. The venue is located at the Department of Information and Media Studies, Aarhus University.

The activities described above could represent a typical day for some people. Although this person is actually not very active with regard to sharing information, there are plenty of data for people in his network—and in part outside of it as well—to make some interpretations and assumptions. One interpretation is that Anders lives in a rural area about 80 km north of Aarhus, and most weekdays he commutes by train to Aarhus where he works at the Department of Information and Media Studies. He is employed in a scientific position that involves writing scholarly manuscripts, and he therefore is likely to hold a PhD degree. There must be a cantina that serves lunch in the nearby INCUBA Science Park Kartrinebjerg. Our example person is probably a father to at least one young child, as he often checks into a playground (the Playground badge is awarded for 10+ check-ins at playgrounds).

The mundane repetition of some of these activities at specific times of the day and at specific locations hints of certain routines and patterns of movement. Also, the general picture of activities might indicate to some that Anders is not among the most experienced users of social media. However, activities that are *not* done as well as tweets and posts *not* made nuance and expand this knowledge. The rarity of check-ins in the evening might emphasize partly that Anders has young children and is therefore simply at home most evenings, and partly that he lives in a rural area with perhaps few places to go at night. Moreover, the absence of check-ins, tweets, and posts during the night indicate a pattern of sleep between roughly 23:00 and 7:00. Most weekdays Anders checks in at the train station and his assumed workplace (Aarhus University), but one or two days a week he does not. However, the tweeting and posting indicate that he is working, so it can be assumed that he works at home some days.

What is constructed through location sharing and online social networking is not a snapshot of someone's life; rather it is a continually unfolding narrative where repetitive activities over a time span form a multifaceted picture. It is the context of activities that makes it possible to form this picture through interpretation, and this is, of course, dependent on how people are related to Anders in the network. For some people the mundane activities described above will just confirm what they already know, and for others the activities will expand knowledge about this person—perhaps as missing pieces that complete the puzzle.

9.3.2. Mixed Places

As discussed in section 9.2.1 the online and offline worlds seem to seamlessly mix into a whole social world. Similarly, location sharing makes it difficult to uphold a sharp division between locations in the physical space and "places" (Facebook) or "venues" (Foursquare) in online social networking.[3]

Locations in online social networking are necessarily tied to a physical location as representations of these. The Foursquare venues mentioned above—e.g., IMV Helsingforsgade 14 Wiener Building, Legepladsen, Stentoften, Troldehaven, INCUBA Science Park Kartrinebjerg—these all have references in physical space. However, this does not mean that these venues are only meaningful *as* a reference to physical space. Often the opposite is the case, and the relation between digital and physical locations is comparable to the relation between geotagged objects and physical locations (de Lange 2009). Geotagged objects add meaning to the physical world, as "physical locations are often visited, defined, and experienced on the basis of geotags and digital metadata" (de Lange 2009, 60). When we share locations online, these places or venues mix with physical locations, and, together, they form augmented locations that can be accessed by our social networks. Comments, suggestions, photos, etc. can augment and thus reconfigure these locations, and these layers of meaning change in accordance with relations in the social networks.

If we revisit the example above we can observe this mixing of places. For example, the Foursquare venue IMV Helsingforsgade 14 Wiener Building is connected to a particular physical location with the address Helsingforsgade 14, 8200 Aarhus N, Denmark, and, as mentioned in above, this address is home to the Department of Information and Media Studies, Aarhus University. When Anders arrives at this venue, his Foursquare network is notified, and in addition to the check-in, he can share information, opinions, or "tips" (Foursquare) with his network. One of Anders' colleagues has tagged the venue with the comment "Damn good coffee!"—which has been acknowledged by a number of other visitors to this place.[4] This simple, knowing statement carries meaning for the network and contributes to a distributed experience of the place, as the stream of shared information reach people regardless of where they are located in physical space. Moreover, the activity itself adds to the shared knowledge in the network about the whereabouts of different people, e.g., who are at the office, who are away for conferences or other external activities, and who are working from home. This is of course not an absolute source of information, as people might not actually check-in even though they are (occasionally) sharing their locations; however, the insight into people's sharing habits contribute to a more precise picture: For example, is Anders in the habit of checking in at IMV Helsingforsgade 14 Wiener Building whenever he is at the office, which means that people in his network can expect to find him at the department when he checks in to Foursquare.

9.3.3. Mapping as Mastering

To better understand what location means to online sharing, it can be useful to view it as a mapping practice. When we share information about activities and locations, this is also a process of mapping parts of our social life. These activities and locations represent a twofold way of mastering: first, as a reduction of complexity where the different events are fitted into a panorama or seemingly "full picture" of the social life. Second, this mapping process is not private, but rather shared with the network, and this aspect can allow for empowerment. The process of mapping is not necessarily limited to any specific SNS, as available information across social platforms is aggregated. Locations, comments, tweets, posts, etc. are documented and archived and, as such, form a history of activities. In a literal sense the mapping is a way to create an overview, which is at the same time a mastering of the social life.

Mapping as mastering is a well-known cultural practice in human history, and as such, location sharing can be compared to the nineteenth-century concept of the panorama where painters strived to give exhausting representations of a given subject (often landscapes or historical events) by creating a wide, all-encompassing view for the audience. Roland Barthes (1997) interprets the panorama as a way of making the world intelligible as part of a pleasurable fantasy of a demystifying overview. It is pleasurable because it structures the world in a certain way that reduces diversity and replaces it with meaning, and the mastering is a fantasy because the panoramic mapping cannot be exhaustive. This can be observed when we consider the aggregated information from SNSs, e.g., the example involving Anders. Although the collected information gives insight into activities, behaviours, interests, and patterns of movement, it is far from a full picture of this person. This is the case even though the collection of information as a whole (including activities that are *not* done) gives more insight than the sum of the individual pieces. It is a consequence of the blurry boundaries between online and offline, different types of spaces and places, that subjectivity and social life is distributed and thus impossible to capture in a single, objectifying perspective. However, the pleasurable activity of mapping as mastering might be seen as a strong motivation for the practice of location sharing online.

The mapping does not result in a *stilleben*, as it is a process where the subjectivity co-shapes the picture. Moreover, the mapping process is not only available to oneself; it is also a sharing process that allows for empowering aspects. When we engage in social interaction online, this is a semi-public process visible to a selected network and perhaps partially visible to the greater Internet-using public. As discussed in section 9.2.2 this more or less broad sharing has a dubious side; however, it also constitutes a way for people to co-construct meaning and identity, as discussed in section 9.2.3. As participants in online social networking, we play a leading role in providing the material that represents us to other people in the network. Compared to for example governmental mapping of citizens (e.g., population register, tax and salary information, address, civil status), social interactions empower people to shape how they appear to others. Mastering as both reduction of complexity and empowerment indicate that *the flâneur*, i.e., the figure of the turn-of-the-century urban observer, is still relevant for understanding the city, mapping, and mastering. The user of location-based SNSs can be seen as a kind of flâneur employing a certain form of perception of urban space that focuses on finding pleasure in the different layers of meaning while still keeping a distance of cool observation.

9.4. CONCLUDING REMARKS

Location sharing is an obvious extension of online social networking that offers an opportunity to connect the potentially empowering self-surveillance practices of social life that is especially observable in the city. The ambition of this chapter is not to describe the abstract power structures inherent in the practices of online sharing; rather the point of departure is the subjectivity that takes part in its own surveillance. The reason for this focus is to better understand why people voluntarily engage in such self-surveillance. It is evident that a vast number of people find it attractive to do so and, thus, it becomes interesting to explore and conceptualize this practice. A qualitative, phenomenological approach has been taken here in order to search for the characteristics of the subjective experience and motivation implicated in location sharing and online social networking.

NOTES

1. http://www.facebook.com/press/info.php?statistics (accessed on October 27, 2010).
2. http://www.facebook.com/help/?page=808 (accessed on October 27, 2010).
3. This is not meant as a classification of the words location and place (and venue) as relating to respectively physical space and cyberspace. I use location, place, venue, etc. synonymously, however, as opposed to (physical, cyber and mixed) spaces. Thus, I lean on the classic understanding of place as

positioned in space, but without a sharp distinction between types of places and types of spaces.
4. In Foursquare terms the other people have "done the tip".

REFERENCES

Albrechtslund, Anders. 2008. Online social networking as participatory surveillance. *First Monday* 13 (3).

Andrejevic, Mark. 2005. The work of watching one another: lateral surveillance, risk, and governance. *Surveillance & Society* 2(4): 479–497.

———. 2006. The discipline of watching: detection, risk, and lateral surveillance. *Critical Studies in Mass Communication* 23 (5): 391–407.

Barthes, Roland and Richard Howard. 1997. *The Eiffel tower and other mythologies.* Berkeley: University of California Press.

boyd, danah and Nicole Ellison. 2007. Social network sites: definition, history, and scholarship. *Journal of Computer-Mediated Communication.* http://jcmc.indiana.edu/vol13/issue1/boyd.ellison.html (accessed on ???).

Ellison, Nicole B., Charles Steinfield, and Cliff Lampe. 2007. The benefits of Facebook friends: social capital and college students' use of online social network sites. *Journal of Computer-Mediated Communication* 12 (4): 1143–1168.

Facebook I Help Center. (n.d.). http://www.facebook.com/help/?page=808 (accessed on August 27, 2010).

Facebook I Statistics. (n.d.). http://www.facebook.com/press/info.php?statistics (accessed on October 26, 2010).

Fuchs, Christian. 2008. *Internet and society: Social theory in the information age.* New York: Routledge.

Gandy, Oscar H. 1993. *The panoptic sort: A political economy of personal information.* Boulder: Westview.

Gates, Bill. 1995. *The road ahead.* New York: Viking.

de Lange, Michiel. 2009. From always-on to always-there. In *Digital cityscapes: Merging digital and urban playspaces,* ed. Adriana de Souza e Silva and Daniel M. Sutko, 55–70. New York: Peter Lang.

Lenhart, Amanda and Mary Madden. 2007. *Teens, privacy & online social networks.* Washington, DC: PEW Internet & American Life Project.

Lyon, David. 2002. *Surveillance as social sorting: Privacy, risk, and digital discrimination.* New York: Routledge.

———. 2006. *Theorizing surveillance: The panopticon and beyond.* Cullompton, Devon: Willan.

Marks, Paul. 2007, July 14. Pentagon sets its sights on social networking websites. *NewScientist.com.* http://www.newscientist.com/article/mg19025556.200 (accessed on ???).

Zimmer, Michael. 2008. Preface. Critical perspectives on web 2.0. *First Monday* 13 (3).

10 What Do IT Professionals Think About Surveillance?

Iván Székely

10.1. INTRODUCTION

A sceptical reader might be tempted to fire back with a "Who cares?" Surveillance exists and is becoming more widespread, independently of what the experts think. In addition to presenting the findings of a recent research project and interviews with information technology (IT) professionals on such issues as surveillance and the handling of personal data and privacy in general, my intention is to frame an argument in favour of making IT professionals' views on these matters count more in the formulation and implementation of the concept of modern surveillance systems.

Another interesting aspect of the topic is that, insofar as research on privacy is concerned, the IT community constitutes something of a white area, and, therefore, our conclusions may enrich the discussions on the subject with some novel viewpoints, hopefully leading to the emergence of new policies, strategies, and areas of intervention for the benefit of the numerous stakeholders. The immediate motive for writing this chapter has, however, been supplied by the BROAD project. This recent research project employed quantitative and qualitative methods alike, and was designed to test the views, the knowledge, and the attitudes of IT professionals.

This chapter also wishes to call attention to the importance of the empirical approach by pointing out that, in addition to purely theoretical constructions, the direct study of reality could also help galvanize speculative methods and engender further interactions between theory and practice.

Once we subscribe to Lessig's (2000) famous view whereby "the Code is the law" in modern information societies, it will follow directly that the coders are the lawmakers in today's society. And if they are indeed the lawmakers, they are likely to produce laws that will reflect their own views, depth of knowledge, and attitudes—naturally, alongside the views of their paymasters. This system has certain boundary conditions, such as economic interests and legal regulations, but those will merely shade the views of the IT professionals, rather than defining them. Experience tells us that the law in general—despite its fundamental role in mediating values— seems to carry very little weight with IT professionals, who tend to regard laws as useless restrictions.

Naturally, the law cannot simply be envisioned as the sum total of abstract rules, as the law must, at some level, relate to the underlying values that determine the workings and the conditions of a society.[1] Individual societies may differ with regard to the closeness and transparency of this relation: it is stronger in legal systems steeped in the traditions of natural law, and weaker in countries preferring a positivist approach. In the case of data protection laws, or in a broader sense privacy laws, the value content is clearly reflected in those internationally accepted legal principles that form the basis of national and international legal documents.

Therefore, if one is to discover what factors are likely to influence the views of IT professionals, one should first have to find out about the depth of their knowledge about data protection or privacy legislation, independent of the actual views they hold about it. Naturally, one would have to learn a great deal more about the members of this professional group before one could form a picture of their views about surveillance, enhanced or in some cases generated by today's ICTs, as well as about the subjects of surveillance and the handling of their data. We must learn about their views on social values, with special emphasis on the ways of their realization in today's ICT environment; we must discover their opinions on data subjects, the users of Internet services, their colleagues, and even themselves. And if we want to extend our research into the causes that give rise to these specific "laws" of information society, we should also study the micro-environment and operational structure in which IT professionals work.

But first we must settle one fundamental question: Who qualifies as an IT professional? Or in a broader sense, who qualifies as an "informatician"? Is it any person who engages in some areas of informatics in ways that are beyond the capacity of an ordinary user? These terms have been slow to take root in the English usage; although the word "informatics" has by now gained general currency, it still smacks of its French origin, l'informatique. And anyone who works in informatics can at best be called an informatician,[2] or perhaps more appropriately an information technologist or an information scientist. The scope of the present chapter does not allow me to analyze the substantive differences between the Anglo-Saxon and the Francophone terminology; nevertheless, we must find a way to draw the boundaries of our research subject.

If we want to limit our study to the circle of IT professionals, then we must be able to define the range of people who belong to that circle. So who is an IT professional? Anyone who has received formal IT training? Anyone who works in IT-intensive jobs? Anyone who is a member of any professional organization? Or anyone who considers himself or herself an IT professional? According to the definition provided by Wikipedia:

> IT professionals perform a variety of duties that range from installing applications to designing complex computer networks and information databases. A few of the duties that IT professionals perform may

include data management, networking, engineering computer hardware, database and software design, as well as the management and administration of entire systems.[3]

We must bear in mind, however, that a social group thus defined possesses neither a central registry nor a coherent pool of statistical data, and, therefore, its members can only be reached through indirect methods, with the result that our population sample in no way can be regarded as a representative one. When we designed the BROAD project, which will be presented in detail later, we decided that instead of striving for representativeness, we would try to identify the characteristic groups of the IT community, engage them in our research, and base our conclusions on their views. In order to select from the vast toolbox of social science studies those elements that are methodologically suitable and practically viable and can empower us to put forward relevant statements on the views of IT professionals, we had to resort to qualitative and quantitative tools alike.

Naturally, we also had to take into account those research preliminaries that either could serve as reference points for our study or help prove that our project has filled a gap in this research area.

10.2. RESEARCH PRELIMINARIES

First it should be noted that a large part of the papers on surveillance are studies conducted from a criminology or law enforcement angle, which means that they tend to take a positive view of surveillance, with an aim to develop efficient strategies to further the social acceptance of surveillance. Some of these studies justify the need for surveillance by drawing general conclusions from cases, which, from the viewpoint of law enforcement, have been perceived as success stories (Hanna and Mattioli 1995; Clark 2009); some others legitimize the practice by analyzing the laws that regulate surveillance (Figliola 2007); whereas still others talk about the natural marriage between law enforcement and the surveillance industry (Enright)—to name but a few examples. We have not covered these studies, partly because instead of taking such a particularistic view we wish to approach the subject of surveillance in a much more general manner, and partly because—although we have done our best to remain objective according to all the rules of our profession—we, the author and his colleagues, consider the prospect of the surveillance society (or its special category, the actuarial society) an unwelcome development that has numerous negative aspects. One such negative aspect is the growing information gap between the observer and the observed; another one is the tendency whereby individuals living in such societies are becoming less and less capable of controlling the fate of their personal data and increasingly lack the capacity to see the impact that these data can have on their lives. Similarly negative, in our opinion, is the approach that prefers a treatment of symptoms to the addressing of the root causes by perceiving everyone as a potential deviant who needs to be placed under constant surveillance.

The research preliminaries included in our study belong to the category of either an area known as surveillance studies[4] or the broader field of privacy studies. We concluded that in most of the cases such studies either take the entire population as their research subject, or focus on some easily identifiable segments, such as young people, consumers, Internet users, or students. With sporadic exceptions, IT professionals as a group have not been investigated in these studies.[5]

Globalization of Personal Data (GPD), one of the most important empirical studies of recent years, was conducted by the Surveillance Studies Centre of Queen's University. The multi-country survey covering Brazil, Canada, China, France, Hungary, Mexico, Spain, the US, and Japan,[6] involved nearly 10,000 respondents and targeted the general population, or the population of telephone users, to be precise.[7] However, the telephone penetration rate is so high in the countries concerned (with the exception of Brazil, China, and Mexico) that this imposed no special filter on the selection of respondents. This was a pioneering project, not only because of its cross-country and cross-cultural aspect, but also in the sense that instead of settling for the recording of the respondents' views, it also probed the depth of their knowledge, as well as their attitudes, values, and beliefs with regard to surveillance and information privacy. To achieve this, they conducted qualitative focus group interviews in each country prior to their survey, which were analyzed quantitatively.[8]

At this point I would like to note that, with regard to the Hungarian data, which was of special interest to me, the findings of the GDP research provided further evidence for the existence of the threshold of abstraction, a concept I introduced (Székely 2010, 167–168). It is well known to researchers conducting empirical studies that face-to-face interviews often yield opinions and attitudes that are different from those obtained through survey-type questionnaires from the same respondents. This is partly explained by the fact that survey-type questionnaires, and most notably those related to surveillance and the handling of personal data, tend to use abstract concepts and refer to abstract situations, the actual content and relevance of which the respondents can comprehend only after receiving detailed explanation, and so the two methodologies yield different opinions. Among others, the acknowledgment of this led the planners of the BROAD project in their decision to complement the online survey with a series of semi-structured face-to-face interviews in two countries. Therefore, the GDP survey targeted the total population, and we cannot extract the data of IT professionals from this sample because of the incomplete information regarding the respondents' occupation.

Another major empirical study completed in recent years was the survey conducted under the aegis of PRIME,[9] a project involving nearly 8,000 respondents from three countries, first and foremost the Netherlands (Leenes and Oomen 2009).

The PRIME survey focused on users' attitudes with regard to trust, privacy, the handling of personal data, and Privacy Enhancing Technologies (PETs). One of the most interesting developments in connection with the survey was that, based on its findings, Oomen and Leenes (2008) created a privacy risk perception index, which offered an alternative to the well-known—and, in its critics' views, somewhat oversimplified—Westin/Harris Privacy Segmentation Index (Harris Interactive 2001).[10] Despite its interesting conclusions and methodological thoroughness, the PRIME survey can be taken as a research preliminary for the BROAD project only in a limited sense. The PRIME survey studied a particular segment of the population, namely higher education students. It approached 388 universities and colleges from three countries—Belgium (Flanders), the Netherlands, and the UK—and their students made up the survey's respondents. The respondents included students studying IT-related subjects, but their views were not separated within the study. Although it would be possible to conjecture the character of training from the respondents' educational background and university, any comparison with the BROAD project's subsample, the IT students, would only have limited usefulness.

The only widely known survey focusing on a particular segment of the community of IT professionals is described in detail by Thomas R. Shaw (2003). In his research work, Shaw studied the attitudes of the webmasters of the world's most visited websites in relation to their decisions affecting the private lives of the users, as well as the their considerations behind these decisions. Although his population sample was relatively small in a statistical sense,[11] his hypotheses and methodology were noteworthy. Shaw conducted his investigations on the basis of the theory of moral intensity. Out of the six dimensions of the theory,[12] he found two to be applicable: those of the magnitude of effect and the social consensus. He complemented the theory with the indicator of proximity, which turned out to be crucial from the viewpoint of organizational consensus and moral attitudes (the role of the organizational consensus was also studied in the BROAD project).

Similarly noteworthy was the methodology Shaw used, as he substituted the study of actual behaviour with the study of attitudes on the basis of the theory of reasoned action, which was developed by Fishbein and Ajzen (1975). He had two reasons to do this: first, the behaviour of the respondents was not easily observable in the given survey situation; and second, self-reported behaviours tend to provide unreliable data. At the same time, the attitudes were directly related to both the moral decisions and the actions arising from them, so they were suitable as substitutes for the direct observation of behaviour. On top of that, in comparison to the rate of technological developments, the attitudes can be described as relatively stable phenomena, and, therefore, they provide suitable material for the prognostication of behaviour in the environment of future technology.

10.3. THE BROAD PROJECT

Carried out by Dutch and Hungarian educational and research institutions (2009–2010),[13] the project Broadening the Range Of Awareness in Data protection (BROAD)[14] has three main action areas: to study the views of IT professionals and to provide feedback to the people concerned; to develop an Internet platform for sharing knowledge and opinions about PETs[15],; and to produce creative artworks to increase people's awareness of surveillance and other privacy evasive phenomena.[16]

The action area designed to study the views of IT professionals (Survey and Feedback) was led by the Tilburg Institute for Law, Technology, and Society (TILT), which is part of Tilburg University. The research consortium's work was actively supported by its two Hungarian members, Central European University and Eotvos Karoly Policy Institute.

The objectives of this activity were to explore in Hungary and in the Netherlands the opinions, values, and attitudes of the target groups that exert a decisive impact on the possibilities and limitations of people's privacy in today's "information society" (multipliers) and to feed back the results to the target groups and common knowledge. To achieve this objective, (a) face-to-face interviews and (b) a dedicated online survey were conducted in two specific target groups in both countries:

1. IT professionals (including those who work in explicit rights-restricting areas such as surveillance systems, border control, etc.)—in other words, those who are *making* (designing and operating) IT systems processing personal data; and
2. Principals, i.e., those who are *commissioning* these systems and paying these IT professionals, namely
    (i)   bureaucrats and decision makers, and
    (ii) business managers of service providers and operators, including small and medium enterprises (SME)

10.4. HYPOTHESES

We started out from the following general hypotheses, which we have advanced partly on the basis of our study of the source materials and partly as a result of our lead researcher's practical experiences deriving from working with information technology professionals for decades:

H1: The opinions, values, and attitudes of IT professionals and their principals have a decisive impact on the IT systems they create and maintain for processing personal data; thus this has a direct impact on data protection/information privacy of the data subjects; and this may have an indirect impact on citizens' opinion and attitudes.[17]

H2: The survey and the interviews will result in significantly different findings ("threshold of abstraction").[18]

H3: [At least in Hungary] the majority of IT professionals are socialized to serve the stronger party (their principals or the information monopolies). However, there exists a small but characteristic "freedom-minded" minority in the IT sector, the members of which have different views.[19]

In working out the detailed plans for the online survey, we stated some further hypotheses (Leenes et al. 2010), with special regard to the findings of earlier surveys:

- There are differences between distinct groups in the sample with regard to their knowledge of the Data Protection Act (DPA).
- Participants who find the DPA relatively more important also have more knowledge of it.
- There are differences between distinct groups in the sample with regard to their concerns about privacy protection.
- Privacy concerns are reflected in people's actual online behaviour and work.
- There is a difference between Dutch and Hungarian respondents with regard to organizational consensus, defined as the overlap between an individual's attitudes about personal data and the attitudes about personal data held in the organization he/she is working in.
- There are differences between distinct groups in the sample with regard to hierarchy in the organization.
- There are differences between distinct groups in the sample with regard to their familiarity with and use of PETs.
- There are differences between distinct groups in the sample with regard to their degree of responsibility, defined as their resistance to carry out decisions about personal data if they disagree with them.
- Responsibility, defined as an individual's resistance to carry out decisions about personal data if he/she disagrees with them, is related to ratings of importance of DPA rights and concerns about privacy protection.
- There are differences in behaviour based on the differences in perceived behavioural control.

Leenes et al. (2010) also worked out a model to explain the interconnections between attitudes, external factors, and behaviours, which is an extended model of Ajzen's theory of planned behaviour (1991).[20]

The BROAD project covered numerous viewpoints, not only at the level of hypotheses and theoretical models, but also in the area of empirical research; the research report in itself could fill a smaller book.[21] The present chapter primarily concentrates on those elements of the research conclusions that are relevant from the aspect of IT professionals' views on surveillance, as well as those that could be of interest from the viewpoint of IT professionals' moral decisions and behaviours.

10.5. METHODOLOGY

Twelve, roughly one-hour-long, semi-structured interviews were conducted in each country, using non-random samples. In the Netherlands, we selected the respondents with the snowball method; the main objective here was to learn the views of people who occupied different positions within the same organizational hierarchy, with a special focus on the study of organizational consensus. In Hungary, the primary aim in selecting the respondents was to ensure that all the relevant groups to be covered in the subsequent survey would also be represented by a typical or characteristic member in the interviews. Because the author knew many of the selected respondents personally, the interviews were conducted by a colleague who was unknown to the interviewees, thus trying to reduce the risk of the respondents' echoing the views of the author.

We prepared an online survey for the qualitative study. Putting together a sample of IT professionals to be interviewed was not an easy task. Because representativeness of the unknown population was a methodological requirement, the sample population was put together in two stages: in the first stage we approached the selected professional groups, relying on the technique of distributing organization-specific tokens[22] (controlled sample); and in the second, we announced the survey on public platforms and the respondents filled out the questionnaire in a form of self-assessment (random sample).

For the quantitative survey, we compiled an online questionnaire, making use of the lessons learned from the interviews. The questionnaire contained 48 questions or blocks of questions, which incidentally turned out to be too many, as many of the respondents lost patience halfway through or lacked the necessary time, which resulted in a number of incompletely filled out questionnaires. The 48 questions were divided into 8 clusters:

1. Current work situation (1 question)
2. You and the organization you work for (5 questions)
3. General description of your work (3 questions)
4. Recent project (15 questions)
5. You and your personal experience with IT (4 questions)
6. Data Protection (10 questions)
7. General attitudes towards the information society (6 questions)
8. Demographics (4 questions)

In carrying out the online survey, we relied on the software Limesurvey.[23] Only active IT professionals were asked to fill out the complete list of questions; IT students and respondents belonging to the category "miscellaneous" (for example, retired IT professionals) automatically skipped clusters 2 through 4, as they had no work environment.

A total of 1,799 respondents filled out the questionnaire in the two countries. There were a large number of incompletely filled out questionnaires, which nevertheless yielded useful information in relation to certain questions. We could not, however, consider questionnaires on which the respondents spent no more than two minutes. The resulting sample contained 1,076 questionnaires for evaluation, which formed the basis of the analysis. The analysis was carried out using the programme IBM PASSWstatistics.[17]

Promotional work in preparation for the survey proved less successful in the Netherlands than in Hungary; as a result, 77.9% of the analyzed sample came from Hungary, and only 22.1% from the Netherlands, which somewhat restricted the validity of the comparative conclusions between the two countries.

10.6. THE INTERVIEWS

In the following we shall focus on a number of specific findings emerging from the analysis of the interviews, with special emphasis on the topic of surveillance, which has been added to the subject matter of the research project as a result of the Hungarian team's marked interest.

The twenty-four respondents represented a broad spectrum of IT applications and job titles. Interestingly, the majority of the respondents, who represent twenty-four IT application areas and came from an age bracket as wide as 27–72, consider themselves IT professionals, despite the fact that most of them have never received any formal education in information technology. Most of them have completed some training course in IT-related subjects or acquired their professional skills in a self-taught manner. The older respondents obtained degrees in electrical engineering or mathematics, which can be considered the predecessors of IT subjects.

> Nowadays just about anybody with a little knowledge about computers can be described as an IT expert, but personally I would continue to insist on linking it to a college degree, as a minimum condition. (Information security expert, HU)

The interviews have revealed that the knowledge of IT professionals on personal data and data protection is equally sketchy in both countries. None of the respondents could provide either a formal or a substantive definition of personal data. Most of them gave a vague, general description, such as "data relating to a person", or mentioned examples of personal data, such as a credit card number. The respondents had similarly hazy notions of data protection. Most of them understood data protection as having to do with data security, although the Dutch respondents proved more critical in this regard. However, even data security proves secondary in the course of their work:

> In the end functionality will also win over security, otherwise your systems are locked up and of no use. (ICT project manager, NL)

The respondents in both countries were also uninformed about data protection laws, with the majority believing that these had no relevance to their work.

> I don't know the data protection law in any great details, but perhaps I know something about its effects, and also what it is about. It does not affect my work. (CEO IT association, HU)

> I have a gut feeling about what can be done and what can't. This is more an ethical norm than a legal one. (Innovator, NL)

Talking about the principles of data protection, one of the Dutch respondents made the following remark:

> I have heard about them, but I cannot name them. It is a feeling in my head. I do however believe that I take these principles into account in my daily work. (Developer, NL)

Another regrettable yet unsurprising finding emerging from the survey is that the active IT professionals also have insufficient knowledge and application experience in the area of PETs:

> We do not really use PETs. There is no demand for them. (Unit manager, NL)

> Not directly. This is the responsibility of the client. (Consultant, NL)

> Clients may eventually ask for them, but we have not heard of requests to insert PETs into our technology. (Business development manager, NL)

10.6.1. Internet Surveillance

Most of the (Hungarian) respondents had no objections to the surveillance of their Internet habits and behaviour; they felt that they "had nothing to hide".

> But personally, I do not consider anything about my life to be out of the ordinary [. . .] If there is anybody out there who wants to observe

me, then he might as well observe all the ten million inhabitants of this country. If I can be a target, so can anybody else. (Marketing and sales manager, HU)

In any case, 98 or 99 percent of the people have nothing to worry, simply because no one cares what they are doing. And as for the remaining one or two percent, they must get used to the fact that this is how the world operates right now. (Chief executive, IT security SME, HU)

Some of them distinguished between surveillance and the various grades of behavioural targeting, for example:

The simple fact that [a robot] watches my Internet habits and clicking patterns and compiles statistics about the pages I visit, effectively treating me as a number, this does not bother me too much. But if someone tied my name to the types of web pages I visit and found me on that basis with a business proposition, say, or if this information came up in the course of a job interview, for example, now that would be troubling. That would truly be troubling (Database expert, HU)

10.6.2. Workplace Surveillance

Contrary to their views on Internet surveillance, the respondents were rather critical about workplace surveillance. Although they considered some forms of workplace monitoring to be permissible, or even necessary, in general they showed solidarity with the employees. This can partly be explained by the fact that the majority of the respondents themselves worked, or used to work, in subordinate positions.

If the employees complete the task that has been assigned to them, they should be allowed to make phone calls or play on the computer a little. (Head of SW development firm, HU)

I am firmly against it. Let's face it, when somebody sits in front of the computer eight hours a day, and does nothing but work and work and work, that's not a good thing. And when this person wants to take ten minutes off to check something out on the Internet, people should not make a big fuss about this. (Web services manager, HU)

When it came to a workplace environment, the respondents took a much more nuanced view of the legitimacy of surveillance than with regard to the Internet, as the quote below can faithfully illustrate:

I hate these methods. Even the mere thought of me monitoring on my central computer terminal how [her secretary] in another office room is spending her time, gives me the creeps. [But] I would reprimand those civil servants who leak material, for example, out of political motivation. (CEO IT association, HU)

10.6.3. Surveillance by the State

The majority of the respondents have considered surveillance by the state both natural and acceptable. The same chief executive of an IT association, who regarded the monitoring of her secretary's work unacceptable, considers surveillance by the state natural:

Obviously, the state needs certain types of information, and it can compile the various databases any time it thinks necessary. There is nothing we can do about that. (CEO IT association, HU)

Although it concerns a public utility company, rather than the state, the rather excessive view below is educational:

Hungary has the strictest privacy protection regime in the world, one that verges on the irrational. [. . .] I mean that this not right that the BKV (Budapest Transport Company) should not be able to install surveillance cameras on its buses, in order to monitor its passengers! [. . .] We are protecting the criminals against the victims. (University professor, HU)

10.6.4. Responsibility

An analysis of the interviews reveals that the majority of the respondents think that they bear no responsibility in ensuring the legality of the system they help to develop or run: the responsibility lies with either the management or the clients, but is in any case outside their competency. We provide a few typical comments:

This is not my area. The responsibility for complying with the law in this respect lies with the management. I do not know enough about it. (ICT innovator, NL)

Besides calling the clients' attention to the legal consequences, is there anything else that you can do or want to do?
No, there isn't, but then again, this is not our job. I think that by doing this we have done all that is expected from us in the matter. (CEO, IT security SME, HU)

Hungarian companies, and especially the smaller ones, don't give a damn about the whole thing. (CEO IT security SME, HU)

Personal, ethical considerations are most likely to pop up in interviews with the Dutch respondents:

> I have a gut feeling about what can be done and what can't. This is more an ethical norm than a legal one [. . .] The main objective for me is to teach the students [and] their teachers how to learn ICT responsibly. (ICT innovator, NL)

In the case of a respondent from the Netherlands, the attitude is manifested in the ethical behaviour, at least in a self-reported manner:

> If a client would want to use the products we advise to target the IT behaviour of individual employees I would not accept the job. (Business development manager, NL)

10.7. SURVEY DATA

The BROAD survey contains 48 questions and more than three hundred variables; even a summary review of their multivariate analysis would considerably exceed the scope of this chapter. On this occasion we have selected three groups of questions: making decisions about the handling of personal data and the compositions of views influencing such decisions in the organizational environment of IT professionals; the respondents' assessment regarding the protection of their information privacy; and the respondents' general ideas about the manifest features of information society.

10.7.1. Decision-Making within the Organization

Three-quarters of the active IT professionals declared that during projects that involved the handling of personal data there were explicit discussions about the specific ways of managing personal data. Nationality, age, and the size of the organization were not factors in relation to the actuality of the discussions. The only difference seems to be that those directly responsible for implementing IT methods are more willing to conduct internal discussions about the handling of personal data than are the leaders of the organization.

The majority of the respondents agree with the decisions made about the handling of personal data throughout the project. Almost all of them claimed that if they happened to disagree with a decision, they would definitely let it be known. However, three-quarters of them said they would go along with the decision, even if they disagreed with it, with only 25% stating that in such a situation they would refuse to implement the decision. With regard to the handling of personal data, we tagged members of the first group as highly responsible, whereas members of the second group were termed as less responsible.

A detailed analysis of the data has revealed that neither nationality nor age appeared to be a factor with regard to responsible behaviour. The only significant difference in the composition of the two groups was related to position within the organizational hierarchy: Managers and IT architects had a higher representation in the high responsibility group than IT engineers and IT testers. However, it is far from self-evident whether the results really reflected the differences of responsible behaviour or merely testified to the fact that people in higher positions were in a better position to refuse to carry out decisions they disagreed with.

In order to identify the underlying values that influence decisions about the handling of personal data within the organization, we asked the respondents to rank the following items on a scale of one to five, from 'completely irrelevant' to 'very important':

1. Freedom of information
2. Security of data
3. Protection of personal data
4. Risk management
5. Cost effectiveness

Respondents rated security of data and the protection of personal data as the most important, followed by risk management, freedom of information, and cost effectiveness; however, the differences recorded on the 5-point scale were insufficient for a precise assessment of the importance of the various items. Using principal component analysis, it was possible to show that two factors played a significant role in the composition of the answers: one factor incorporated freedom of information, security of data, and protection of personal data (we termed this the security & data protection factor), and the other was a combination of risk management and cost effectiveness (the risk management factor).

A study of the respondents' opinions about the views of their bosses, subordinates, and professional peers in connection with the ranking of the above items has revealed that the security & data protection factor weighed little in their assessment of their colleagues. In other words, the respondents felt that they rated these values higher than their colleagues did.[24] At the same time, with regard to risk management and cost effectiveness, they apparently believed that these mattered more to them than they did to their subordinates, but they still mattered less than their bosses and clients seemed to think. This opinion was independent of their position, their age, the size of their organization, and their national identity.

A difference in the general attitude of the two national groups has been measured in that, in comparison to their Hungarian colleagues, the Dutch IT professionals attached greater importance to the extent their peer group valued the security & data protection factor, and also that the managers— irrespective of nationality—assessed the importance these items had in the eyes of their clients significantly higher than their colleagues employed as IT engineers did.

Organizational consensus refers to the degree to which an individual's attitudes coincide with the general attitudes within an organization. In our case we studied this consensus in relation to the importance attached to the assessment of the above values. An analysis of our data has revealed that neither age nor gender affected the organizational consensus. What did affect it, however, was nationality: according to their own assessment, the Dutch respondents were more in agreement with their colleagues than their Hungarian counterparts seemed to be. This conclusion, therefore, failed to support our general hypothesis, whereby the IT professionals in Hungary are more likely to identify with the views and value systems of their bosses than those of their colleagues who have been socialized in established democracies.

10.7.2. Perceived Behaviour Regarding One's Own Privacy Protection

According to the evidence of the face-to-face interviews, the majority of IT professionals believe that IT professionals can protect their information privacy better than others. So we posed the following question to the survey's respondents: How closely do you agree with the suggestion that IT professionals can protect themselves in the Internet environment? Half of the respondents were convinced that they could adequately defend themselves on the Internet, whereas one-quarter definitely disagreed; the rest could not answer.

We also examined whether those who thought that they could protect themselves on the Internet made use of PETs in their own practice more than the rest of the respondents. We reached the conclusion that there was no significant difference in the use of PETs between members of this group and the others. Furthermore, we studied whether those who thought they could adequately protect themselves on the Internet actually used more PETs in the IT applications created or supervised by themselves than the others did. Here, too, we found that there was no significant correlation between subjective assessment and workplace behaviour.

10.7.3. General Attitudes Towards the Information Society

We inquired about the respondents' level of concern for the following issues of apparent social significance:

- Quality of health services
- National security/terrorism
- Standard of education
- (Mis)use of personal data
- Environmental issues

- Unemployment
- Immigrants and asylum seekers
- Discrimination and equality
- Limitation to the freedom of speech
- Emergence of a surveillance society

Of the listed items, quality of health services, standard of education, and (mis)use of personal data received the highest scores.

Next we asked our respondents to indicate on a 5-point scale—from strongly disagree to strongly agree—the extent of their agreement with the following statements in relation to privacy and the handling of personal data:

- People have lost control of the way their personal data is being collected
- New technologies provide better privacy protection
- Privacy used to be better protected
- The protection of privacy has increased in the last couple of years
- The protection of privacy has decreased over the last couple of years
- Ordinary Internet users do not know how to protect their data on the Internet
- Privacy can be traded in against benefits
- Government and organizations collect personal data to gain control over people
- The protection of privacy undermines national safety
- IT professionals know how to defend themselves on the Internet
- There is too much hype about the handling of personal information
- The modern world is the end of privacy, you must live with it
- People are not interested at all in what happens to their data
- Internet users are themselves responsible for the way their data is handled on the Internet

Our principal component analysis has revealed the presence of five factors, which we marked with the terms 'changes', 'hype', 'lost control', 'disinterest', and 'own responsibility'. According to the evidence of our analysis, the respondents agreed that the average Internet users had no idea how to protect themselves on the Internet and were not too bothered about the issue ('disinterest'). The respondents also concurred with the view that people lost control over the handling of their personal data and that the government and various organizations were collecting personal data in order to increase their influence over people ('lost control').

At the same time, it should be noted that one-third of the respondents could not decide whether they were concerned with the content of the listed statements; this indicates a considerable lack of interest for the handling of personal data.

In another list of items, we asked the respondents how big a role the following values played in their everyday lives:

- Freedom of information
- Security
- Protection of personal data
- Risk management
- Personal freedom
- Democracy
- Trust between people and government
- Trust between organizations and their customers
- Social order
- Cost effectiveness

The majority of the respondents rated all the listed items as valuable, without showing significant variations. In the detailed analysis we relied on the distribution of answers to select three factors, which we marked with the terms 'democracy', 'cost effectiveness', and 'security'. Of these three items, the values comprising the factor 'democracy' received the highest score, albeit with a small margin.

Finally, we checked whether the answers to the items list could be correlated and found that the answers to the following four items—each incorporated in a different question—show significant correlation: concerns about the misuse of personal data, concerns about the emergence of a surveillance society, concerns about people having lost control of the way their personal data is being collected, and concerns about a decrease of privacy in the last couple of years. Using these four questions, we created a new variable, which we termed 'privacy concern'.

We have concluded that significant variations exist in the respective views of the groups of respondents from three different aspects: nationality, student status, and age. Respondents in the Netherlands were significantly more concerned about privacy than the Hungarian respondents were. Additionally, IT professionals were more concerned about privacy than IT students. Respondents between 35 and 49 years old were significantly more concerned about privacy than younger participants. At the same time, age, gender, the size of the organization, and work position did not play any role in the level of privacy concern.

We also compared the level of privacy concern with various elements of self-reported behaviour. We found that the level of privacy concern was not related to whether people used pseudonyms in their online activities, whereas there was a positive correlation between the level of privacy concern and people's—habitual or occasional—tendency to provide false personal information on the Internet.

10.8. LESSONS LEARNED—AND THINGS TO DO

Within the framework of the BROAD project, we have studied the views of people representing a profession generally regarded as influenced by the global technical development in two different social and cultural environments. In numerous cases, nationality proved irrelevant to both the final conclusions and the quantitative cataloguing of the answers; in other cases, however, it revealed significant differences. Therefore, some of our conclusions can be regarded quite general, whereas others emphasize the importance of the social and cultural differences between the two environments.

Foremost among our general conclusions is the recognition that IT professionals play a pivotal role in the implementation of projects that involve the handling of personal data, and that they possess great potentials to foster the rights and opportunities of the data subjects, a circumstance they themselves seem to be keenly aware of. IT professionals, regardless of age, gender, and organizational background, had the same level of concern for data protection rights in both countries. They also held similar, rather pessimistic views about the knowledge and skills of Internet users in the area of personal data protection. However, when it came to the protection of their own privacy, they claimed to be more cautious than the rest, with half of the respondents thinking that they were capable of protecting themselves on the Internet.

The respondents from both countries shared a willingness to voice their concerns in case decisions irreconcilable with their views on the handling of personal data were discussed in their presence. However, the majority of the respondents in both countries admitted that in spite of such a disagreement they would carry out any final decisions.

In the areas of data protection and PETs, the Dutch IT professionals have shown themselves more knowledgeable than their Hungarian counterparts; they are also more concerned with the effects on the private sphere; and there is a wider agreement among them in professional matters.

It can be concluded that the attitudes of the IT professionals only marginally influence their actual behaviour, at least in the areas covered by the study. Those who care more about privacy do not appear to be using more PETs in their own online activities or in the products they have helped develop. On some occasions, such as workplace discussions, they appear to be more active.

As for our general hypothesis, whereby the IT professionals who design, build, or operate the systems that manage personal data have a crucial role in the way these systems handle the personal data of the people concerned, this is fully in line with our collected data. As for the assumption that on certain issues the interviews and the survey yield substantially different information, this will need further clarification in the course of the detailed analysis. Our analysis regarding organizational consensus has failed to support our original hypothesis, whereby IT professionals—at least in Hungary—tend to identify with the value system of their bosses or clients; here, however, further investigation would be necessary before we can settle the issue.

One of our detailed hypotheses, whereby there are differences between distinct groups in the sample with regard to their concerns about privacy protection, has partially been borne out by our data: the Dutch and the older IT professionals are significantly more concerned with the protection of privacy than the rest. Our other hypothesis, whereby privacy concerns are reflected in people's actual online behaviour and work, proved correct only to a limited extent, as the attitudes only marginally affect people's behaviour, according to our data. Our research results supported our expectations regarding national differences in organizational consensus.

Our hypothesis claiming that there are differences between distinct groups in the sample with regard to their degree of responsibility, defined as their resistance to carry out decisions about personal data if they disagree with them, has essentially been unsupported by our data; the level of responsibility, which we have defined as someone not carrying out any decision that goes against his or her views on the handling of personal data, has turned out to be equally low in all groups.

But before we turn to drawing our final conclusions, we ought to run through the limitations of our research. One such limitation results from the specific nature of the sample: using qualitative methods, we have investigated a sample population of interviewees selected either by us or by their own colleagues, and we studied another, semi-controlled sample using quantitative methods. Several factors distorted our sample: it was possible that only those who had attached great importance to the topic from the start, or only those who wished to conform to certain expectations, emanating either from the heads of their organization or from their teachers, filled out our online questionnaire. The demographical composition of the survey sample was also uneven, and on the basis of the lessons learned from the analysis of the responses, certain modifications in some of the questions ought to be considered for any subsequent surveys. Finally, another limitation was the fact that only a few indirect comparative analyses could be carried out because of the pioneering nature of the research.

After all, what do IT professionals think about surveillance? The emerging picture is rather complex, and for the time being we only see the details. The one thing that seems clear is that we can describe the role of IT professionals as neither "outright positive" nor "outright negative"; as a whole, they stand neither "for" nor "against" surveillance. What seems perfectly obvious, however, is that if we want to control or limit the emergence of surveillance society, especially in the Internet environment, then the only viable strategy must include the inculcation of IT professionals, or at least a large part of them, so as to encourage them to develop their knowledge and change their attitudes—and we need to do this not in a didactic way, but by taking into account their existing interests.

The results of one research project will not suffice to achieve this; we need educational programs, professional platforms, and civil initiatives, as well as a meaningful dialogue between IT professionals and the other stakeholders in society. Naturally, we also need further research projects, either by repeating the BROAD survey in other countries or by improving its methods. In the interest of furthering this goal, the research consortium has decided to make available its raw data for all researchers interested in the topic.

NOTES

1. See for example Dyzenhaus et al. (2007).
2. In the author's own definition, a "social informatist"—even if this expression cannot be found in any of the English dictionaries.
3. http://en.wikipedia.org/wiki/Information_technology (accessed on September 27, 2010).
4. By now, this multi-disciplinary field has produced a number of highly acclaimed research and learning centres, such as the Surveillance Studies Centre at Queen's University (Kingston, Canada) and City University London, which runs an MA course in Surveillance Studies; the academic field has a prestigious professional forum in the *Surveillance and Society Journal*, and its researchers and research centres can keep in touch through the Surveillance Studies Network (http://www.surveillance-studies.net).
5. One part of the available studies deals with computer ethics or organizational ethics in general, which may include privacy- or surveillance-related aspects with regard to the views and behaviour of IT professionals. In this category the study of Collins and Stahl (2002) deserves particular attention, in which the authors analyze the moral problems of employee surveillance and the role of codes of conduct in influencing the behaviour of IT professionals within the organization. Studies have also been published about the potential risk posed by the IT professionals to the security of the organization, such as the annual "Trust, Security and Passwords" survey and analysis prepared by Cyber-Ark Software (2007–2010), implicitly suggesting that IT professionals themselves should be kept under surveillance. A significant exception to the negligence of researchers in the area of exploring IT professionals' own views about surveillance and the management of personal data in general is Shaw's empirical study of webmasters' attitudes (2003).
6. The data collection project conducted simultaneously in eight countries in the summer of 2006 was extended to Japan in December 2007; however, the (online) methodology used in the latter country was different.
7. The survey interviews in Canada, France, Hungary, Spain, and the US were conducted over the phone by professional pollsters.
8. The results of the research have been published in a book (Zureik et al. 2010).
9. Privacy and Identity Management for Europe (PRIME) was a project supported by the European Comission's Sixth Framework Program (2004–2009) aimed at developing privacy-enhancing identity management solutions (http://www.prime-project.eu). As part of the project, the Tilburg Institute for Law, Technology, and Society (TILT) led empirical research on user attitudes relating to privacy.
10. For a critical analysis, see Kumaraguru and Cranor (2005) or EPIC (http://epic.org/privacy/survey) (accessed on ???).
11. From the nearly 5,000 webmasters successfully reached through e-mails, Shaw received a total of 359 usable responses (Shaw 2003, 309).
12. Magnitude of effect, social consensus, probability of effect, temporal immediacy, proximity, and concentration of effect (Jones 1991).

13. The project was supported by the Fundamental Rights and Citizenship Program of the European Commission.
14. http://www.broad-project.eu (accessed on ???).
15. This is the trilingual PET Portal & Blog, http://pet-portal.eu (accessed on ???).
16. The professional videos are registered under Creative Commons license and can be freely downloaded from http://pet-portal.eu/video (accessed on ???).
17. This is supported by the findings of researchers, for example Collins and Stahl (2002) or Shaw (2003), who have studied the moral considerations, intra-organizational relations and self-reported attitudes of IT professionals.
18. This hypothesis rests on a certain realization, termed by the author the "threshold of abstraction", whereby the answers depend not only on the severity of the breech of privacy, but also on the degree of abstraction, otherwise the level of palpability, associated with the violation. Typical survey questions dispense with most of the details, which means that they appear far more abstract than the problems outlined in an interview. A similar phenomenon emerged from the GPD survey (Székely 2010).
19. We have advanced this hypothesis on the basis of the author's decades-long work as an expert and lecturer.
20. We must point out here that the BROAD project, similarly to any research projects using interviews and surveys, has been designed to measure self-reported behaviour, rather than actual actions. Therefore, researchers under such circumstances need a hypothesis, which establishes the connection between the observable and the inferred elements, namely the knowledge, the attitudes, and the actual acts—in this regard we have borrowed the conclusions of Shaw's research, and also adjusted the general Fishbein-Ajzen model to our own research environment.
21. At the moment, the manuscript forms part of the closing report of the BROAD project.
22. These tokens make the categorization of the anonymous responses from the various organizations possible; they also allow a comparison of the replies from the individual organizations.
23. http://www.limesurvey.org (accessed on ???).
24. In all probability the fact that people tend to judge their own attitudes more positively than their colleagues' has a lot to do with this finding. Because the questionnaire and the general topic of the survey convey the importance of the topic, the respondents are probably inclined to see themselves as more interested and responsible in this area than they see their colleagues.

REFERENCES

Clark, M. Wesley. 2009. Pole cameras and surreptitious surveillance. *The FBI Law Enforcement Bulletin,* November 2009. http://findarticles.com/p/articles/mi_m2194/is_11_78/ai_n42126009/ (accessed on ???).
Collins, Dervla and Bernd Carsten Stahl. 2002. The importance of codes of conduct for Irish IS/IT professionals' practice of employee surveillance. In *The transformation of organisations in the information age: Social and ethical implications,* ed. Isabel Alvarez et al., 67–82. Proceedings of ETHICOMP 2002, Lisbon, Portugal.
Cyber-Ark Software. Annual trust, security and passwords surveys 2007–2010. http://www.cyber-ark.com/constants/white-papers.asp (accessed on ???).

Dyzenhaus David, Sophia Reibetanz Moreau, and Arthur Ripstein. 2007. *Law and morality: Readings in legal philosophy.* Buffalo: University of Toronto Press.

Electronic Privacy Information Center (EPIC). 2005. Public opinion on privacy. http://epic.org/privacy/survey (accessed on ???).

Enright, Henry. *The winning partnership: law enforcement & video surveillance systems.* The McMorrow Corporate Facilities Management Report. http://mcmorrowreport.com/articles/lawenforce.asp (accessed on ???).

Figliola, Patricia Moloney. 2007. *Digital surveillance: the Communications Assistance for Law Enforcement Act.* CRS Report for Congress. http://www.fas.org/sgp/crs/intel/RL30677.pdf (accessed on ???).

Fishbein, Martin and Icek Ajzen. 1975. *Belief, attitude, intention, and behavior: An introduction to theory and research.* Reading, MA: Addison-Wesley.

Hanna, Michael J. and Ronald P. Mattioli. 1995. Tactical surveillance with a twist. *The FBI Law Enforcement Bulletin,* August, 1995. http://findarticles.com/p/articles/mi_m2194/is_n8_v64/ai_17482629/ (accessed on ???).

Harris Interactive. 2001. Privacy on & off the Internet: what consumers want. Technical Report. November 2001. New York: Harris Interactive.

International PET Portal and Blog. http://pet/portal.eu (accessed on ???).

Jones, Thomas M. 1991. Ethical decision making by individuals in organizations: an issue-contingent model. *The Academy of Management Review 16* (2): 366–395.

Kumaraguru, Ponnurangam and Lorrie Faith Cranor. 2005. Privacy indexes: a survey of Westinís studies. Pittsburgh, PA: Institute for Software Research International, School of Computer Science, Carnegie Mellon University. http://reports-archive.adm.cs.cmu.edu/anon/isri2005/CMU-ISRI-05-138.pdf (accessed on ???).

Leenes, Ronald and Isabelle Oomen. 2009. The role of citizens: what can Dutch, Flemish and English students teach us about privacy? In *Reinventing data protection?* ed. Serge Gutwirth et al., 293–316. Springer Science+Business Media B.V.

Lessig, Lawrence. 2000. *Code and other laws of cyberspace.* New York: Basic Books.

Oomen, Isabelle and Ronald Leenes. 2008. Privacy risk perceptions and privacy protection strategies. In *Policies and research in identity management,* ed. Elisabeth de Leuw, Simone Fischer-Hübner, Jimmy Tseng, and John Borking, 121–138. Boston: Springer.

Shaw, Thomas R. 2003. The moral intensity of privacy: an empirical study of webmasters' attitudes. *Journal of Business Ethics 46:* 301–318.

Székely, Iván. 2010. Changing attitudes in a changing society? information privacy in Hungary 1989–2006. In *Surveillance, privacy and the globalization of personal information: International comparisons,* ed. Elia Zureik et al., 150–170. Montreal: McGill-Queen's University Press.

Zureik, Elia, Linda Harling Stalker, Emily Smith, David Lyon, and Yolande E. Chan (eds.). 2010. *Surveillance, privacy and the globalization of personal information: International comparisons.* Montreal: McGill-Queen's University Press.

11 Fields, Territories, and Bridges

Networked Communities and Mediated Surveillance in Transnational Social Space

Miyase Christensen and André Jansson

11.1. INTRODUCTION

The rise of new media networks in general and the widespread appropriation of "web 2.0" applications in particular have not only altered the agenda of media studies, but also contributed to the growing osmosis between the discipline and its surroundings. Although it is relatively easy to identify the technological affordances of these media, especially in terms of global connectivity, the social consequences are notoriously ambiguous to pin down, and cannot be conceptualized without venturing into the broader interdisciplinary discourses of surveillance and community making.

Let us, as a case in point, consider Andreas Wittel's (2001) assertive analysis of "network sociality"; a concept pointing to the distinctly new forms of disembedded sociality allowed by the affordances of networked means of communication. Wittel's work is grounded in empirical data gathered in urban middle-class settings around the heydays of the "new economy" and depicts an order directly opposed to *Gemeinschaft*. Network sociality is based on an "exchange of data" rather than on mutual experience and narration—which, however, is not to be understood as an entirely pessimistic diagnosis: "Instead of perceiving this process as de-socialization, I suggest a shift away from regimes of sociality in closed social systems and towards regimes of sociality in open social systems" (Wittel 2001, 64). Clearly, Wittel's study in many ways foresaw what was to come in terms of growing opportunities for (commodified) social networking and increasingly deterritorialized forms of coordination. However, through the combination of converging (online) media industries, diversified genres of social media, and the pervasive, yet socially stratified everyday saturation of these media, Wittel's claim as to the more general shift towards "sociality in open systems" seems to be increasingly problematic to sustain, and also deserves further sociological contextualization.

Three types of complexity have surfaced since Wittel published his analysis. First, there is evidence that the "exchange of data" that occurs at social networking sites such as Facebook (not invented when Wittel conducted his study) is just as much about "narrational" relation building, and the maintenance of communities, as it is about ephemeral encounters. Online interaction unfolds through diverse channels within a broad social spectrum, attaining the signs of durability (time bias) as well as expansion (space bias). This means that *social control* in the traditional sense of *Gemeinschaft* is still an influential social desire, even fuelled by growing experiences of insecurity (Abe 2009).

Second, to the extent that network sociality does occur, in Wittel's sense, it is usually entangled with processes of *social exclusion and closure*. Although social "networking" per se attains an expansive bias, it always takes place within more or less institutionalized social fields (Bourdieu 1972/1977, 1979/1984) where the quest for influence and status necessitates various forms of symbolic boundary maintenance and distinction (Christensen 2011; Jansson 2011). There is also a technological side to this: whereas the diversification and sophistication of digital networking tools ensure increasingly global forms of connectivity, the very same development allows for refined regimes of closure, and the making of (deterritorialized) enclaves.

Finally, the expansion of online social networks is inherently dependent on commoditized forms of *interactive surveillance*, meaning that media users are commercially monitored and targeted through their own representational activities (here, referring to actions and transactions taking place within the online realm) (Andrejevic 2007). This condition has established a new complexity of gazes, where the "data subjects" may enjoy the sights of the simulated "data doubles" of themselves and others (Deleuze 1992; Bogard 1996, 2006; Best 2010), while the same data is also accumulated and processed for further monitoring purposes within the industry. Integral to the participatory, even emancipatory, expressions of convergence culture advocated by Henry Jenkins (2006) and others, is thus the rise of complex "surveillant assemblages" (Haggerty and Ericson 2000), often critically assessed in terms of for instance "digital enclosures" (Andrejevic, 2007).

Altogether, whereas "network sociality" seems a valid theoretical concept, the current developments of "web 2.0" call for a deeper problematization of the social interdependency of surveillance and community within a regime of mediated networking. This becomes a particularly critical challenge in a world marked by the multiplication of global mobility, where the bonds and bridges between people must often be regained and reformulated at new geographical locations, either by free will or out of coercive necessity. Here, the everyday saturation of online media and interactive surveillance is both a driver and a social response (see Urry 2003)—mediating between the exhilarating prospects and possibilities of a freewheeling cultural identity and the fears of community loss and dissolution.

The key for thinking about these approaches together, we argue, is to pay closer attention to the moral and ideological spaces within which people negotiate the various affordances of interactive technologies and manage the tension fields between community making, networking, and surveillant practices. In addressing the three areas of inquiry in all their complexity and in the context of web 2.0 surveillance, we adopt a theoretical approach based on both political-economic and more postmodern considerations in order to account for the dualistic character (i.e., technologies of freedom *and* control) of late-modern surveillance practices and processes. Whereas Andrejevic (2007) points to a growing pre-eminence of, for example, digital enclosures, Haggerty and Ericson (2000), with their metaphor of "surveillant assemblages" draw attention to the diffuse and disconnected (or rhizomatic) nature, hence potentially democratizing, potential of surveillance systems. Lyon's (2003) analysis makes reference to systems of social sorting, and Jenkins (2006) stresses new potentials for community building and creativity in the interactive era.[1] These moral and ideological spaces are the spaces (always socially materialized, see Silverstone et al. 1992) through which various degrees of "complicity" (Christensen 2011) or resistance to different forms of surveillance emerge (compare: Best 2010). Here, we will in particular incorporate Bourdieu's (1972/1977, 1979/1984) theory of social fields as an intermediary realm for making sense of the social construction of online territories and the associated expressions of symbolic capital. In doing so, we will weave together theoretical assessments and empirical findings from fieldwork conducted in two transnational contexts.

The first study deals with transnational migrants (of Turkish/Kurdish origin) residing in urban Sweden and involves qualitative, in-depth interviews conducted in 2008 and 2009. The interview data utilized in this chapter from this study involves six individuals (three men and three women), who are either professionals or students of higher education institutions, and who have either lived in Sweden their entire lives (second-generation immigrants) or moved to Sweden for professional/educational purposes. Their ages range between mid- to late-20s to early 40s, and they are well-educated, well- to fairly well travelled, and have considerable cultural and social capital. All six individuals are long-time media technology users and are active in diasporic representative formations (offline formal institutions and/or online identity-based groupings) either in more formal capacity (for example, as institutional board members) or as administers of/active users in online social media groups.

The second study was conducted in 2008 within a Scandinavian expatriate community in Managua, Nicaragua, that was linked to a global development business. One of the authors of this chapter spent four months working and living in Managua and experienced the expatriate life conditions. The interview data referred to in this chapter consist of six individual interviews with persons working for non-governmental organizations, and thus represent a formal structure and ethico-political project in which cosmopolitan ideas are ingrained (see Nowicka and Rovisco 2009, 7). As the informants are part of a well-educated class faction tied to the "global civil society" (Kaldor 2003), their affluence resides in cultural capital rather than economic capital (as seen from a Western perspective). In addition, they all have substantial previous experience working and living abroad. Demographically, the group includes three men and three women within the age-span of mid-20s to mid-50s.

At their first level, these studies provide comparative views of how online interaction in general, and the everyday management of surveillance (through personal communication technologies) in particular, pertain to the constitutive logic of (transnational) social fields.[2] Together, these case studies exemplify the ways in which surveillance operates at the "subjective level"—a lesser explored area in studies of surveillance—in an interactive media environment, and how individuals regard various key notions such as privacy and visibility vis-à-vis surveillance. The examples also provide a basis to consider how online social networking, personal management of individual data, and various surveillance practices function as mechanisms of both deterritorialization and reterritorialization through re/construction of and prying into a variety of digital spaces.

11.2. ON TRANSNATIONAL FIELDS AND BOURDIEUIAN SOCIOLOGY

Parallel to the global-scale rise of trans-border activity and penetration of technologies of virtual mobility, both situated, geographically demarcated experiences of "elsewheres" and technologically mediated communicative exchange have become central elements underlying social relations and social playing fields across the board. Within transnational and transmigratory contexts, where social reality is further marked by various forms of multiplicities (of spatial belonging; of political representation; of identity), the adoption and use of communication technology takes on a more intense meaning. Most recent research on transnational groups and their media use centre on the significant role played by ICTs and diasporic media in the management of identity and social relations (compare Georgiou 2005, 2006; Bailey et al. 2007; Titley 2008).

Whereas the globalization paradigm has provided a convenient discursive tool in articulating both the fundamental macro dynamics and social instances of such multiplicities and virtual and actual border-crossings, scholarship within its scope has tended to adopt an overly generalizing, at times poetic, discourse that has been counter-productive in capturing particularities. We are reminded here of Bourdieu's antagonism to "theoretical system building" (in Calhoun 1993, 44) or "theoretical theory", which involves conceptualizations that have no or little practical and analytical purchase. For one, in relation to human and labour flows, globalism has strived to draw attention to (a) discontinuities and ruptures in the social order by way of underscoring areas and processes where the nation state (as a meta-field) is presumably absent, and (b) the realm of social imaginaries

(Taylor 2004) that feed from such flow and flux. Here, in an attempt to locate and articulate the ensemble of new modes of sociality, structural elements and industry-pushed practices that (re)produce both systems of social control/monitoring and new arenas of social dynamism, first, we take on board conceptual apparatus from two distinct veins of thought: the paradigm of transnationalism and Bourdieuian sociology.

Transnationalism, which we take as a departure point here (and, despite its own shortcomings which we hope to alleviate in our larger study), allows for social analysis in which the puzzling role of the nation-state, alongside other social actors and in the grand scheme of mobilities, is understood more precisely and in relation to specific social instances of both its absence and ambiguous presence. The discourse of transnationalism also enables an analytical lens to pinpoint cross-locational elements that go into forging and maintaining socio-political formations beyond the confines of nation-state-centric frameworks *and* methodological nationalism (Beck, 2004/2006), which dominated social-scientific research over the decades. Most importantly, unlike in many accounts produced by the globalization paradigm, spatio-temporal and contextual specificity and "difference" remains integral to social analysis in transnationalism—and, as such, complements the Bourdieuian transhistoricity and lack of attention to epochal, spatial, and cultural particularity in his discussion of capital.[3]

This said—and, without following transnationalism into the depths of its analytic/paradigmatic confines—this vein of research has produced its own reductionisms and rigidities. It remains the case that in the body of literature produced on diasporas and migrant groups, the multiple complexities that structure transnational existence and everyday sociality are often explored in terms of geographic dualities. Such an approach is based on a linear logic of origin/destination paradox readily attributed to migrant or transient (as in the case of development workers) subjects and their (assumed) cultures/identities: home vs. host; sending country vs. receiving country; and, home culture (or national identity) vs. adopted culture are only a few of such categorizations that go into the formulation and operationalization of research agendas. An adjacent shortcoming of research on transborder/translocal groups has been the pervasive inclination towards defining transmigrant communities based on their ethnicity and presumed embracement of their national/cultural identity—considering those who do not fit in these frames exceptions to the rule.

Apart from the general problem of epistemological reductionism inherent in dichotomizing logics, such an understanding of migrant or transient subjectivities and their territorial multiplicity in terms of an attribute of absolute ontological interruptedness also maps onto methodological approaches to the geography of technology and mediation in transnational and diasporic contexts (i.e., the analysis of reception/consumption of transnational media). Although it does hold true that media (broadcast and print media, in particular) from the migrants' geo-linguistic region play a significant role not only in their capacity as information and entertainment sources but also in structuring sociality and power relations in social fields, the complexity of (new) media use by far exceeds the analytic potential that can be accommodated by the simple home vs. host duality.

A multiplicity of spatialities (the home departed, the city of residence, neighbourhood, home, school/work, places of social togetherness/pass-time), and a multiplicity of individual positionalities (class, gender, race/ethnicity, generation, sexual preference, politics/ideology, cultural taste, shopping habits, to name but few) shape technology use. And, each constituent, with its own morality, ideology, and economy, adds an autonomous dimension to the shape sociality takes. One good example was provided by a young Turkish man when he described how he created different groupings on his Facebook page to prevent his relatives from seeing photos tagged by his friends in Sweden and elsewhere and vice versa (in this case, to protect his privacy about his sexual preference and lifestyle), thereby creating different embodiments of his public and private self (male in his 20s), as we will further discuss later in the chapter. Similar tendencies were found in the Nicaraguan study, where the embedded code of Facebook, the fostering of peer-to-peer surveillance, was even considered too problematic to manage, and thus (implicitly) a threat to the autonomy of the social field. In some cases these experiences eventually led to passive uses of Facebook, in order not to get too involved.

As such, "the subjective geography of technology" (in Morley 2007, 250) as a structured and structuring force in transnational social fields remains key (yet under-researched) in understanding mediated social practice. Added to this are other forms of complexities brought about by systems of sorting and practices of web 2.0 surveillance that are increasingly part and parcel of the quest for belonging and positioning engaged in by individuals. In order to make sense of the social construction of online territories, accompanying expressions of symbolic capital and the structuring character of digitality, we turn to Bourdieu's (1972/1977; 1979/1984) theory of social fields as an intermediary realm. And, we do so for two reasons: first, the Bourdieuian conception of field is based on an understanding of power, its unequal distribution and the forms of domination/subordination it enables. Such a configuration of power and power relations remains key in constituting society, social relations and sociality. Second, although Bourdieu himself did not address "the transnational" per se as a realm where non-nation-state-centric fields take shape, his notion of the field allows for a construction of transnational social formations as fields with flexible boundaries, making room for the kind of multiplicities (rather than dualities) we discussed above. In terms of how they qualify as "fields", in the strict sense of the word, there are differences between the social realms represented by the two studies. Whereas the construct of field could be more directly associated with the domain of international development work that, in our case, involves the Scandinavians in Nicaragua, employing the term in discussing the diasporic spatio-social realm constituted by the Turkish groups in Sweden necessitates further elaboration.

A two-tiered approach encapsulates our inclination towards seeing clear linkages between how fields operate and the ways in which community-building and sociality structure, and are structured by, deeply ingrained codes and regimes in diasporic contexts—hence, engendering field-like struggles and positionalities. First, despite the fact that diasporas and the mobility that precedes their formations are not instigated by institutionalized, formal fields, if we are to take fields, akin to Jenkins (1992, 85), as social arenas defined by "the stakes that are at stake", then the similarities between any differentiated field and the specific spatialities and regimes of being/becoming generated by diasporic dynamics become obvious ones. Diasporic constellations, which are constituted of very complex, intricately embedded aggregates of networks (and, networks of networks) operate every bit as arenas characterized by collective and individual struggles (based on various conventions and individual/group tactics for capital conversion towards symbolic accumulation) to achieve power and domination through legitimatization, affirmation, and representation (in the meta-field of the nation state; internationally and transnationally; and, amongst the subgroups within the diaspora). Second, despite the wide-ranging differences in economic, social, and cultural, hence symbolic, capital that exist between the individuals and the groups that constitute transmigrant/transient groups (a point we try to underscore throughout the chapter), their agents, in general, are stakeholders to similar goals and aspirations and similar motives: a collective quest for dignified image and recognition in the larger social field (representative power) on the one hand; and, inter/intra group and individual struggles for symbolic power accumulation within the field itself. Further, the individuals interviewed for this study are active members in the diasporic arena and they embody a heightened sense of reflexivity about the inner workings of this particular diasporic group.

In short, the findings from the two empirical studies highlight how communicative, networked sociality is simultaneously delimited and enhanced by structural elements inherent in the transnational field/s (strategies) and by reflexive modulations and technologically induced interventions at the subjective level (tactics),[4] ultimately giving way to highly complex modes of surveillance and encapsulation.

11.3. TERRITORIES AND FIELDS: SOCIAL NETWORKING AS SPATIAL PRODUCTION AND CONTROL

The concepts of *territory* and *field* provide different, but also overlapping, connotations of spatial production. Whereas territory is most prominently associated with spatial enclosure, achieved through sharp boundaries that separate the rules and regimes of the inside from those of the outside, field tends to be associated with open space; an open-ended area of social possibility, agency and change. The field attains no distinct boundaries, and thus remains more or less open towards its vicinities, which also implicates that the division between "insiders" and "outsiders" becomes more diffuse, a matter of symbolic negotiation and visibility (see e.g., Tuan, 1977). This is to say that territory and field (within the present sociological context) signify different spatial orders of interaction and control. In directly observable social contexts, however, the relationship between these two horizontal understandings of space is much more complex. On the one hand, archetypal territories, such as nation states and institutionalized social enclaves, are never entirely sealed and homogenous entities, but marked by various, more or less regulated, in- and out-flows of people and information, as well as internal struggles for defining the means, ends, and limits of the territorial construct as such. Territories are thus always contested by various forces of deterritorialization, which destabilize pre-existing regimes of spatial control. On the other hand, in a social space such a thing as a completely open field can never exist, because social interaction always brings with it the establishment of codes and conventions, which in turn have a tendency to agglomerate into more or less compartmentalized sets of rules. As the competition for spatial order and control increases, fields (and parts of fields) may thus successively attain more territorial characteristics.

Although the concepts of field and territory can be analytically applied as separate spatial orders of interaction, the relationship between them must be understood as a social continuum rather than as a dichotomy. This point is comprehensively illustrated in Bourdieu's (for example: 1980/1990) discussions of the *social field*, which attains an intermediary position between the bounded social territory and the more open-ended system of exchange and flow. Whereas the social field provides a common ground for the circulation, exposition, and exchange of certain mutually recognized assets, that is, symbolic capital of a certain kind, it also constitutes a social battleground where different actors compete for centrality and power. Gaining access to a certain field is not a matter of crossing any absolute borders but rather about successively internalizing the rules and schemes of classification through which the power structures of the field are maintained. Bourdieu (1980/1990, chapter 4) has famously described this process of accommodation in terms of acquiring the "feel for the game"—a process of symbolic naturalization that comes easily to those with the right social *habitus*, whereas others are effectively prevented from accessing, or even imagining themselves as part of the field. This underscores not only that social fields attain certain territorial qualities, in the sense that they are "the products of a long, slow process of autonomization" (Bourdieu 1980/1990, 67), but also that boundary maintenance and remaking is an ever enduring socio-cultural battle.

Furthermore, territories and fields can coexist and overlap in complex ways. Analyzing any spatial construct, such as a village or a city—or for that matter a seemingly coherent and bounded online community—always involves the risk of making simplified claims as to what kinds of spatial orders actually prevail, and how different forms of social change, such as transnational mobility or the appropriation of new means of surveillance, influence those orders. The problem is particularly critical as such claims are always bound up with the representation of power. In the case of global, linked cities (Sassen 2001), for instance, the expansion of communication networks and the parallel rise of an online realm of network sociality cannot be separated from the logic of territoriality. In our case studies of transnational spaces of interaction there is evidence of how the deterritorializing affordances of new means of mobility and networking are paralleled by a socio-spatial development towards "software-sorted geographies" (Graham 2005) and what De Cauter (2004) calls "capsularization" (see also Jansson 2011). These mechanisms of segregation, which are to be seen as integral to the expansion of surveillant assemblages (Haggerty and Ericson 2000), imply that different mobile class factions are separated from one another, not only when travelling, but also when dwelling and interacting online as well as offline.

Our study of Scandinavian development workers in Managua, which will be discussed in the remainder of this section, confirms that expatriate professionals are typically targeted by relatively little, or "soft", administrative surveillance, whose purpose is primarily to ensure smooth passages, frictionless mobility, secure home environments, and a sense of "exitability", that is, the opportunity to leave the country if things would get too risky or complicated (Urry 2007, 201). Even though the professional, cosmopolitan ethos of development workers makes them inclined to engage with the poor, "motionless" areas of cities like Managua, their day-to-day presence in the city thus largely converges with the bounded routes and capsules of the global just-in-time city (compare Ciccolella and Mignaqui 2002, 322).

The logic of this condition can be further explicated through Bourdieu's conception of the social field (for example, Bourdieu 1972/1977, 1979/1984, 1980/1990). Although Bourdieu's writings do not provide any account of the role of globalization and transnational flows in relation to the (re)production of social fields, one can certainly argue that the logic of certain fields, such as the above-mentioned field of international development aid, is constituted precisely through the premise of global mobility, and thus follows a transnational set of rules.[5] The various actors and organizations that operate within the development sector all contribute to the consecration and legitimization of certain practices, competencies, and possessions as markers of symbolic capital (here broadly understood as the capacity to define and influence international development practices in a variety of transitional contexts), through which, in turn, the social positions of the actors and organizations are themselves classified. Typical indicators of capital are those skills and experiences that express individual mastery of cross-cultural interaction and translation, not least language skills and the experience of having worked in a variety of transitory societies (compare Eriksson Baaz 2005). For those in possession of such qualities the field operates as a vehicle and an arena for transnational mobility, as well as "motility" (Kaufmann 2002; Kaufmann et al. 2004), and thus for the further accumulation of the type of symbolic capital through which the field reproduces itself.

Through a closer scrutiny of the everyday practices of this group we can also grasp how the use of networked media implies the continuous interplay, at different spatial levels, between boundary maintenance and transcendence. On the one hand, Internet use tends to reinforce the transnational logic of the field—a tendency that is unambiguously expressed among those with longer experience of transnational professional mobility, that is, those who attain well-established positions within the field. These individuals testify to a slow process of accommodation, through which regular environmental changes and an increasingly globalized network of friends and acquaintances are turned into a natural part of one's biography, and thus an embodied expression of *habitus*. Here, networked media attain a key function for the time-space coordination of everyday job-related tasks; the monitoring of potential career opportunities within the field; and the maintenance of a global social network. For example, several informants mention that they often keep a chat window open via Skype or a webmail account when working in their offices, in order to enable swift communication within the professional context. In spatial terms their everyday work space thus expands from the local Nicaraguan setting to the rest of Central America, and to significant nodes in the rest of the world. There is no explicit mentioning of being under surveillance; on the contrary, these professional peer-to-peer monitoring practices, which might be subsumed under the term 'interveillance' (Jansson, 2010) to indicate their horizontal character, contribute to a deepening sense of integration within the field.

On the other hand, the opening of those transnational media spaces is paralleled by specific regimes of enclosure. First, whereas mediated interaction within the social field is experienced as smooth and liquid, many efforts to interact beyond the field are successively being compartmentalized, positioned as exceptional, ritualized events. Such a thing as "keeping in touch" with family and old friends is partly experienced as a social obligation and a pressure that has to be reflexively managed. One informant mentions that she has ritualized a Saturday Skype call with her parents in Sweden. Another informant describes how she sometimes opens the chat function in order to lower the threshold for making contact:

> The continuous communication gets more spread out the longer you are away. After a while you get immersed into this new world and then it becomes less important to communicate everything. [. . .] For some reason it's also nice sometimes to keep the worlds apart. There might

be a pressure to keep in touch [with those back home], and when you're finally ready to do that there must be something really exciting and emotionally precious to tell—but you may not feel that way, it may be a pressure actually, and then it's sometimes easier just to open a chat. It can take the edge of all that—that 'now I have to call home and inform them about everything'. (Female project leader in her 30s)

When Sofia talks about immersion it is to be understood not only in terms of local immersion, the experience of leading one's life under everyday conditions that are radically different from those of one's old friends and family, but perhaps more prominently in terms of field integration. Among those informants who are most thoroughly integrated within the field, for whom the prospects of returning to their home country is becoming an increasingly obscure idea (as the very idea of *the* "home" loses its significance) the social pressure of connectivity also loses its strength. The social trajectory of transnational professionals implies that the social network converges with the structures of the field, which means that the social network, together with an ensemble of other (mediated) relations and practices, increasingly operates as symbolic capital.

This brings us to the second point, which has to do with the mediated territorializing processes that occur *within* the field. Engaging with relevant blogs, e-mail lists, and online news flows are key symbolic practices that not only manifest the logic of the field, the "rules of the game", but also produce distinct online territories of belonging. As expressed by one of the informants, when reading the blogs of people he trusts and identifies with, he can "read between the lines" and thus gather a more nuanced picture than through mainstream media. By contrast, the margins of the field, and the socially restricted applicability of the rules of the game, become evident when the informants describe their experiences of networking platforms such as Facebook. Part of the problem with Facebook, as they describe it, is that it is too difficult to territorialize, and too complicated to manage the socio-technological imperatives of the surveillant assemblage:

> About Facebook . . . I was invited and signed up, but I have a problem with Facebook. [. . .] One thing I find especially clever about digital media is that you don't have to be simultaneous. That pertains to email or a blog—I can write when I want to, and somebody can comment when he or she has the time. Facebook does also work a bit like that, but I also feel that people try to drag me into things I don't have time for nor any interest in. [. . .] Facebook takes away parts of what I see as the good things about digital media—that I control my filters! (Male consultant in his 50s)

This approach appears to be typical. Other informants have even tried to restrict their profiles, activate filter functions, etc, but still find Facebook problematic. A woman in her 30s stated that she was "in two minds for a start" and decided to include only those she knew well, "so that not just anybody should be able to enter and see pictures, or that others should be able to publish pictures [of her]". Since then she has also realized that most of her job-related friends do not use Facebook very much.

This does not mean that Facebook is non-significant among those working within the development sector. But one obvious dilemma is that interaction through Facebook cannot occur within the *practical sense*, "social necessity turned into nature", of the field (Bourdieu 1980/1990, 69). Instead, the confrontation with diverse logics of practice leads to negative experiences of peer-to-peer monitoring ('interveillance' as social control), boundary transgression, and the mixing of worlds that preferably should be kept apart. Our findings in this regard underscore the ambiguous spatial nature of surveillant practice, and may be compared to the conclusions that Abe (2009) reached in a study of the Japanese social networking site *mixi*, where the users (whose social features are not specified in the study) were found, on the one hand, to "joyfully consume the peer-to-peer surveillance enabled by the system", but, on the other hand, seemed to be "obsessed with ascertaining security concerning their interactions with strangers" (Abe 2009, 86). We argue that a further scrutiny of how the logics of different social fields are played out within online spaces is needed in order to reach beyond too broad, and sometimes techno-deterministic, claims as to what orders of interaction social media sustain, and how users cope with various extensions of the surveillant assemblage (which would then also involve a critical problematization of the situated phenomenological *meaning* of surveillance and social control).

The picture is equally (if not more) complicated if we turn to our second case study. Although there is no professional field, as we discussed earlier, that precedes the agentic quest for mobility, and pursuits of representation and community building in diasporic contexts, the very acts of everyday, mundane online activity and social networking are bound up with in-group positioning, seeking belonging and identification (or the rejection of it), and creating alternative proximities through (virtual) geographic enclaves, as will be exemplified in the next section. In such cases, when "actual" (Morley 2011) spaces of being and living do not/or do partially map onto places of identification and physical territories of belonging, virtual geographies may end up embodying more closure and more rigorous regimes of border and activity control, thereby attracting certain groups and individuals who crave security through such closure and repelling certain others who merely seek the ontological comfort and practicality that come with online socialization (social network attributes) but wish to avoid structuring regimes of naturalization and control (field attributes). In the case of the Turkish diaspora in Stockholm, the two realms seem to be highly intertwined.

11.4. SOCIAL BRIDGES IN TRANSNATIONAL FIELDS: BETWEEN COMPLICIT SURVEILLANCE AND COMMUNICATIVE SOCIALITY

As we argue throughout this chapter, whereas web 2.0 affords new forms of communal/interpersonal interaction and creative sociality, such social formations need to be understood within the broader context of *social control,* processes of *social exclusion* and *closure,* and the complex forms of *surveillance* that they lead into. The transformation of existing norms and regimes and the emergence of new ones is always part and parcel of a social negotiation process that takes shape in moral and ideological spaces with both "complicity" (Christensen 2011) and resistance (compare: Best 2010) involved, hence various forms and scales of power relations always play a restructuring role. In this section, in addressing questions related with technologically enhanced communicative sociality and freedom vis-à-vis surveillance and closure in transmigratory contexts, we offer a discussion of online territorial constructions in specific contexts and perceptions of privacy and visibility.

Our fieldwork on Turkish diasporic subjects in Sweden illustrates a highly complex scenario of technology use and subjective positioning through which (a) existing identificatory categories are enforced and maintained; (b) new categories of identification and inclusion are instigated; and, (c) strategies for less-overt association/identification are made possible. The interviews reveal intensely contested notions of communal identity that mark social relations and power struggles within the larger diasporic field. Although offline institutions such as Turkiska Riksförbundet (Federation of Turkish Workers) Turkiska Ungdomförbundet (Turkish Youth Federation) have taken on representative roles over the decades, relatively new social constellations on online networking sites such as Facebook reflect the dynamic process of a quest for new spaces of belonging and identification, particularly amongst the younger individuals.

"Isvecli Turkler (Swedish Turks)", "Isvec Turkleri (Turks of Sweden)", "Turkar i Stockholm (Turks in Stockholm)", "Isvec'te Yasayan Turkler (Turks living in Sweden)", "Isvec'teyiz (We are in Sweden)" moderated by the offline Sweden Idea and Culture Association, and "A Group for the Swedish Turkish" constituted some of the popular Facebook groups at the time of the fieldwork. In addition, offline institutions such as Turkiska Student och Akademikerföreningen (Turkish Students and Academics Association) also have their own Facebook groups, carrying their existing offline networks to a larger field with more visibility. All the groups noted here incorporate spatial and ethnic signifiers in their titles.[6] Yet, there is a wide range of sentimentality and various degrees of identification with the labelling amongst the informants. Whereas some informants noted that they joined certain groups for the very purpose of seeking belonging and "like-minded company" (female in her 40s) beyond what the offline institutions can provide, some others commented that they avoid becoming members (yet, use the posts and information that is circulated within the group) as they "don't want to take on an identity *like that*" (female in her 20s).[7]

Merely being involved and active in one of many these domains bring with it symbolic assets that structure social relations and positions in intricate ways. Mediation takes the form of both practical resource and symbolic means (i.e., status marker through mere visibility and/or social influence). Activity online (or carving communicative space, as we discussed earlier); that is, profile maintenance, posting of information, clips, photos, messages, announcements, etc., equals symbolic capital actualization and accumulation. As such, activity online always translates into mis/recognition, is an immediate signifier for status, and inevitably coterminous with surveillance both at a vertical, and horizontal, subjective, and desired level.[8] This is particularly the case with younger and/or (cultural)capital-rich individuals in diasporic/transnational settings who, by moving into domains of "virtual togetherness" (Bakardjieva 2003) to either enhance offline status quo and visibility or to bypass various forms of coerced allegiances (for example to national identity, territorial/ethnic origin, religious identification) and symbolic violence, de facto enter into playing fields structured by a complicit form of surveillance and where a different "feel for the game" (Bourdieu 1980/1990, 66) is needed to mobilize capital conversion (into power) to pursue symbolic struggle. One informant who administered a Facebook group noted an overt example:

> When I took over I sent information about [this new group] to the other existing groups. But one of them seems to delete all the messages I have been sending so I stopped sending them. . . . (Female in her 40s)

The complicity in question here, beyond the incriminating connotations it carries, is in referring to the agentic character of current modes of surveillance that is conceded (or ignored) by the users. In the Turkish study, most of the individuals (despite being long-time, savvy users) had little to no awareness about the perverseness of surveillance on social networking sites[9] and commodification of private data. Yet, most were very critical of more visible forms of surveillance: "I am not a luddite. . . . but I don't buy the arguments put forth by politicians to promote applications like security cameras. . . . I believe they shouldn't be used" (male in his 40s).

> I lived in London and there are CCTV cameras everywhere. Actually, the fact that there are cameras everywhere makes you feel that there is a security issue. When there are no cameras, it implies that you live in a safe and secure society and that surveillance is not needed. (Male in his 30s)

234 Miyase Christensen and André Jansson

The attitudes towards horizontal visibility and monitoring online ranged between indifference and knowing approval amongst the informants. More interestingly, the mediated deployment of various sets of private, digital data as a symbolic pursuit emerges as a tactic commonly used to both off-set borders and avoid exclusion, and to create "wittingly or unwittingly" (Bourdieu 1977, 79) new enclosures.

One informant noted that although he was aware of the privacy issues on online social domains, paying too much attention to it would cripple his ability to socialize, thus creating spatial limitation (male in his 20s). Like-wise, other informants expressed preferences (based on different criteria) toward modulating *who*, in their circles, sees their private information and *to what extent*, rather than considering total withdrawal of personal data.

> MC: What does privacy mean to you?
> I: That I, as an individual, have control over . . . well, . . . that I have a sense of control over what people know about me and about my private life. So it's sort of like I have a private sphere and a public sphere and some facts about me can be accessible publicly and I guess I usually know what depth of information is available about me in public. And whatever is not available is in my private sphere. . . . And, I have to be careful in certain contexts. About what people know about me. I am member of a Turkish associa-tion for example and there people can be very curious. They ask questions about you and talk to each other about you.
> MC: How do you feel about privacy and surveillance on social net-working sites?
> I: I heard a discussion about it a year and a half ago in Sweden. That's when I became aware of it. But I must say that I am not that knowledgeable about the terms and conditions [on Face-book]. I haven't read them properly. I must say that if they use it [private data] for commercial purposes, then I guess I am OK with it. But, I mean if it has my name on it, if they use my name, then it's a different matter. (Male in his 30s)

11.5. CONCLUDING REMARKS

Based on our broader concern with surveillance on the one hand and networked communicative practice on the other, we have in this chapter explored two cases of mediated community making in transnational con-texts. Such contexts of mobile life biographies and long-distance social-ity could be predicted to incorporate this tension field in a particularly pregnant way, both at the general level, and at the level of distinct forms of situated transnational practice (here Scandinavian expatriate profession-als in Nicaragua and Turkish diasporic subjects in Sweden). Implementing

Bourdieu's theory of social fields our field-work has demonstrated not only the enduring need to analyze the intersecting logics of surveillance and networking within a framework of social place-making and territorialization, but also that an understanding of the distinct, yet overlapping, logics of symbolic struggle and boundary maintenance must be empirically grounded at the local, even phenomenological, level.

Above all, our studies have unveiled how the management of converging social media reproduces segregating modes of community maintenance. In referring to Scannell (1989), Barnett (2004) suggests that "broadcasting cultivates a form of *reasonable* subjectivity, characterized by a willingness to listen and openness to other viewpoints that is essential to the maintenance of a shared public life" (65, *emphasis added*). By contrast, as we have showed in this chapter, new online social media cultivate an exclusivist subjectivity marked by a desire to control the inflow and outflow of public utterance, engendering a paradoxically traditional *and* novel sense of *Gemeinschaft*. Here, our studies reveal the existence of complex norms and dynamics that govern privacy control at the user end in the face of expanding surveillant practices: In that privacy (as well as various connectivities) emerges as an asset, akin to symbolic capital, which is (often creatively) modulated for the purposes of border control, thus maintenance of power and status—and hence, *complicity* in surveillant practice. This form of subjectivity and reflexivity (expressed through various modulations of information) stands in sharp contrast with the kind of subjectivity and public intimacy engendered through the older, few-to-many applications (such as portals) for communal interaction that are imbued with a broadcasting style publicness.

What must also be noted here, however, is that the very articulations of this form of subjectivity vary significantly between different social fields, and that reflexivity as such is not always the desired logic of practice. On the contrary, as told particularly by the case of expatriate professionals, the technologically imposed management of online social networks (such as Facebook) and accompanying surveillant spaces is often regarded with great scepticism, even seen a threat to the socio-spatial order and practical sense of the field. In the case of the Turkish diaspora, by contrast, such practices of spatial remediation and reflexive negotiation were rather shown to entail the promise of more field-like structures to evolve, taking on a new relevance beyond the confinements of territorial communities. Although one should be wary of extrapolating the findings of these two case studies, our analyses clearly indicate a need to consider the transnational condition in close relation to surveillance. For mobility, home-making, and the simultaneous transcendence *and* craving of everyday mundane fixity (all of which are part and parcel of transnational life) are increasingly managed and negotiated through personal technologies that de facto lead to a social context deeply marked by a surveillant logic and personal management/appropriations of it. We could further suggest that the ease, speed, and ephemerality of mediated proximity and boundary maintenance conceal both the temporal (for example the persistent longevity of data) and the spatial (for example the presence of data in multiple digital locales) aspects of surveillance and systems of sorting, even in cases where a heightened sense of reflexivity is demonstrated by the users, thus raising further questions. Larger scale, phenomenologically informed studies would help illuminate the complex nature of the ways in which surveillance operates at subjective, contextual, everyday levels.

NOTES

1. Whereas these considerations (that both complement and stand in stark contrast with each other) provide a starting point for our overall thinking of web 2.0 surveillance in its complex forms, we do not necessarily closely follow or empirically employ each and every one of these terms in our analysis.
2. This study is part of the ongoing research project *Secure Spaces: Media, Consumption and Social Surveillance,* conducted by André Jansson and Miyase Christensen with funding from the National Bank of Sweden. The authors are grateful to the persons who volunteered to participate as interviewees within the two case studies, as well as to the anonymous reviewers for their comments on the first version of this chapter.
3. Due to lack of space, we cannot offer a detailed discussion of the relative richness and analytic impasses in Bourdieuian theory of field. Taken together, transnationalism and field provide a more holistic account of the issues at stake here. The latter helps illuminate the workings of in-group dynamics and subjective positionalities in transmigratory contexts. The former contextualizes a discussion of both moments of transformation and culturally/locationally specific practices of conversion of capital into power.
4. In the sense of De Certeau (1984).
5. Even though the international development sector clearly shows qualities that make it possible to analyze it in terms of a field, this is of course a tentative conclusion. The more precise dynamics, boundaries, and capital forms of such a field will not be assessed in this chapter.
6. For some groups, the convenience of using an ethnic label as an interaction-starter and an easy marker for a meeting point for individuals with the same general transnational background is one practical reason. For some other groups, the label harbours deeper sentiments.
7. This informant, a university student, occupies an active position at one of the largest representative institutions.
8. This has to do with the fact that (a) social networking sites are ultimately marked by a top-down surveillant logic (industry/state surveillance of users for various gains and purposes) regardless of the degree to which users are aware of such monitoring, and (b) what underlies user practices is a regime of personal data management to allow for various degrees of visibility and peer-monitoring.
9. By the industry, the state, and other social actors. The informants also had little knowledge of the possible longevity of personal data on social networking sites; of the various degrees of privacy that can be modulated through use of privacy settings; and of the fact that their online social network friends and their privacy settings can have serious consequences for their own privacy of personal data.

REFERENCES

Abe, Kiyoshi. 2009. The myth of media interactivity: technology, communications and surveillance in Japan. *Theory, Culture and Society* 26 (2–3): 73–88.

Andrejevic, Mark. 2007. *iSpy: Surveillance and power in the interactive era*. Lawrence: University Press of Kansas.

Bailey, Olga, Myria Georgiou, and Ramaswami Harindranath, eds. 2007. *Transnational lives and the media: Re-imagining diaspora*. London: Palgrave.

Bakardjieva, Maria. 2003. Virtual togetherness: an everyday life perspective. *Media, Culture and Society* 25 (3): 291–313.

Barnett, Clive. 2003. *Culture and democracy: Media, space and representation*. Edinburgh: Edinburgh University Press.

———. 2004. Neither poison nor cure: space, scale, and public life in media theory. In *Media/Space: Place, scale and culture in a media age*, ed. Nick Couldry and Anne McCarthy, 58–74. London, Routledge.

Beck, Ulrich. 2004/2006. *The cosmopolitan vision*. Cambridge: Polity.

Best, Kirsty. 2010. Living in the control society: surveillance, users and digital screen technologies. *International Journal of Cultural Studies* 13 (1): 5–24.

Bogard, William. 1996. *The simulation of surveillance*. Cambridge: Cambridge University Press.

———. 2006. Welcome to the society of control: the simulation of surveillance revisited. In *The new politics of surveillance and visibility*, ed. Kevin D. Haggerty and Richard V. Ericson, 55–78. Toronto: University of Toronto Press.

Bourdieu, Pierre. 1977. *Outline of a theory of practice*. Cambridge: Cambridge University Press.

———. 1979/1984. *Distinction: A social critique of the judgement of taste*. London: Routledge.

———. 1980/1990. *The logic of practice*. Cambridge: Polity.

Calhoun, Craig. 1993. Habitus, field and capital: the question of historical specificity. In *Bourdieu: critical perspectives*, ed. Craig Calhoun, Edward LiPuma, and Moishe Postone, 61–88. Cambridge: Polity.

Christensen, Miyase. 2011. Online social media, communicative practice and complicit surveillance in transnational contexts. In *Online territories: Globalization, mediated practice and social space*, ed. Miyase Christensen, André Jansson, and Christian Christensen, 224–240. New York: Peter Lang.

Ciccolella, Pablo and Iliana Mignaqui. 2002. Buenos Aires: sociospatial impacts of the development of global city functions. In *Global networks, linked cities*, ed. Saskia Sassen, 309–326. London: Routledge.

De Cauter, Lieven. 2004. *The capsular society: On the city in the age of fear*. Rotterdam: NAi.

Deleuze, Gilles. 1992. Postscript on the societies of control. *October 59*: 3–7.

Eriksson Baaz, Maria. 2005. *The paternalism of partnership: A postcolonial reading of identity in development aid*. London: Zed Books.

Georgiou, Myria. 2005. Mapping diasporic media cultures: a transnational cultural approach to exclusion. In *Media, technology and everyday life in Europe: From information to communication*, ed. Roger Silverstone, 33–53. Hants: Ashgate.

———. 2006. *Diaspora, identity and the media: Diasporic transnationalism and mediated spatialities*. New York: Hampton.

Graham, Stephen. 2005. Software-sorted geographies. *Progress in Human Geography* 29 (5): 562–580.

Haggerty, Kevin D. and Richard V. Ericson. 2000. The surveillant assemblage. *British Journal of Sociology* 51 (4): 605–622.

Harvey, David. 1982. *The limits to capital*. Oxford: Blackwell.

———. 1990. *The condition of postmodernity*. Cambridge, MA: Blackwell.

Jansson, André. 2007. Texture: a key concept for communication geography. *European Journal of Cultural Studies* 10 (2): 185–202.

———. 2010. Interveillance and identity: the social forces of interactive surveillance. Paper presented at the 3rd ECREA Conference, Hamburg, Germany, October 12–15.

———. 2011. Cosmopolitan capsules: mediated networking and social control in expatriate spaces. In *Online territories: Globalization, mediated practice and social space*, ed. Miyase Christensen, André Jansson, and Christian Christensen, 241–257. New York: Peter Lang.

Jenkins, Henry. 2006. *Convergence culture: Where old and new media collide*. New York: New York University Press.

Jenkins, Richard. 1992. *Pierre Bourdieu*. London: Routledge.

Kaldor, Mary. 2003. *Global civil society: An answer to war*. Cambridge: Polity.

Kaufmann, Vincent. 2002. *Re-thinking mobility: Contemporary sociology*. Aldershot: Ashgate.

Kaufmann, Vincent, Manfred M. Bergman, and Dominique Joyce. 2004. Motility: mobility as capital. *International Journal of Urban and Regional Research* 28 (4): 745–756.

Lyon, David. 2003. *Surveillance as social sorting: Privacy, risk and digital discrimination*. London: Routledge.

Massey, Doreen. 1993. Power-geometry and a progressive sense of place. In *Mapping the futures: Local cultures, global change*, ed. John Bird, Barry Curtis, Tim Putnam, George Robertson, and Lisa Tickner, 59–69. London: Routledge.

Morley, David. 2007. *Media, modernity and technology: The geography of the new*. London: Routledge.

———. 2011. Afterword. Electronic landscapes: between the virtual and the actual. In *Online territories: Globalization, mediated practice and social space*, ed. Miyase Christensen, André Jansson, and Christian Christensen, 275–292. New York: Peter Lang.

Nowicka, Magdalena and Maria Rovisco. 2009. Introduction. Making sense of cosmopolitanism. In *Cosmopolitanism in practice,* ed. Magdalena Nowicka and Maria Rovisco, 1–16. Farnham: Ashgate.

Sassen, Saskia. 2001. *The global city: New York, London, Tokyo*. New York: Princeton University Press.

Silverstone, Roger, Eric Hirsch, and David Morley. 1992. Information and communication technologies and the moral economy of the household. In *Consuming technologies: Media and information in domestic spaces*, ed. Roger Silverstone and Eric Hirsch, 15–31. London: Routledge.

Stromer-Galley, Jennifer and Rosa Martey. 2009. Visual spaces, norm governed places: the influence of the spatial context online. *New Media and Society* 11 (6): 1041–1060.

Taylor, Charles. 2004. *Modern social imaginaries*. Durham, NC: Duke University Press.

Titley, Gavan. 2008. Media transnationalism in Ireland: an examination of Polish media practices. *Translocations: Migration and social change* 3 (1): 29–49.

Tuan, Yi Fu. 1977. *Space and place: The perspective of experience*. Minneapolis: University of Minnesota Press.

Urry, John. 2003. Social networks, travel and talk. *British Journal of Sociology* 54 (2): 155–175.

———. 2007. *Mobilities*. Cambridge: Polity Press.

Wittel, Andreas. 2001. Toward a network sociality. *Theory, Culture & Society* 18 (6): 51–76.

12 When Transparency Isn't Transparent

Campaign Finance Disclosure and Internet Surveillance

Kent Wayland, Roberto Armengol, and Deborah G. Johnson

12.1. INTRODUCTION

For many scholars who are concerned about surveillance of Internet users, demanding transparency (or greater transparency) in data-mining practices may seem a promising approach (Lyon 2007, 181–1833; Danna and Gandy 2002).[1] The hope is that transparency about data collection practices would serve as an antidote to the erosion of online privacy. The argument is: when data-collection practices are revealed, users become aware of how they are being watched, and adjust their behaviour accordingly. They may opt out of the activity, change their behaviour, protest, or take some other action. They also might be able to negotiate changes to data uses. Transparency empowers, so the story goes.

In this chapter we challenge the idea that transparency always or necessarily protects the public good and will therefore protect Internet users. We claim that when transparency is constituted on the Internet, the accounts produced are never simply the "truth" about what is happening as the term "transparency" might suggest. We use the case of campaign finance disclosure (CFD) in US elections to show that, in effect, transparency is not transparent. Put differently, transparency systems do not construct glass houses that allow others to see what is happening inside; rather, they pull data about people and institutions into a house of mirrors in which the observer can "see", at best, a partial construction—a mediated glimpse—of what those being watched are doing. The "house of mirrors" metaphor serves to describe and analyze what happens in transparency accounts, and to understand the limitations as well as the promise of transparency on the Internet.

Elsewhere, we have argued that transparency systems have important structural similarities to surveillance systems and, consequently, the distinction between these two types of systems is blurry (Johnson and Wayland 2010). Indeed, our analysis of CFD illustrates how a system instituted for transparency of campaigns gets used for surveillance of donors. The analysis here begins with some background on CFD, its underlying metaphor, and its workings, before presenting the house of mirrors model and using it to analyze the CFD system.

12.2. CAMPAIGN FINANCE DISCLOSURE LAW

Campaign finance disclosure is a central component of election law in the US and in many other countries. These laws require campaigns to disclose the names (and other identifying data) of those who contribute to a campaign and to specify how donated funds have been spent. Such regulations fall under the general category of "sunshine" laws. More specifically, CFD is thought to be a form of transparency, in the sense that it enables the populace to "see" what candidates are doing, which in turn functions as an important means by which democratic governments are held accountable to their electorates. CFD is, perhaps, the epitome of a transparency system aimed at democratic accountability because it involves the ultimate moment of accountability in any democracy, the moment when citizens exercise their voting power.

Focusing just on the US, the first federal campaign disclosure law was the Publicity Act of 1910, also referred to as the Federal Corrupt Practices Act. This law required disclosure of contributions to national party committees or multi-state committees, but not until after the election (Corrado 2005, 8). Congress amended the law the following year to require disclosure immediately prior to and after an election. In 1925, the Federal Corrupt Practices Act introduced quarterly reporting to the disclosure regime (Corrado 2005, 9). Yet these rules went largely ignored because they were not enforced (Potter 2005, 125). Federal disclosure law changed little until the Federal Election Campaign Act of 1971, followed by major amendments in 1974 and 1976. These subsequent acts of Congress greatly expanded the requirements for who must disclose funding details, covering all large federal campaigns and committees, not just national or multi-state committees. Further, the acts established the Federal Election Commission (FEC) as the regulator of this new system.

In 1995, Congress required the FEC to create a technological and regulatory structure that allowed campaigns to file their reports electronically, and a 1999 law made electronic filing mandatory. Most recently, the Bipartisan Campaign Reform Act of 2002, better known as the McCain-Feingold bill, extended disclosure provisions to third-party "issue advocacy" campaigns and required the FEC to post reports on the Internet within 48 hours of receipt.

Because we will focus later on a particular campaign in California, it is important to note that campaign finance laws have a longer history in California. In 1893, California state legislators introduced a disclosure system that foreshadowed the Federal Corrupt Practices Act (Ansolabehere 2007, 169; Thompson 1953). Indeed, California made disclosure the central element of its anti-corruption efforts. Unlike the federal system, between 1949 and 1988 the state placed no limits on the size or source of contributions, although the state legislature did briefly limit the amount that campaigns could spend. A 1988 law added limits on donations to candidates, but not to ballot initiatives (Baber 1989). And electronic disclosure of donations became law in 2000 (CA GOVT § 84605 (a)).

The basic rationale for campaign finance laws has been upheld in court, with the Supreme Court case *Buckley v. Valeo* (1976) establishing the prevailing wisdom. That case evaluated whether the restrictions of the FEC legislation were justified, given the burden they placed on political expression protected by the First Amendment. The ruling laid out three compelling arguments for disclosure. First, disclosure would help deter corruption. Second, it would aid enforcement of anti-corruption laws. Third, disclosure would provide the public with useful information about political candidates, increasing "voter competence". The courts have sustained, with some alterations, these basic justifications over the years in the face of a variety of challenges (Potter 2005). Indeed, in a recent case, *Citizens United v. Federal Elections Commission* (558 U.S. 50 (2010)), the Supreme Court struck down long-standing restrictions on corporate spending on elections but explicitly stated that such spending could still be subject to disclosure.

Putting campaign donation data on the Internet is believed to improve the efficiency of managing this information, though some would argue that the most significant benefit of putting information about campaign contributions online is that it makes the information available to regulators and the general public (including public interest groups) in a medium that allows them to analyze the data more effectively. This effectiveness derives from combining powerful data-mining techniques with the speed of electronic disclosure (Holman and Stern 2000).

Still, those who support posting CFD data on the Internet tend not to focus on the consequences of increased efficiency. In a 2000 report titled "Access delayed is access denied", the watchdog group Public Citizen acknowledged a curious side benefit to the campaigns themselves: now the candidates, too, could more easily mine their own donation data for targeting donors with greater precision (Holman and Stern 2000). This use of the data goes well beyond the stated rationale of the system and thereby hints at the potentially profound consequences of pushing for increased efficiency.

12.3. CAMPAIGN FINANCE DISCLOSURE, TRANSPARENCY, AND THE IMPLICATIONS

Transparency has been prevalent in governance theory going back to Jeremy Bentham (1748–1832), who first used the term in this way, although he was echoing earlier ideas from as far back as the ancient Chinese and Greeks (Hood 2006). In recent decades, however, transparency has become a much more common concept in endeavours to improve government and reduce corporate malfeasance. In tandem with notions of good governance, transparency has mostly been embraced as a positive public policy, even a necessary one for a globalizing world (Florini 1998). Various forms of "government in the sunshine" laws and corporate disclosure requirements are said both to foster the confidence of citizens and investors, and to reduce health and safety risks for consumers.

"Transparency" is a metaphor that borrows from the domain of sight and optics: by casting light on campaign financing we bring into view what has before lurked below the surface. Shedding light on the activities of institutions and political leaders is said to reveal their inner workings and allow the public to better understand, manage, and evaluate the object of this gaze. This optic metaphor is often coupled with a cleansing theme, exemplified by Justice Brandeis's oft-quoted comment that "sunshine is said to be the best of disinfectants" (Brandeis 1914, 92). In this sense "light" exposes and destroys wrongdoing, whether in the form of corporate fraud or political corruption. The fundamental rationale for transparency, then, is to reveal the otherwise obscure workings of power, subjecting the powerful to public scrutiny and reducing the likelihood that they might abuse their positions or hide their intent. In forcing political leaders to reveal their activities and the type of people who support them, according to this argument, the public and other interested parties will be able to hold them accountable. Campaign finance laws, in particular, aim to hold candidates and campaigns accountable to their constituencies. In knowing which groups and citizens donate to political campaigns, we are supposed to better know the campaigns themselves and thus be better able to detect corruption in the democratic process. Supporters of such systems argue that they discourage deal-making in "smoky back rooms", where wealthy supporters use donations to influence a candidate's positions on issues of interest to them. In addition, by knowing who supports a candidate, the public is supposed to better understand the candidate's political leanings.

For decades, CFD reports were difficult to access and therefore examined only by the most diligent journalists. They were difficult even for regulators to use. However, when CFD information is posted on the Internet, it is much more easily accessible and, consequently, much more widely viewed. The reports are, in effect, broadcast. Once the campaigns' data are put into electronic databases, journalists, interest groups, and regulators can more easily search for patterns in the timing or the sources of donations that might suggest some corruption.

Importantly, due to this searchability of electronic databases, it is not just campaigns that are scrutinized. Donors also are subject to a new level of examination. The donation reports are large collections of accounts about individual contributors—including their names, hometowns, postal codes, occupations, and employers. Thus, both campaigns and donors become "watched" entities, and the wide electronic availability of accounts of both attracts an array of "watchers".

The addition of these watchers creates entirely new forms of account-ability. Donors suddenly are watched not only by campaigns (who target them for more donations and for possible volunteer work), but also, potentially, by neighbours, professional colleagues, friends, and family, all of whom can easily view the information on the Internet. These uses of donor data take transparency far beyond simply attesting to the ethical or unethical influence of money on politicians. These practices make transparency into a system for further tracking of individuals. In short, the transparency system becomes a surveillance system.

The distinction between surveillance and transparency, we acknowledge, can be vague. We use the term surveillance to invoke the common understanding of surveillance as a negatively valued exercise of power. Such a tactic calls attention to the radical shift that takes place as the system focuses on individual citizens in addition to political parties and candidates. We roughly distinguish surveillance from transparency in the following way. Generally, surveillance systems track and monitor individuals' behaviour, sort them into groups, and treat them on the basis of generalizations about the group. Further, surveillance takes place largely without the consent of the individual being watched. Transparency, on the other hand, is generally understood to refer to practices in which organizations (and sometimes individuals) reveal information about their behaviour. Whether they do so because it is required by law or because they are trying to control their public image, the organizations or individuals have some control over the information that they disclose.

In the shift from paper and ink accounts of campaign finance to electronic records posted on the Internet, new actors (both watched and watchers) are drawn into the system, and new rationales and new forms of accountability are constituted. The challenge of Internet studies is to understand what happens when information, individuals, practices, or institutions are constituted online. Although it might seem that the newly constituted systems are more transparent because the information is widely available, the language of transparency is misleading. Accounts of campaigns are being constituted, and they are being distributed widely, but the process can hardly be characterized as "laying bare" or seeing into what is actually going on. Most information theory recognizes that informating shapes what is produced (Zuboff 1985).

If not providing the glass through which viewers can "see" what is going on, what happens when campaign finance disclosure is instrumented on the Internet? The system may be best characterized as a house of mirrors.

12.4. THE HOUSE OF MIRRORS

What does it mean to say that campaign finance accounts are produced in a house of mirrors? A house of mirrors is full of reflection and imaging; a person standing in a house of mirrors sees aspects of his or her body elongated, shortened, exaggerated, multiplied, fragmented, and reconfigured. The house of mirrors is a complex of projection, bouncing, highlighting, and shading that produces a surprising portrait of a person. One sees oneself in what seems like a distorted version, a rendering that is out of whack with ordinary experience. Of course, the distortion is far from random; it is the result of the nature of mirrors, the positioning of the mirrors in question, the lighting, and so on. In everyday life, houses of mirrors are often built as a form of amusement. Hence the colloquial term "funhouse".

Using the house of mirrors as a metaphor gives us a novel way of understanding Internet-based data systems. Paper and ink data have very different properties from data constituted and processed on the Internet. Playing out the metaphor, at least four processes can be identified in the production of Internet-instrumented information systems: entry, bouncing, highlighting and shading, and rendering. Although each of these processes might be thought of as architectural (i.e., resulting from the nature of information technology), they are socio-technical processes; cultural assumptions and norms always guide both the workings of the system and the meanings derived from them. The outcome of these processes constitutes an account (or accounts) delivered in the name of transparency, but processed and infused with system-specific assumptions and values. The case of campaign finance disclosure illustrates these processes.

12.4.1. Entry

The first thing that occurs when a person enters an actual house of mirrors is that an image of the person is reflected off of the mirrors. The individual can then see an image of herself in a mirror (or mirrors). Similarly, when someone donates to a campaign, the campaign creates a record (a reflection of the donor). This initial record-creation is a legal requirement. In the US system, donors must supply five items of personal information; campaigns are required to gather and record this information. Although the donor may not "see" the record created in the campaign database, their donation means that they have entered a system. An image—a reflection—of the donor has been created. Indeed, multiple images have been created because the *record* of the donation is also a record of the campaign; the *reflection* of the donor is a reflection of the campaign.

Donors are required to supply their name, employer, occupation, home address, and the amount donated. In this respect, the reflection of the donor (and campaign) is selective and limited. It is a reduction of the person, as any representation, informated or not, must be. In requiring certain information, American CFD law singles out certain aspects of donors that are deemed relevant. That it is a reduction can be seen clearly when we consider what citizens might want to know about donors and campaigns, but is not required in CFD. For example, the required information does not include a donor's motivation in contributing to the campaign, the percentage of the person's total wealth that is donated, the person's country of birth, age, gender, or party affiliation.

The reduction of individual donors into the required information is the expression of a set of cultural values and norms about which aspects of campaigns need to be monitored. Each of these data points derives from a set of assumptions about human nature, interests, and corruption. The overriding norm is that of the entrepreneurial individual; that is, persons have material interests that they seek to further. Donations to political candidates are a central way through which they can pursue their interests. In American democracy, some forms of influence are legitimate (supporting candidates for their beliefs) and others are not (seeking a *quid pro quo*). Thus, the data first tie the donation to an individual person to make sure that no individual exceeds the maximum donation. Once the individual is isolated, his or her interests can then be identified, starting first with occupation and employer. Occupational role is thought to be the major driver of influence-seeking, and collecting this information therefore helps regulators and the public look for undue influence. Transparency supports democracy by not letting such influence go on in the dark. By attending to these particular data, however, the system draws attention away from any number of other possible motives for seeking influence. These might include religious or social values, community interests, or wealth not tied to a specific occupation, among other motives. Instead, the system's norms presume that citizens need to know who contributes to campaigns, what the donors do for a living, and for whom they work.

That the campaign creates an account of itself (by gathering the required information about its donors) may seem insignificant because the data gathered are simple and required. However, the fact that campaigns develop accounts of themselves is important because it points to a feature of transparency systems that, as we have seen, differentiates them from surveillance systems. Campaigns are watched, but they are watched through information that the campaign produces and turns over to others. In most surveillance systems, those who are being watched are passive in the data collection process; others develop accounts of them and use those accounts to make decisions about the watched and/or give those accounts over to others. Yet in this transparency system, the data provided by campaigns easily become reflections of individual donors. Simply by reflecting donors, CFD—a system developed in the name of transparency—comes to resemble a surveillance system.

In short, then, when individuals make a donation to a campaign, they enter a house of mirrors. Entry involves creation of a record, a record that is a reduction insofar as it is based on a selective set of data, and the selection has been made on the basis of ideas, theories, values, and concerns that, presumably, justify the selection. In other words, embedded in the reflection are norms about "what matters" in political campaigns and what constitutes political corruption. Whether she likes it or not, the record of a donor's contribution may be taken as a public expression of political patronage.

12.4.2. Bouncing

For people moving through a house of mirrors, one of the oddities of the experience may be sharing the misshapen or distorted image of themselves with companions. The image bounces off the mirror to the person's own eyes, as well as to the eyes of others, and sometimes it even merges with other reflections from nearby mirrors. The images might appear in a fragmented way to others in the house who are strangers. This may happen even without the person's knowledge, for example, when someone sees an image of you, but you cannot or do not see that they do.

There are parallels in the "digital" house of mirrors. Once a record of a donation has been created by a campaign, it is merged with records of other donations (received in a period of time); the merged information is then submitted to the FEC; and the FEC posts the report on the web. Once posted on the web, the original reflection of the donor (and thereby, the campaign) is bounced (replicated) from one location to another, without the consent or control of the donor. This bouncing nicely parallels what seems like an infinite regress of images when two mirrors are positioned face to face. Once posted on the web, campaign finance data can be copied, reformatted, and reposted ad infinitum. It can move to unexpected places, with unpredicted results.

In American CFD, because the information is posted on public websites, entries on individual donations bounce from the databases of the campaign to those of regulators to those of watchdog groups, journalists, law enforcement, neighbours, family, and friends. This is possible because of the affordances of IT (see boyd 2008). At each place, the data can be easily and almost perfectly replicated and transmitted. When the FEC posts the reports online, journalists, watchdog groups, other data repositories, and even citizens can download them in their entirety. The data can be searched quickly, and they can be mined for relationships that might not be immediately apparent. People can search within their neighbourhood to find what their neighbours are doing. Campaigns and political consultants can link the donation databases to other databases to better target fund-raising and advertising. Finally, the data persist in web-linked databases, ready to be recalled when an interested user searches for them.

How the information bounces and becomes available for unexpected purposes can be illustrated with a recent example from California. In 2008, a ballot initiative in California known as Proposition 8 sought to ban gay marriage. Many groups poured resources into advertising for or against the controversial measure. When the proposition passed (effectively banning gay marriage), many opponents of the ban were outraged with the result, and sought to figure out how proponents had succeeded. Because state campaign finance laws require CFD data to be posted online, these opponents were able to develop a database of people who had funded the campaign in favour of the new law. An anonymous programmer mashed up the names and geographic locations of the donors with Google maps, producing www.eightmaps.com, a site where any visitor could see who in what neighbourhoods contributed to the campaign. With some fairly simple coding, then, the record of a donor's contribution was "bounced" to a wide and very interested audience. As a result many of the individual donors were targeted with insults, threats, and boycotts (Stone 2009).

It is one thing to explain the bouncing of images in a house of mirrors that is intentionally designed to create fun, and quite another to explain why campaign finance information moves so freely on the Internet. Part of the explanation no doubt has to do with the nature of the Internet. Free flow of information on the Internet is part of the Internet's architecture and history; it is, in some sense, what was sought after in building the Internet. Still, the fact that the Internet makes free flow of information possible does not explain why the decision was made to post CFD information on the web. This decision may best be understood as a coalescing of Internet capability with transparency (and democratic) theory. Ideas about the role of transparency and its deleterious effects on corruption must have played a role in the decision to post contribution data in a medium that would allow for so much bouncing.

So, once data are put into a digital house of mirrors, they bounce all around. When the data bounce from location to location, from user to user, changes in the meaning or significance and use of data occur. Arguably in the case of the Proposition 8 campaign, a system of transparency was transformed into a system of surveillance. What originally had been an explicit disclosure of information by the initiative-supporting campaign, meant to better inform voters, became a means of profiling individual donors and targeting them for retribution. Nevertheless, the full significance of bouncing cannot be seen until the highlighting and shading that go on in the process are described.

12.4.3. Highlighting and Shading

The images that bounce through a house of mirrors are transformations of the initial reflection of a person. The transformations that occur might be thought of as highlighting and shading. In a real house of mirrors, this has comic effects. One sees one's nose as the largest component of one's face, or one sees oneself with big feet, but essentially no legs. In the digital house of mirrors, the effects are less comical and can be more profound and enduring. As reflections are bounced from place to place, the information is recontextualized and repurposed according to the interests and actions of the watchers. Once information is available on the web, additional watchers may shine light on the individual or entity in unpredictable ways and at unexpected times, neglecting aspects that were important in the original context, and drawing attention to what was minor or poorly understood information in the original. The ramifications of the highlighting and shading are significant. Among other things, data collected for one purpose may be used for another, that is, those who gave the data for one purpose may discover that they have revealed something they had no idea they were revealing.

As already mentioned, CFD donor information is bounced to innumerable others. These others can use the information for whatever purpose they like, with the exception that they cannot be used for commercial purposes (2 U.S.C. §438(a)(4)). They can mine the data, merge them with other data, and redistribute the results. Anyone can become an intermediary and the intermediaries may or may not have anything to do with CFD and why the system was created. Even if their motivation is consistent with the intent of CFD, intermediaries can use the data in ways unimagined in the decision to post the data online.

The press is one of the most powerful intermediaries, and reporters routinely scour disclosures for signs of influence and indications of a candidate's political leanings. Watchdog groups, too, pore over this information looking for threats to the public interest. Opposing candidates and opposition researchers also probe the data seeking any hint of scandal tied to individual donors, such as contributions from corrupt business leaders or ineligible donors. Opponents may look for classes of donors, such as trial lawyers, health care organizations, or oil companies, who could shape or fit into a narrative that reflected poorly on the candidate. In some cases, especially in major national elections, a candidate may be forced to publicly denounce acquaintances formed largely for financial expedience. Such was the case in the 2007 US presidential primaries, when then-candidate Hillary Rodham Clinton decided to return $850,000 in funds raised for her campaign by the Democratic operative Norman Hsu. Hsu was charged and later convicted in a pyramid scheme that bilked investors out of $20 million. Senator Clinton claimed that she was unaware of Hsu's crimes, but she continues to face scrutiny regarding her relationship to him (Flaherty 2009; Solomon 2007). In this way, the availability of donor data in digital form facilitated highlighting and shading that repurposed the data, reaching well beyond the prevention or rooting out of corruption.

Sometimes a person or an aspect of a person in a house of mirrors is highlighted simply because the person stands in a particular place within the architecture of the building. In the CFD digital house of mirrors, donor contributions are, through intermediaries, accessible on the web through Google's search engine. In this architecture, highlighting and shading become a function of a complex variety of factors that, in some sense, have nothing to do with CFD. If one searched on Google for "Kent Wayland" (one of the authors of this paper) in 2009, one of the top results would have been a link to a database available at The Huffington Post, an online newspaper, where users could access campaign donation information by name, zip code, date of donation, campaign season, etc. The web tools available at the site would allow the user to browse recent political donations downloaded from the FEC, repackaged, and indexed by Google's web crawler. Although Wayland's campaign donations were relatively minor, they made up a significant component of his online identity due to the high ranking Google gave these search results. Information on Wayland's contributions were a highlighted aspect of his web presence because of the combination of the way Google works, The Huffington Post's popularity, and other incidental factors: Wayland's name is not especially common and his web presence was not especially extensive.

Returning to the Proposition 8 example, although only the minimal required information was collected on donors to the pro Proposition 8 campaign, that information, when combined with another system (Google Maps), highlighted the locations of the donors. This highlighting made the donors available for intimidation and reprisals. In effect, the website rendered all donors equivalent, tarring them all as antigay and shading other possible motives for a donation. Other possible motives could be, for example, the desire to create a favourable impression on some third party, the desire to distract attention from one's own sexual preference, or the willingness to follow the suggestion of a pastor or other advisor. In all likelihood, donors had not imagined that the record of their contributions would lead to the inference that they were antigay zealots, or that it would lead to personal harassment. Indeed, the use of donor data in this way seems antithetical to democratic elections, as the US Supreme Court recognized when, in the *Buckley v. Valeo* case, it allowed for an exception to disclosure when donors might be targeted for unpopular views. It may also be seen as encroaching on the privacy of the vote (Regan, Johnson, and Wayland 2011).

The CFD digital house of mirrors is, then, like a real house of mirrors insofar as certain aspects of a person are highlighted and shaded. This highlighting and shading takes place as a result of the architecture of the Internet, the design of the databases, and the relationship of these components to human interests and purposes. The initial reflection created upon entry into the system is bounced to a variety of audiences who in turn highlight and shade it according to their own interests.

12.4.4. Rendering of Accounts

Eventually, when a person exits a real house of mirrors, the generation, bouncing, highlighting, and shading of images stop. The experience one had in that house of mirrors might be likened to seeing a cubist or surrealist portrait of oneself. Features were selected, fragmented, and reconfigured into a very different representation of one's body (self). The individual may remember a series of these images or a concatenation of images that make her see herself differently.

In the case of the digital house of mirrors, what results is not a memory of one's distorted body, but an account (or many accounts) that has been rendered. "Render" here carries the connotation of something (someone) being taken apart and then transformed into something different. The rendered accounts—the equivalents of cubist or surrealist portraits of donors and campaigns—are the outcome of reduction, bouncing, and highlighting and shading.

Posting CFD data on the web means that many different watchers can render many different accounts: accounts of donors and campaigns, accounts produced by a range of actors, accounts that are used for a variety of purposes. There may, in fact, be no exit from this house of mirrors because the data persist, ever-ready for the rendering of additional accounts. Further, any of the rendered accounts may become the starting place for new matching and mining processes and new interpretations of the data that lead to yet more renderings (accounts). Reflections of individuals can, thus, get caught in an infinite loop.

Referring to what is produced as an account—or multiple accounts—has the benefit of suggesting that what is going on is accounting; it makes explicit that what is at stake is accountability. In the case of CFD, donors and campaigns are being held accountable. As we have argued elsewhere (Johnson and Wayland 2010), accountability can be thought of as a triad in which there are watchers, watched, and accounts. Renderings are selective, processed accounts of those who are watched, and they are used by watchers in powerful ways: they lead to consequences for the watched (such as accusations of corruption).

The renderings produced in the digital house of mirrors draw on specific cultural assumptions and norms, as we have shown in earlier stages. These cultural assumptions and norms will vary with different watchers who are pursuing different ends as they render accounts. In the case of Proposition 8 in California, the data about donors supporting the Proposition 8 campaign—when combined with the cultural assumption that donating to this cause was an affirmative act of resisting gay marriage—rendered those donors as antigay people who deserve scorn, protest, or even retaliation.

The rendering of accounts, then, is the final step. It involves the final pulling together of all the bounced, highlighted, and shaded images into an account that is tailored to and coherent for the purposes of a particular watcher. Furthermore, the multiplicity of the system means that a number of different watchers can render their own accounts, based on their own cultural assumptions and norms. They use this rendered account to effect some consequence, to hold the watched accountable in some way.

12.4.5 The Role of the House of Mirrors Metaphor

Although the house of mirrors metaphor has the potential to be used in many different contexts, including those involving transparency as well as other systems instrumented on the Internet, the metaphor should not be interpreted as more than it is: an extended metaphor. It is a heuristic device used to uncover some of the ways that data are transformed and repurposed. The metaphor might be thought of as a technique used to get at what happens behind the scenes (backstage) of systems instrumented on the Internet. In this respect the metaphor is targeted to counter the tendency to think that the Internet provides unmediated access.

The four processes identified—entry, bouncing, highlighting and shading, and rendering—are not the only processes that might be identified behind the scenes of any given system. Yet the four processes are inextricably intertwined. This can be seen by contemplating changes that might be made in a system. Perhaps the most powerful stage is entry. When information is entered into a database, it becomes available for bouncing, highlighting, and shading, and rendering. Different data (less or more or of a different kind) mean different consequences for bouncing, shading/highlighting, and rendering. Similarly if bouncing is restricted, for example, when data are posted in read-only form, then the possibilities for highlighting and shading are constrained as well, and this, in turn, means constraints on accounts rendered.

12.5. CONCLUSION: THE IMPLICATIONS OF TRANSPARENCY AS A HOUSE OF MIRRORS

What, then, is the significance of thinking about transparency as a house of mirrors? One obvious answer is that it allows us to see that transparency is not transparent. The notion of transparency suggests that we see persons or institutions as they are. This is misleading. What we see in the case of CFD is a system (aimed at transparency instrumented through the Internet) rendering accounts of individuals and campaigns that can be likened to cubist paintings. The accounts rendered involve reduction, selection, multiplication, highlighting and shading, and recontextualization, a dramatic transformation. Hence, we draw the conclusion that transparency is not transparent.

Does this mean that transparency should be rejected as a goal or potential remedy for Internet surveillance? Such a conclusion does not seem justified; it overextends what the house of mirrors metaphor allows us to see. In fact, the house of mirrors metaphor offers a better way to achieve what is often aimed at in transparency systems. When we stay with the metaphor, we are more likely to see and ask how the mirrors might better be arranged. We should be asking not for transparency per se, but for systems that reveal information appropriate to the context and without unintended consequences. For example, one general rule of thumb might be to limit, as a matter of policy and of computer coding, the extent to which digital information travels, so that it cannot move too far beyond its original or appropriate context. Fung et al. (2007) argue for just this kind of "targeted" transparency, and thinking in these terms might provide a useful way of keeping the information from bouncing too far within the house of mirrors.

In campaign finance disclosure, recognizing the structure of the system as constituted suggests that we consider either collecting more information and placing tighter controls on it or, paradoxically, collecting far less information. For example, one way of rearranging the mirrors in campaign finance disclosure would be to allow only government enforcement agencies access to identifying information about individual donors, while publicly releasing useful systemic and aggregated information about campaign donors. Such information might include more data points than are currently collected and thus capture a broader picture of how candidates might be influenced, without compromising the privacy of individual donors. Voters might be interested to know the relative income of donors, for example, whether they are homeowners, what their race or ethnicity is, etc. On the other hand, greater secrecy and less information might afford a more practical solution to the problem of transparency in campaign funding. Here, we might imagine, as others have proposed, candidates funding their campaigns from something like a blind trust (Ayres 2000). In that scenario, donors would support campaigns by donating to the trust, and their donations would remain anonymous both to the public and, crucially, to the campaign itself. If the reflection does not bounce to the campaign, then elected officials cannot reward their patrons. With no reflection, there is no possibility of corruption, at least in the traditional form of a quid pro quo. (This approach, it must be said, would not address the recent controversy over anonymous corporate funding of political ads in the US.)

Of course, each of these proposals carries with it some peril or disadvantage, not least of which is the probable need for greater regulation. The ultimate moral of this story might be, as Lessig has suggested, that we do away with the notion of transparency entirely and revolutionize such systems. At the very least, the US could consider adopting campaign finance policies used in other countries. In the UK, for example, for the most part there are no limits on fund-raising but rather on spending. Individual office-seekers need only report individual contributions of more than £1,000, whereas for parties the threshold is higher, £5,000 (Fiekert 2009). By the same token, however, candidates may not purchase ads of any kind on broadcast or in the mainstream print media. Instead, the government requires TV and radio stations to provide free and equal airtime to candidates around a relatively abbreviated election season. In France, public financing of campaigns is accomplished by way of tax credits to individual donors, covering up to 60% of their contributions (Atwill 2009). In this way, electors "vote with their pocketbooks" about which campaigns to invest taxpayer dollars in, and how much to invest. Copying such policies wholesale, of course, would face a steep uphill battle in the US, given the political climate and recent court decisions on campaign financing.

Finally, although the case of CFD indicates that transparency is not transparent, the underlying goal of transparency is accountability. In the case of CFD, the accountability at issue is essential to democracy. In this respect, CFD is a good case to learn from for Internet surveillance. Those operating on the Internet—especially those engaged in surveillance—should be accountable for what they are doing. Hence, the lessons of CFD should be helpful for figuring out antidotes to Internet surveillance. A number of lessons can be found in this chapter, but the most important is, perhaps, that what we call transparency is really a house of mirrors.

NOTES

1. This material is based upon work supported by the National Science Foundation under Grant No. 0823363.

    Any opinions, findings, and conclusions or recommendations expressed in this material are those of the author(s) and do not necessarily reflect the views of the National Science Foundation. The grant has funded discussion and collaboration among a team of researchers composed of the three authors and Priscilla Reagan, Siva Vaidhyanathan, Alfred Weaver, and Kathleen Weston.

REFERENCES

Ansolabehere, S. 2007. The scope of corruption: lessons from comparative campaign finance disclosure. *Election Law Journal* 6 (2): 163–183.

Atwill, Nicole. 2009. *Campaign Finance: France*. Washington, DC: Library of Congress.

Ayres, Ian. 2000. Disclosure versus anonymity in campaign finance. In *Designing democratic institutions*, ed. Ian Shapiro and Stephen Macedo, 19–55. New York: New York University Press.

Baber, Bill. 1989. California's new campaign finance law: is section 85303(C) the life of the party. *California Western Law Review* 26 (2): 425–447.

Brandeis, Louis D. 1914. *Other people's money: And how the bankers use it*. New York: Frederick A. Stokes.

boyd, danah m. 2008. *Taken out of context: American teen sociality in networked publics*. PhD dissertation. Berkeley: University of California.

Corrado, Anthony. 2005. Money and politics: a history of federal campaign finance law. In *The new campaign finance sourcebook*, ed. Anthony Corrado, Daniel R. Ortiz, Thomas E. Mann, and Trevor Potter, 7–47. Washington, DC: Brookings Institution.

Danna, Anthony and Oscar H. Gandy. 2002. All that glitters is not gold: digging beneath the surface of data mining. *Journal of Business Ethics* 40 (4): 373–386.

Fiekert, Clare. 2009. *Campaign finance: United Kingdom*. Washington, DC: Library of Congress.

Flaherty, Peter. 2009. Hsu convicted but no reckoning for Hillary.National Legal and Policy Center, Promoting Ethics in Public Life. May 20, 2009.

Florini, Ann. 1998. The end of secrecy. *Foreign Policy* 111 (Summer): 50–63.

Fung, Archon, Mary Graham, and David Weil. 2007. *Full disclosure: The perils and promise of transparency.* New York: Cambridge University Press.

Holman, Craig B. and Robert M. Stern. 2000. Access delayed is access denied: electronic reporting of campaign finance activity. *Public Integrity* 11 (Winter). https://www.citizen.org/documents/electronic_reporting2000_new.pdf (accessed September 5, 2010).

Hood, Christopher. 2006. Transparency in historical perspective. In *Transparency: The key to better governance?* ed. Christopher Hood and David Heald, 3–24. Oxford: Oxford.

Johnson, Deborah G. and Kent Wayland. 2010. Surveillance and transparency as sociotechnical systems of accountability. In *Surveillance and democracy*, ed. Kevin D. Haggerty and Minas Samatas, 19–33. London: Routledge.

Lessig, Lawrence. 2009. Against transparency. *The New Republic*, October 21. http://www.tnr.com/print/articles/books-and-arts/against-transparency (accessed October 12, 2009).

Lyon, David. 2007. *Surveillance studies: An overview.* Cambridge: Polity.

Potter, Trevor. 2005. Campaign finance disclosure laws. In *The New Campaign Finance Sourcebook*, ed. Anthony Corrado, Thomas E. Mann, Daniel R. Ortiz,and Trevor Potter, 123–160. Washington, DC: Brookings Institution.

Johnson, Deborah G., Priscilla M. Regan, and Kent Wayland. 2011. Campaign disclosure, privacy and transparency. *William and Mary Bill of Rights Journal* 19 (4). forthcoming.

Solomon, John. 2007. Clintons to return $850,000 in Hsu funds. In the trail: a daily diary of campaign 2008. *The Washington Post Online Edition.* Sept. 10, 2007.

Stone, Brad. 2009. Prop 8 donor web site shows disclosure law is 2-edged sword. *New York Times*, February 8.

Thompson, Bruce A. 1953. Campaign contributions and expenditures in California. *California Law Review* 41 (2): 300–319.

Zuboff, Shoshana. 1985. Automate/informate: the two faces of intelligent technology. *Organizational Dynamics* 14 (2): 5–18.

13 Privacy, Surveillance, and Self-Disclosure in the Social Web

Exploring the User's Perspective via Focus Groups

Monika Taddicken

13.1. INTRODUCTION

It has become common practice today to use the Internet, not only for retrieving information, but also for providing information. Internet users have developed new ways to utilize the Internet. The social web—that is, web applications such as social networking sites, blogs, and wikis—offers opportunities for participation and collaboration, but requires the user's willingness to reveal private information.

On one hand, the manifold possibilities of the Internet can enhance life in many ways. On the other hand, those very possibilities raise new concerns. The heightened disclosure of personal information on the Internet places one's privacy at risk. Therefore, the reasonable handling of personal information on the social web has become an important topic in media and society. Privacy and surveillance concerns have increased. These include the competence and ability of users regarding their handling of personal information in the society as well as in the literature, especially in the context of social networking sites and adolescent users (Barnes 2006; Paine et al. 2006; Lampe et al. 2007; Lewis et al. 2008; Krämer and Winter 2008; Thelwall 2008; Tufekci 2008; boyd and Hargittai 2010).

It is reasonable to expect privacy and surveillance concerns to influence the social web user's behaviour. Recent studies show that social web users ascribe high importance to privacy (Barnes 2006; Tufekci 2008; Debatin et al. 2009). However, considerable uncertainty still exists regarding the notion of privacy on which users base their social web activities. Little is known about the adaptation of privacy concerns to the user's behaviour. So far, there is relatively little evidence that users translate concerns about data abuse into privacy-enhancing behaviours while online (Acquisti and Gross 2006; Tufekci 2008; Debatin et al. 2009; boyd and Hargittai 2010). This is called the "privacy paradox" (Barnes 2006; Awad and Krishnan 2006; Norberg et al. 2007). Moreover, it is unclear if and in what way concerns about surveillance influence users.

For this reason the explorative method of focus groups was used to examine the perception of privacy by social web users. The findings are presented in this paper and are reviewed in connection with the concepts of surveillance and self-disclosure. To establish a theoretical background, these concepts are first discussed in theory and transferred to the social web, after which the focus groups' findings are presented.

13.2. THEORETICAL BACKGROUND: PRIVACY, SURVEILLANCE, AND SELF-DISCLOSURE

Privacy can be defined in many different ways. Basically, it can be seen as "the right to be let alone" (Warren and Brandeis 1890). Despite this general definition, various dimensions and perspectives of privacy have been analyzed by researchers of various scientific perspectives (for an overview, see Newell 1995). Although various attempts have been made to create a synthesis of the existing approaches to defining privacy (for example, Parent 1983; Schoeman 1984; Burgoon et al. 1989), a unified single account has yet to emerge (Paine et al. 2007).

Most notable are the works by Westin (1967) and Altman (1975, 1976, 1977). Both researchers focus on control and regulation of access to private information. According to Westin, privacy is "the right to prevent the disclosure of personal information to others" (Westin 1967, 7). The desire to keep personal information out of the hands of others is central to this concept of privacy (Westin 1967). Altman, on the other hand, defines privacy as a "selective control of access to the self or to one's group" (Altman 1975, 18). According to him, the regulation of privacy is a dynamic process of optimization, which is influenced by two basic psychological needs: On the one hand, the individual has the need to preserve one's privacy and control access to and distribution of personal information, but on the other hand, one also has the need to interact socially and, therefore, to disclose personal information. Accordingly, privacy is perceived as being at its optimum when both needs can be united and the desired and the actually achieved levels of privacy correspond (Altman 1975, 1976). Consequently, the regulation of privacy is not to be understood as a process of retreat, nor is an optimum degree of privacy equal to the highest possible control over one's personal information. Individuals, rather, strive for different degrees of self-disclosure in different situations.

Self-disclosure is an integral component of every social interaction and can be described as "any message about the self that a person communicates to another" (Wheeless and Grotz 1976, 338). Self-disclosure, therefore, is a part of the communication process and has to be considered in relation to specific individuals, namely the communication partners (Wheeless 1976, 47; Cozby 1973, 73). In general, self-disclosure is the basic pre-condition for every social relationship because it is part of every communication, and the passing on of information about oneself, one's thoughts, and one's feelings is necessary to create social proximity (Altman and Taylor 1973;

Laurenceau et al. 1998). This means that self-disclosure and the perception of privacy are closely related.

Another concept that is strongly connected to this topic is surveillance. Whereas privacy can be seen as a concept that is based on the individual's perception and the individual's behaviour, and self-disclosure as a concept that highlights the relevance of social interaction and relationships, the concept of surveillance focuses on the societal phenomenon. Literally, surveillance means "to watch over", and as such it is an everyday practice in which individuals engage routinely (Lyon 2007, 449). Although it should be noted that some surveillance relies on physical watching, much is nowadays automated and digitized (Lyon 2002, 1). That is why some authors argue that today we have a "surveillance society" (Lyon 2001; Norris and Armstrong 1999). Surveillance can be understood in a neutral way as "any focused attention to personal details for the purpose of influence, management, or control" (Lyon 2007, 449). According to Foucault, surveillance means that someone "is seen, but he does not see; he is the object of information, never a subject in communication" (Foucault 1977, 200). However, surveillance is related to questions of power and social control: Those who hold access to large data sets of personal information have a crucial tool that allows them to influence the behaviour of those whose data is being held (Stalder 2002). Therefore, surveillance can also be defined as "a negative term that denotes the collection [. . .] of data about individuals or groups in order to control and discipline their behaviour by the threat of being targeted by violence or to establish or reproduce domination" (Fuchs 2010, 174; Fuchs 2008, 269).

In modern societies, surveillance is primarily conducted by political and state institutions, such as the police and the military, and by corporations. Whereas the state's interest in gathering data about their citizens is the effective organization of bureaucracy and the effective prevention of crime, corporations are interested in information about their staff and consumers in order to optimize working processes and maximize profits (Fuchs 2010, 174). But even if surveillance appears justified from a societal perspective, at the individual level it means an invasion of privacy, as the individuals do not have the possibility to control and regulate the access to their monitored personal information.

On a theoretical level, the three concepts of privacy, self-disclosure, and surveillance are strongly interconnected with privacy as the central concept.

13.3. PRIVACY, SURVEILLANCE, AND SELF-DISCLOSURE ON THE SOCIAL WEB

Culnan (1993) recommends examining privacy in varying contexts. This seems to be especially true for the context of the Internet. Given the rapid technical and ongoing changes in usage, the Internet has to be acknowledged as a very dynamic medium. In particular, the emergence of the social web may have caused changes in the users' perceptions of privacy. More than ever, users are required to disclose information about themselves. Typically for the social web, making the self known to other users is critical for being accepted as a part of the community. Self-disclosure can be seen as a part of the functionality of the system itself. It is assumed that the users' perceptions of privacy affect their self-disclosing behaviours—and vice versa.

According to Etzioni (1999), the first step in analyzing privacy is to determine whether or not there is a problem. Because of the easy availability of private information on the Internet and the seemingly great readiness of social web users to disclose personal data, it seems that the protection of privacy is not a priority for users. Empirical evidence can be found, however, that social web users are actually quite concerned about their privacy (Barnes 2006; Tufekci 2008; Debatin et al. 2009).

Despite these findings, empirical research suggests that the individual need for privacy only has a small influence on online behaviour. This is what is called the "privacy paradox" (Barnes 2006; Awad and Krishnan 2006; Norberg et al. 2007). It means that an extensive concern about the safety of one's private data does not necessarily coincide with intensified security measures, such as reducing the accessibility of one's social web profile, changing the privacy settings if possible (Acquisti and Gross 2006; Tufekci 2008; Debatin et al. 2009; boyd and Hargittai 2010), or decreasing one's self-disclosure (Debatin et al. 2009).

The reasons for this are manifold. On the one hand, they include a lack of problem awareness (Debatin et al. 2009; boyd and Hargittai 2010) or of media competence, such as ignorance of privacy settings (Debatin et al. 2009) and uncertainty about the audience (Acquisti and Gross 2006). On the other hand, it can be assumed that social web usage offers many advantages and gratifications that increase in direct proportion to the degree of self-disclosure. Lampe et al. (2007) confirm that the quantity of disclosed information in social networking sites is linked to the degree of networking. This leads to the conclusion that the revelation of private information is rewarded with social gratification (Taddicken and Jers in press).

An additional reason for the fact that many studies find empirical evidence for a high degree of privacy concerns, but none for corresponding behaviour, could be the difficulty of measuring these attitudes. As explained above, privacy and self-disclosure are subject to situational processes of negotiation. In relation to that, Joinson et al. (2008) showed that situational cues are the main factors influencing the users' self-disclosures. It can be assumed that the concept of privacy, upon which social web behaviour is based, is likewise influenced by these situational cues.

Furthermore, privacy must be seen as a subjective measure that differs from individual to individual (Buchanan et al. 2007). Recent research has found connections with the individual's demographics, such as gender (Sheehan 1999; Rodgers and Harris 2003), age (Bellman et al. 2004), and education (Wang and Petrison 1993; Milne and Gordon 1994). Other studies examined the influence on privacy concerns of the individual's experiences with the Internet (Miyazaki and Fernandez 2001; Singh and Hill 2003; Bellman et al. 2004). Furthermore, it must be assumed that privacy concerns are affected by the individual's interests, values, and norms (Introna and Pouloudi 1999). Moreover, it was shown that external factors such as nationality and national culture influence Internet users' privacy concerns (Cho et al. 2009). In summary, privacy concerns on the Internet are a function of a wide and multidimensional variety of an individual's aspects and characteristics.

To make it even more complex, the user's privacy concerns are additionally connected with the user's behaviour. Buchanan et al. (2007) suggest that attitudes and behaviour in this field are related (159). An example they give is providing false or incomplete personal information when registering on some websites instead of giving a real name and address. Additionally, Paine et al. (2007) present empirical findings that privacy concerns are related to behaviour regarding privacy protection. They found that some people reported that they were not concerned about privacy, and when asked why, they stated that they had taken action to protect their privacy in the Internet.

Given that social web applications have become an integral part of the Internet—and will most likely continue to be—it is vital to explore the user's perception of privacy in this context. In this context the concept of surveillance and its awareness have to be considered as well. In the social web, problems, such as state surveillance after 9/11, or economic surveillance, such as the commodification of personal data in the form of spam and advertising, are important in this context. So far, however, the corporate surveillance mechanisms of for example social networking sites, such as targeted advertising, have hardly been studied (Fuchs 2010, 173). This assumption makes it all the more necessary to employ explorative methods to study social web users' understanding of privacy and surveillance as well as the aspects that influence self-disclosure on the Internet.

13.4. METHODOLOGY

To answer these questions, five qualitative focus group discussions were conducted. This qualitative approach provides the opportunity to measure the subject's individual opinions and perceptions in detail. Furthermore, focus groups allow interaction. With this method, even subliminal attitudes and motives may be accessed and verbalized. Moreover, repressions, fears, and resistance can be reduced by virtue of group dynamics. The qualitative method of focus groups thus provides deep insight into the users' perceptions and evaluations as well as their attitudes and thought processes. Therefore, this method is promising for investigating users' awareness of privacy and surveillance issues as well as perceived benefits and risks of self-disclosure.

The composition of the groups was varied. The users' levels of activity were taken into account. For this, the concept of social web activity of Shao (2008) and Taddicken and Jers (in press) was applied (see also: Jers et al. 2009; Taddicken et al. 2009): According to this concept, producing users (active users) are people who use at least one kind of social web application actively, meaning that they produce content, such as running their own blog or writing blog articles. Consuming users (passive users) are people who use the social web as regular web content, meaning that they are only consumers and merely read or watch the social web content. People who make use of the active possibilities of the social web by evaluating things or writing comments are called participating users (semi-active users); they are participating in an active way but not generating new, original, and elaborate content. For this study, producing and participating users were interviewed in separate focus groups.

The participants of the focus groups were selected on the basis of their activity level as well as their sex, age, and education. Thirty males and sixteen females, aged 18 to 44, with different levels of education participated in the study. For recruitment, flyers were distributed in many households in Stuttgart, Germany. Additionally, the study was promoted in blogs and web forums that were somehow related to Stuttgart. In total, 961 people were interested. They had to answer a Web survey that was used as a screener to find out about their socio-demographics and their Internet activities in order to classify them as producing, participating, or consuming users.

The group size was about eight to ten. Each focus group lasted approximately two hours. Two females were moderating with a flexible questionnaire routine, meaning the participants were mostly able to discuss the aspects they preferred.

Each discussion was transcribed in three stages via audio and video records. The transcripts were then analyzed via qualitative content analysis. As the idea of this study was to learn about the social web users' attitudes towards privacy, surveillance, and self-disclosure on the Internet, the following tactics were used for generating meaning: noting patterns and themes, seeing plausibility, and clustering (Miles and Huberman 1994, 245). The categories were derived inductively. The MAXQDA software was used for this process.

13.5. FINDINGS

The participants started talking about the privacy topic directly in the beginning of each focus group, although the moderator's introduction did not even broach the issue of privacy. After this first phase, however, the participants only returned to this topic periodically. It seemed to be important for the participants to have talked about this issue, but during the discussions privacy issues became less salient. The topic of surveillance was only occasionally the subject of the discussion.

The participants mainly reported general, unspecific concerns regarding privacy on the Internet and the social web. They showed great uncertainty about how their online revealed data might be used or misused by others.

> One just doesn't know what happens to one's data. And who uses them. (Female, 25, producing user)

This uncertainty was expressed and regarded as important by many participants. At the same time, only a few participants were aware that the Internet "does not forget" and that the revealed information is available online for a long time.

Specific concerns in relation to this problem were reported only by a few participants. Some of these were, for example, that e-mail providers would scan private e-mails. Also, some participants reported being afraid that their personal content was stored somewhere on the Internet and could be viewed by unauthorized people. This concern was especially true for photographs.

Some of the participants, though, were not aware of privacy and surveillance risks beforehand. It was during the discussions they thought about the possibilities of data abuse on the Internet and the social web for the first time.

> One does that because one does not even get the idea that it could have such consequences, and that is why one is willing to use things even though one takes a certain risk which one is not even aware of at that moment. [. . .] I feel like my eyes are being opened right now. (Female, 43, producing user)

A few participants even explained that they found it stressful to worry about the privacy of their personal data or to think about the consequences of disclosing their information. They clearly displayed a low awareness concerning the problem of disclosure of personal information. Some persons expressed the opinion that there was nothing bad about full disclosure because they had nothing to hide.

> I think it is silly to pay attention to that. I just think if someone is interested in my life, I don't care, because I have nothing to hide. (Male, 23, producing user)

Many participants did not have a deep knowledge about data abuse and threats to privacy and, therefore, did not realize the risks of self-disclosure.

I, too, think that the thing with the pictures is overrated. If one posts normal pictures, I mean one does not post nude pictures or something like that on the Internet, like of the last vacation leaning against a palm tree and one wants people to see those, what's the harm? I mean what bad can even be done with pictures like that? (Female, 29, participating user)

Moreover, concerns that something bad could be done with the disclosed information were sometimes classified as exaggerated and excessive compared with other problems of data protection.

Maybe I'm a bit naive but I thought that hype, 'oh my God, they want to steal our data,' was completely exaggerated. [. . .] I don't think anything like that could happen to me. (Female, 22, participating user)

However, those judgments were assessed as being poor and naive by those participants who were more careful. They mentioned a lack of the ability to reflect and, most importantly, a lack of life experience as possible reasons for the carelessness of others.

I believe that younger people disclose more information about themselves because they don't think about the possibility that when they start working, someone from the human resource department might take a look at what they do in their private time. A 17 or 18 year old who is still in school or has just started studies at a university does not think about something like that because it does not concern him yet. I have witnessed that among my friends. When the students started doing internships or something like that, they blocked their names in studiVZ [M.T.: a popular German social networking site] or made it more anonymous somehow. Only then did they realize how much of themselves they had presented online. (Male, 25, participating user)

In relation to other Internet users, this phenomenon was described as an effect of "dis-inhibition. Some speculated that persons who disclose a lot of information about themselves on the Internet have lost control.

I find it fascinating what the Internet can do to people. One loses control, I think. (Female, 25, producing user)

In fact, most of the participants stated that their self-disclosing behaviour on the Internet had changed over the course of time. One participant explained how he had learned to protect his privacy. In cases like this, personal experiences as well as the experiences of friends and relatives, seem to be relevant regarding interference with privacy on social websites.

Accordingly, participants explained that they used the technical options for privacy settings more often than before. Still, some reported to feel helpless in regard to the disclosure of their personal information by others. One participant brought an interesting argument into the discussion by explaining how he would stay in control of his privacy:

> I post pictures and I sometimes even post pictures that are not suitable for being found by, for example, a staff manager. Because [. . .] if I post that picture then hopefully no one else does, but others can just link to it. This means, if I delete it, it's gone. (Male, 19, participating user)

He tried to preserve the right over his own information and, with that, the control over who received that information by self-disclosing his information, which is indeed accompanied by a loss of control. In fact, this is a case of paradoxical behaviour that gives the actor a feeling of control, which he does not actually possess since the saving, duplication, and distribution of the disclosed contents by others cannot be ruled out.

Another cluster of comments focused on people's privacy concerns in daily life. Among these, many participants emphasized their need for privacy in general. They often referred to having similar caution in "real life", for example, in talking with strangers, using ATMs, or similar situations. This shows that the participants were sensitive when it came to their personal data in general but not specifically in connection with social web activities. For example, one participant claimed that he would only disclose information on the social web that he would tell a stranger he met while waiting at the train station. These participants did not differentiate between disclosing personal information on the Internet and disclosing personal information in an offline context, such as when participating in a sweepstakes.

In general, participants focused on the individual perspective of privacy during discussions. Privacy as a social or cultural value was almost never mentioned. Some participants expressed concern about the fact that there is so much easily accessible personal information on social websites, but even those participants thought that the individual advantages outweigh the risks. A change in perception and importance of the concept of privacy over time is stated but not critically assessed.

> It is just part of the time that it is not as private anymore as it used to be. (Male, 23, participating user)

Some few remarks regarding criminal activities on the social web provide an exception. They show a perceived helplessness towards the social web mechanisms of circulation. These participants noted that personal information on the social web cannot be easily removed from the Internet and can, therefore, threaten individual privacy or reputation. Concurrently, the mechanisms and institutions of supervision are perceived as powerless.

Users do not perceive state surveillance but rather the state's inability to fulfil its duty of preventing and investigating crime.

> Yes, I think that there are a lot of pictures showing violent acts on YouTube and elsewhere. They just spread in [. . .] the video is not even online for an hour and already 10,000 people have watched it and it is suddenly displayed on 500 other websites. And one can never know what happens to the pictures. Principally, everyone could copy the desktop information [. . .] even if you protect your pictures, they are very quickly online, either way. (Female, 25, producing user)

> I think false information or information that should not be online is one of the biggest problems. But if there are enough people or enough criminal energy to keep it there, then it is impossible to erase anymore. (Male, 19, producing user)

Concerns about surveillance were reported regarding economic information. The participants were aware of the need of commercial social web providers to make profits with their services, but on the whole they were still unsure of the purposes for which the providers would use that information. This lack of transparency was considered the biggest problem.

> I think the problems regarding studiVZ [M.T.: a popular German social networking site] are not limited to the disclosure of information. I am always asking myself who is behind this project and what do they want this information for. [. . .] you have to ask yourself what those people want to do with it and to what purpose they gather all that information. (Male, 21, participating user)

The gathering of information by social web providers was compared to loyalty card systems like Miles and More or Payback, but individual views concerning participation in such commerce-oriented voluntary revelations of information differed: Some participants described a vague feeling of uneasiness regarding becoming a "glass human".

> It has nearly become common standard to disclose private data, even if one orders on the Internet, it does not matter if it is from a mail-order house or somewhere else, everyone can access the private data and can see what one buys so that one even gets swamped with advertisings according to one's preferences. (Female, 29, participating user)

Others, however, even viewed the commercial purposes of data usage, such as placing of personalized advertising, as an advantage. This view changed, though, as soon as pull-communication developed into push-communication. The latter is regarded as an interference with one's individual privacy.

> If it is just one commercial that is shown on the browser, okay, but if it goes further and one would get sent mails or get a call and . . . things like that, [. . .] that would just be too much. (Male, 22, participating user)

> Advertising can still be ignored somehow [. . .], but if somebody calls you or writes you an e-mail, [. . .] that would be a clear interference with privacy. (Female, 22, participating user)

Some participants reported conducting surveillance themselves. They brought up the point that the social web gives users the opportunity to observe other people, whether known (e.g., friends) or unknown (strangers).

> One visits a site of a person one does not even know but still gets a pretty good idea of this person just by looking at their site. What do they like and dislike. Partly even political views or something like that. I think that is reason for concern, but still [. . .] this is a good platform for exchange. (Male, 23, participating user)

This quotation also shows that the perceived benefits of the social web are, in fact, a decisive aspect of self-disclosure on social websites. Accordingly, many participants, especially producing users, stated that they know about problems concerning data protection and other social web risks by now, but that the advantages that come with use are more important to them.

> But I mean everybody produces such a vast quantity of data on the Internet, probably, at least someone who is not that careful, but surfs relatively free, produces a lot of data and maybe even a lot of contradictory data, but I don't know. I don't think that is good, I don't like it, but I think the service and the functions are so good, that I am willing to partly give up my privacy. (Male, 30, producing user)

In this case, users made deliberate decisions and chose benefits over privacy, as opposed to those who worried vaguely about endangerment of privacy through self-disclosure. Only a few participants, however, and exclusively producing ones, voiced their decision this clearly. Many users indirectly admitted that the services and benefits they can enjoy while using social websites outweigh that vague feeling of insecurity concerning their privacy.

The perceived gratification for the individual user seems to be closely tied to aspects of the social context. The participants reported that the usage and self-disclosing behaviour of their social offline context are one of the main drivers in their use of social websites. They explained that they register for and use the same social web applications as their peer group.

Many participants indicated worries about not being socially integrated if they were to be the only one not using a social website. For example, one participant explained that he would feel socially excluded if he did not use the same social networking site as his friends and colleagues.

> If you're not a member in a social networking site you are completely socially excluded, well, I can talk about myself. [. . .] That's where the whole life takes place. (Male, 24, participating user)

Networking and social integration were reported as the main gratifications in using social websites.

> It's these contacts with people you don't see very often or you actually are hardly in contact with. Then you can write short messages back and forth. To attend friendships a little bit. (Female, 24, participating user)

An important part of that interaction is the exchange of information. The social web is perceived as an enormous help in gathering information. That is the reason why so many users are willing to post their problems on the Internet in order to discuss their options with other users. The possibility to simplify and bundle communication processes through social websites is also an important reason to display personal information on these sites.

> I was abroad for three months last year and everyone has always asked me: Can you post some new pictures? I want to see what it looks like there. It was also a question of communication. I did not have to write everyone an e-mail. I just said I have been here and there and the police already busted me on the first day and then I just posted some pictures and that was it. Everyone just took a look at it. (Male, 23, producing user)

Purposes like documentation or archiving were also given as reasons for disclosure of personal information. This was most true for archiving pictures and experiences. It was likewise seen as a gratification that the contact details of one's social acquaintances can be archived on social websites. It was also acknowledged that this service can only be used sensibly if users state their contact details honestly. The building and maintenance of social relationships also requires the disclosure of personal contacts. Most participants named that as the main reason to post their own contact details.

Moreover, there are social norms that dictate how a member of a certain social web application has to act, especially regarding the level of self-disclosure. This rule of conduct is perceived as such, even before registering, and is respected by the users if they decide to register.

> Yes, one certainly takes a look at how other users are registered. I mean, if I enter a forum and let's say most of the users are registered under nicknames then I am also going to register under a nickname. If I want

to use Xing I don't have to register before being able to look at certain things, okay there everybody uses his real name and has posted a basic level of information. I think to take a look at that would be my guideline to determine how much to reveal. (Male, 27, producing user)

Another important aspect concerning the question of self-disclosure seems to be the perception of the respective social web application. In this context respectability of an application was given as a reason, but none of the participants could articulate which concrete criteria they used to judge it. An indefinite feeling of security due to a familiar atmosphere, as well as widespread popularity of the website, was mentioned. An unclear design and layout and a lack of trustworthiness in atmosphere, on the other hand, led to a decrease in activity and information disclosure.

13.6. DISCUSSION

Starting from the fact that a lot of personal information about users is revealed on social websites, one has to wonder how and if users can combine that with the protection of their privacy. In the theoretical part of this paper, it was assumed that control over and regulation of access to personal information is the core characteristic of privacy. However, it must further be assumed that the perception of privacy is subject to certain processes of negotiation between the individual need for privacy and the concurrent need for self-disclosure and social interaction. Accordingly, social web users have to weigh the advantages and disadvantages. It has been the aim of this study to look at the perception of this process against the backdrop of privacy, surveillance, and self-disclosure.

The conducted focus groups delivered a deep user insight about these questions. To summarize, the findings present proof that social web users perceive privacy as an important issue. Most users are concerned about privacy invasion, but their fears and concerns are mostly on a general level. Therefore, the perceptions of online privacy concerns are linked with privacy concerns in general. Users translate their general concerns about information security in everyday life into the online context. A high level of uncertainty and a lack of knowledge about concrete risks are shown. Accordingly, some users feel helpless or overstrained by worry about their personal data. Participants exhibit different ways of managing the dilemma of partaking in the social web, with its required self-disclosure and its risk of compromising one's privacy. For example, some users trivialize the perceived risk. Others report that they have changed their usage behaviour and value technical privacy options more. Again others take the privacy risk consciously because of the gratifications.

During the discussions, the issue of privacy became less salient for the participants. Each discussion started with this topic, but the participants then began focusing more and more on the different ways of using social web services and the perceived benefits of usage. Although the privacy risks are perceived somewhat vaguely, participants report that the usage of, and the self-disclosure on, the social web provide gratification in a multitude of forms. Socially oriented gratifications are perceived as especially important. Users feel strong social pressure to participate in social web applications like others do. It can be assumed that for many users, refusal to participate in the social web is not perceived as a possible alternative. For example, to decide which social web application to use, participants often relied on the recommendations of their social context. A high degree of popularity for a specific social website among one's personal social context is generally equated with high respectability and credibility in the social web provider. Objective criteria like displaying privacy policies or technical options to secure privacy (privacy settings) are not that important.

Surveillance issues were discussed seldom, but more concretely than privacy aspects. Users do not perceive a state surveillance; they rather perceive state institutions as helpless and overstrained when it comes to their connection with the social web. Mechanisms of economic surveillance were discussed differently. Non-invasive instruments such as targeted advertising banners are tolerated or even evaluated positively whereas invasive instruments such as spam mails are clearly not. The lack of transparency in the corporate usage of data seems to be the biggest problem in this context. Further, participants highlighted the possibility to observe other users via social web applications. This can be seen as a private mode of surveillance, or as Albrechtslund (2008) puts it, as "participatory surveillance."

The users' low level of knowledge and awareness about the utilizations of personal information by social web providers can be seen as one of the main problems. It is not surprising that users rate the gratifications higher than the privacy risks because the perceived benefits are far more concrete than the very general and somewhat vague perceived privacy risks. Further, a lack in media competence and, accordingly, a perceived helplessness, become apparent. Additionally, the social orientation seems to be the main driver for the usage of social websites. Users perceive strong social pressure to participate.

13.7. CONCLUSIONS

This study provided users' insights by choosing a qualitative approach. The results are important for society and politics because they provide understanding of which aspects must be regulated to protect social web users' privacy. Users have to manage a dilemma, which is called the "privacy paradox". It was shown that the lack of knowledge of users concerning the use and the possibilities of misuse of their personal information can be seen as the most important starting point in terms of persuasive and educational campaigns. The individual's level of media competence must be increased.

Further, social web providers should offer mechanisms to raise their users' awareness of the fact that their disclosed information is (more or less) open to the public. Users should be asked during the revealing process about who should actually have access to it.

Providers, too, should increase their credibility by making their utilizations of users' data more transparent (Awad and Krishnan 2006). For example, providers could explain how they make use of their users' information in detail. Even, this could be subject of the terms of use.

Still more research about privacy and especially surveillance concerns and self-disclosure in the social web is needed to understand the users' behaviours. It was shown that social circumstances play an important role in the process of negotiation about privacy versus self-disclosure. Those circumstances should assume a more prominent role in future scholarly discussion about this topic. In addition, it was shown that users feel helpless because of the social pressure for usage. Because users need to self-disclose at least some personal information for using most social web platforms (Staksrud and Lobe 2010, 36), it must be emphasized that both the economic actors, such as the providers, and political institutions need to meet their responsibility, for example, by making utilizations of users' personal data more transparent and by solving the problems of online data security by law.

ACKNOWLEDGMENTS

This research was supported by the German Research Foundation and conducted at the University of Hohenheim, Germany.

REFERENCES

Acquisti, Alessandro and Ralph Gross. 2006. Awareness, information sharing, and privacy on the Facebook. Paper presented at the 6th Workshop on Privacy Enhancing Technologies, June 28–June 30, 2006, Cambridge, ???.

Albrechtslund, Anders. 2008. Online social networking as participatory purveillance. *First Monday* 13 (3). http://firstmonday.org/article/view/2142/1949 (accessed August 3, 2010).

Altman, Irwin. 1975. *The environment and social behavior: Privacy, personal space, territory, crowding.* Monterey, CA: Brooks/Cole.

———. 1976. Privacy: a conceptual analysis. *Environment and Behavior* 8 (1): 7–29.

———. 1977. Privacy regulation: culturally universal or culturally specific. *Journal of Social Issues* 33 (3): 67–83.

Altman, Irwin and Dalmas A. Taylor. 1973. *Social penetration: The development of interpersonal relationships.* New York: Holt, Rinehart and Winston.

Awad, Naveen Farag and M.S. Krishnan. 2006. The personalization privacy paradox: an empirical evaluation of information transparency and the willingness to be profiled online for personalization. *MIS Quarterly* 30 (1): 13–28.

Barnes, Susan B. 2006. A privacy paradox: social networking in the United States. *First Monday* 11 (9). http://firstmonday.org/htbin/cgiwrap/bin/ojs/index.php/fm/article/view/1394/1312 (accessed on August 3, 2010).

Bellman, Steven, Eric J. Johnson, Stephen J. Kobrin, and Gerald L. Lohse. 2004. International differences in information privacy concerns: a global survey of consumers. *The Information Society* 20 (5): 313–324.

boyd, danah and Eszter Hargittai. 2010. Facebook privacy settings: who cares? *First Monday* 15 (8). http://www.uic.edu/htbin/cgiwrap/bin/ojs/index.php/fm/article/view/3086/2589 (accessed on August 3, 2010).

Buchanan, Tom, Carina Paine, Adam N. Joinson, and Ulf-Dietrich Reips. 2007. Development of measures of online privacy concern and protection for use on the Internet. *Journal of the American Society for Information Science and Technology* 58 (2): 157–165.

Burgoon, Judee K., Roxanne Parrott, Beth A. LePoire, Douglas L. Kelley, Joseph B. Walther, and Denise Perry. 1989. Maintaining and restoring privacy through communication in different types of relationship. *Journal of Social and Personal Relationships* 6 (2): 131–158.

Cho, Hichang, Milagros Rivera-Sanchez, and Sun Sun Lim. 2009. A multinational study on online privacy: global concerns and local responses. *New Media and Society* 11 (3): 395–416.

Cozby, Paul C. 1973. Self-disclosure: a literature review. *Psychological Bulletin* 79 (2): 73–91.

Culnan, Mary J. 1993. "How did they get my name?" An exploratory investigation of consumer attitudes toward secondary information use. *MIS Quarterly* 17 (3): 341–363.

Debatin, Bernhard, Jennette P. Lovejoy, Ann-Kathrin Horn, and Brittany N. Hughes. 2009. Facebook and online privacy: attitudes, behaviors, and unintended consequences. *Journal of Computer-Mediated Communication* 15 (1): 83–108.

Etzioni, Amitai. 1999. *The limits of privacy.* New York: Basic Books.

Foucault, Michel. 1977. *Discipline and punish.* New York: Vintage.

Fuchs, Christian. 2008. *Internet and society: Social theory in the information age.* New York: Routledge.

———. 2009. *Social networking sites and the surveillance society: A critical case study of the usage of studiVZ, Facebook, and MySpace.* Salzburg: Unified Theory of Information Research Group. http://fuchs.icts.sbg.ac.at/SNS_Surveillance_Fuchs.pdf (accessed on August 3, 2010).

———. 2010. StudiVZ: social networking in the surveillance society. *Ethics and Information Technology* 12 (2): 171–185.

Introna, Lucas D. and Athanasia Pouloudi. 1999. Privacy in the information age: stakeholders, interests and values. *Journal of Business Ethics* 22: 27–38.

Jers, Cornelia, Monika Taddicken, and Michael Schenk. 2009. "Why do I use the social web?" exploring the motives of active and passive users via focus groups. Paper presented at the General Online Research Conference (GOR), April 4–April 5, 2009, Vienna.

Joinson, Adam N. 2001. Self-disclosure in computer-mediated communication: the role of self-awareness and visual anonymity. *European Journal of Social Psychology* 31 (2): 177–192.

Joinson, Adam N., Carina Paine, Tom Buchanan, and Ulf-Dietrich Reips. 2008. Measuring self-disclosure online: blurring and non-response to sensitive items in Web-based surveys. *Computers in Human Behavior* 24: 2158–2171.

Krämer, Nicole C. and Stephan Winter. 2008. Impression management 2.0: the relationship of self-esteem, extraversion, self-efficacy, and self-presentation within social networking sites. *Journal of Media Psychology* 20 (3): 106–116.

Lampe, Cliff, Nicole B. Ellison, and Charles Steinfield. 2007. *A familiar Face(book): Profile elements as signals in an online social network.* Proceedings of the SIGCHI Conference on Human factors in Computing Systems, 435–444. New York: Association for Computing Machinery.

Laurenceau, Jean-Philippe, Lisa Feldman Barrett, and Paula R. Pietromonaco. 1998. Intimacy as an interpersonal process: the importance of self-disclosure, partner disclosure, and perceived partner responsiveness in interpersonal exchanges. *Journal of Personality and Social Psychology* 74 (5): 1238–1251.

Lewis, Kevin, Jason Kaufman, and Nicholas Christakis. 2008. The taste for privacy: an analysis of college student privacy settings in an online social network. *Journal of Computer-Mediated Communication* 14 (1): 79–100.

Lyon, David. 2001. *Surveillance society: Monitoring everyday life.* Buckingham/Philadelphia: Open University Press.

———. 2002. Editorial. Surveillance studies: understanding visibility, mobility and the phenetic fix. *Surveillance & Society* 1 (1): 1–7.

———. 2007. Surveillance, power, and everyday life. In *The Oxford handbook of information and communication technologies,* ed. Robin Mansell, Chris Anthi Avgerou, Danny Quah, and Roger Silverstone, 449–472. Oxford/New York: Oxford University Press.

Miles, Matthew B. and A. Michael Huberman. 1994. *Qualitative data analysis: An expanded sourcebook.* Thousand Oaks/London/New Delhi: Sage.

Milne, George R. and Mary Ellen Gordon. 1994. A segmentation study of consumers' attitudes toward direct mail. *Journal of Direct Marketing* 8 (2): 45–52.

Miyazaki, Anthony D. and Ana Fernandez. 2001. Consumer perceptions of privacy and security risks for online shopping. *Journal of Consumer Affairs* 35 (1): 27–44.

Newell, Patrica Brierley. 1995. Perspectives on privacy. *Journal of Environmental Psychology* 15 (2): 87–104.

Norberg, Patricia A., Daniel R. Horne, and David A. Horne. 2007. The privacy paradox: personal information disclosure intentions versus behaviors. *The Journal of Consumer Affairs* 41 (1): 100–126.

Norris, Clive and Gary Armstrong. 1999. *The maximum surveillance society: The rise of CCTV.* Oxford: Berg.

Paine, Carina, Ulf-Dietrich Reips, Stefan Stieger, Adam Joinson, and Tom Buchanan. 2006. Internet users' perceptions of 'privacy concerns' and 'privacy actions'. *International Journal of Human-Computer Studies* 65 (6): 526–536.

Parent, William A. 1983. Privacy, morality and the law. *Philosophy and Public Affairs* 12 (4): 269–288.

Rodgers, Shelly and Mary Ann Harris. 2003. Gender and e-commerce: an exploratory study. *Journal of Advertising Research* 43 (3): 322–329.

Schoeman, Ferdinand David. 1984. Privacy and intimate information. In *Philosophical dimensions of privacy,* ed. Ferdinand David Schoeman, 403–417. Cambridge: Cambridge University Press.

Shao, Guosong. 2008. Understanding the appeal of user-generated media: a uses and gratifications perspective. *Internet Research* 19 (1): 7–25.

Sheehan, Kim Bartel. 1999. An investigation of gender difference in online privacy concerns and resultant behaviors. *Journal of Interactive Marketing* 13 (4): 24–38.

Singh, Tanuja and Mark E. Hill. 2003. Consumer privacy and the Internet in Europe: a view from Germany. *Journal of Consumer Marketing* 20 (7): 634–651.

Staksrud, Elisabeth and Bojana Lobe. 2010. *Evaluation of the implementation of the safer social networking principles for the EU. Part I: General Report.* Brussels. http://ec.europa.eu/information_society/activities/social_networking/docs/final_report/first_part.pdf (accessed August 10, 2010).

Stalder, Felix. 2002. Opinion. Privacy is not the antidote to surveillance. *Surveillance & Society* 1 (1): 120–124.

Suler, John L. 2004. The online disinhibition effect. *CyberPsychology and Behavior* 7 (3): 321–326.

Taddicken, Monika and Cornelia Jers. (in press). Uses and gratifications of privacy issues online: obtaining social web gratifications = taking a loss of privacy? In *Privacy online: Theoretical approaches and research perspectives on the role of privacy in the social web*, ed. Sabine Trepte and Leonard Reinecke. New York: Springer.

Taddicken, Monika, Cornelia Jers, and Michael Schenk. 2009. Social web and self-disclosure = participation vs. privacy? Exploring how users manage this dilemma via focus groups. Paper presented at the General Online Research Conference (GOR), April 4–April 5, Vienna.

Tidwell, Lisa C. and Joseph B. Walther. 2002. Computer-mediated communication effects on disclosure, impressions, and interpersonal evaluations: getting to know one another a bit at a time. *Human Communication Research* 28 (3): 317–348.

Tufekci, Zeynep. 2008. Can you see me now? audience and disclosure regulation in online social network sites. *Bulletin of Science, Technology and Society* 28 (1): 20–36.

Utz, Sonja. 2009. Resolving the privacy paradox? How privacy concerns, strategic self- presentation, and norms influence the choice of privacy settings. Paper presented at the General Online Research Conference (GOR), April 4–April 5, 2009, Vienna.

Wang, Paul and Lisa A. Petrison. 1993. Direct marketing activities and personal privacy: a consumer survey. *Journal of Direct Marketing* 7 (1): 7–19.

Warren, Samuel D. and Louis Brandeis. 1890. The right of privacy. *Harvard Law Review* 4 (5). http://www.lawrence.edu/fast/boardmaw/Privacy_brand_warr2.html (accessed October 29, 2009).

Westin, Alan. 1967. *Privacy and freedom*. New York: Atheneum.

Wheeless, Lawrence R. 1976. Self-disclosure and interpersonal solidarity: measurement, validation, and relationships. *Human Communication Research* 3 (1): 47–61.

Wheeless, Lawrence. R. and Janis Grotz. 1976. Conceptualization and measurement of reported self-disclosure. *Human Communication Research* 2 (4): 338–346.

14 How Does Privacy Change in the Age of the Internet?

Rolf H. Weber

14.1. INTRODUCTION

14.1.1. New Privacy Challenges

Information technology has fundamentally changed society. Communications have become much easier and faster with the advent of the Internet and mobile phones. Such change brings uncertainty with it, in particular because directing, controlling, and enforcing traditional norms has become more difficult, even if risks to privacy in the digital environment were sounded some time ago (presaged in George Orwell's 1984 and earlier in Bentham's Panopticon). Indeed, the loss of privacy is particularly obvious in social networks; therefore, light must be shed on the research question of how privacy needs and surveillance requests can be adequately reconciled.

The dichotomy between personal privacy and free access to information must be tackled in light of the described developments (Kleve and De Mulder 2007, 331f). In addition, privacy has also come under pressure from actors who advocate other political objectives, such as combating organized crime and terrorism, improving health care, and implementing e-government. Even if predictions of the "death of privacy"[1] or of the "perils of social networking"[2] seem to be exaggerated, the traditional privacy concept is challenged, and new protective measures must be developed. The rapid progress made in the field of information technologies, for example concerning developments such as fingerprinting, network monitoring, bio-awareness systems, electronic data processing, and creating extensive data bases, have facilitated the collection and storage as well as the processing and interlinking of personal data[3]; however, technical measures can also serve—if properly applied—as means of privacy improvement.

14.1.2. Meaning and Function of Privacy

The term "privacy" encompasses a large number of concepts and ideas.[4] The objective of an individual (or enterprise) to control access to his/her/its personal information[5] can be achieved by infrastructure security (as a shield against unwanted signals), by letting the person have the freedom to make self-defined choices in respect to data dissemination without state interference and by giving the person control over processing data (Kang 1998, 1202–1211).[6] Control and access, however, can be looked at from two sides: On the one hand, holders of private information are interested in controlling it and (in case of third party control) accessing it; on the other hand, third persons might have a legitimate right to make information transparent.

The three basic features of privacy are secrecy (information known about an individual), anonymity (attention paid to an individual), and solitude (access to an individual) (Weber 2009, 237). Privacy is not a value in itself, but the decisive factor (the spatial issue) consists in the relation between a person and a specific information (Weber 2002, 150). In particular, sensitive data vary in relevance depending on the person in question, because information always has a certain value in the information society (Reidenberg 2000, 1323; Posner 1978, 395). Ultimately, the most important objective of privacy is the prevention of improper use of personal information (Kang 1998, 1214f).

Surveillance is to be understood as a repeated surveying of certain activities. Supervisory bodies usually do have an "official" task, encompassing the objectives and legal means of surveillance. In principle, such activities are designed to protect individuals (in the short or the long run).

14.1.3. Weaknesses of the Present Legal Framework

As mentioned, new technologies, such as click streams and cookies, bear the risk that the concerns of individuals regarding privacy will no longer be properly taken into account in the digital environment. The large volumes of electronic transactions facilitate data warehousing; nowadays it is possible to collect and disseminate data (information and communications) from and to a potentially worldwide community through global networks at quite a low cost, leading to digital distress (Weber 2009, 148f). The corresponding threats that already exist in the real world have undergone a qualitative and quantitative shift in the age of cyberspace, i.e., privacy-destroying technologies can cause ubiquitous surveillance (Froomkin 2000, 1475ff). Furthermore, digital information can hardly be fully deleted; data tracks partly remain (if information has been copied before) even after a deletion exercise (Mayer-Schönberger 2009, 50ff).

Apart from the technical developments provoking legal problems, the law as such is confronted with "internal" failures:

1. A main weakness of the present legal framework consists in the fact that the law does not cope with rapid technological developments. Legal rules are static; technology is dynamic. Consequently, if a new legal framework is established, usually after a lengthy legislative

process, it's possible that the new norms are already technologically outdated (Weber 2010, 488).

2. Another weakness can be seen in the fact that privacy rules are mainly national, whereas technology is global. This fact is known for many segments of the society (for example: financial markets, e-commerce); however, the territoriality principle is particularly problematic in the field of privacy because the moral understanding related to the extent and scope of protection of secret information considerably deviates amongst different nation states in the world (Weber 2002, 164f).

3. The law often is not equipped with the legal instruments needed in a technologically new world; for example law does not (yet) properly respond to the question of who would be the owner of data in web 2.0.

14.2. PRIVACY AND SECURITY

Privacy allows keeping certain information and data confidential. However, security might call for data collection efforts, at least if surveillance is in the public interest. Because due process must ensure that the collection of data does not produce political abuses, an interest balancing test should apply, notwithstanding the fact that the yardsticks of such "trade-offs" are often rather discretionary (Weber 2009, 240).[7] In order to adequately balance the interests, a short look into the technical possibilities of protecting privacy is necessary.

14.2.1. General Requirements

Privacy has a close connection with security, insofar as technical security measures are suitable to improve privacy. Generally the following security and privacy requirements need to be taken into account:

1. Resilience to Attacks: The system has to avoid single points of failures and should adjust itself to node failures (Weber and Weber 2010, 45).
2. Data Authentication: Retrieved address and object information must be authenticated.
3. Access Control: Information providers must be able to implement access control on data provided.
4. User Privacy: Measures need to be taken that only the information provider is able to infer from observing the use of the look-up system related to a specific user.

In view of the importance of technical measures for the establishment of a high privacy level, the most applied technologies and protective measures are briefly described hereinafter.

14.2.2. Privacy Enhancing Technologies (PET)

}A number of technologies have been developed in order to achieve information privacy goals. Privacy Enhancing Technologies (PET) can be oriented on the subject, the object, the transaction or the system (for a more detailed overview, see Bennett and Raab 2006, 180–202). Subject-oriented PET aim at limiting the ability of other users to discern the identity of a particular organizational entity, object-oriented PET endeavour to protect identities through the use of a particular technology, transaction-oriented PET have the goal to protect transactional data through, e.g., automated systems for destroying such data, and system-oriented PET want to create zones of interaction where users are hidden and objects bear no traces of data streams handling them nor records of interaction (Samuelson 2000, 1668; see also Froomkin 2000, 1528–1553; Schartum 2008, 20f).

A fifth category is being developed by the World Wide Web Consortium (W3C) and is called a Platform for Privacy Preferences (P3P) (Bennett and Raab 2006, 195f). This server-based filtering tool is supposed to enable individuals to program their browsers to identify which information they are willing and unwilling to disclose the owners of websites (Samuelson 2000, 1668). Thereby, identification and protection against deviations from the applicable legal framework in the privacy field are possible.

In the meantime, a large number of technical systems and measures have been developed;[8] for example, the following mechanisms can be mentioned:[9]

1. Public Key Infrastructure: The most common technical measure is the implementation of a PKI-like hierarchical certification system that serves as the data authentication, in order to fulfil the requirement of user privacy needs. The technical and legal regime is based on a reliable infrastructure of two mathematically related keys for each communicating party (a public and a private key) providing for secure channels separated from the general communication channels (Weber and Weber 2010, 47; Bennett and Raab 2006, 187–189).

2. Virtual Private Networks: VPN are extranets which can be established by closed groups of (private, professional, political) partners. The closed circle increases the confidentiality; however, this solution does not allow for a dynamic global exchange that takes into account scalability issues and cost savings.

} 3. Transport Layer Security: TLS, based on an appropriate global trust structure, could improve confidentiality and integrity of data streams; however, a new TLS connection needs to be established for each new delegation step and negatively affects the search of information.

4. DNS Security Extensions: Using DNSSEC, delivered information, transmitted by applying public-key cryptography, can guarantee origin authenticity and data integrity; however, DNSSEC does not

address confidentiality issues and has so far not been widely adopted (lack of scalability and of building chains of trust between servers of different organizations).

5. Onion Routing: The main idea of onion routing is to encrypt and mix Internet traffic from many different sources; data is wrapped into multiple encryption layers, using the public keys of the onion routers on the transmission path. However, onion routing has a negative effect on performance issues.

6. Private Information Retrieval: PIR Systems could conceal which user is interested in which information; however, in a globally accessible system, problems of scalability and key management make these methods impractical.

7. Peer-to-Peer Systems: P2P Systems allow for the exchange of data between different (equal) participants; in the meantime the most advanced forms of P2P operate without a centralized server. They generally show good scalability and performance in the applications, but it is important to establish some form of access control; authenticating the user can be done by issuing shared secrets or applying public-key cryptography.

14.3. PRIVACY IN THE FUNDAMENTAL RIGHTS' SYSTEM

A human society should be based on the values of human rights in all of their normative dimensions. As addressed at the outset, privacy is part of the human rights framework because it corresponds to a global value extending to the dignity of all individuals and their equal and inalienable rights.

14.3.1. Privacy as a Human Right

The right to privacy is enshrined in Article 12 of the Universal Declaration of Human Rights (UDHR),[10] Article 17 of the International Covenant on Civil and Political Rights (ICCPR),[11] as well as Article 8 of the European Convention on Human Rights (ECHR).[12]

The right to privacy encompasses the protection of individual privacy free from national and international surveillance. Taking up this idea, the German Supreme Court in its decision of February 27, 2008, has constituted an independent fundamental right of confidentiality and integrity related to info-technical systems.[13] Moreover, the right to privacy includes the right of individuals to control the way in which their data is being used. Amongst others, individuals need to be able to deactivate their own tags (so-called "silence of the chip") (Weber and Weber 2010, 53).

Human rights are not unlimited because the exercise of a human right by an individual can interfere with the human right of another individual; so, rights and freedoms are limited by the corresponding values of others.[14]

Furthermore, restrictions related to the exercise of human rights may also be imposed by principles of morality or of public order. In particular, as mentioned in the introduction, privacy can come into a conflict with transparency; in the words of Brandeis "the right to be let alone" eventually contradicts the "sunlight". The enhancement of transparency as an objective is generally acknowledged in order to establish a satisfactory governance system for all of the individuals and enterprises involved. An interest balance test between privacy and transparency will have to be done in case of diverging objectives.

14.3.2. Scope of Human Rights' Application

According to the classical understanding of human rights the scope of protection is directed against states and governmental bodies that unduly interfere with fundamental rights of individuals. Consequently, human rights are only protected from interference by non-state actors if the relation between a state and an individual person can be analogously used to express the relation between private individuals and/or legal persons. Insofar as two possibilities exist under the international legal framework (Cheung and Weber 2008, 418–423, with further references): (a) either non-state actors can be directly bound by human rights, which is sometimes known as "direct horizontal effect", or (b) states can be obliged to protect human rights from violations committed by non-state actors.

A few human rights provisions explicitly mention not only the state, but also the society or the family (Cheung and Weber 2008, 420). Furthermore, the interpretation of provisions related to the freedom of expression in different human rights treaties allows the conclusion that human rights obligations are not necessarily limited to state actors. Even without having specific sanctions and enforcement mechanisms, non-state actors can still be bound by the material provisions of a human rights treaty, regardless of whether and to what extent legal consequences from an international institution can occur. In fact, rules that stipulate that no provisions may be interpreted to imply that any state, group, or person has a right to engage in any activity or to perform any act aimed at the destruction or limitation of the codified human rights may also be considered as an indication that non-state actors can be bound by them (Cheung and Weber 2008, 422).

A further differentiation concerns the question of whether there is an obligation of states to protect human rights from violations committed by non-state actors. Looking at wording such as to "secure to everyone within the jurisdiction, the rights and freedoms . . ." it can be acknowledged that states have to actively secure the protection of human rights in their territories as well as observe their general obligation to refrain from violating human rights provisions. To this extent, the classical "negative" perception of human rights and freedoms is complemented by positive obligations (Cheung and Weber 2008, 423).

4.4. REGULATORY MODELS AND SCENARIOS

14.4.1. Present Situation

14.4.1.1. Governmental Regulations

An internationally binding agreement generally covering privacy does not exist. Nevertheless, international human rights instruments usually embody the essence of privacy, at least to a certain extent (Weber 2009, 235; Grewlich 1999, 280f). The already mentioned[15] International Covenant on Civil and Political Rights of the United Nations and the European Convention on Human Rights address matters related to privacy; for example, respect for private life is ensured, exposure to arbitrary or unlawful interference is rejected, and rules legally protecting privacy are introduced.[16]

More specific international instruments are the economically oriented OECD Guidelines of 1980 entitled "Guidelines Covering the Protection of Privacy and Transborder Flows of Personal Data",[17] the (regional) Convention for the Protection of Individuals with Regard to Automatic Processing of Personal Data of 1981 issued by the Council of Europe,[18] and most comprehensively, the EC Directive on the Protection of Personal Data of 1995.[19] The main principles of the EC Directive concern the proper collection of data, the observance of high data security standards, data integrity (purposeful use of data), and the proportionality of data collection.

Because an overarching international legal framework is missing, governmental regulations are mainly based on national laws having the disadvantage of a geographically limited scope of application due to the territoriality principle. Furthermore, privacy "cases" are often not easily suited to court proceedings, due to high costs or to personal reluctance to present private information to judges. Therefore, only a few cases have been decided by national courts.[20]

Consequently, the legal framework is very fragmented and the development of new approaches is necessary. On the one hand, the implementation of a privacy framework should be based upon a sophisticated technological architecture; on the other hand, the appropriate legal challenges need to be addressed. The basic questions of the agenda can be phrased as follows (Schmid 2008, 200): (a) Is there a need for (international or national) state law, or are market regulations sufficient? (b) Is existing/traditional legislation adequate or is there a need for new laws? (c) Which kind of laws are required, and what is the time frame for implementation?

14.4.1.2. Privately Introduced Rules

Due to the weaknesses of governmental regulations, privately introduced rules, which do have an impact on privacy, have gained importance (Bennett and Raab 2006, 151–175). Such rules, supported by technical measures, allow improved privacy. An example is TRUSTe, an independent non-profit initiative, which imposes specific standards on organizations collecting personal data (Froomkin 2000, 1525–1527). The TRUSTe Privacy Seal Program assures consumers that visited websites are compliant with fair information practices; the "control" is done by means of a validation page (Jasper 2009, 35f). In case of non-compliance, a complaint can be filed, and TRUSTe will contact the website, eventually requiring the participating company to change its privacy practices (Jasper 2009, 36, 58). Another service is the BBBOnLine Seal Program promoting trust and confidence related to compliance with privacy principles on the Internet through the BBBOnLine Trustmark.[21] Furthermore, publicly available privacy protection tools, such as Pretty Good Privacy (PGP), could be applied.

Experience shows that the effectiveness of self-regulatory schemes varies depending on the private entities, organizational structures, and governmental bodies involved (Weber 2009, 243). Codes of conduct could also be tailored to particular industries and evolve as technology develops. In fact, such self-regulation is already a common tool and is also supported by intergovernmental organizations such as the OECD (Grewlich 1999, 292, footnote 86). Alternative approaches to codes of conduct are standardized contractual clauses dealing with the treatment of personal data. Often, such clauses are called "Binding Corporate Rules" (Grapentin 2009, 693). A set of standardized contractual clauses would gain general acceptance and importance if approved by an official entity; this approach has been chosen by the European Commission related to the transfer of personal data to third countries (so-called cross-border information flow); several decisions outline the adequate contents of standardized privacy clauses and the procedural issues to be taken into account when delivering personal information to third countries.[22] Such standardized contractual clauses would lead to more legal certainty and could even be enlarged to safe havens if the principle of mutual recognition is applied (Grapentin 2009, 698).

Particularly related to business transactions or merchandise over the Internet, commercial entities are collecting manifold personal information. In order to reach an adequate level of transparency, a privacy statement should describe the way in which the website collects, shares, and protects personal information. A well-drafted privacy policy would have to encompass the following aspects (Jasper 2009, 32–34): (a) information being collected, (b) whether the information is personally identifiable, (c) reasons for information collection, (d) appropriateness of information collection, (e) manner of collection, (f) eventual consumer choice regarding the type and quantity of collected information, (g) eventual use of cookies and maintenance of weblogs, (h) the way that collected information is used, (i) eventual use of information for a secondary purpose, (j) information and approval of the concerned person for a secondary use, (k) eventual offering of different kinds of services depending on privacy preferences, (l) access to the collected information, (m) possibility of correcting inaccurate data, (n) length of the storage of collected information, (o) complaint procedures, (p) contact information of the data collector, (q) laws governing data collection.

14.4.2. Changing Concepts

The evaluation of the present situation has shown that the realization of new concepts in the field of privacy laws is unavoidable. Fresh approaches need to be taken into account, and new formats of privacy regulations are to be considered.

1. Experience has shown that a more user-centric approach to privacy is needed. When users click, it should be clear what happens, to whom and where personal information is sent, who is collecting this personal information, and if and how such personal information is being transferred to third parties. Furthermore, users should be provided with understandable and (in the light of good faith principle) acceptable terms of services including options to influence the collection of personal information. Furthermore, the environment is constantly producing information about persons, creating identities without the participation and awareness of the data subject; in this respect, more transparency needs to be realized.[24]

In the light of these facts, a number of general principles should be taken into account as milestones of an online privacy system (Basho 2002, 1510).

- *Choice*: Individuals should have the choice of sharing or not sharing their information.
- *Ease of use*: The technical system should be designed so that the execution of choices by individuals is not too cumbersome in respect to privacy protection.
- *Notification*: Individuals whose information is used by third persons must be notified about such use.
- *Verification*: The legal framework should provide means to verify whether the information is correct and whether existing privacy policies are followed.
- *Enforcement and redress*: The legal framework should provide mechanisms that ensure compliance with privacy policies and give recourse for legal action.

In this sense, privacy is a "value" that needs to be understood as an aspect of autonomy of individuals containing both freedom from undue demands to conform and freedom to control one's own information (Cheung 2009, 209). Amongst the different constituents of privacy, autonomy is a key element; however, threats are not only coming from the Big Brother of the Orwellian State, but also from all the little "dictators" around the individuals (Cheung 2009, 209, with further references). Examples include collection of information and data for shopping, telecommunication, and leisure purposes.

The more user-centric approach has caused legal scholars to apply contractual theories, encompassing elements of trade secrecy laws; this approach could lead to default licensing rules of personal information, thus ensuring that individuals retain their control (and power) over their information (Samuelson 2008, 1125f). Thereby, flexibility could be preserved, based on accepted mechanisms rather than relying on complex (and partly rigid) legal tools (Mayer-Schönberger 2009, 142). Another voice proposed to focus on the context in which information gathering and dissemination takes place; thereby, rights protecting individuals' control of information could ensure that information is not disconnected from its context (corollary to the purpose limitation principle) (Nissenbaum 2004, 119f). Consequently, it is argued that the concept of property is sufficiently flexible and adjustable to work for information privacy (Schwartz 2004, 2055ff). Looking at it from this angle, privacy is understood as a bundle of interests related to information property that can be shaped through the legal system (Mayer-Schönberger 2009, 143).

2. The implementation of adequate protective principles is important not least due to the fact that privacy more and more concerns the identity of a person as such. In view of the growing number of services provided over digital infrastructures, citizens increasingly have quasi-digital lives, moving in and out of analogue and digital spaces. Therefore, the electronic identity is becoming a key component of the digital economy and governmental structuring (Hoikkanen et al. 2009, 84–86). These new developments require that we seek new and more efficient privacy concepts because traditional data protection rules qualify identity only in relation to the behaviour of controllers with respect to personally identifiable information, which is partly due to the fact that data protection deals hierarchically with information privacy rather than horizontally with physical privacy and decisional privacy. The present privacy rules also offer no assurance concerning contextual integrity of identity (Hoikkanen et al. 2009, 87). Consequently, privacy risks related to electronic identity need to be tackled on the basis of a separate concept.

3. In addition, more attention should be paid to the perspective of understanding information privacy in a functional sense as a type of public good because it benefits and shapes society. From this vantage point, information privacy acquires characteristics of a commons that requires some degree of social and legal control to construct and then maintain (Schwartz 2004, 2088; Solove and Schwartz 2009, 61).[25] Consequently, the privacy commons is a multidimensional "territory" that should be ordered through legislation structuring anonymous and semi-anonymous information spaces (Schwartz 2004, 2088). Based on such appreciation it becomes apparent that the propertization of personal information should be limited to the extent it undermines the privacy commons (Schwartz 2004, 2088).

Furthermore, it can be argued that privacy is also a public value in that it has value not just to the individual or to all individuals in common, but also to the democratic political system (Regan 1995, 225). In other words, privacy derives its value equally from its usefulness as a restraint on the government or on the use of power (Regan 1995, 225).

14.4.3. Formal Categories of Privacy Regulations

Due to global challenges to privacy through new technologies and different identity threats, the outreach of privacy regulations should not be limited to territorial boundaries. The "globalization" of the legal framework, however, cannot easily be achieved. Ongoing efforts need to be made in order to improve the situation. Apart from the geographical scope of privacy regulations, formal structuring is another topic that merits further discussion. Different categories of rule-making approaches can be considered:

1. Future legislation encompassing privacy and data protection issues could be based on five different approaches[26]:

(i) *Right-to-know legislation*: This approach has the purpose of keeping the concerned persons informed about the technological environments and the consequences of daa streams, i.e., a person should know which data are collected and should also have the option to deactivate any tags.

(ii) *Prohibition legislation*: This concept introduces provisions that envisage forbidding or at least restricting the collection and distribution of data in certain scenarios. Such an approach is traditional in state legislation if the public community dislikes certain behaviour; enforcement of the prohibition is possible (at least in the books).

(iii) *IT-security legislation*: This approach encompasses initiatives that demand the establishment of certain IT-security standards that should protect persons from unauthorized disclosure of data. Provisions of this kind can be introduced by the state legislature, and also by self-regulatory mechanisms; typically, industry standards are developed by the concerned market participants, who therefore have the chance to be observed by respective developers. Technologically, a new "fourth-generation" framework of data protection protocols should be developed and should allow stringent safeguards as to reporting and frequent audits of measures.

(iv) *Utilization legislation*: This concept intends to support the collection of data in certain scenarios (contrary to the prohibition-legislation); however, such legislation must fine-tune an appropriate balance between utilizable and prohibited data collections.

(v) *Task-force legislation*: This approach encompasses legal provisions supporting the technical community's investment in the resources of the given legal challenges; the purpose of this approach consists in a better understanding of the relevant problems.

2. Another fundamental regulatory choice concerns the decision about what kinds of rules to select for the formulation of privacy provisions. In relation to data protection, legal doctrine distinguishes amongst four layers, correspondingly based on each other (Schartum 2008, 10):

Table 14.1   Layers of Data Protection Regulation

D General and holistic data protection regulations
C Sectoral and holistic data protection regulations
B Regulations regarding specific personal data filing systems
A Mixed regulations with miscellaneous data protection provisions

Layer A covers most aspects of privacy, e.g., the data protection principles. Layer B also contains comprehensive regulations but is limited to a specific sector of the society. Layer C comprises "traditional" data protection regulations, and layer D addresses specific privacy aspects such as professional confidentiality (Schartum 2008, 10/11). Layers A and B are of a mainly system-oriented nature, whereas layers C and D encompass specific but less comprehensive regulations.

3. A further taxonomy is based on the transactional scenarios and distinguishes amongst information collection (surveillance, interrogation); information processing (aggregation, identification, insecurity, secondary use, exclusion); information dissemination (breach of confidentiality, disclosure, exposure, increased accessibility, blackmail, appropriation, distortion); and invasion (intrusion, decisional interference) (Solove 2006, 478, 490). This concept begins with the data subject (the individual) from which various entities (other people, governments, and businesses) collect information. The qualification of the processing of information depends on the harmfulness of the respective activities. The next step consists in information dissemination, which brings the potential control of the information even further away from the concerned individual. Finally, privacy could be (illegally) invaded by third persons (Solove 2006, 488–491). This taxonomy follows the structuring of many data protection laws quite closely by putting the major emphasis on the question of to what extent the infringement of privacy could be considered as harm being the basis for further legal action.

14.4.4. Substantive Objectives of Privacy Regulations

In developing the idea of minimum standards, the establishment of an intergovernmental "General Agreement on Information Privacy" could be considered, introducing an international organism that builds a high-level negotiating forum for consensus-based decisions (Reidenberg 2000, 1360). The substantive principles should cover the following issues (Reidenberg 2000, 1326f; see also Hosein 2006, 134; Drezner 2007, 103ff; Weber 2009, 241):

- The data collector must be accountable for all personal information in its possession.

- Purposes for which the information is processed should be adequately identified.
- The information collection must be limited to the extent necessary for pursuing the identified purposes.
- The data collector should gather information with the knowledge and consent of the concerned individual.
- The information should only be used for the purposes specified and should be destroyed if no longer necessary.
- The data collector must ensure that personal information is kept accurate, complete, and up-to-date.
- The data collector is responsible for the appropriate security safeguards.
- Individuals must have access to their (collected) personal information, with a right to amend it if necessary.

Any new form of networked privacy governance encompassing the afore-mentioned substantive objectives and partly overcoming the limitations of territorial sovereignty must be thoroughly assessed. Relying on networked relations across organizational boundaries for privacy does need to include the interests of the individual citizen and the civil society leading to a more user-centric approach of privacy regulations.[27]

Looking at the fact that the development and establishment of international agreements in the field of privacy is quite difficult and time-consuming, the self-regulatory approach should be more strongly supported (Mueller 2008, 15; Weber 2009, 242).[28] The governance of the Internet generally takes place by means of informal, cooperative relationships among technical experts, non-profit organizations, and private sectors including the civil society. The steersmen ("kybernetes") are mainly actors who have direct operational control of some form of access to the Internet (such as controllers of service, routers, bandwidth, domain names) and assume the functions within cooperative frameworks (Weber 2009, 242).

Several elements can be combined to create a cooperative system of self-regulation, encompassing substantive privacy aspects and procedured privacy issues. Possible elements of a self-regulatory scheme may include the following topics (Grewlich 1999, 294ff):

- Codes of conduct for Internet privacy should be negotiated by market participants; preferably not only data collectors, but also users should have an influence.
- Such codes of conduct must contain rules for best practice, released in accordance with at least minimal substantive privacy principles.
- Data collectors should establish internal control procedures, to be in a position to continuously check compliance with the codes of conduct.
- Setting up hotlines to handle complaints from the public will help build confidence in self-regulation.

- The codes of conduct should be transparent and become a quality standard for good behaviour.

The fact that self-regulatory efforts merit to support is also underlined by the acceptance of privacy as a specific topic in the Internet Governance Forum (IGF) framework. Privacy has become a high-ranking discussion topic and plays an important role in the baskets of the annual conferences of the IGF (Bendrath and Jørgensen 2006, 363, 635ff). Furthermore, a Dynamic Coalition on Privacy has been established as a stakeholder group in the context of the IGF process (Weber 2009, 245). The Dynamic Coalition on Privacy addresses emerging issues of Internet privacy such as digital identities, the link between privacy and development, and the importance of privacy and anonymity for freedom of expression.[29] Apart from research work made available in draft form, modular human-readable privacy rights agreements are available for consultation.[30]

Notwithstanding the merits of self-regulatory efforts, some weaknesses should not be underestimated (for further details see Weber 2000, 84f). The quality of the legislative process can hardly be judged, a democratic deficit is likely to occur. Furthermore, self-regulation tends to concentrate on case-by-case rules rather than general rules, and its mechanisms are not directly binding in legal terms. The main problem of self-regulation concerns the lack of enforcement procedures; non-compliance with "private norms" does not necessarily lead to sanctions.

14.4.5. Strengths and Weaknesses of the Different Approaches

The foregoing evaluation of the present situation has shown that the influence of technology requires a more coherent legal concept of privacy, in which a broad scale of privacy problems can be designated (Solove 2006, 477ff). The chosen approach has to become more user-centric, meaning that the legal framework should encompass the concept of a relational privacy (Kleve and De Mulder 2007, 340). In particular, autonomy about the collection and dissemination of personal information must be given to individuals and so lead to a concept of contextual integrity of identity; a clear policy encompassing standardized codes of conduct could help to allocate more emphasis on choices made by individuals. This appreciation is even truer in relation to web 2.0, which is largely outside of the scope of state influence.

Looking at the formal categories of privacy regulations, the pure approach of prohibition has not produced satisfactory results in the past. Moreover, a mixture of right-to-know legislation and IT-security legislation seems to be more promising. The regulatory approach that refers to specific needs of data protection has the disadvantage of being at risk of being rapidly overcome by technological developments. A general approach has the merit to more easily comply with new technologies. A taxonomy based on transactional scenarios mainly takes up the challenges of the present privacy threats without fully tackling new developments such as digital identity or RFID-chips (Radio-Frequency Identification) in the context of the Internet of Things.

In an overall appreciation, a framework of substantive key principles set by a legislator at the international level, complemented by the private sector with more detailed regulations, seems to be the best solution. Through such a framework, general pillars of law-making principles can be set for everyone, which may then need to be supplemented by the individuals concerned in a way that covers their current needs. Furthermore, the inclusion of an international legislator in the process also ensures the continued involvement of the public sector, contributing at least by monitoring the process (Weber and Weber 2010, 67/68).

14.5. SPECIFIC IMPLEMENTATION TOPICS OF PRIVACY

A few specific topics related to privacy are worth discussing in more detail.

14.5.1. Transparency

As Supreme Court Justice Louis D. Brandeis (Brandeis 1914, 92) said in 1912, "Sunlight is said to be the best of all disinfectants". The transparency principle also relates to privacy even if it seems to be the contrary at first instance. Protective measures can be introduced in an efficient way if the eventual collection of personal information is made transparent. The respective aspects include notifying a supervisory authority about data collection as well as eventually registering data collections.[31]

Historically, Brandeis saw transparency as a remedy of otherwise illegal or objectionable behaviour; transparency has indeed long been recognized as a key element of governance and is essential in rebuilding and maintaining trust (Kaufmann and Weber 2010, 770f). "Publicity" implies many elements of transparency concepts related to government actions and business methods in general by shedding light on activities of state institutions as well as private entities with regard to data collection and dissemination (Kaufmann and Weber 2010, 780).

Transparency helps us to acknowledge and appreciate whether there is surveillance by technologies, what the scope of that surveillance would be, who is carrying out the surveillance, and what will be done with the data (Kleve and De Mulder 2007, 346). If general principles such as choice, notification, and verification are in place as milestones of an online privacy system, individual behaviour can be adjusted in a user-centric manner.[32] Without transparency regarding information gathering, it is quite possible that citizen feel more vulnerable rather than less;

that would inhibit the assimilation process, which could become detrimental to technological developments improving privacy (Kleve and De Mulder 2007, 347).

14.5.2. Security/Safety and Privacy

Security and safety interests do have an impact on privacy.33 Efforts to safeguard security might create barriers and roadblocks to others' freedom of action; shielding data from others eventually impinges on their ability to learn and to make decisions that protect their interests (Mueller 2008, 5). Furthermore, extensive privacy might cause problems in case of criminal behaviour of certain persons and could even lead to an evasion of accountability from harm done to others; particularly, as far as the fight against cyberterrorism is concerned, governments need to have access to data and have to be enabled to collect the data necessary for the surveillance in the public interest (Weber 2009, 240).

Obviously, due process must ensure that the collection of such data does not produce political abuses. Incontestably, an interest balancing test usually applies. However, the yardsticks of any kind of "trade-offs" are often rather discretionary; therefore, attempts to bridge the wide discretion and to develop guidelines for an interest balancing test are of importance (Weber 2009, 214).

At the end, the question arises how much privacy individuals are prepared to surrender in order to increase security. Privacy and security do not have to be opposites, but the one can affect the other (Kleve and De Mulder 2007, 342, 346). However, a situation in which differing concepts of privacy and security are adequately taken into account can only be achieved if civil society and government are clear about how control should be exercised, namely with regard to who is observing whom, how, and for how long (Westin 1968, 7; Cheung 2009, 194).

The relation between security/safety on the one hand and privacy on the other hand is probably the most important challenge for future privacy legislation. Law cannot be successful without taking into account and using technology. In this context, a concept having been developed in order to protect intellectual property, namely digital rights management (DRM), could be revitalized.34 Markets (for example music, movies, and games) did not really appreciate DRM systems for many reasons (amongst others for the fact that these systems could be easily circumvented); therefore, the success of the technology has been remote. Even considering this aspect, the respective idea should not be dismissed at once; to the contrary, it would be worthwhile to create a technical and organizational digital privacy rights infrastructure through which individuals could control the use of their personal information (Laudon 1996, 92f). With such a system, individuals would be able to add meta-data to their personal information detailing who can use it, for what purpose, and, eventually, for what price (Mayer-Schönberger 2006, 145f). Obviously, such a digital privacy rights infrastructure would have to be stable and reliable as well as easy to handle.

14.5.3. Social Control and Solidarity

Very clearly, the use of information technology makes daily lives more effective and efficient. This simple fact leads to the assumption that something that is useful or more useful than it used to be, may lead to a certain shift in norms. This development can be mainly seen in the example of Facebook: Social control and cohesion, which were typical of civil society several decades ago and no longer exist, at least not in the same form, experience some kind of revitalization; users of Facebook recognize that social control and social cohesion may have a useful function (Kleve and De Mulder 2007, 344; see also Garry et al. 2009, 236ff).

Furthermore, it is no longer possible to implement complex legal projects without the use of technology. The automation of processes itself imposes certain requirements and restrictions; however, new technologies may also contribute to social advantages. A new kind of solidarity could occur because creating and keeping consensus depends on the correct implementation of new technologies (Kleve and De Mulder 2007, 345).

14.6. OUTLOOK

Privacy is an "important currency" (Schwartz 2004, 2056). As in the case of a traditional "currency", privacy does not only encompass values, but also technological issues derived from the fact of circulation. Currencies need to be cleared in a cross-border setting through technical mechanisms; the flow of personal data must go through an infrastructure allowing protecting privacy interests.

Referring to the research question of reconciling privacy and surveillance, addressing the impact of new technologies is crucial. Apart from self-regulatory initiatives (including possible certification systems), the data controller's responsibility as well as their task of cooperating with other governmental agencies should be enhanced. Special data protection rules are needed in the field of police and judicial cooperation.

Furthermore, global consensus should encompass some generally acceptable principles such as legality in operation of the system, openness in personal data systems, responsibility of the data keepers and application of the proportionality principle (no excessive data collection, i.e., principle of ensuring data minimization) (Rule 2010, 263f). An adequate privacy concept necessarily needs to be based on the right to informational self-determination giving individuals the control over every phase and stage of the use of their personal information (Mayer-Schönberger 2009, 137). Such a concept would also enlarge the well-known term, the "privacy-watchers" (Rule 2010, 261f, 274), covering not only supervisory authorities but all individuals who could also apply the principle of information ecology in the sense of digital abstinence.[35]

NOTES

1. "Death of privacy" is, for example, mentioned in titles by Froomkin (2000) and Garfinkel (2000).
2. "Perils of social networking" is mentioned in a title by Garrie et al. (2009, 236).
3. Garfinkel (2000, 37–67) refers to "absolute identification".
4. For a recent overview see Cheung (2009, 191f) with references.
5. In the seminal article of 1890, Warren and Brandeis (1890, 205) refer to the right to be let alone; for a discussion of Warren and Brandeis see Solove and Schwartz (2009, 10–12); Richards (2010, 27–34); in general also Hosein (2006, 122–125 and 131–135).
6. The problem has already been addressed by a large number of philosophers; see, for example, Mill (1869) and Arendt (1958).
7. See also 14.5.2.
8. This legal contribution cannot address the technical systems in detail; as examples from the vast literature see McDonald et al. (2009); Raghavan, et al. (2009); Kosta et al. (2009); Androulaki and Bellovin (2009); Muntermann and Rossnagel (2009).
9. For a more detailed overview see Weber and Weber (2010, 47–50); see also Rubinstein et al. (2008, 274–280).
10. Universal Declaration of Human Rights, December 10, 1948, adopted by the General Assembly Resolution 217 (III), UN Doc.A/810 (1948), UN GAOR, 3rd Sess. Supp. No. 13, http://un.org/Overview/rights/html (accessed on ???); see also Rule (2010, 5–7).
11. International Covenant on Civil and Political Rights, GA Res. 2200 Annex (XXI), UN GAOR, 21st Session, Supp. No. 16, opened for signature December 16, 1966, 999 UNTS 171.
12. European Convention for the Protection of Human Rights and Fundamental Freedoms, November 4, 1950, ETS No. 5, 213 UNTS 221.
13. See Decision 1 BvR 370/07 and 1 BvR 595/07.
14. This also corresponds with a Kantian liberalist perception of freedom.
15. See 14.3.1.
16. For further details, Weber 2002, 154.
17. See OECD Guidelines Governing the Protection of Privacy and Transborder Flows of Personal Data, September 23, 1980, http://www.oecd.org/document/18/0,3343,en_2649_34255_1815186_1_1_1_1,00.html (accessed on ???).
18. Convention for the Protection of Individuals with regard to Automatic Processing of Personal Data, January 28, 1981, ETS No. 108, 20 ILM 377 (1981).
19. EC Directive 95/46/EC of the European Parliament and of the Council of October 24, 1995, on the Protection of Individuals with regard to the Processing of Personal Data and on the Free Movement of such Data, OJ 1995 L 281/31.
20. For example in the UK the case Applause Store Productions, Ltd. and Anor v. Raphael [2008] EWHC 1781 (QB); see also Garrie et al. (2009, 238–239).
21. For further details see Jasper (2009, 36–37).

22. Commission Decision of June 15, 2001, on standard contractual clauses for the transfer of personal data to third countries, under Directive 95/46/EC, 2001/497/EC, OJ 2001 L 181/19 of July 4, 2001; Commission Decision of December 27, 2001, on standard contractual clauses for the transfer of personal data to processors established in third countries, under Directive 95/46/EC, 2002/16/EC, OJ 2002 L 6/52 of January 10, 2002; Commission Decision of December 27, 2004, amending Decision 2001/497/EC regarding the introduction of an alternative set of standard contractual clauses for the transfer of personal data to third countries, 2004/915/EC, OJ 2004 L 385/74 of December 29, 2004.

23. See also Cheung (2009, 192), advocating a re-examination of privacy as a concept because geographical boundaries have dissolved and ethnographical uniqueness is dwindling in the Internet world.

24. See 14.5.1.

25. Critical to this approach Etzioni (1999, 59–61, 594, 623).

26. The following comments are based on Schmid (2008, 207–209) and Weber and Weber (2010, 60–62).

27. See 14.4.2.

28. For further details see 14.4.1.2.

29. See http://www.intgovforum.org/cms/index.php/dynamic-coalitions/69-privacy (accessed on ???).

30. See http://www.wiki.igf-online.net/wiki/Privacy-rights-agreements (accessed on ???).

31. See also 14.4.2.

32. See 14.4.2. (1).

33. See also 14.2.1 and 14.2.2.

34. For further details see Mayer-Schönberger (2006, 181ff).

35. For further details see Weber (2003, 23 et seq.) and Mayer-Schönberger (2009, 157 et seq.).

REFERENCES

Androulaki, Elli and Steven Bellovin. 2009. An anonymous credit card system. In *Trust, privacy and security in digital business*, ed. Simone Fischer-Hübner, Costas Lambrinoudakis, and Günther Pernul, 42–51. Berlin/Heidelberg.

Arendt, Hannah. 1958. *The Human Condition*. 38. 2nd edition. Chicago/London: University of Chicago Press

Basho, Kalinda. 2000. The licensing of our personal information: is it a solution to Internet privacy? *California Law Review* 88 (5): 1507–1545.

Bendrath, Ralf and Rikke Frank Jørgensen. 2006. The world summit on the information society—privacy not found? *SCRIPT-ed* 3 (4): 355–369.

Bennett, Colin J. and Charles D. Raab. 2006. *The governance of privacy: Policy instruments in global perspective*. Cambridge: MIT Press.

Brandeis, Louis D. 1914. *Other people's money and how the bankers use it*. New York: Bedford/St. Martin's.

Cheung, Anne S.Y. 2009. Rethinking public privacy in the Internet era: a study of virtual persecution by the Internet crowd. *Journal of Media Law* 1 (2): 191–217.

Cheung, Anne S.Y. and Rolf H. Weber. 2008. Internet governance and the responsibility of Internet service providers. *Wisconsin International Law Journal* 26 (2): 403–477.

Drezner, Daniel W. 2007. *All politics is global, explaining international regulatory regimes*. Princeton/Oxford: Princeton University Press.

Etzioni, Amitai. 1999. *The limits of privacy*. New York: Basic Books.

Froomkin, A. Michael. 2000. The death of privacy? *Stanford Law Review* 52 (4): 1461– 1543.

Garfinkel, Simson. 2000. *Database nation—the death of privacy in the 21st century*. Beijing: O'Reilly.

Garrie, Daniel B., The Honourable Maureen Duffy-Lewis, Rebecca Wong, Mari Joller, and Richard L. Gillespie. 2009. Impersonation of life: the perils of social networking. *Convergence 5* (2): 236–249.

Grapentin, Sabine. 2009. Datenschutz und Globalisierung—Binding Corporate Rules als Lösung? *Computer und Recht Issue* 11: 693–699.

Grewlich, Klaus W. 1999. *Governance in "cyberspace": Access and public interest in global communications*. The Hague: Kluwer Law International.

Hoikkanen, Anssi, Margherita Bacigalupo, Ramón Camañó, Wainer Lusoli, and Ioannis Maghiros. 2009. New challenges and possible policy options for the regulation of electronic identity. In *Legal discourses in cyberlaw and trade*, ed. Sylvia Kierkegaard, 84–98. Malta: IAITL.

Hosein, Gus. 2006. Privacy as freedom. In *Human rights in the global information society*, ed. Rikke Frank Jørgensen, 121–147. Cambridge: MIT Press.

Jasper, Margaret C. 2009. *Privacy and the Internet: Your expectations and rights under the law*. 2nd edition. New York: Oceana.

Kang, Jerry. 1998. Information privacy in cyberspace transactions. *Stanford Law Review* 50 (4): 1193–1294.

Kaufmann, Christine and Rolf H. Weber. 2010. The role of transparency in financial regulation. *Journal of International Economic Law* [forthcoming].

Kleve, Peter and Richard De Mulder. 2007. Privacy protection and the right to information: in search of a new symbiosis in the information age. In *Cyberlaw & security privacy*, ed. Sylvia Kierkegaard, 201–212. Beijing: IAITL.

Kosta, Eleni, Christos Kalloniatis, Lilian Mitrou, and Evangelia Kavakli. 2009. Search engines: Gateway to a new "panapticon"? *In Trust, privacy and security in digital business*, ed. Simone Fischer-Hübner, Costas Lambrinoudakis, and Günther Pernul, 11–20. Berlin/Heidelberg.

Laudon, Kenneth C. 1996. Markets and privacy. *Communications of the ACM 39* (9): 92–104.

McDonald, Aleecia M., Robert W. Reeder, Patrick Gage Kelley, and Lorrie Faith Cranor. 2009. A comparative study of online privacy policies and formats. In *Privacy enhancing technologies*, ed. Ian Goldberg and Makhail Atallah, 37–55. Berlin/Heidelberg.

Mayer-Schönberger, Viktor. 2006. Beyond copyright: managing information rights with DRM. *Denver University Law Review* 84 (1): 181–198.

———. 2009. *Delete*. Princeton/Oxford: Princeton University Press.

Mill, John Stuart. 1869. *On Liberty*. 12–13, 74–75. London: Longman, Roberts & Green.

Mueller, Milton. 2008. Securing Internet freedom: security, privacy, and global governance. *Inaugural Address*. Technology University of Delft. http://faculty. ischool.syr.edu/ mueller/opzet1.pdf (accessed August 18, 2010).

Muntermann, Jan and Heiko Rossnagel. 2009. On the effectiveness of privacy breach disclosure legislation in Europe: empirical evidence from the US stock market. In *Identity and privacy in the Internet age,* ed. Audun Josang, Torleiv Maseng, and Svein Johan Knapskog, 1–14. Berlin/Heidelberg.

Nissenbaum, Helen. 2004. Privacy as contextual integrity. *Washington Law Review* 79 (1): 119–157.

Posner, Richard A. 1978. The right of privacy. *Georgia Law Review* 12 (3): 393–422.

Raghavan, Barath, Tadayoshi Kohno, Alex C. Snoeren, and David Wetherall. 2009. Enlisting ISPs to improve online privacy: IP address mixing by default. In *Privacy enhancing technologies*, ed. Ian Goldberg and Makhail Atallah, 143–163. Berlin/Heidelberg: Springer.

Regan, Priscilla M. 1995. *Legislating privacy: Technology, social values and public policy.* Chapel Hill/London: University of North Carolina Press

Reidenberg, Joel R. 2000. Resolving conflicting international data privacy rules in cyberspace. *Stanford Law Review* 52 (5): 1315–1371.

Richards, Neil M. 2010 The puzzle of Brandeis, privacy, and speech. *Vanderbilt Law Review* 63: 1295–1352.

Rubinstein, Ira S., Ronald D. Lee, and Paul M. Schwartz. 2008. Data mining and Internet profiling: emerging regulatory and technological approaches. *The University of Chicago Law Review* 75 (1): 261–285.

Rule, James B. 2010. Introduction and Conclusion. In *Global privacy protection*, ed. James B. Rule and Graham Greenleaf, 1–14 and 257–275. Cheltenham/Northampton: Edward Elgar.

Samuelson, Pamela. 2000. Privacy as intellectual property? *Stanford Law Review* 52 (4): 1124–1173.

Schartum, Dag Wiese. 2010. Designing and formulating data protection laws. International Journal of Law and Information Technology 18 (1): 1–27.

Schmid, Viola. 2008. Radio frequency identification law beyond 2007. In *The Internet of things,* ed. Christian Floerkemeier, Marc Langheinrich, Elgar Fleisch, Friedemann Mattern, and Sanjay E. Sarma, 196–213. Berlin/Heidelberg: Springer.

Schwartz, Paul M. 2004. Property, privacy, and personal data. *Harvard Law Review* 117 (7): 2055–2128.

Solove, Daniel J. 2006. A taxonomy of privacy. *University of Pennsylvania Law Review* 154 (3): 477–560.

Solove, Daniel J. and Paul M. Schwartz. 2009. *Information Privacy Law.* 3rd edition. Austin: Wolters Kluwer.

Warren, Samuel D. and Louis D. Brandeis. 1890. The right to privacy. *Harvard Law Review* 4 (5): 193–220.

Weber, Rolf H. 2002. *Regulatory models for the online world.* Zurich: Schulthess.

———. 2003. *Rechtsfragen rund um Suchmaschinen.* Zurich: Schulthess.

———. 2009. *Shaping Internet governance: Regulatory challenges.* Zurich/Berlin: Schulthess/Springer.

———. 2010. *E-Commerce und Recht.* 2nd edition. Zurich: Schulthess.

Weber, Rolf H. and Romana Weber. 2010. *Internet of things—legal perspectives.* Zürich/Berlin: Schulthess/Springer.

Westin, Alan. 1968. *Privacy and freedom.* London: Bodley Head.

PART III
Conclusion

15 Postface
Internet and Surveillance

Kees Boersma

"Wipe The Slate Clean For 2010, Commit Web 2.0 Suicide". On December 31, 2009, a web 2.0 suicide was announced: "Are you tired of living in public, sick of all the privacy theater the social networks are putting on, and just want to end it all online? Now you can wipe the slate clean with the web 2.0 Suicide Machine" (Schonfeld 2009).

This message was put on TechCrunch, a Rotterdam-based weblog on new technologies (http://moddr.net/), a new media space for artists, hackers, and filmmakers. The TechCrunchies guarantee that any individual user of web 2.0 sites (like Facebook, Twitter, and YouTube), enabled by a simple computer program, can wipe out all his/her personal codes, passwords, and login codes. The goal is to commit virtual suicide in order to get back to the "real" life and to escape from the web, from web-based alienation, virtual friendships, and Internet-mediated surveillance. That is the idea.

At first sight, the proposed web 2.0 suicide seems to be a silent protest against the increasing influence of the Internet on our private life and privacy. At the same time the web 2.0 suicide machine can be seen as a destructive call. Like the followers of Ned Ludd, who, in the late eighteenth century, destroyed stocking frames in the UK (Jones 2006), the virtual suicide initiators simply oppose the new technology. Their neo-Luddist solution is not to join the positive forces of the new media and to transform the dark side of web 2.0 into a bright side by active political action, but to completely abandon communication technology itself. Yet, although a call for suicide is a quite extreme protest, even if it is virtual, it is not surprising that it focuses on the impact of the new media on our lives. The Internet, no longer a one-way information provision system, is intruding on our privacy. Everyone who is in one way or another active in the virtual space would agree: the Internet—and especially its new generation web 2.0 associated with interaction, user-centred design, self-expression, and self-monitoring—has an impact on our private life. Web-based information about individuals is collected, stored, and by means of profiling translated for marketing purposes. For security reasons, Internet data is used in ways that potentially threaten civil rights.

This book presents political, sociocultural, and economic analyses of Internet surveillance. In the introduction to this book, it has been argued that computing, and especially the Internet, enables various forms of surveillance. Researchers, from various backgrounds, in this book pay attention to the role of Internet technology, the new media, and the interactive web of surveillance. The key question of their studies is: How does the Internet transform surveillance? How can research about Internet surveillance advance the state of knowledge about the surveillance society? And: how can its impact be understood, analyzed, and, if possible, influenced and democratized?

Surveillance is a fundamental quality of modern society and an outcome of historical processes of inclusion and exclusion (Wagenaar and Boersma 2008). In pre-modern times, surveillance was about physical watching. In the modern age, automation has become the dominant force driving surveillance (Beninger 1986). Surveillance has become part of a technical infrastructure, in which the many watch the few and the few watch the many (Lyon 2007, 157). What makes the Internet special is the fact that surveillance becomes mediated by a technology that transforms social order by transcending time and space: it makes interaction and networking over long distances possible. Surveillance can take place at any time, continuously, and from any location. Apparently, new Internet-based technologies further define the expanding character of surveillance. Looking for a terminology to describe this phenomenon, scholars came up with descriptions such as dataveillance, panautomaticon, and electronic superpanopticon (see for example: Poster 1990; Lyon 1994). Yet, given the dynamic character of the new media and its development, it is hard to grasp or even to define Internet surveillance.

The new generation of the Internet—which is also termed "social media" or "web 2.0"—makes research about the Internet and surveillance even more challenging. Some advocates of web 2.0 argue that the current generation of the Internet will result in a more interactive, and therefore democratic, virtual environment (Shirky 2008; Tapscott and Williams 2006). After all, the users of personal blogs and interactive websites are able to express themselves; disseminate views against established views; use the wisdom of the crowd to answer the most exotic questions; create a dynamic and ever-growing web of information systems, such as the Wikipedia encyclopedia; join social movements; become members of virtual, transnational communities of any kind; mobilize protest to further propagate political ideas; share their experiences about urban life, popular music, and travelling. These are just a few examples, some of which are mentioned in this book, that illustrate the democratic potential of web 2.0. Web 2.0 holds the potential to make the Internet more interactive, less static, more polyphonic, and thus more democratic.

Arguably, the interactive and dynamic character of the new generation of the Internet resonates with the liquidity of our modern times (Bauman 2000).

On the Internet, the social is negotiable and malleable. Through social media representations of the self get a new dimension. Reinforced by the more popular views on new media, the idea that web 2.0 can/will contribute to a more democratic (virtual) society has taken root in some accounts of media change. However, this book shows that the Internet also has a dark side: it is used in ways that contribute to increasing surveillance.

15.1. DIFFERING VIEWS OF THE INTERNET

Internet Surveillance Studies is a growing subfield of Internet Studies and Surveillance Studies. Although it is hard to predict how the Internet will look in five or ten years, most scholars and observers agree that it is certainly not a temporal phenomenon. Even if one sees the Internet and web 2.0 as hype, it is one that sets the agenda for further surveillance and control (Boersma, Meijer, and Wagenaar 2009). Only by studying the special nature of the Internet and of web 2.0, and how it evokes strong and opposing reactions, will we be able understand how these technologies impact surveillance. Internet Studies is currently shaped by a debate about the effects of web 2.0 on society. One can find utopian and dystopian views in web 2.0 studies.

On the one hand we see strong *utopian* views of web 2.0. In this view, the new generation Internet contributes to the well-being of our digital selves. The new utopian view of web 2.0 parallels the web 1.0 optimism of the 1990s before the dot.com crisis (Negroponte 1995). Internet technologies, in this view, contribute to a safer and more transparent world. Technicians emphasize the enabling effect of Internet-based techniques on surveillance (see for example Räty 2008). Iván Székely, in this book, unravels the rather instrumental views of software developers on these issues. For them, a solely technical rationality is the driving force behind the further development of the Internet. Social scientists also see promising elements in the new media, arguing that it has the potential to contribute to the ideal of communicative action (for a critical analysis, see: Murray 2010). It is the Internet and the wisdom of the crowd, they argue, that enable interaction, creativity, and innovation (Shirky 2008). On another level, it is argued that web 2.0 can contribute to safety and resilience in modern society, for example when citizens work together through emergent, online communities in situations where formal organizations fail (for example: Comfort 2007 on the aftermath of Hurricane Katrina).

At the other hand, there are strong *dystopian* views about the Internet, web 2.0, and social networking sites. These views are echoing a tradition of technological pessimism: the expanding force of technology will result in a total institution, in which we are completely encapsulated. Well-known dystopian ideas about our future technological society are expressed in Huxley's *Brave New World* (1932), Orwell's *1984* (1954), and Kurt Vonnegut's

Player Piano (1999 [1954]). In their own way, each emphasizes the dark side of our times: our individual autonomy, privacy, and our right to be left alone are at stake. The recently published novel *Little Brother* by Cory Doctorow (2008), in which the new technology plays a major role, builds upon this tradition. In this book, young citizens of California use the new media to fight increasing surveillance by the US Department of Homeland Security and the government of California.

Less apocalyptical dystopian thinkers argue that the Internet makes us—the current generation—less creative, more stupid, and narcissistic (Carr 2010; Twenge 2006)—or even violent (Serazio 2010). And there is more: the web 2.0 social media like Facebook and YouTube are increasingly *defining* our identity: Who are you? Where are you? And: What is in your mind? Even when you are not quite active on the Internet, the answers to these questions increasingly come from the virtual realm. Web 2.0 is mastering the body, mind, and soul. Dystopian views can provoke strong actions to oppose the dark side of the technology. The 2010 movie, *The Social Network*, about Facebook is revealing in this respect. It shows that given the enormous (economic) potential of web 2.0, this technology will promote, enable, and reinforce more surveillance in future times.

Other than web 2.0 utopias and dystopias, the contributors to this book show that it is important to go beyond dystopian and utopian approaches and to see the Internet as a field that is shaped by power and conflicting interests. In order to overcome the dark side of web 2.0, for example the unfettered surveillance, we need to develop a more balanced view (and take similar action). In David Lyon's words: "A careful exploration of the social and material realities of cyberspace does induce cynicism about utopian visions, but this by no means paints social analysis into dystopian corner" (2007, 100). In other words, a study of Internet Surveillance must pay attention to the ways the Internet changes society.

15.2. THE CONSTITUTION, CONDITION, AND CONSEQUENCES OF THE INTERNET

In general the Internet and web 2.0, like any other technology, can be understood by an analysis of three dimensions: its *constitution*, its *condition*, and its *consequences* (compare Boersma and Kingma 2011; Boersma, Kingma and Veenswijk 2007).

The *constitution* of the Internet (and web 2.0) refers to the material time/space dimension of the new technology. This (material) dimension of the Internet greatly defines the way it is used. But although the Internet, like any other technology, has scripts—standard technological procedures (Akrich 1992)—in the end the Internet only becomes meaningful in the actual use of the Internet. It is therefore that it is useful to speak about Internet (2.0) *in-use* (following Orlikowski 2000).

The actual use of the Internet and web 2.0 technologies reveal its *condition*: the integration of social domains through the virtual, which makes new interactions possible. In the context of this book this means that the virtual dimension of the Internet (Shields 2002; Woolgar 2002) not only makes new social interaction between individuals possible, it also means the introduction of new modes of surveillance.

Finally, the Internet has far-reaching *consequences,* both intended and unintended for surveillance practices. It is not surprising that it is mainly the consequences of the Internet that are hotly disputed. Whereas on the one hand the Internet can lead to a more active involvement of citizens in society, on the other hand it can lead to an increased panoptic control. A social networking site can contribute to participation, interaction, and self-expression, but at the same time its content can and will be seen as a commodity. Web 2.0 can reveal detailed information about governmental bodies to become more transparent, whereas at the same time the information is coloured and distorted. The Internet (2.0) in use can lead to inclusion and exclusion, to empowerment and coercive power, to shared identity and weakened social relationships at the same time (Hier 2008).

The authors of this book present various dilemmas of the Internet and surveillance such as the *user/owner* problem (David Arditi); the *knowledge* problem (and the lack of knowledge among users: Monika Taddicken); the *privacy* problem (Rolf Weber); the *inhumanity* problem (David Hill using the work of Lyotard); and the *transparency* problem (Kent Wayland, Roberto Armengol, and Deborah Johnson) of Internet surveillance. Most important, they all show that Internet is a new architecture of panoptic control and disciplinary forces that make new surveillance practices possible.

15.3. TWO PERSPECTIVES ON INTERNET SURVEILLANCE

Web (2.0) is contested terrain, so much is clear after reading this book. In studying the new Internet-based surveillance practices, the authors of this book use—roughly speaking—two perspectives or approaches to Internet and surveillance that go beyond the one-sided utopian-dystopian debate.

On the one hand there are approaches that employ a *critical political economy approach* for studying Internet surveillance. Many authors in this book find this perspective meaningful. For example, Christian Fuchs, Mark Andrejevic, Marisol Sandoval, and Thomas Allmer explicitly build upon a Marxist tradition. The focus is on the ownership and the ownership-structure of the Internet. Most of the interactive Internet sites are owned by private organizations and enterprises with an increasing influence that they use in an undemocratic manner. But Google, Facebook, Twitter, YouTube, and Blogspot are not only products of private corporations, the content of these sites is also a commodity. The individual user's information, through profiling and social sorting (Lyon 2003), is used by private enterprises for capitalist ends. Moreover: the users of web 2.0 who voluntarily put their information online, are to be seen—in Marxist terms—as *free labour force*. After all, they are not paid for what they are delivering and are not involved in the decision-making processes about the use of the information they provide. The political implication arising from this perspective is: how can we oppose this web of coercive power and the influence of private enterprises on the Internet? How can alternatives be established?

On the other hand there are approaches that focus on the analysis of the *social dimension of Internet surveillance*. The main idea that can be found in such approaches is that users of the Internet employ its potential to be creative, interactive, and connected. Being active on the Internet, in this view, is about adding information through identity-work. In this book, Daniel Trottier and David Lyon use Facebook as a case study to explore this phenomenon. In this way they are able to trace the liquidity of surveillance. The argument is that on the Internet, surveillance has lost its static, centralized character. Miyase Christensen and André Jansson use the idea of networked sociality to analyze transnational social spaces. Finally, Anders Albrechtslund argues in this book that interactive forms of Internet stand for more democratization and *participatory* surveillance. The question that arises from this perspective is: who is actually actively participating in web 2.0 and under what conditions? Can we indeed speak about participatory surveillance on the Internet, and how can this concept be concisely defined?

15.4. THE PANOPTICON AND INTERNET SURVEILLANCE

It is interesting to see that the metaphor of the panopticon is used in both perspectives. The panopticon, Bentham's best-practice concept for prisons, which was used by Foucault for describing the genealogy of power, remains an important metaphor for systems of surveillance, rules, and disciplinary power. However, surveillance scholars use the metaphor of the panopticon in different ways, depending on the way surveillance is conceived. Representatives of political economy approaches in this book define surveillance as a (by definition) negative process of domination, control, violence, and coercive power (in this book: Christian Fuchs, Mark Andrejevic, Marisol Sandoval, and Thomas Allmer). They cannot be put in the dystopian corner, because they do not argue that there are not positive potentials of the Internet, but they reject using the term surveillance for these potentials. Rather, they suggest using other terms for positive potentials and reserving the notions of surveillance, Internet surveillance, and web 2.0 surveillance for a critique of coercive power structures. Similar understandings of surveillance as a negative concept can be found in the chapters that are grounded in critical studies approaches, as for example the ones by David Arditi and David Hill. A similar definition of surveillance can also be found in the chapters by Monika Taddicken and Kent Wayland/Roberto Armen-gol/Deborah Johnson. The latter make a conceptual distinction between surveillance as form of domination and transparency of power structures.

This view is not shared by everyone in Surveillance Studies and not by all authors in this book. Some portray surveillance more broadly (see for this tradition: Lyon 2007, 163; Lyon 1994, 19). Surveillance, according to them, must be defined dualistically, as a phenomenon and activity that has enabling, positive effects (for example the surveillance of patients in hos-pitals, self-expression, and emancipation in situations of dictatorship) and negative effects.

To see both the enabling as well as the constraining elements of sur-veillance is in line with what Giddens (1984) calls the dialectic of control (see also Lyon 2007, 163; Lyon 1994, 77). Giddens' idea is that control and power always result in various forms of counter-power. For example, counter-surveillance initiatives on the Internet, like the whistle-blowing site *WikiLeaks,* which reveals state and corporate secrets, show how citizens "talk back" and try to hold governments and companies accountable in a critical manner. End-users of web 2.0, who try to build, maintain, and own non-commercial social networking sites try to oppose the dominant force of private enterprises. *Kaioo,* a non-profit social networking site, is men-tioned in this book by Christian Fuchs and Thomas Allmer as an example of such counter-forces. Another example, mentioned by Christian Fuchs, is the alternative social networking site project Diaspora. Finally David Arditi writes about file sharing, an alternative Internet practice. Surveil-lance in this more balanced situation has not disappeared from society, but the counter-forces contribute to "sublate" (in Hegelian terms "aufheben": to eliminate, to preserve, and to uplift at the same time) surveillance.

Given the complexity of Internet surveillance, one can ask oneself whether or not the panopticon is the best metaphor to describe Internet surveillance. In reflecting upon our surveillance society, Haggerty and Eric-son (2000) prefer to speak of the surveillant *assemblage.* They follow the theory of Deleuze and Guattari (1987) and argue that it is the multiplic-ity of heterogeneous objects that together form a functional entity of sur-veillance. Surveillance assemblages consist of discrete flows of forces that are temporal, come and go, and that are fluid. Latour introduced the term *oligopticon*—to describe the separate, local places of control, where little is seen well (Latour 2005). In their seminal study of the rise of CCTV, Norris and Amstrong argue that it is an empirical question to see if/how panop-tic potential is linked to other disciplinary techniques so that the result is complete control (1999, 6). Critics of Foucault's critics, however, argue that the panopticon should not be understood as a form of technology, but that although the technologies of control and surveillance have become more decentralized, the social relations of surveillance are still dominated by powerful actors, especially companies and state institutions. They main-tain that collective actors such as the state and capital are still the most powerful surveillance actors and that a refined version of the notion of the panopticon should still be used today. They especially stress that the Foucauldian tradition in surveillance studies should not be abandoned in order to preserve its critical character.

Most of the authors in this book agree that, on the technological level, the Internet represents forms of surveillance that are rather liquid, decentralized, dynamic, and dispersed. We can speak with Heraclitus: everything on the Internet flows. We cannot step twice into the same website, and moreover, users can decide if, when, and how to contribute to the virtual world. No single social entity can completely control the Internet and its content. Private enterprises are dominant actors in terms of ownership of social media sites. There are also end-users who try to establish alternative Internet projects because they are critical of negative consequences of Internet surveillance.

It is clear that the new media and information technologies have fundamentally restructured the way panoptic power works and is executed (see also Whitaker 1999 on the Internet as cybernetic Panopticon). Although the authors of this book differ in the ways that they define Internet surveillance, all of them agree with the idea that web 2.0 and Internet surveillance is shaped by power, conflicts, and contradictions. Social choices, contradictions, inclusion, and exclusion are important elements of the virtual world (Shields 2002). The Internet leads to more surveillance—surveillance of various forms. This book shows that it is important to focus on the political implications of Internet surveillance, aspects of power, and everyday struggles of end-users.

15.5. A POLITICAL ANALYSIS OF WEB (2.0) SURVEILLANCE

A comprehensive analysis of the Internet and surveillance is multidimensional. The Internet as a technology is neither good nor bad, but can evolve into different modes within frameworks of domination at the one hand or democratization at the other hand. The chapters in this book show that it is important to avoid a techno-centric analysis and to focus on the analysis of the power structures underlying Internet surveillance. The Internet *has politics*, to borrow Langdon Winner's expression about artifacts having politics (1999 [1986]). The main questions about Internet surveillance, as the chapters in this book show, concern power, domination and democratization (Clegg, Coupasson, and Phillips 2006, chapter 13). When the Internet is dominated by hierarchical control and domination, the outcome will be more manipulation and repression and what Habermas (1981) terms the colonization of the lifeworld.

There are also potentials of the Internet to support development in society towards a more democratic life-world. This does not mean that we should embrace opportunistic cyberlibertarianism as if complete liberty is possible on the Internet. It means that it is important to advance broad participation, deliberation, and participatory decision-making in society and to find ways that the Internet can support such developments. A political analysis recognizes that the Internet confronts us not just with questions of how to act, but also with questions about ourselves, about citizenship, and about the way we perceive the society we live in (Winner 1996). A democratic life-world can contribute to a more critical awareness about the intended and unintended consequences of the Internet in the context of surveillance. The authors in this book agree that this is an important political task.

Google today defines to a great deal the answers we get for an online search, which is why we need a critical understanding of its underlying ideology. More and more elements of our digital selves are used by bodies that are hard to control. That is why it is important to advance counter-forces that question these developments. The state is intervening in our virtual lives in various ways, and social movements oppose possible abuse of state power. Corporate enterprises are the dominant owners of social media. At the same time one finds expressions of alternatives on the Internet. The Internet is a contested space. Users have the moral right to be informed about and to politically question the forces that lead to increasing surveillance. They also have the right to be protected against the abusive power of surveillance.

Our lives are being watched more than ever before. But the technology, the Internet, will never completely determine our lives. This book shows that the Internet has brought new elements to our surveillance society. The Internet is adding a virtual dimension to surveillance that opens up possibilities for surveillance and counter-power that were unknown before. This book also shows that an analysis of the condition and constitution of Internet surveillance (what kind of surveillance is possible, enabled, and by whom) is not enough. We have to consider its consequences: the willingness to examine dominant patterns of Internet surveillance.

Critical awareness is key here. The process of democratization that follows is not a guarantee for absolute freedom as such, but a pre-condition for the (self) protection of citizens (i.e., the electronic information of citizens mediated by the Internet) against arbitrariness, exploitation and the tyranny of state institutions and private corporations. The authors of this book argue that citizens and users need to be protected from the abuse of power.

Democratization of the Internet means awareness, participation, the creation of safe spaces, and stimulating diversity and opposing views. This requires a more active and critical role of consumers and civil society. Public awareness and informed scepticism about Internet surveillance is needed. This book shows the importance of this debate.

REFERENCES

Akrich, Madeleine 1992. The de-scription of technical objects. In *Shaping technology/building society*, ed. Wiebe Bijker and Trevor Pinch. Cambridge: MIT Press: 205–224.

Bauman, Zygmunt. 2000. *Liquid modernity*. Cambridge: Polity.

Beninger, James R. 1986. *The control revolution: Technological and economic origins of the information society*. Cambridge, MA: Harvard University Press.

Boersma, Kees and Sytze Kingma. 2011. Organizational learning facilitation with Intranet (2.0): a socio-cultural approach. In *Encyclopaedia of knowledge management*, ed. David Schwartz and Dov Te'eni. Hershey, London: Idea Group: 1280–1289.

Boersma, Kees, Albert Meijer, and Pieter Wagenaar. 2009. Unravelling and understanding the e-government hype. In *ICTs, citizens & governance: After the hype!* ed. Albert Meijer, Kees Boersma, and Pieter Wagenaar. Amsterdam: IOS: 256–266.

Boersma, Kees, Sytze Kingma, and Marcel Veenswijk. 2007. Paradoxes of control: the (electronic) monitoring and reporting system of the Dutch High Speed Alliance (HSA). *Project Management Journal* 38 (2): 75–83.

Carr, Nicolas. 2010. *The shallows: What the Internet is doing to our brains*. New York/ London: W.W. Norton.

Clegg, Stewart, David Courpasson, and Nelson Phillips. 2006. *Power and organizations*. London: Sage.

Comfort, Loise K. 2007. Crisis management in hindsight: cognition, communication, coordination, and control. *Public Administration Review* 67 (s1): 189–197.

Deleuze, Gilles and Félix Guattari. 1987. *A thousand plateaus: Capitalism and schizophrenia*. Minneapolis: University of Minnesota Press.

Doctorow, Cory. 2008. *Little brother*. New York: TOR.

Giddens, Anthony. 1984. *The constitution of society*. Cambridge: Polity.

Habermas, Jürgen. 1981. *The theory of communicative action*. London: Beacon.

Haggerty, Kevin and Richard Ericson. 2000. The surveillant assemblage. *British Journal of Sociology* 51 (4): 605–622.

Hier, Sean. 2008. Transformative democracy in the age of second modernity: cosmopolitanization, communicative agency and the reflexive subject. *New Media & Society* 10 (1): 27–44.

Huxley, Aldous. 1932. *Brave new world*. London: Penguin.

Jones, Steven. 2006. *Against technology: From the Luddites to Neo-Luddism*. London: Routledge.

Latour, Bruno. 2005. *Reassembling the social: Introduction to actor-network-theory*. New York: Oxford University Press.

Lyon, David. 1994. *The electronic eye*. Minneapolis: University of Minnesota Press.

———, ed. 2003. *Surveillance as social sorting*. London: Routledge.

———. 2007. *Surveillance studies: An overview*. Cambridge: Polity.

Murray, Andrew. 2010. *Information technology law: The law and society*. Oxford: Oxford University Press.

Negroponte, Nicholas. 1995. *Being digital*. New York: Vintage.

Norris, Clive and Gary Amstrong. 1999. *The maximum surveillance society: The rise of CCTV*. Oxford/New York: Berg.

Orlikowski, Wanda J. 2000. Using technology and constituting structures: a practice lens for studying technology in organizations. *Organization Science* 11 (4): 404–428.

Orwell, George. 1954. *1984*. Harmondsworth: Penguin.

Poster, Mark. 1990. *The mode of information: Poststructuralism and social context*. Cambridge: Polity.

Räty, Tomi. 2008. *Architectural improvements for mobile ubiquitous surveillance systems*. Espoo: VTT.

Schonfeld, Erick. 2009. Wipe the slate clean for 2010, commit web 2.0 suicide. http://techcrunch.com/2009/12/31/web-2-0-suicide/ (accessed on ???).

Serazio, Michael. 2010. Shooting for fame: spectacular youth, web 2.0 dystopia, and the celebrity anarchy of Generation Mash-up. *Communication, Culture & Critique* 3: 416–434.

Shields, Rob. 2002. *The virtual*. London: Routledge.

Shirky, Clay. 2008. *Here comes everybody*. London: Penguin.

Tapscott, Don and Anthony D. Williams. 2006. *Wikinomics: How mass collaboration changes everything*. London: Penguin.

Twenge, Jean. 2006. *Generation me*. New York: Free Press.

Vonnegut, Kurt. 1999/1952. *Player piano*. New York: Dell.

Wagenaar, Pieter and Kees Boersma. 2008. Soft sister and the rationalization of the world: the driving forces behind increased surveillance. *Administrative Theory & Practice* 30(2): 184–206.

Whitaker, Reg. 1999. *The end of privacy*. New York: New Press.

Winner, Langdon. 1996. Who will we be in cyberspace? *The Information Society* 12 (2): 63–72.

———. 1999/1986. Do artifacts have politics? In *The social shaping of technology*, ed. Donald MacKenzie and Judy Wajcman, 28–41. Philadelphia, PA: Open University Press.

Woolgar, Steve, ed. 2002. *Virtual society? Technology, cyberbole, reality*. Oxford/New York: Oxford University Press.

Contributors

Anders Albrechtslund holds a BA & MA in philosophy (University of Odense, Denmark, 2003) and a PhD in Information Studies (Aalborg University, Denmark, 2008). He has published work on surveillance, new technologies, social media, and ethics. Currently, he is an Assistant Professor at Aarhus University's Department of Information and Media Studies. His research interests include surveillance technologies in urban spaces and ways to conceptualize surveillance. He is a member of the Management Committee of the EU COST Action "Living in Surveillance Societies" (2009–2013).
Website: http://www.albrechtslund.net/
Contact: alb@hum.au.dk

Thomas Allmer has studied media and communication at the University of Salzburg and the Victoria University of Melbourne. Allmer is a member of the Unified Theory of Information Research Group (UTI) and participates in the working group Living in the Surveillance Age of the European Cooperation in Science and Technology Action Living in Surveillance Societies. He currently is a PhD student at the University of Salzburg and a research associate in the project "Social Networking Sites in the Surveillance Society", funded by the Austrian Science Fund (FWF). His research interests are critical theory, critical media and communication studies, information society research, and surveillance studies.
Website: http://www.uti.at/thomasallmer
Contact: thomas.allmer@uti.at

Mark Andrejevic is an Associate Professor in the Department of Communication Studies at the University of Iowa. He is the author of *Reality TV: The Work of Being Watched* (2004) and *iSpy: Surveillance and Power in the Interactive Era* (2007), as well as numerous articles and book chapters on surveillance, new media, and popular culture. Mark studies television and new media from the perspective of critical theory and cultural studies. His recent work focuses on surveillance and monitoring in the digital economy. Topics include interactive media, surveillance, digital art, and reality TV.
Website: http://www.uiowa.edu/~commstud/people/faculty/andrejevic/andrejevic.shtml
Contact: mark-andrejevic@uiowa.edu

David Arditi is a PhD student in the Cultural Studies program at George Mason University where he also teaches classes on globalization and culture. He received his MA in Political Science from Virginia Tech in 2007. His Master's thesis was published as a book entitled *Criminalizing Independent Music: The Recording Industry Association of America's Advancement of Dominant Ideology*. Arditi is particularly interested in researching the intersections of music, technology, and politics and is serving as the Graduate Student Representative to the Board of Visitors at George Mason University.
Contact: darditi@gmu.edu

Roberto Armengol is a PhD Candidate in Anthropology at the University of Virginia. His dissertation research focuses on everyday life and exchange in Cuba after the collapse of the Soviet Union. He also is a member of an interdisciplinary work group examining IT-based surveillance and transparency systems as accountability systems.
Contact: armengol@virginia.edu

Kees Boersma is an Associate Professor at the Faculty of Social Science of the VU University Amsterdam. His research interests are science and technology studies, the organization of surveillance and security, and organizational power. He has published widely on R&D history, organizational learning, enterprise-wide systems, and organizational safety culture. He teaches the courses Organizational Politics, Organizational and Management Theory, and Technology and Culture. He is a management committee member and working group leader in the EU COST Action Living in Surveillance Societies.
Website: http://keesboersma.com
Contact: f.k.boersma@vu.nl

Miyase Christensen is a Professor of Media and Communication studies at Karlstad University. She is the author and co-editor of a number of international articles and books, including *Shifting Landscapes: Film and Media in European Context* (2008); *Connecting Europe: Politics of Information Society in the EU and Turkey* (2009); *Online Territories: Globalization, Mediated Practice and Social Space* (2011, with André Jansson and Christian Christensen); and *Understanding Media and Culture in Turkey: Structures, Spaces, Voices* (forthcoming, with Christian Christensen). Her current research focuses on social theory and globalization/transnationalization processes and social surveillance and the media. Current research includes a funded project entitled Secure Spaces: Media, Consumption and Social Surveillance (with André Jansson) and a second project on the environment and the media funded by FORMAS.
Contact: miyase.christensen@kau.se

Christian Fuchs is Chair Professor in Media and Communication Studies at Uppsala University's Department of Informatics and Media. He is also a board member of the Unified Theory of Information Research Group, Austria, and editor of *tripleC (cognition, communication, co-operation): Journal for a Global Sustainable Information Society* (http://www.triple-c.at). He studied computer science at the Vienna University of Technology from 1994 to 2000 and completed his PhD there in 2002. From 2000 to 2006, he was a lecturer for Information Society Studies at the Institute of Design and Technology Assessment of the Vienna University of Technology and was a research associate in the same department in 2002–2004. At the University of Salzburg, he was assistant professor in 2005–2007 and associate professor from 2008 to 2010 in the field of ICTs and Society. His main research fields are social theory, critical theory, political economy of media, information, technology, information society studies, ICTs, and society. He is author of many academic publications, including *Internet and Society: Social Theory in the Information Age* (New York: Routledge 2008) and *Foundations of Critical Media and Information Studies* (New York: Routledge, 2011). He is coordinator of the research project "Social Networking Sites in the Surveillance Society" (2010–2013), which is funded by the Austrian Science Fund FWF, and management committee member of the EU COST action "Living in Surveillance Societies".
Website: http://fuchs.uti.at
Contact: christian.fuchs@im.uu.se

David W. Hill is a PhD student at the Department of Sociology, University of York, UK. His PhD thesis explores the place of the ethical in contemporary social theory through an examination of the new media environment. His research interests include contemporary social theory (particularly work on technology, violence, and ethics); poststructuralism; media theory; urban studies; and the thought of Emmanuel Levinas, Zygmunt Bauman, and Jean-François Lyotard. David previously studied Philosophical Studies: Knowledge and Human Interests (BA Honours) at Newcastle University, UK, and Philosophy (MA) at Durham University, UK.
Website: http://www.york.ac.uk/depts/soci/research/reshill.htm
Contact: dwh501@york.ac.uk

André Jansson is Professor of Media and Communication Studies at Karlstad University, Sweden. He currently leads two research projects: Rural Networking/Networking the Rural (FORMAS, with Magnus Andersson) and Secure Spaces: Media, Consumption and Social Surveillance (National Bank of Sweden, with Miyase Christensen). He has published several books and articles in the field of media and cultural studies, with a special focus on communication geography. Among his publications in English are the co-edited books *Online Territories: Globalization, Mediated Practice and Social Space* (with Miyase and Christian Christensen, 2011); *Strange Spaces: Explorations into Mediated Obscurity* (with Amanda Lagerkvist, 2009); and *Geographies of Communication: The Spatial Turn in Media Studies* (with Jesper Falkheimer, 2006). Contact: andre.jansson@kau.se

Deborah G. Johnson is the Anne Shirley Carter Olsson Professor of Applied Ethics and Chair of the Department of Science, Technology, and Society in the School of Engineering and Applied Sciences of the University of Virginia. Trained in philosophy, Johnson's scholarship focuses broadly on the connections between ethics and technology, especially the ethical issues arising around computers and information technology. Two of her books were published in 2009: the 4th edition of *Computer Ethics* (Prentice Hall) and *Technology and Society: Engineering our Sociotechnical Future,* co-edited with J. Wetmore (MIT Press). As an interdisciplinary scholar, Johnson has published over fifty papers on a wide range of topics and in a variety of journals and edited volumes. Currently Johnson serves as co-editor of the journal *Ethics and Information Technology* published by Springer and on the Executive Board of the Association for Practical and Professional Ethics. Johnson received the John Barwise prize from the American Philosophical Association in 2004; the Sterling Olmsted Award from the Liberal Education Division of the American Society for Engineering Education in 2001; and the ACM SIGCAS Making a Difference Award in 2000. Contact: dgj7p@virginia.edu

David Lyon is Director of the Surveillance Studies Centre at Queen's University, Kingston, Ontario, Canada. Surveillance Studies has been Lyon's major research area for the past twenty years. David Lyon's research, writing, and teaching interests revolve around major social transformations in the modern world. Questions of the information society, globalization, secularization, surveillance, and postmodernity all feature prominently in his work. His latest books are: *Identifying Citizens: ID Cards as Surveillance* (Polity 2009); and, co-edited with Elia Zureik and Yasmeen Abu-Laban, *Surveillance and Control in Israel/Palestine* (Routledge 2010); and with Elia Zureik, Lynda Harling Stalker, Emily Smith, and Yolande Chan, *Surveillance, Privacy and the Globalization of Personal Information* (McGill-Queen's University Press 2010). Other publications include *Surveillance Studies: An Overview* (Polity 2007); *Surveillance after September 11* (Polity 2003); *Surveillance Society: Monitoring Everyday Life* (Open University Press 2001); *The Electronic Eye: The Rise of Surveillance Society* (Polity 1994); *Postmodernity* (Open University Press 1994); *The Information Society: Issues and Illusions* (Polity 1988). Website: http://www.queensu.ca/sociology/?q=people/faculty/full-time/lyond
Contact: lyond@queensu.ca

Thomas Mathiesen, born 1933, became professor of sociology of law at the University of Oslo in 1971 and has been professor emeritus since 2003. He is the author of a number of books on sociology of law, criminology, media, prisons, power and counter-power, and surveillance. Six of them have been published in English: *The Defences of the Weak: A Sociological Study of a Norwegian Correctional Institution* (Tavistock Publications 1965); *Across the Boundaries of Organizations* (Glendessary Press 1971); *The Politics of Abolition* (Martin Robertson/Norwegian Universities Press/ Wiley 1974); *Law, Society and Political Action* (Academic Press 1980); *Prison on Trial* (Sage Publications 1990/Waterside Press 2000/2006); *Silently Silenced* (Waterside Press 2004). Mathiesen is founder of KROM—the Norwegian prisoners' association, where he is still active.
Website: http://folk.uio.no/thomasm/
Contact: thomas.mathiesen@jus.uio.no

Marisol Sandoval is member of the Unified Theory of Information Research Group. She graduated in Communication Studies from the University of Salzburg in 2008 with a master's thesis on critical media theory and alternative media. From 2008 to 2010 she worked as a research fellow at the ICT&S Center at the University of Salzburg. Currently Marisol is recipient of a DOC-scholarship from the Austrian Academy of Sciences for her PhD research, which critically questions the concept of Corporate Social Responsibility (CSR) with a special focus on the (new) media industry. She is member of the working group Surveillance Technologies in Practice of the COST Action Living in Surveillance Societies. Marisol's research interests are critical social theory, critical political economy of media and information, alternative media, ideology critique, business ethics and CSR, as well as Internet and surveillance.
Website: http://www.uti.at/sandoval
Contact: marisol.sandoval@uti.at

Iván Székely, social informatist, is an internationally known expert in the multidisciplinary fields of Data Protection and Freedom of Information. A long-time independent researcher, consultant and university lecturer, as well as former chief counsellor of the Hungarian Parliamentary Commissioner for Data Protection and Freedom of Information, Székely is at present Counsellor of the Open Society Archives at Central European University and associate professor at the Budapest University of Technology and Economics. A founder of the newly democratic informational-legal system in Hungary, Székely was a leader of the first privacy and data protection research in Hungary and in the region (1989–1990). Since 1992 he has been participating in the advisory work for preparation of information and communication-related laws in newly democratic European countries. Székely is member of several international research groups, among others, the Broadening the Range Of Awareness in Data protection (BROAD), Ethical Issues of Emerging ICT Applications (ETICA),

European Privacy and Human Rights (EPHR), and Living in Surveillance Societies (LiSS) projects of the EU, and advisory board member of Privacy International, the Eötvös Károly Policy Institute, Access Info Europe, and the European Privacy Institute. His studies and publications, as well as his research interests, are focused on information autonomy, openness and secrecy, privacy, identity, and archivistics.
Contact: Székelyi@ceu.hu

Monika Taddicken works as a researcher at the Institute of Journalism and Communication Research and the cluster of excellence Integrated Climate System Analysis and Prediction (CliSAP) at the University of Hamburg, Germany. Previously, she was a researcher and lecturer at the University of Hohenheim, Department of Communication Science and Social Research, and the Research Centre for Media Economy and Communication. In 2008 and 2009, she coordinated the research project The Diffusion of the Media Innovation Web 2.0: Determinants and Effects from a User's Perspective, funded by Deutsche Forschungsgemeinschaft [German Research Foundation]. She studied social sciences in Göttingen, Germany, and Galway, Ireland, and worked as a junior researcher in the field of commercial online research. She then joined the University of Bamberg as a lecturer and research assistant in the Marketing Department. She received her doctor's degree in 2008 from the University of Hohenheim. Her dissertation is about mode effects of web surveys. Her main working fields are online research, audience research, and methodology.
Website: http://www.journalistik.uni-hamburg.de, http://www.wiso.uni-hamburg.de/index.php?id=9914#c38241
Contact: monika.taddicken@uni-hamburg.de

Daniel Trottier is a postdoctoral fellow in the Department of Sociology at the University of Alberta in Edmonton, Alberta, Canada. He completed his PhD in the department of Sociology at Queen's University in Kingston, Ontario, Canada. Under Dr. David Lyon's supervision, his doctoral research explored information exchange and social media, using Facebook as a case study. Daniel is affiliated with the Surveillance Studies Centre research group, and has completed his previous degrees at McGill University and Concordia University in Montréal, Quebec.
Website: http://www.queensu.ca/sociology/?q=node/135
Contact: 5dt14@queensu.ca

Kent Wayland, an anthropologist, is a Postdoctoral Research Associate in the Department of Science, Technology, and Society at the University of Virginia. His current research includes an interdisciplinary project analyzing surveillance and transparency as accountability systems, an ongoing examination of the cultural politics and technological practices

of restoring World War II warplanes, and a curriculum development program aimed at preparing engineering students for engaged scholarship and intercultural exchange.
Contact: kaw6r@virginia.edu

Rolf H. Weber is Chair Professor for Civil, Commercial and European Law at the University of Zurich and Visiting Professor at the University of Hong Kong. He is director of the European Law Institute and the Center for Information and Communication Law at the University of Zurich. Since 2008 Weber has been a member of the Steering Committee of the Global Internet Governance Academic Network (GigaNet) and, since 2009, a member of the High-level Panel of Advisers of the Global Alliance for Information and Communication Technologies and Development (GAID). He is also engaged as an attorney-at-law and as a member of the editorial board of several Swiss and international legal periodicals.
Website: www.uzh.ch
Contact: rolf.weber@rwi.uzh.ch

Index

Published by Routledge, an imprint of the Taylor & Francis Group, an
informa business

© COST Office, 2011. COST Action IS0807—The Internet and Surveillance
2011

ISBN: 978–0-415–89160–8 (hbk)

ISBN: 978–0-203–80643–2 (ebk)